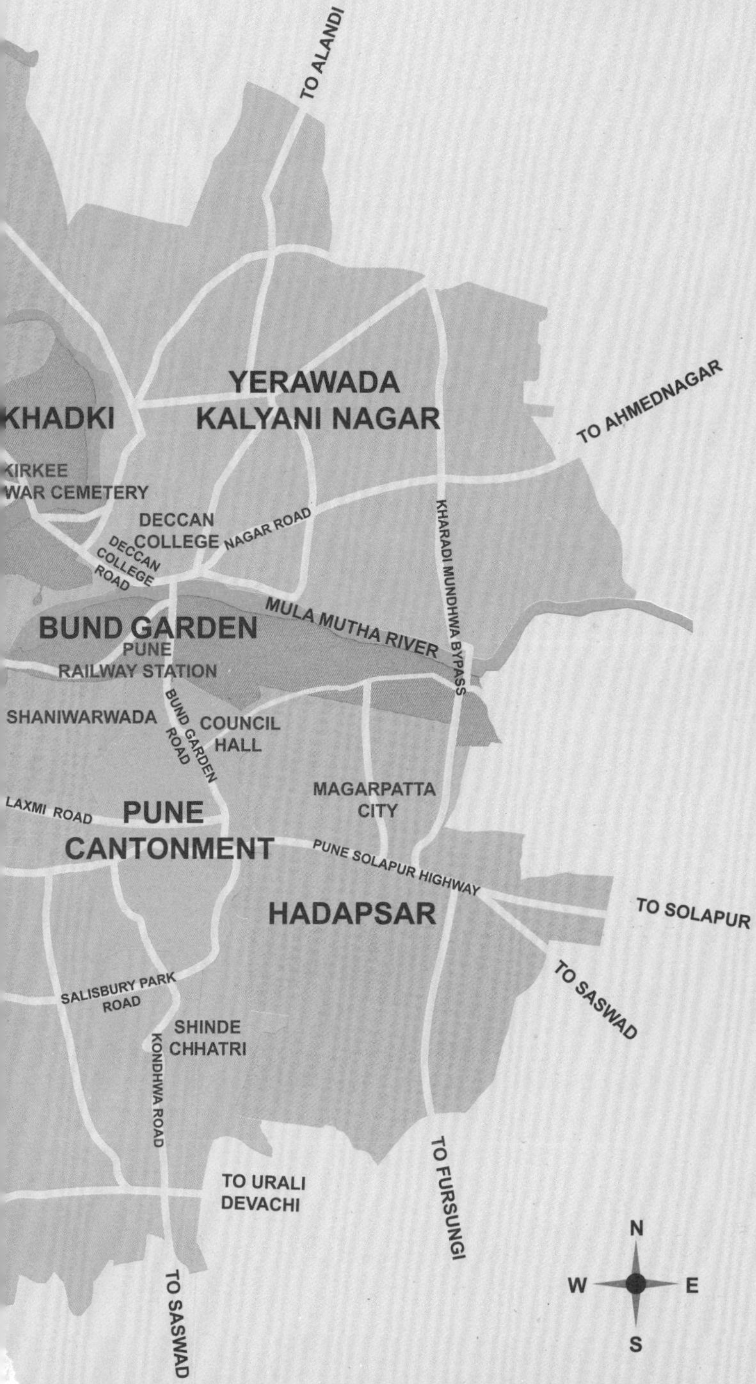

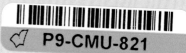

TO ALANDI
YERAWADA
KALYANI NAGAR
KHADKI
TO AHMEDNAGAR
KIRKEE
WAR CEMETERY
DECCAN
COLLEGE
NAGAR ROAD
DECCAN
COLLEGE
ROAD
KHARADI MUNDHWA BYPASS
BUND GARDEN
MULA MUTHA RIVER
PUNE
RAILWAY STATION
SHANIWARWADA
BUND GARDEN
ROAD
COUNCIL
HALL
MAGARPATTA
CITY
LAXMI ROAD
PUNE
CANTONMENT
PUNE SOLAPUR HIGHWAY
HADAPSAR
TO SOLAPUR
TO SASWAD
SALISBURY PARK
ROAD
SHINDE
CHHATRI
KONDHWA ROAD
TO URALI
DEVACHI
TO FURSUNGI
TO SASWAD
N
W
E
S

Intach Presents

My PUNE पुणे Travel Book

Discover Pune like never before!

elephant

mccia

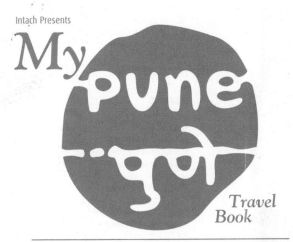

elephant

Published by
Elephant Design Pvt. Ltd.
13 Kumar Srushti
S. No. 1 Pashan-NDA Road
Bavdhan Pune 411 021 India
Tel: +91–20-22951055 / 59 / 22951914
Telefax: +91-20-22951160
info@elephantdesign.com
www.elephantdesign.com
www.punebook.com

mccia

Co-published by
Mahratta Chamber of Commerce
Industry and Agriculture
505 & 506, A & B Wing, 5th floor,
MCCIA Trade Tower,
International Convention Center,
403 - A, Senapati Bapat Marg,
Pune 411016 Tel: 25709000
Email: info@mcciapune.com
Website: www.mcciapune.com

Printed at Pragati Press India

First Edition 2006
Reprint 2007

ISBN 81-87693-01-0

Disclaimer

Every effort has been made to ensure that this book is as up to date as possible at the time of going to press. However change in schedules, prices, telephone numbers, and other details is inevitable. Places may also change, some for the better and some for the worse, while some may even close down. We request you to contact us at **update@punebook.com**, if you come across any outdated information, so that we can verify and update it in the next edition. All the maps and graphs in this book are indicative and are not to be used for reference.

No part of the **My Pune Travel Book** is an advertisement and all places listed herein are at the discretion of the Publishers.

The Publishers cannot accept responsibility for any consequences arising directly or indirectly from the use of this book.

My Pune पुणे

Travel Book

Publisher's Note

Around seventeen years ago a few of us, fresh graduates from the National Institute of Design, came to Pune to start a design firm. We called it Elephant Design.

Pune was then an unknown place to us and to the world of designers. We came here because of the promise of growing industrial opportunities, and the proximity to the business and financial capital of India.

Founder Directors of Elephant Design

Thus began an adventure that became intertwined with the city of Pune, for as we began to explore the city and its nuances, we started falling in love with this captivating place. The culture so open yet so traditional, the people so intellectual yet so down to earth, the cityscape dotted with modern buildings and interjecting temple spires.

As Pune grew at a significant pace so did Elephant. Both progressing steadily towards a bigger, better future armed with optimism and backed by intelligent hard work, and the ability to assimilate, learn and adapt to new opportunities.

The process of discovering the city that we now called home was ongoing while on the path of progress. In our unravelling of the city, we discovered that there was no comprehensive document tracing the urban development of Pune in the recent past. There were records of different periods and eras, which could be gleaned from various sources but this information had never been put together.

Pune Queen of Deccan

So, on the occasion of our 10th anniversary, we published a book called **'Pune Queen of the Deccan'** authored by **Jaymala Diddee** and **Samita Gupta** and photographed by **Sandesh Bhandare.** It was our way of saying thank you and giving something back to the wonderful city of Pune. The book became an instant success. So path breaking was the information in this book that it became a reference book for anyone who wanted to study Pune's development.

Two years later we decided to publish **'Pune 30 Picture Cards'**, a unique book that was a photo documentary on Pune city by ace photographer **Sandesh Bhandare**. This book too became an instant hit.

Pune 30 Picture Cards

Today Elephant has grown to become a multi-dimensional design firm of international repute. We have to our name an outstanding portfolio of brand work and a good list of clients. Pune too has progressed full steam towards becoming a well-rounded city of international standing, and is on the threshold of becoming a global city.

Travellers frequent Pune for business and leisure purposes and there is a constant influx of people from all over the country who are coming here to be part of Pune's bright future.

We too have travelled to many cities of the world and gained new perspectives. We have found one lacuna faced by any traveller coming to Pune, a book that comprehensively documents Pune city from the perspective of a newcomer. One that not only gives a glimpse of Pune's glorious past but also provides information on what Pune is today, a single book that can highlight every aspect of this colourful city.

Intach supported the project with information and pictures, and MCCIA agreed to partner the publication with Elephant.

Put together with care to ensure that no aspect of Pune, its history, its people, or life here is missed out, the **'My Pune Travel Book'** is perfect for anyone who wants to know all about the city of Pune.

This book would not have materialised without the enthusiastic support of Arti Kirloskar and Ravi Pandit, and my partners Ashish, Partho and Ashwini.

We hope you enjoy reading this book, find it useful, and get to know and love Pune like we at Elephant do.

The **'My Pune Travel Book'** is not an authority on the city, nor an exhaustive directory of it. It is meant to illustrate the commitment to the city we all love. However, we may have inadvertently missed out some vital aspects of Pune. Therefore, we would appreciate your response to the book at **update@punebook.com**

Sudhir Sharma
Elephant Strategy + Design
Publisher

Elephant Design office at Bavdhan, Pune

Contents

Business in Pune 204-215

My Pune 216-248

Selective Directory 249-287

Pune Overview

- Location • Climate • History • Ecology • Government • Language
- Identities • People • Communities • Cuisine • Fashion • Real Estate
- Sister Cities • Holidays • Commonwealth Youth Games
- Cultural Calendar • Ganesh Festival

Location

Nestled amidst the Sahyadri Hills in the large, prosperous Indian state of Maharashtra, Pune has a population of over 45 lakh. Situated at a height of 560m above sea level at the confluence of the Mula and Mutha rivers, it is surrounded by hills, valleys and historic forts. Pune is the second largest city in Maharashtra, after capital Mumbai.

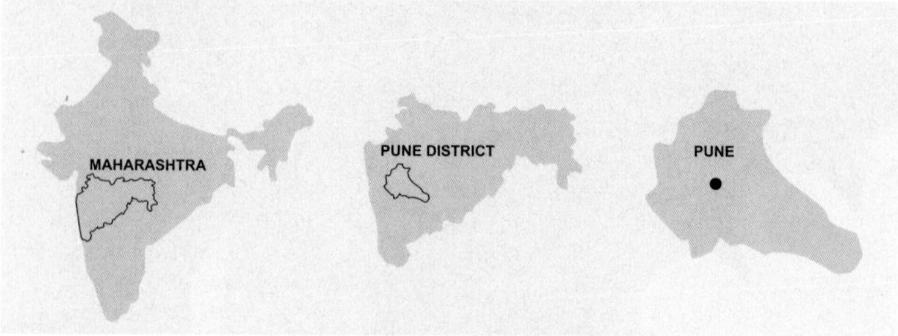

Climate

Pune has a pleasant climate almost all through the year, except during the summer months of April and May, when temperatures can soar to 40^{0} C. It is best to stay indoors between noon and 4 pm in the height of summer. Winter temperatures can dip to as low as 5^{0} C at night but the days are balmy and agreeable. The monsoon, from June to early September, is characterised by moderate to heavy rain and cool days and nights.

History

Pune has a glorious past. From the celebrated times of legendary warrior king Chhatrapati Shivaji and 18th century rulers, the Peshwas, to the historic era of eminent freedom fighters, social reformers and educationists, the city has played a leading role in the growth of the region and country.

Prehistoric Pune

Human civilisation in Pune started early, almost 100,000 years ago according to the findings of archaeologist Dr. S. N. Rajguru who excavated along the Mutha riverbed in the 1970s. Although very little is known about Pune in prehistoric times, the earliest mention of the city was made in records of the Satavahana dynasty (235 BC-225 AD), which set up its capital in Junnar, close to Pune. There are also references to Pune in sacred texts like the Puranas (400 AD).

Early Pune

The Rashtrakutas were one of the earliest rulers of Pune. They were great patrons of art and architecture and built many famous structures in the region, including the Ellora temple near Aurangabad, and the Pataleshwar Caves in Pune. Later Pune came under the rule of the Yadava dynasty followed by the Muslim Mughals. In the mid-seventeenth century, the local Marathas united and emerged as a supreme power under the command of Shivaji, one of India's most celebrated and valorous emperors.

Timeline : Pune and surroundings

100,000 BC	1000 BC	300 -100 BC	200BC - 200 AD

Hand Axe Paleolithic Lower Era-Old Stone Age	**Megaliths** Neolithic Era-New Stone Age	**Carla Bhaja Caves**	**Artifacts of Pune** Satavahana Period

In Shivaji's Times (1643-1680)

Founder of the mighty Maratha Empire, Shivaji spent his early childhood in Pune. Under the expert guidance of his teacher Dadaji Kondadev and the inspirational upbringing of his mother Jijabai, Shivaji grew up to be a great and ambitious warrior.

In 1643, at the age of 16, he made his first military foray and captured the fort of Torna, a part of Mughal territory. This started a lifelong battle with the Mughals and other Muslim powers. Skilfully using guerrilla warfare, he seized a large part of the Mughal Empire and set up one of the most powerful independent states in India. In 1674, at a ceremonious coronation, the young man was crowned sovereign king and given the symbolic title of Chhatrapati, or the 'umbrella-bearer'.

Tales about Shivaji have become part of the nation's folklore, narrated to children even today. His heroic exploits include slashing his enemy's waist with a tiger claw and decamping from Mughal ruler Aurangzeb's prison by hiding in a fruit basket.

Shivaji died in 1680, bringing to an untimely end the reign of one of the country's greatest rulers.

The Progressive Peshwas (1713-1818)

Shivaji's son Sambhaji ruled for a short while on the death of his father. He was in turn succeeded by his son, Chhatrapati Shahu who handed over the responsibility for Pune to his prime minister (Peshwa) Balaji Vishwasnath in 1710. A new era commenced under the Peshwas, who made Pune their socio-political and cultural capital and enriched the city with attractive temples and gardens, civic amenities and public utilities.

Under Peshwa Thorale Bajirao, an extremely ambitious and able warrior, the Maratha Empire expanded up to Delhi in the north and Hyderabad in the south. Pune once again featured prominently on the map of India.

The third Peshwa Balaji Bajirao, alias Nanasaheb, contributed extensively in urbanising Pune. He set up the administrative wards or *peths*, built the famous Parvati Temple complex, and developed aqueducts (still in use today) that brought water from the Katraj Lake to the city.

The downfall of the Peshwas began with the arrival of the British in Pune. In 1817,

Pune probably derived its name from the word *punya* or auspicious. According to Hindu beliefs, the confluence or *sangam* of two rivers is auspicious. Since Pune is located at the confluence of the Mula and Mutha rivers, it is considered a *punya vishaya* (auspicious region). Some of its other earlier names were Punaka Wadi, Punaka Desh and Punya Nagari.

Timeline : Pune

800-900 AD

Pateleswar Caves
Rashtrakuta Dynasty

1000 AD

Marathi developed as a language of the people

1290 AD

Sant Dnyaneshwar

1607-1650 AD

Sant Tukaram

at the Battle of Kirkee, the British ousted the last Peshwa and hoisted the Union Jack, ending a remarkable, century-old reign.

The British Raj (1817-1947)

The British, led by Mount Stuart Elphinstone, Governor of Bombay Presidency, established the British Raj in this region. They brought with them their educational and administrative systems and soon declared Pune their 'Monsoon Capital', anglicising the city's name to 'Poona'. In the decades leading up to the Independence movement leaders like Bal Gangadhar Tilak, Mahadev Govind Ranade, Gopal Krishna Gokhale, and Mahatma Jyotirao Phule spearheaded the freedom struggle.

Pune Today

Today, Pune continues to be at the forefront of development in areas ranging from business and education to arts and culture. It has evolved from a provincial township into a multifaceted, vibrant city that embraces modernity with as much ease and élan as it retains its rich heritage.

Ecology

Pune is said to be the fourth greenest city in India. Surrounded by verdant hills, valleys, forests, rivers and lakes, it enjoys an enviously rich biodiversity seldom found in the urban sprawl of a city.

Located on the leeward side of the Western Ghats, it boasts thick forest parks (Bhamburda and Parvati-Pachgaon), huge swathes of green cover in areas such as the cantonments, the Pune University and National Defence Academy, numerous lakes (Pashan, Model Colony, Katraj, and Khadakwasla), and over 100 gardens (Empress Garden, Osho Park).

Hills of Pune

1. Parvati Hill
2. Law College Hill
3. Taljai Hill
4. Vetalbaba Hill
5. Malwadi Hill
6. Katraj Hill
7. Chaturshringi Hill
8. Ramtekdi
9. Fergusson Hill
10. Baner Hill

Pune has an amazing wealth of flora and fauna. More than 400 species of birds have been recorded in and around the city, along with 65 wild mammal species, among the highest in any Indian city. Pune is also home to over 104 different varieties of butterflies including the Blue Mormon and Plain Puffin, around 380 tree species, and an astounding range of amphibians, reptiles, fish and insects.

Pune is built on Deccan Trap Basalt formed by volcanic lava flows. The multiple layers of these stratified rocks can be distinctly seen on some of the hills surrounding the city. The basalt rocks also host the cavity mineral, Zeolite. Red soil predominates, though black and brown soil is also found.

The splendid example of urban

Timeline : Pune

1627-1680	1637	1712-1721	1721-1740

Chhatrapati Shivaji Maharaj	**Shivaji** comes to Lal Mahal at Pune	**First Peshwa, Balaji Vishwanath -** Prime minister of Shahuji, Shivaji's grandson	**Peshwa Bajirao** son of Balaji

biodiversity in Pune is being threatened by the acute development drive, despite efforts of vocal environmental pressure groups to maintain an ecological equilibrium.

Government

The city is administered by the Pune Municipal Corporation (PMC) set up in 1950. The PMC is in charge of the civic needs and infrastructure of the city. The executive power of the Corporation is vested in the Municipal Commissioner, an IAS officer appointed by the State government. The city is divided into 48 panels or municipal wards, each electing three corporators to the PMC. The Mayor is the titular head of the PMC and has few executive powers.

The city also houses three military cantonments (Pune, Khadki and Dehu Road). They are administered by the Cantonment Boards formed by the Ministry of Defence, and are not under the jurisdiction of the PMC.

Pune and the neighbouring townships of Pimpri-Chinchwad share a symbiotic relationship and are often perceived as one unit. The PMC and the Pimpri Chinchwad Municipal Corporation (PCMC) often work together to promote development of the region.

Language

Marathi is the official language of the state of Maharashtra, and is spoken by a vast majority in Pune. Signboards of all shops, commercial establishments, restaurants, and even private offices are written in both Marathi and English.

However, since Pune also has a large non-Maharashtrian population, Hindi and English are extensively heard, understood and used.

Identities

Known variously as the 'Cultural Capital' of the state, the 'Oxford of the East' or 'Pensioner's Paradise', Pune has many different identities, depending on who is talking about it.

Oxford of the East

Recognised as the 'Oxford of the East', Pune is a premier seat of learning with some of the oldest and finest educational institutes in the country. Scholars from all over the world are drawn to its renowned universities (such as the University of Pune, and Symbiosis Deemed University), large number of famous colleges (including Deccan College, and Fergusson College) and pioneering research institutes (among them the National Chemical Laboratory, and the Inter-University Centre for Astronomy and Astrophysics).

Pune provides superior technical and professional education especially in disciplines like engineering, electronics, computers, management, medicine and chartered accountancy. It is also home to the Film and Television Institute of India, the largest and most reputed such institute in Asia.

While Pune is an academic city, the huge population of students has given the city an interesting, intelligent and youthful quotient. Not surprisingly, Pune has the highest number of foreign students in the

Timeline : Pune

1745-1750

Parvati temple by Peshwa Nanasaheb

1782

Nana Phadnavis builds Pune's drainage system

1811

Vishrambag Wada is built

1817-1818

Third Anglo-Maratha war won by the British

country hailing from over 70 nations and contributing over Rs. 30 million in foreign exchange annually.

Cultural Capital

Pune is the hub for traditional Maharashtrian culture, and has nurtured some of the best work in Marathi theatre, dance, music and literature. Icons like P.K. Atre, P. L. Deshpande, Bal Gandharva, and Bhimsen Joshi have built a rich cultural tradition that is enthusiastically kept alive even today.

Marathi theatre, known to be among the most progressive in India, finds its roots in this city. Indian classical music has scores of followers here, and aficionados hold sacred the 53-year-old Sawai Gandharva music festival, held in the winter months every year.

People from across the globe come here to attend the many vibrant festivals and thriving cultural activities such as the Ganesh Mahotsav, Shaniwarwada Festival, Pulotsav, Purushottam Karandak, international film festivals and inter-collegiate cultural carnivals. Like true connoisseurs, Punekars enjoy ethnic *natyasangeet* as much as they do modern avant-garde productions.

Pensioner's Paradise

A significant number of retired people from across India opt to make Pune their home, drawn to its verdant surroundings, salubrious climate, peaceful lifestyle, and healthy blend of convention and modernity.

Comprising retired professionals, government officers, defence personnel, and other empty-nesters, the senior citizens of Pune are a remarkably active and aware community. The Association of Senior Citizens' Organisations of Pune, a nodal agency, started with seven groups in 1992 and counts among its members over 100 organisations today. A Senior Citizen's Academy conducts programmes, seminars, workshops, and study circles for older people with time on their hands.

Pune has the distinction of building the first housing complex exclusively for senior citizens, the Athashree society in Pashan.

Received enthusiastically, the project was followed by others including Golden Nest in Kalyani Nagar.

Defence Hub

The city is one of the foremost bases for defence organisations in the country. It is the headquarters of the Southern Command of the Indian Army; it has three military Cantonments (Pune, Khadki, Dehu Road); and an air base for Jaguar, Mig29 and Su30 aircraft of the Indian Air Force.

Pune also has a large number of unique, nationally renowned defence institutes and associations including the National Defence Academy, Defence Research and Development Organisation, College of Military Engineering, and Military Intelligence Training School.

The medical services wing of the military has a significant presence in the city, led by the Armed Forces Medical College, the Artificial Limb Centre, the Paraplegic Rehabilitation Centre, and other

Timeline : Pune

1851

Deccan College is established

1853

Railway from **Pune to Mumbai** constructed

1856-1920

Lokmanya Bal Gangadhar Tilak

1858

Pune Municipality established

military hospitals.

The cantonment areas of Pune have an old-world charm, with beautiful colonial houses in sprawling gardens, and clean, well-maintained public areas. Pune has always, had a sizeable defence presence in and around the city, and is proud of their amazing discipline and overall proficiency.

People

It is the people who live here that define the city. Pune has many identities, each of which is also a definition of its inhabitants. This is a city of retired government officers, motivated professionals, dedicated social workers, dynamic servicemen, talented artistes, gifted scientists and educationists, and vibrant students.

Once a Maharashtrian bastion, it is now a melting pot of different communities, each contributing to the unique ethos of the city. A blend of tradition and modernity, the city is home to diverse people, ranging from the deeply conservative Punekar to the more

contemporary and open minded Puneite. While pockets of the inner city reflect a more traditional ambience, you will find a more cosmopolitan outlook in the newer areas of the city and the cantonments.

Pune's inhabitants have varying interests, ranging from theatre and classical music to environmental activism and outdoor activities.

A very local phenomenon is the 'Katta', or meeting place. People from all walks of life gather at their favourite restaurant, or under a shady tree, around a park bench or wall, to discuss everything from the latest films and eateries to politics, philosophy, and national passion, cricket!

Pune is welcoming to visitors, and has a long tradition of playing host to a variety of people from across the country and globe.

Vasudev

Potraj

The people of Pune are warm and caring. If invited into their homes, be prepared for generous hospitality that it would be boorish to refuse. In general, the man on the street is approachable and willing to help. Service staff in stores and restaurants is courteous and helpful, but you might come across some less friendly examples in the traditional quarter of the city!

Some traditional Indian families follow the practice of removing footwear at the door to their home. If you are unsure about what to do, it is best to enquire with your host if he would prefer you to remove your footwear on entering his home.

Timeline : Pune

1870

Yerawada Jail is built

1875

MES Society's High School is established

1875

Department of Meteorology office shifts to Pune from Simla

1885

Fergusson College is established

Communities

Pune is a unique blend of many communities who have retained their individual identities and flavour. Collectively, they make the city colourful and cosmopolitan.

Among the first settlers in the city of Pune were the Marathas, a warrior class loyal to the ruling Brahmin Peshwas. They set up home near Shaniwarwada and Tulsibaug, which once housed the administrative offices of the Peshwas.

Along with the warriors came the priestly class, the Maharashtrian Brahmins, who have contributed extensively to the city's rich academic, literary and cultural identity. The Maharashtrian presence is strong in the inner city and Deccan Gymkhana areas.

The Bohris who came from Gujarat and Mumbai during the Peshwa era and began trading in construction material, set up shops in what came to be known as Bohri Ali (lane). Here they dealt in everything from door fittings to cement. Today many have shifted residence to Kondhwa, and other places around the city but their business presence in Bohri Ali remains strong.

The Muslim stronghold is in Camp and its surrounding areas. During Ramzan a visit to Mominpura is a must - colourful temporary shops serve a delightful assortment of food items ranging from mutton chops, fish *tikkas,* and *biryani*, to *firnis, kebabs* and *dal gosht*. As the city grew, the Muslim community also began to move to other areas of the city such as Kondhwa.

A large number of Parsis (Zoroastrians) have made Pune their home, setting up important educational institutes and other landmarks like the popular Kayani Bakery and Dorabjee restaurant. Parsis tend to prefer the Camp area where their fire temples are located. A philanthropic race, Parsis in Pune have done their bit to keep alive the sounds of Western classical music and have contributed to the fledgling theatre scene.

As elsewhere in the country, you will find Christians living near their churches where several community activities are held in addition to religious services. In Pune the Christian community is clustered in the Camp area, and now in newer areas such as Fatima Nagar, Wanowrie and Wadgaon Sheri. With their love for music, food and wine, they are a happy and warm community.

Even while most Indian Jews have migrated to foreign shores, around 300 of them still consider Pune home. They are a close-knit community and their lives revolve around the two synagogues, Ohel David Synagogue in Camp, and Succath Shelomo in Rasta Peth.

Timeline : Pune

1887

First modern **steel plant opens** in **Kutti**

1892

Aga Khan Palace is built by **Sultan Mohmad Shah Aga Khan III**

1893

Rajabahadur Motilal Pittie starts **first textile mill** in **Pune**

1896

Raja Ravi Varma, legendary artist, starts his litho press at **Malavli,** near **Lonavla, 50 km from Pune**

Timber Market in Raviwar Peth and Gultekdi Market are where you will find Pune's trading community - the Marwaris. A hard working and religious people, they have built several beautiful Jain temples like the Goadiji Parasnath Temple in Guruwar Peth.

A large number of Sindhi families migrated to Pune after the Partition of India and Pakistan, setting up refugee camps on the outskirts of the city. Today they have a strong presence in Pudumjee Park, Bhawani Peth, Pimpri-Chinchwad, and Aundh. Sindhis have contributed much to Pune's spiritual mood, primarily through the Sadhu Vaswani Mission and its various social efforts.

Enter the bylanes of Rasta Peth and the tantalising smell of freshly ground coffee beans will welcome you. This Tamilian enclave offers the essence of South India, from traditional meals to the Ayyappa temple, which draws flocks of devotees.

The Kannadigas, whose contribution to the city by way of Udupi restaurants and schools cannot be ignored, are not restricted to any one area. One of their most famous sons is Suresh Kalmadi, MP, and the man behind Pune's image as a sports city.

Pune's Keralites have preferred to stay away from the main city and reside mainly in Khadki, Pimpri-Chinchwad and Nigdi where various associations have kept their distinct cultural identity intact through community activities and celebrations.

The majestic Gurudwara in Ganesh Peth and the automobile spare parts business in Nana Peth bear testimony to the zestful presence of the Punjabi and Sikh communities. While Cycle Society near Nana Peth remains one of the Punjabi strongholds, other areas like Kondhwa, Aundh and Camp also seem to find favour with these two communities.

The earliest Bengalis in Pune settled in Khadki where they were employed in the ammunition factory. A large number of Bengalis can still be found here, their lives centering around the famous Kalibari temple. Organisations like Kolkata Nostalgia and others have kept their culture alive through theatre shows and the promotion of Rabindra Sangeet. Twelve public Durga Poojas are organised across the city, testifying to the large presence of Bengalis in Pune.

Many more communities live harmoniously together in Pune. For all the cultural diversity of the people of Pune they are one in joy and in sorrow, and fiercely proud of the city they call home.

Cuisine

Pune offers the gamut of cuisines, and the gastronome will be in culinary heaven if he has the time to sample all the tempting fare that is served up here. A visitor to Pune can't leave without tasting some typical Puneri fare, recipes for which have been handed down through the generations.

Typical Maharashtrian preparations in Pune include *Puran Poli,* a sweet flatbread

stuffed with a mixture of jaggery and lentils; *Alu chi Vadi,* a preparation of steamed colocassia leaves fried in tangy spices; *Pithla Bhakri,* a gramflour gravy eaten with flatbread made out of a healthy combination of various cereals; *Aamti,* a sweet and spicy lentil dish; and the ubiquitous *Varan Bhat,* a

Timeline : Pune

June 22nd 1897

The first assassination of a British official in **India's freedom struggle** by the **Chaphekar brothers** takes place on Ganeshkhind Road

1907

Poona Agricultural College is started

1910

Bharat Itihas Samshodhak Mandal is formed

1916

S. P. College is started

preparation of rice and lentils. Small eateries and specialty restaurants throughout the city serve up their versions of all these.

If you simply want to snack, try *Missal Pav,* a spicy gravy made from lentils and served with bread; or the extremely popular *Wada-Pav*, a potato patty served in bread, much like a burger, only cheaper. These are the staples of the people of Pune, and are available at every street corner. *Chaat,* a piquant mixture of different ingredients, is also very popular and various versions such as *Bhel Puri, Pani Puri* and *Shev Potato Dahi Puri* are sold in restaurants and off handcarts.

Pune is renowned for a drink called *Mastani,* a delicious combination of milk and ice cream available in several flavours. Another favourite is *Shrikhand,* a sweet, subtly flavoured yoghurt that is typically eaten along with a meal. If you happen to be here during a festival, you will be treated to typical festive fare at any home you visit, ranging from *chaklis* (savoury pinwheels) and *shankarpali* (spicy or sweet fried preparation) to sweet *karanjis* (flour envelopes stuffed with coconut).

Visitors to Pune always carry back savoury *Bakarwadis,* or *Laxmi Narayan Chiwda,* an appetising blend of puffed rice and other ingredients. Pune is famous for a host of bakeries, and topping the shopping lists of regular visitors to the city are Shrewsbury biscuits, wine biscuits, cheese biscuits, and macaroons.

Pune is also a large agricultural centre and a variety of fruits and vegetable are available throughout the year. By far the most awaited fruit is the sumptuous mango, especially the Alphonso variety known as the king of mangoes. Available in summer and early monsoon (April to June), the mango is eaten with relish. An entire range of mango-based sweetmeats such as *barfi, aam papad, amrakhand,* and *aamras* are quickly snapped up in the season.

Fashion

Like most large Indian cities, Pune has become significantly westernised in its manner of dress. While conservative Punekars prefer to dress in traditional attire, even that is being adapted to suit modern lifestyles. The traditional *navvari* (nine-yard sari) once worn by women throughout Maharashtra, can hardly be seen in Pune these days, except among the elderly.

Women generally wear *saris* or the popular *salwar kameez* (loose tunic and pants) ensemble. Indo-western fusion clothing is also popular. Some professionals prefer western wear, and favour skirt- or trouser-suits for office wear. Students and youngsters are partial to casual wear including t-shirts, blouses and shirts, and trousers, jeans, capris and skirts. Visitors to

Timeline : Pune

1917

Development of Laxmi Road and Tilak Road

1920

Deccan Gymkhana and **other colonies** are formed

1924

Law College is started

1928

The **Mumbai-Pune Deccan Queen** makes her **first run**

The Pune Sari and the Paithani

Woven in a distinctive style, the Pune sari is an elegant cotton creation in bright colours and embellished with a contrasting brocade or silk border. Synonymous with Pune, it is a must on the shopping list of every fashion conscious visitor to the city.

The Paithani, a magnificent silk and brocade creation, is the sari of choice for Maharashtrian brides, and a favourite for other special occasions. A heavily brocaded Paithani sari takes anywhere from six months to one-and-a-half years to weave.

the city will not find it difficult to fit in with the crowd if they dress modestly. Anything too outrageous or revealing will draw unwelcome attention.

A majority of men in Pune have discarded traditional attire for more comfortable western wear, especially at the workplace. Contemporary Indian fashion, both formal and casual is also getting popular, and many men sport the *churidar kameez* ensemble for an evening out or formal function.

A vast and varied range of branded clothing, footwear and accessories for men and women is available at malls and specialty stores across the city. Readymade ethnic wear and fabrics in colourful hues and textures are also widely available.

Real Estate

The unprecedented property market boom in Pune has radically altered its topography. The small-town landscape of yesteryears has become a sophisticated metropolitan stretch marked by swanky residential towers, integrated townships, chic malls, glass-and-chrome offices, and sprawling info-tech parks.

The city recorded nearly 40% growth in real estate, both residential and commercial in 2005-2006 largely driven by the blazing growth of the IT-ITES sector.

An estimated 75% of the total commercial space in Pune is occupied by the infotech industry. With the BPO and IT workforce drawing attractive salaries, the demand for high-end houses has also escalated phenomenally.

Pune is expected to lead the mall culture in the country with as many as 20 malls in the pipeline. It will witness a significant surge in retail activity over the next few years, and is already seeing the development of niche or specialised malls like the 10-acre Ishanya Mall in Yerawada, being developed as India's number one

Timeline : Pune

1932

Nowrosjee Wadia College is established

1932 - 1933

Gandhi is incarcerated in **Yerawada jail**

1942

Quit India Movement begins

1944

Kasturba Gandhi dies at **Aga Khan Palace**

international design centre.

Area under construction (2006)

10 million sq. ft. – IT

3.9 million sq. ft. – Retail

27 million sq. ft. - Residential

Some of the world's leading property consultants like Knight Frank and Trammell Crow Meghraj have set up shop here. Investors from Mumbai and overseas are clamouring to buy property in Pune. Real estate appreciation has also witnessed a record high with prices in some areas shooting up by almost 20-30% in 2005-2006.

The graph shows comparitive real estate values of different areas in Pune.

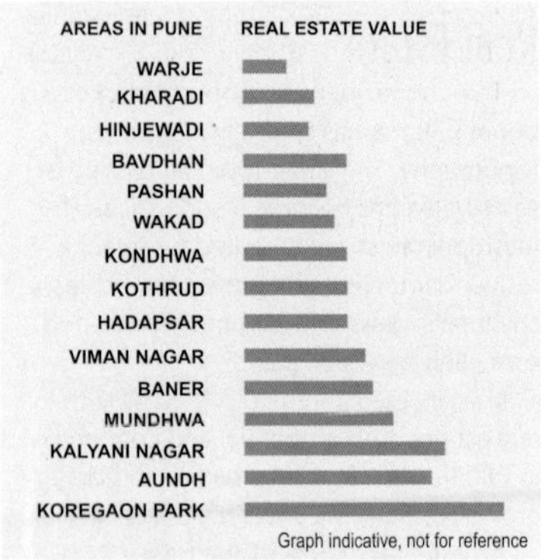

Source: Times Property

With the city area saturated, massive construction activity is focused on peripheral areas like Hadapsar, Kharadi, Yerawada, Kalyani Nagar and Viman Nagar at the eastern end and Aundh, Baner, Bavdhan, Balewadi and neighbouring annexes like Sus and Wakad on the western front.

Sister Cities

Pune has Sister City Affiliations with two cities:

Bremen, Germany: Pune enjoys a very close relationship with Germany. German is among the most popular foreign languages being taught in the city and the Max Mueller Bhavan plays a important role in the promotion of art, theatre and culture. German industries and associations have a significant presence here.

San Jose, USA: The Pune-San Jose connection began to develop with the large migration of young Puneites to Silicon Valley in California. Today, one of the most famous gardens in San Jose, the Guadalupe River Park, boasts a statue of Shivaji Maharaj gifted by the Mayor of Pune.

Holidays

Republic Day	–	January 26
Maharashtra Day	–	May 1
Independence Day	–	August 15

Indians celebrate the birth anniversary *(jayanti)* of their favourite gods and national icons with great fervour. Banks and other public institutions may remain closed on these days.

Shivaji Jayanti	–	February 19
Mahavir Jayanti	–	March/April
Hanuman Jayanti	–	March/April
Buddha Jayanti	–	April/May
Dr Ambedkar Jayanti	–	April 14
Gandhi Jayanti	–	October 2
Gurunanak Jayanti	–	Oct/Nov

(Some dates vary according to lunar calendar)

Timeline : Pune

1947

India gains Independence

1948

AFMC starts

1949

National Chemical Laboratory starts functioning

1950

The National Defence Academy is founded

Commonwealth Youth Games

III
Commonwealth
Youth Games
PUNE
2008
INDIA

Elephant Design has created the branding, identity and mascot for this grand event.

It is matter of immense pride that Pune will be the first city in Asia to host the Commonwealth Youth Games.

Pune scored over several other cities to host the prestigious Third Commonwealth Youth Games in 2008. This international event will enhance the youthful and sporting ethos of the city considerably.

Over the years, Pune has sprinted ahead spectacularly in multiple fields to create a niche for itself both nationally and internationally. It has successfully hosted several world-class events some of which are now part of the city's annual event calendar.

The Games will be held from October 12 to 18, 2008 and will feature nine disciplines, namely athletics, badminton, boxing, shooting, tennis, weightlifting, swimming, table tennis and wrestling.

Around 1,000 athletes and 250 officials from 71 countries will participate in this event. The city will also witness an assemblage of representatives from international federations, print and electronic media.

The venue for the games will be the 153-acre Shiv Chhatrapati Sports Complex that has world-class sports amenities and infrastructure. Pune is availing the services of international consultants for the up gradation and creation of new infrastructure. The city is getting full support from the government, for the betterment of the Sports Complex and the city.

Timeline : Pune

1950	1950	1958	1961

PCMC is formed	Pune Municipal Transport (PMT) begins operations	Maharshi Dhondo Keshav Karve wins the Bharat Ratna	Floods of Panshet disrupt life in Pune

Cultural Calendar

Pune is a city of celebrations and its cultural calendar is crammed with interesting events and festivals. Some are unique to the city such as the Sawai Gandharva (classical Indian music festival), Pune Festival (cultural extravaganza), Purushottam Karandak (inter-collegiate theatre competition), and Ganesh Chaturthi (festival to honour Lord Ganesh).

Exact dates for Hindu festivals are not available since they follow the lunar calendar where the dates vary from year to year.

January

Makar Sankranti

The year begins with the Hindu festival of Makar Sankranti celebrated on January 14. On this day the Sun starts moving into the northern hemishpere, heralding the beginning of the auspicious half of the year, characterised by increasing daylight. *Til laddoos* (sweets made of sesame and jaggery) are exchanged along with greetings of *'Til-gul ghya, god god bola'*, which means 'Accept these sweets and speak sweet words'.

Bakri Id

The highlight of this Muslim festival is the sacrifice of a *bakri* (goat) in commemoration of Prophet Ibrahim's willingness to sacrifice his son as ordained by God. In the days before the festival, a common sight around the city is that of sacrificial goats tethered to trees and poles. Prayers and feasts mark the day.

The Pune International Film Festival

Celluloid fans eagerly anticipate the Pune International Film Festival that brings world-class cinema and international film personalities to the city. The schedule is announced in advance and season passes are available.

February

Shaniwarwada Dance Festival

This two-day festival showcases some of the top artistes of the country against the majestic backdrop of the historic Shaniwarwada.

Verve

In a city known for its college festivals, Verve is among the most popular. Backed by big sponsors, this high-profile inter-collegiate festival features a mélange of dance, music and theatre performances, and other interesting activity.

Mahashivratri

Mahashivratri literally means 'The great night of Shiva'. Of the several legends attached to this festival, one of them celebrates the marriage of Shiva and Shakti. On this day, devotees throng the temples of Lord Shiva, like the Pataleshwar caves on J.M. Road or the Vishweshwar temple at Appa Balwant Chowk.

Muharram

Muharram marks the beginning of the Islamic New Year. The 10-day festival honours the martyrdom of Hazrat Imam Hussain, the grandson of Prophet Mohammed. On the last day processions of *tazias* (glittering replicas of the martyr's tomb) are taken out in the city and the Imambara in Camp draws many devotees.

March

Holi

Holi is the most colourful festival of the Hindus and heralds the arrival of Spring. The night before Holi, a bonfire or Holika is burnt on street corners to symbolise the victory of good over evil. On the next day, also known as Dhulivandan, people spray coloured water on each other and distribute sweets.

Rang Panchami

This festival, which comes five days after Holi, is celebrated with great fervour in Pune. Highlights include music, dance, colourful powder, lots of water and hot *jalebis* (popular sweetmeats fried in oil).

April

Gudi Padwa

One of the most auspicious occasions in the state of Maharashtra, Gudi Padwa heralds spring and the New Year. It is

celebrated on the first day (Padwa) of the Hindu month of Chaitra. Devout families welcome the New Year by worshipping the *gudi* set up at the entrance of the house and by consuming neem leaves. Symbolising victory or achievement, the *gudi* comprises a pole or bamboo staff decorated with saffron or green silk cloth, neem and mango leaves, *gathi* (sweets made from sugar) and an upturned brass or silver pot.

Ramnavami

This celebrates the birth of legendary Hindu king Ram, considered to be an incarnation of Lord Vishnu, and worshipped with fervour as a God. The Tulshibaug Ram Mandir comes alive with *bhajans, kirtans* and devotees on this special day.

May

Maharashtra Day

May 1 is celebrated as the foundation day of the state. A holiday, it is marked by the hoisting of the Indian flag at government and local political party offices and the city resounds with celebratory cries of 'Jai Maharashtra'.

June

Vat Purnima

This is an important festival for married Hindu women, who ceremoniously worship the banyan *(vat)* tree and pray for the long life of their husbands.

July

Guru Purnima

On this day students, especially of music and dance, venerate their *'guru'* or teacher through special functions and ceremonies.

August

Shravan

Shravan is the fifth month of the Hindu calendar and has always been regarded as especially holy. Almost all the days of this month are auspicious and several religious festivals and ceremonies are held in homes across the city. During this month you will see large crowds of worshippers at Shiva temples throughout the city on Mondays, while on Fridays the crowds gather at the Chaturshringi and Jogeshwari temples, dedicated to incarnations of Goddess Laxmi.

Independence Day

Every Indian citizen proudly celebrates 15th August to mark the freedom of the country from British rule.

Nag Panchami

On this day, people pray to the *Nag-Devata* (snake god) and offer milk to snakes carried in cane baskets by snake charmers across the city.

Gokulashtami

Also known as Janmashtami, this festival celebrates the birth of Lord Krishna, one of the most popular gods in the Hindu pantheon. In several areas of the city you will see *dahi-handis,* pots of yoghurt and butter, strung high across the streets and young men

forming a human pyramid in an effort to reach out and break open the pot. The SNDT College on Karve Road puts up a pyramid display with the exclusive participation of girls.

Raksha Bandhan

A widely celebrated festival all over India, it involves sisters tying beautifully decorated threads or *rakhis* on their brothers' wrists to signify an eternal bond between the siblings.

Purushottam Karandak

This unique and prestigious inter-collegiate Marathi theatre festival is held over a period of three days. It provides an excellent platform for budding actors, scriptwriters and directors to showcase their talent. A Purushottam Karandak trophy has a special cachet and is a ticket to greater things in showbiz.

Navroz

'Nav' means new, and 'roz' means day. Parsis celebrate their New Year by offering prayers at the Agiaries (fire temples) in Camp and Rasta Peth, and exchanging sweets. A number of restaurants in the city hold Parsi food festivals featuring favourites like *Patrani Machhi* (steamed fish wrapped in banana leaves) and Sali Boti (little meat chunks cooked in a gravy and decorated with potato straws).

September

Ganesh Chaturthi

Held to honour Lord Ganesh, the Hindu 'God of New Beginnings', this is the biggest and most colourful festival in the city, marked by community celebrations at every street corner.

The Pune Festival

Coinciding with the ten-day Ganesh festival is the internationally acclaimed Pune Festival, an extravaganza of dance, music and culture.

October

Navratri

Celebrated over nine nights, this festival is dedicated to Hindu goddess Durga or Shakti. Revellers dressed in their finery gather in the evening to join in the lively group folk dances called *garba* and *dandia-ras*.

Chaturshringi Fair

Held annually during Navratri at the base of the Chaturshringi Temple on Senapati Bapat Road, this fair attracts thousands of devotees. Chanting praises in the name of the Goddess, they queue up through the night for a chance to worship in the temple, joining joyfully in the revelry afterwards.

Dussehra

Dussehra signifies the victory of good over evil. According to the ancient epic *Ramayana,* it is the day on which Lord Ram killed the demon Ravana. Cars and homes are decorated with strings of yellow and orange marigolds, and people worship the tools of their trade including vehicles, machinery, books and even computers.

Ramzan Id

Devout Muslims undertake fasts during the holy month of Ramzan, only eating late in the evening or before sunrise. Every evening during this month, the lanes of Mominpura area in Camp and Bohri Ali in the inner city become lively food courts with stalls selling delicacies like *kebabs, biryani* and sweets.

November

Diwali

Held to celebrate the return home of Lord Rama after 14 years of exile, Diwali is one of the most beautiful Indian festivals. Homes are lit with *diyas* (oil lamps) and lanterns to dispel darkness and welcome light and prosperity. People don new clothes, visit relatives and friends, and exchange sweets that have been painstakingly prepared at home. For children, lighting colourful and often noisy firecrackers is the highlight of the festival.

December

Sawai Gandharva

Thousands of people from all backgrounds flock to this celebrated Hindustani classical music festival. Braving the winter chill, they sit entranced through the night, savouring performances by some of the leading maestros of the country. Held over three days every year, it was started in 1953 by Pt. Bhimsen Joshi in memory of his teacher Shri Sawai Gandharva. Marked by hot coffee, warm blankets and soul stimulating music, this is truly a heady experience.

Pune International Marathon

A high profile and colourful event, the Marathon draws almost 30,000 participants, ranging from celebrated athletes to enthusiastic youngsters and the fitness conscious.

Christmas

Over the past few years Christmas celebrations have extended beyond the homes of Christian families in the city. Shops and commercial establishments enter the spirit of the season, putting up lights and colourful decorations much in advance. Most five and four star hotels in the city organise a lavish Christmas lunch complete with Christmas pudding and turkey and all its trimmings.

New Year's Eve

Enthusiastic celebrations ring in the New Year, with parties ranging from intimate gatherings to high-decibel bashes in hotels and clubs.

Vintage Car Rally

While there is no fixed date for the annual Vintage Car Rally, it is eagerly awaited by motor enthusiasts from across the country. Among the well-maintained beauties that feature in the Rally are some dating back to 1919.

Ganesh Festival

Kasba Ganpati

Tambdi Jogeshwari

Guruji Talim

Tulsibaug

Kesariwada

The two things that Punekars are unanimously passionate about are Shivaji, the great Maratha warrior King; and Ganeshotsav, the most widely celebrated festival in the city. Ganeshotsav / Ganesh Chaturthi is celebrated in August-September to mark the birth anniversary of Lord Ganesh, lovingly known as Ganpati, one of Hinduism's most revered gods.

In 1882, revolutionary Lokmanya Bal Gangadhar Tilak revived the festival primarily to stir patriotic sentiments among the populace. Since then the 10-day Ganeshotsav has been celebrated as a *sarvajanik* or community festival across the city.

Ganpati idols are set up in over 3,000 *mandals* (public stalls) across the city. While most *mandals* are lavishly decorated, others feature tableaux of current affairs. Several undertake charitable work, such as distributing books and clothes among the underprivileged.

At the end of the festival, on Anant Chaturdashi day, the idols are carried across the city in a ceremonious procession for immersion in the river. Rapturous cries of *'Ganpati bappa morya. Pudchya varshi lavkar ya'* (Beloved Lord Ganesha, visit us again early next year) rent the air as thousands of devotees throng the streets to bid farewell to their favourite God.

Ganpatis of Honour

The five oldest and most sacred Ganpati idols of Pune are called the *Manache Ganpatis.* Each over a hundred years old, they are venerated by all, and a true devotee

Shrimant Dagdusheth Halwai Ganpati

One of the most high-profile idols in the city is the Shrimant Dagdusheth Halwai Ganpati at Budhwar Peth. Its widespread reputation attracts people in ten thousands, including dignitaries and celebrities like superstar Amitabh Bachchan who is believed to have donated gold ear ornaments for the idol. A jeweller donated eight kilos of gold for the *dhoti* (loincloth) worn by the idol.

Timeline : Pune

1970-80

Pune rapidly establishes itself as the **Oxford** of the **East.**

1971

Symbiosis Education Society is formed

1974

Bhagwan Rajneesh comes to **Pune &** **starts the Osho Commune**

1988

Pune Festival coinciding with **Ganesh Chaturthi** is launched

will begin his tour of the *mandals* in the city by praying to these five idols. They are also the first five to be immersed at the end of the festival in the following sequence:

1. **Kasba Ganpati:** Located in the heart of the city at Kasba Peth, it is the Gramdevata or the presiding deity of Pune. According to legend it was consecrated by Jijamata, Chhatrapati Shivaji's mother. Traditionally the first invitation for auspicious occasions and wedding ceremonies is offered to the Kasba Ganpati.
2. **Tambdi Jogeshwari Ganpati** at Budhwar Peth.
3. **Guruji Talim Ganpati** on Laxmi Road.
4. **Tulsibaug Ganpati** at Shukrawar Peth.
5. **Kesariwada Ganpati** at Narayan Peth.

Sarasbaug Ganpati

Also high on the visitor's list is the Sarasbaug Ganpati located in the midst of the scenic Sarasbaug, a popular garden that draws many people in the evenings.

Modak

A favourite of Lord Ganesh, the *modak* is an indispensable part of the festival. Made from rice flour, it is stuffed with coconut, sugar and other condiments, and deep-fried or steamed.

Pune Festival

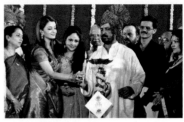

Alongside the traditional Ganeshotsav celebrations, Pune also plays host to a contemporary cultural fiesta to welcome Lord Ganesh. The Pune Festival is a weeklong carnival showcasing the best of art and culture, music and dance, custom and tradition. It has evolved into one of India's landmark cultural happenings and is promoted as a tourist attraction. Visitors can feast on local cuisine and pick out the choicest Maharashtrian textiles and handicrafts. A village festival including bullock cart races and wrestling also forms part of the celebrations.

Timeline : Pune

1998

Pune's first flyover is inaugurated at **Dashabhuja Ganapati Chowk, Kothrud**

1999

The **500 acre Software Development Park** is developed near **Hinjewadi** where **IT** giants like **Wipro & Infosys** set up shop

April 2000

Pune-Mumbai Expressway opens to public

Dec 2005

First international flight takes off from **Pune**

People

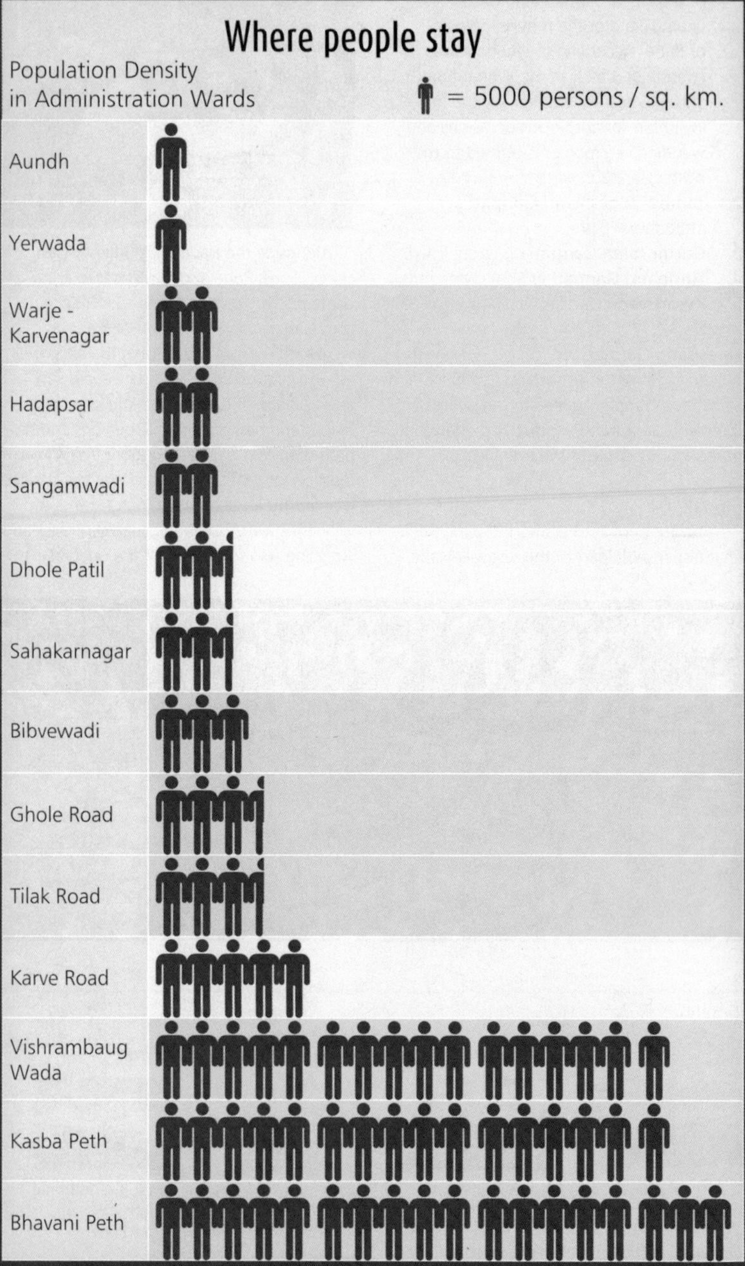

Graph indicative, not for reference (Source: ESR 2004-05)

Age of the People

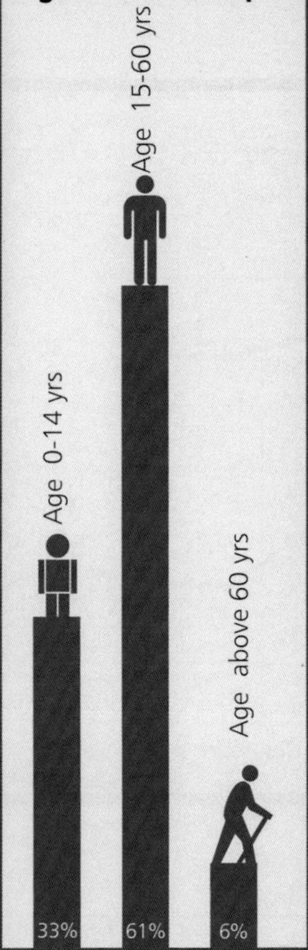

Working People

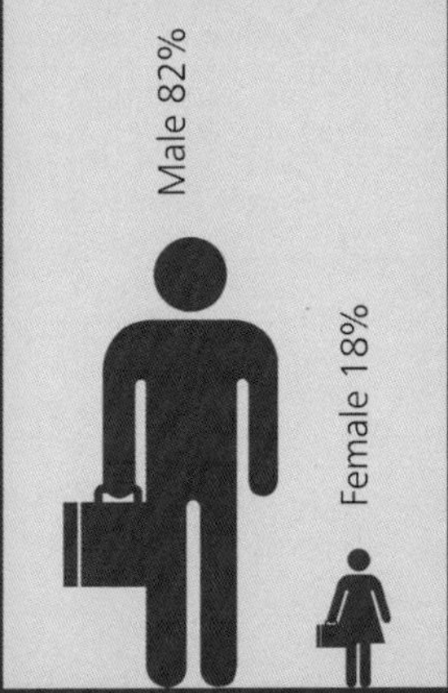

Where People Work

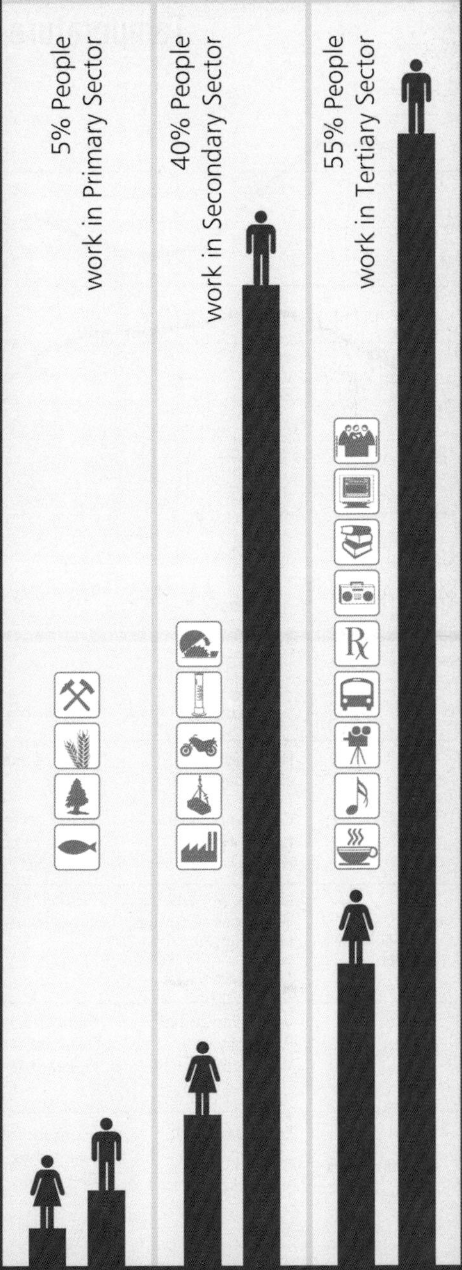

Graph indicative, not for reference (Source: ESR 2004-05)

Seasons

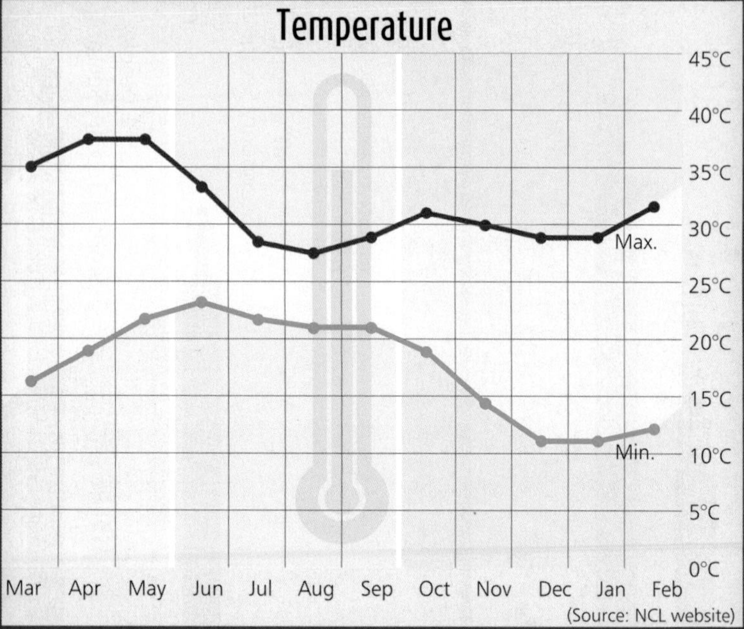

	Summer	Monsoon	Winter
Clothes	Hot days & warm nights Cotton and linen fabrics in light colours.	Warm & humid climate Water resistant jackets or coats, or umbrellas.	Cold nights & pleasantly warm days Warm clothes and light jackets, pullovers, sweaters or shawls.
Vegetables & fruits	Mango, Strawberry, Watermelon, Grapes, Muskmelon.	Citrus Lime, Groundnuts.	Apple, Sugarcane, Cabbage, Guava, Sweet Lemon, Grapes, Oranges, Cauliflower.
Festivals	Guddi Padva, Holi, Rang Panchmi, Vat Pournima.	Independence Day, Ganesh Chaturthi, Gokulashtami.	Navratri, Diwali, Christmas, New Year, Ramzan Id.
Discount Sales	Season End Sale.	Monsoon Sale, Sale before Ganesh Chaturthi.	Sales at Diwali Christmas and New Year.

Graph indicative, not for reference

Pune's Geography

Temperature in Pune

Highest temperature recorded in Pune is 43.3° C on 30 April 1987

Lowest temperature recorded in Pune is 1.7 °C on 17 January 1935

Altitude of Pune & surrounding areas

(Unit: Metres)

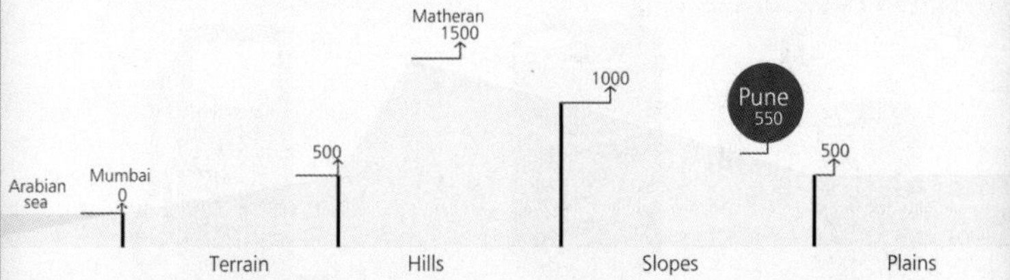

Altitude of places in Pune

(Unit: Metres)

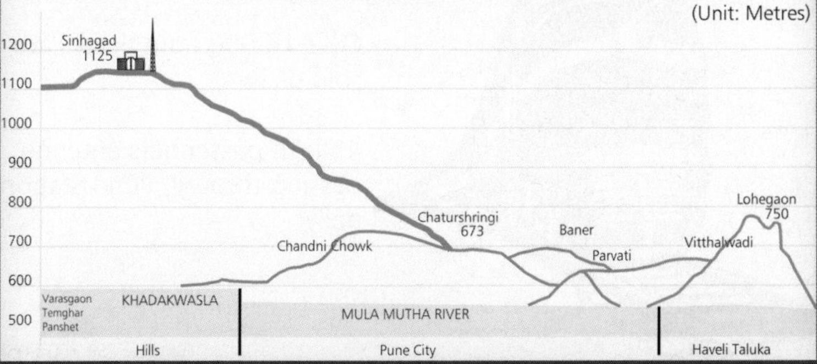

Graph indicative, not for reference (Source: Mashal)

Transportation

% Distribution of vehicles

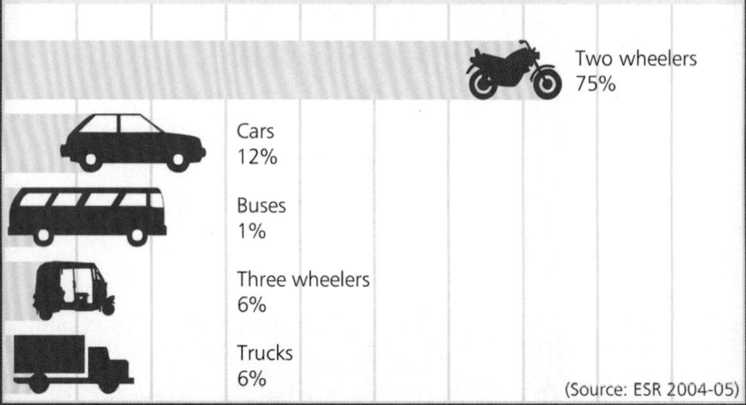

(Source: ESR 2004-05)

Pune's fuel needs

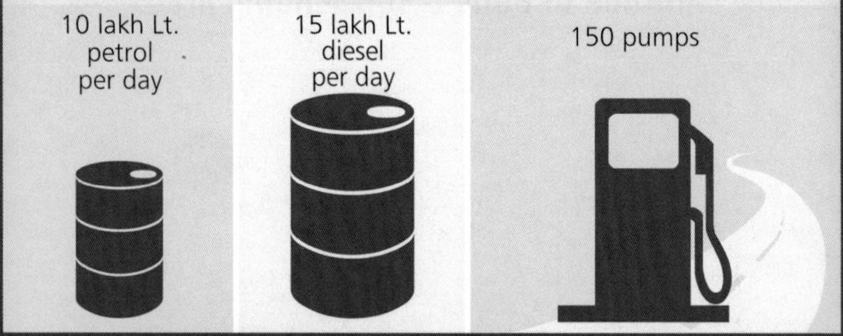

(Source: Pune Petrol Pump Dealers Association)

Over 16,000 train tickets are sold daily

45 lakh passengers entering, passing through Pune Station daily

(Source: ESR 2004-05)

Graph indicative, not for reference

Vehicles in Pune

More than 53% of the households in Pune have two-wheelers

All vehicle registration nos. in Pune begin with MH 12

(Source: RTO)

Flying time from Pune in Hours

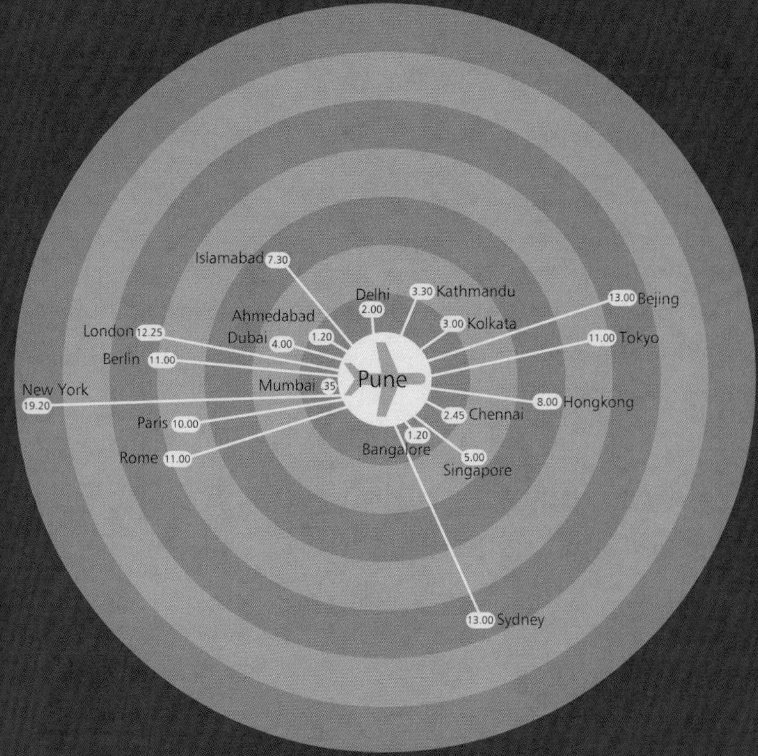

Graph indicative, not for reference

Education

Number of colleges & students in Pune

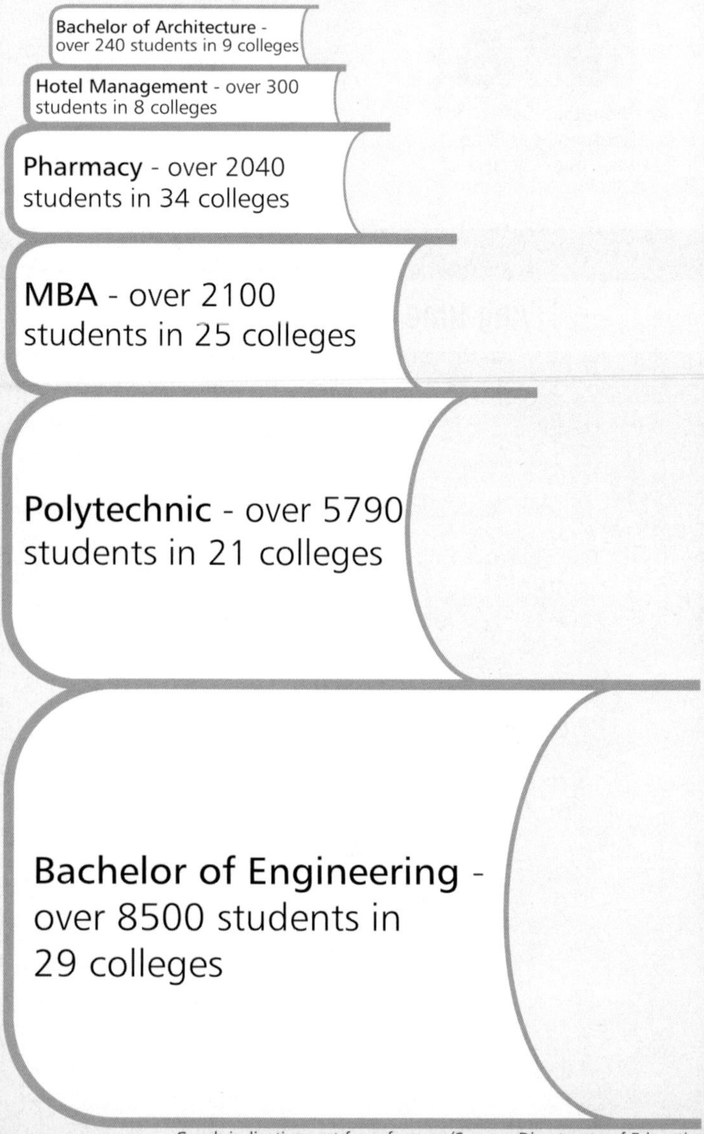

Graph indicative, not for reference (Source: Directorate of Education)

Foreign students coming to Pune

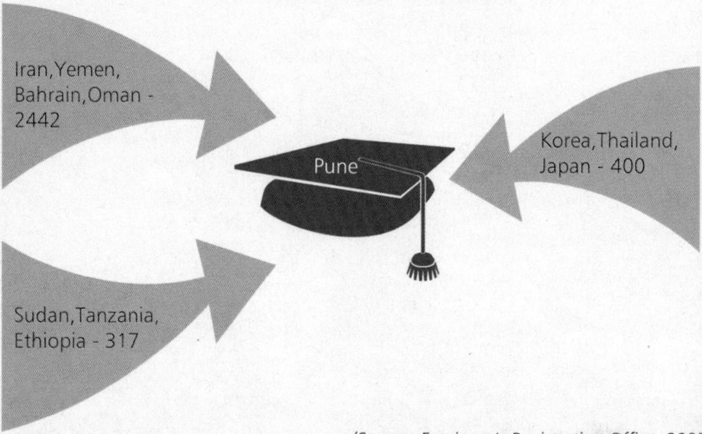

(Source: Foreigner's Registration Office, 2005)

PC penetration in Pune

PC penetration among households of Pune is highest in the country

(Source: Hindu Business Line)

परिहार

Pune by Area

Aundh & Surroundings · Bund Garden-Koregaon Park, *Osho Resort*

Central Pune, *Peths, Shaniwarwada* · Deccan-Shivajinagar

Hadapsar-Solapur Bazaar · Khadki · Kondhwa-Wanowrie-Bibvewadi

Kothrud-Erandwane · Pimpri-Chinchwad · Pune Cantonment

Yerawada-Nagar Road

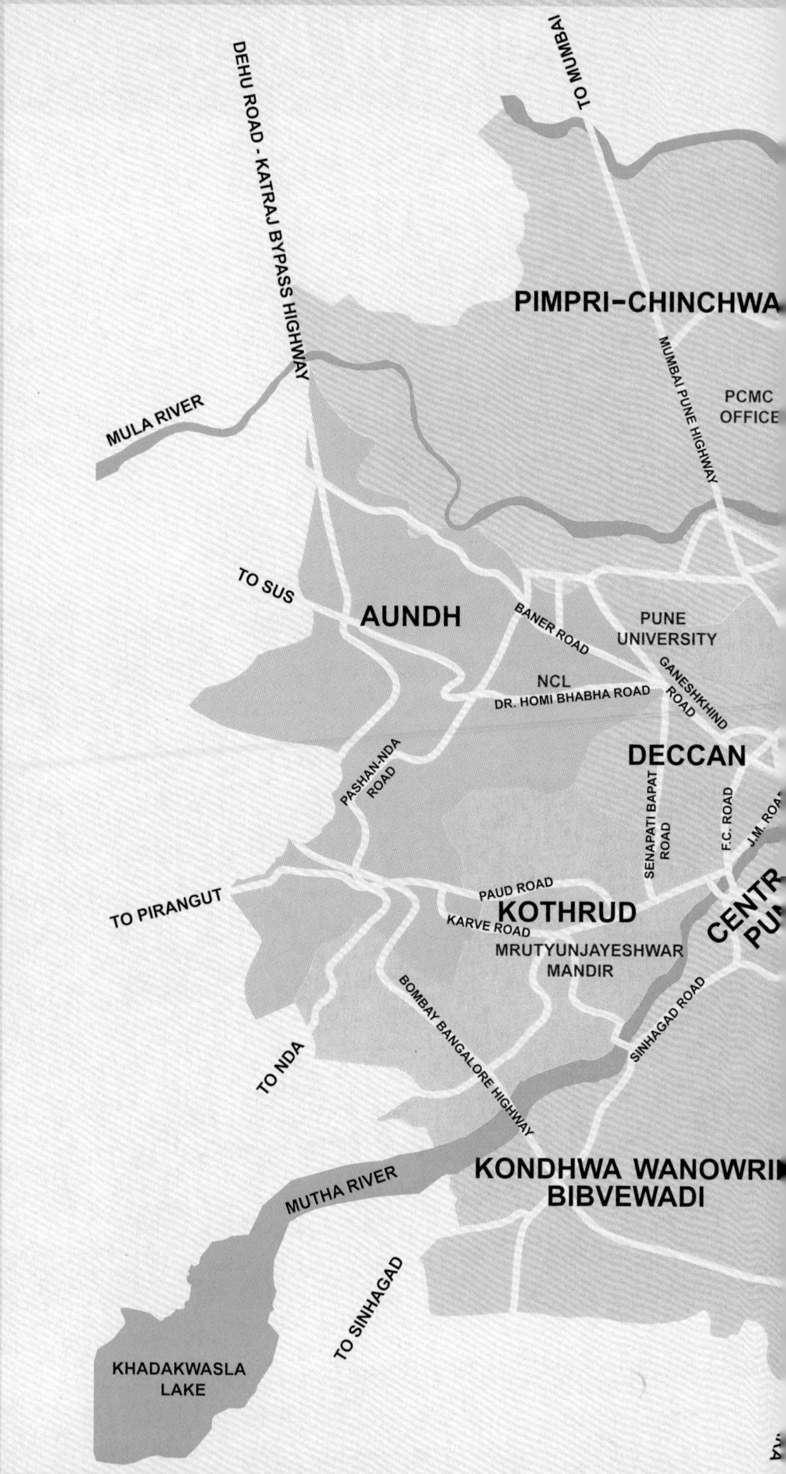

TO MUMBAI
DEHU ROAD - KATRAJ BYPASS HIGHWAY
PIMPRI–CHINCHWA
MUMBAI PUNE HIGHWAY
PCMC
OFFICE
MULA RIVER
TO SUS
AUNDH
BANER ROAD
PUNE
UNIVERSITY
GANESHKHIND
ROAD
NCL
DR. HOMI BHABHA ROAD
PASHAN-NDA
ROAD
DECCAN
SENAPATI BAPAT
ROAD
F.C. ROAD
TO PIRANGUT
PAUD ROAD
KOTHRUD
KARVE ROAD
MRUTYUNJAYESHWAR
MANDIR
SINHAGAD ROAD
BOMBAY BANGALORE HIGHWAY
TO NDA
KONDHWA WANOWRI
BIBVEWADI
MUTHA RIVER
TO SINHAGAD
KHADAKWASLA
LAKE

Pune by Area

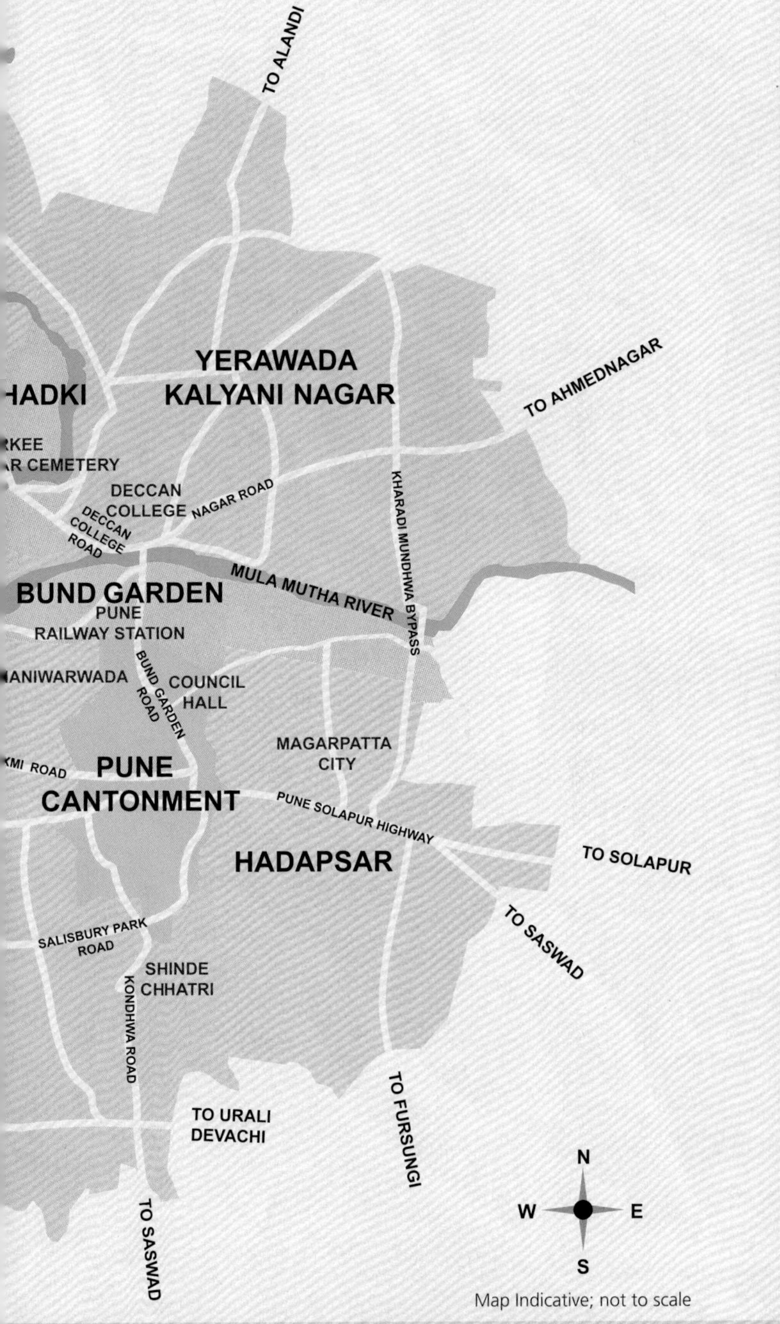
TO ALANDI
YERAWADA
KALYANI NAGAR
HADKI
TO AHMEDNAGAR
KEE
R CEMETERY
DECCAN
COLLEGE
NAGAR ROAD
DECCAN
COLLEGE
ROAD
KHARADI MUNDHWA BYPASS
MULA MUTHA RIVER
BUND GARDEN
PUNE
RAILWAY STATION
ANIWARWADA
BUND GARDEN
ROAD
COUNCIL
HALL
MAGARPATTA
CITY
KMI ROAD
PUNE
CANTONMENT
PUNE SOLAPUR HIGHWAY
HADAPSAR
TO SOLAPUR
SALISBURY PARK
ROAD
TO SASWAD
SHINDE
CHHATRI
KONDHWA ROAD
TO URALI
DEVACHI
TO FURSUNGI
TO SASWAD
N
W
E
S

Map Indicative; not to scale

Aundh & Surroundings

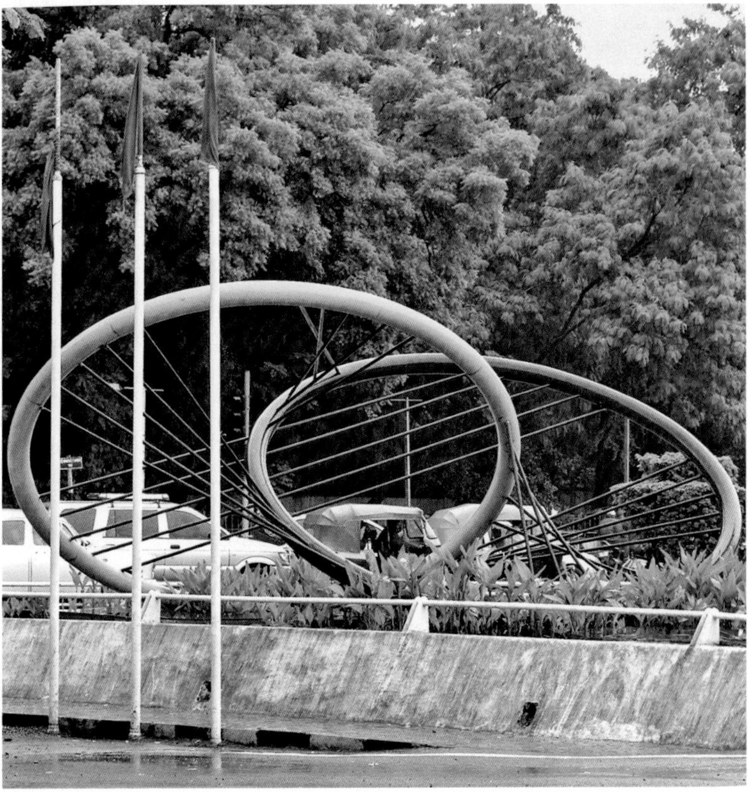

Once considered a far-flung suburb, Aundh and its neighbouring areas have undergone a rapid transformation. This northwestern part of the city is now an upmarket, cosmopolitan residential area with its own share of snazzy departmental stores, shops, and restaurants. Its proximity to the Mumbai-Pune expressway and the growth of the IT Park at Hinjewadi nearby has accelerated its pace of development. Today it has become the area of choice for professionals and pensioners alike.

In the past five years areas around Aundh, including Baner, Balewadi, Sus Road, and Bavdhan have also seen quick development. Construction activities have increased manifold, and several exclusive residential colonies are coming up in the area. Since they fall on the outskirts of the city, these areas can still lay claim to abundant greenery and have access to the last few open spaces in the city.

Prominent Localities

Aundh

One of the most sought after areas in the city, it is a mélange of diverse living spaces and growing commercial activity.

Pashan-Sus Road

Pashan has long been home to some of the nation's major research institutes, such as the National Chemical Laboratory (NCL), and Defence Research and Development Organisation (DRDO).

Bavdhan

Developed as a residential area along a hillside, Bavdhan is also the preferred location for several large companies.

Baner

In the last few years Baner has shot to prominence as the area of choice for several IT companies, and the landscape is dominated by imposing glass and concrete structures.

Balewadi

The sprawling Shiv Chhatrapati Sports Complex built for the 1993 National Games was what first brought this area into the public eye. Today it is developing into a prime residential area.

Wakad

Adjacent to Aundh, this small village has of late seen a spurt in construction thanks to its proximity to Hinjewadi.

Hinjewadi

Unknown till just a few years ago, the area is now synonymous with the world class IT park where leading international and national companies have set up office.

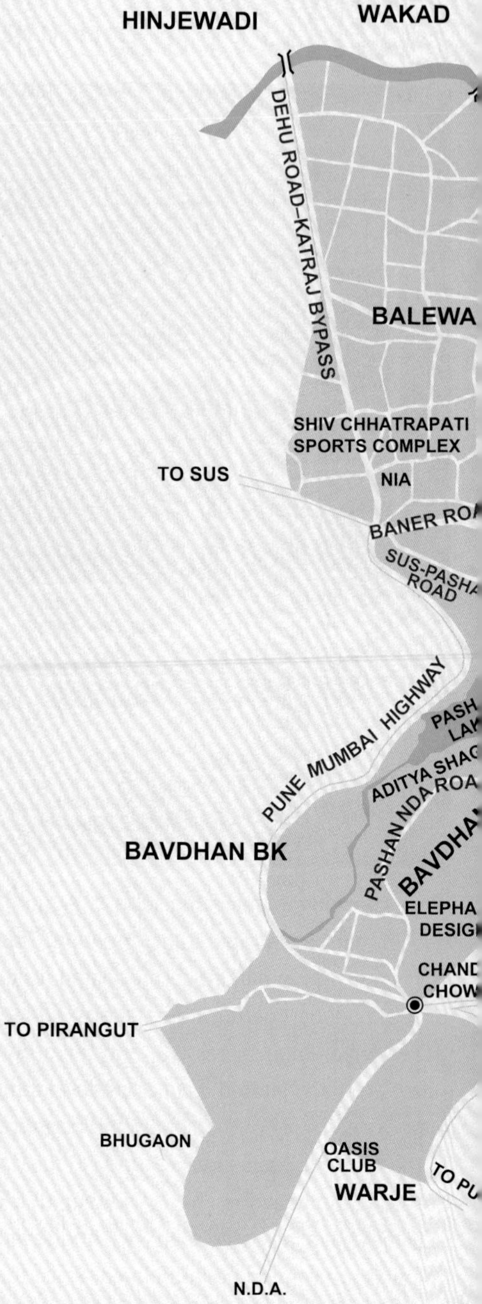

Aundh & Surroundings

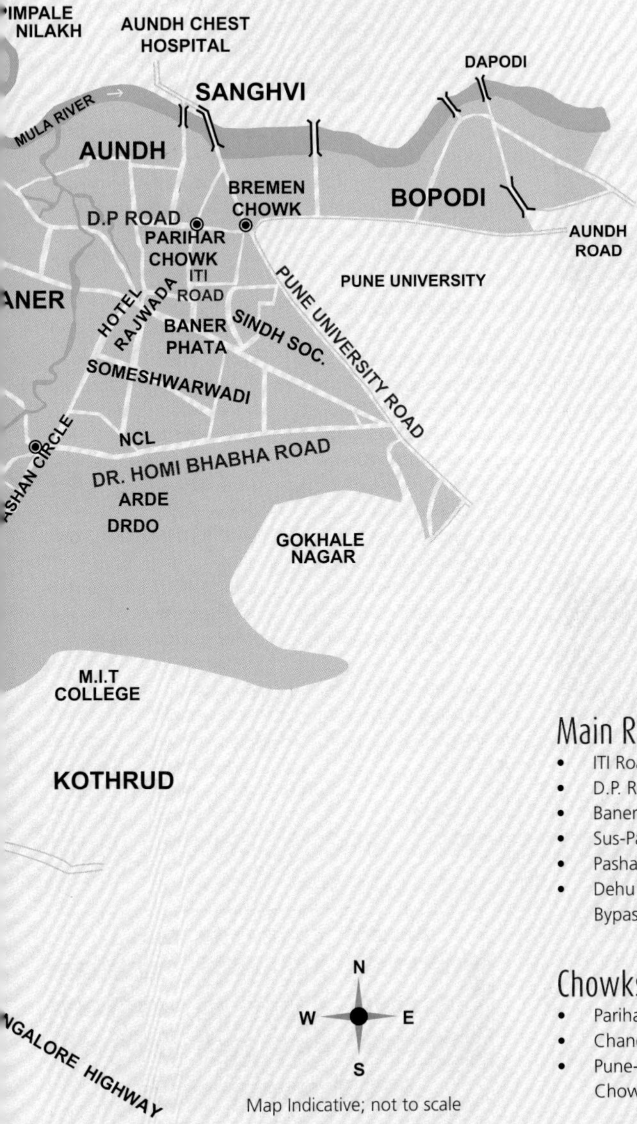

Map Indicative; not to scale

Main Roads

- ITI Road
- D.P. Road
- Baner Road
- Sus-Pashan Road
- Pashan-NDA Road
- Dehu Road-Katraj Bypass

Chowks

- Parihar Chowk
- Chandni Chowk
- Pune-Bremen Maitri Chowk

Landmarks

Aundh has a number of government research institutes of national importance. With their large campuses and well-maintained gardens they have become major landmarks in the area.

Yashwantrao Chavan Academy of Development Administration (YASHADA)

This is an apex-training institute of the Government of Maharashtra to prepare senior officials in development administration. Raj Bhawan Complex, Baner Road, Pune 411007 Tel: 25608000 / 25608612

Indian Institute of Tropical Meteorology

Once a distinct part of the Indian Meteorological Department, IITM received autonomous status in 1971 Its main area of research is monsoon meteorology and many of its studies are of national and international importance. Dr Homi Bhabha Road, Pashan, Pune 411008 Tel: 25893600/25893825

Armament Research and Development Establishment (ARDE) Explosive Research and Development Authority (ERDA) Defence Research and Development Organisation (DRDO)

These establishments conduct extensive research and devise programmes to build new weapons and improve national security. 108/Necklace Area, Armament, Pashan, Pune 411021 ARDE Tel: 25881914 DRDO Tel: 27150882

High Energy Material Research Laboratory (HEMRL)

Located in the vicinity of DRDO, HEMRL is into research and development of powerful warheads for munitions. The institute also specialises in development of propellants for missile systems and has also made anti-thermal and anti-laser smoke bombs. Sutarwadi, Pashan, Pune 411021 Tel: 25869828

Raj Bhavan

A sprawling complex of colonial buildings, the Raj Bhavan is the residence of the Governor of Maharashtra who spends the monsoon months here. Ganeshkhind Road, Pune 411007 Tel: 2565 0188/ 1330 / 6813

Rural Police Headquarters

The Pune district rural police headquarters are located on Pashan Road. The large campus also houses a training centre and residential quarters for police personnel. The Centre for Police Research is also located in the vicinity.

National Chemical Laboratory (NCL)

NCL is part of the Council of Scientific and Industrial Research (CSIR). It is a research, development and consulting organisation essentially for chemical engineering and chemistry. 264 Main Building, Dr Homi Bhabha Road, Pashan, Pune 411008 Tel: 25893300 / 25893053

Dr Homi Bhabha Road,
Chavan Nagar, Pashan,
Pune 411008 Tel: 25657878

Places of Worship

Loyola Chapel
A charming little chapel located on the campus of Loyola High School.
Dr Homi Bhabha Road,
Pashan, Pune 411008
Tel: 25656699

Balaji Temple
Near Mont Vert, Sus Road
Pune 411021

Someshwar Temple
Someshwarwadi,
Baner Road, Pune 411008

Education

Loyola High School

One of the oldest schools in the area, it was set up by the Jesuits and is as well known for its picturesque campus as its discipline.
Dr Homi Bhabha Road,
Pashan, Pune 411008
Tel: 25656699

St Joseph's High School
Set up under the Convent of Jesus and Mary, this all-girls school is considered one of the best convent schools in the city.
Dr Homi Bhabha Road,
Pashan, Pune 411008
Tel: 25655505

DAV Public School
Run by the acclaimed DAV Society, which runs schools all over the country.
Opp. Spencer's Daily,
D.P. Road, Aundh,
Pune 411007
Tel: 25893377 / 25890081

Vidya Valley School
A relatively new school, it is gaining popularity for its radical teaching methods.
Sus Road, Pashan,
Pune 411021
Tel: 56339986/56339985

Orchid School
Backed by experienced educationists, the school offers unique teaching methods and caters basically to the children of young professionals.
Baner Road, Baner,
Pune 411045
Tel: 27292701 / 30926464
www.theorchidschool.org

Spicer Memorial School and College
The Spicer College campus also houses a school. The college is affiliated to the University of Pune and attracts many international students for its degree and diploma programmes.

Besides academics, the college has also become popular for its confectionery.
Aundh-Khadki Road,
Aundh, Pune 411007
College Tel: 25691383
School Tel: 25692384

Mercedes-Benz International School
Started by the German automobile premier Daimler Chrysler India Pvt. Ltd. primarily for their employees' children. It follows an international syllabus and is open to all.
Pune Infotech Park, MIDC,
Phase 1, Hinjewadi,
Pune 411057
Tel: 22934420 / 30

Art Galleries

Indiaart Gallery
This is a popular venue for painting exhibitions. Art workshops for children are also conducted here.
Sarjaa Restaurant Lane,
Off ITI Road, Aundh,
Pune 411007
Tel: 25896503

Vaishwik Art Environment
A multicultural centre, it is the first art gallery in Pune to provide a platform for young artists, including potters, sculptors and calligraphers.
Survey No 246, House No 1982, Saket Society,
D.P. Road, Aundh
Pune 411007
Tel: 27298182

Books

Jungle Book
A great library and activity centre for kids.

Also conducts classes in elocution, drama, music and drawing.
Avni Arcade, Gaikwad Nagar, Aundh,
Pune 411007 Tel: 25882223

Jagtap Library
One of the oldest libraries in the area, it offers a selection of Marathi and English books and periodicals.
Gaikwad Nagar, Aundh,
Pune 411007

P40
Part of a chain of libraries, it houses a diverse selection of English books and magazines.
Clarion Park, Aundh,
Pune 411007
Tel: 32948175

Twist 'n' Tales
A neighbourhood bookstore catering to all tastes and age groups.
Gaikwad Nagar, Aundh,
Pune 411007
Tel: 25881465
Closed on Monday.

Crossword
Part of a chain of snazzy bookstores, it also stocks music and stationery.
ITI Road, Next to Ozone,
Aundh, Pune 411007
Tel: 66028013/25883501

Pashan Lake
An ornithologist's delight, the lake attracts an amazing variety of birds like the black-winged stilt, painted stork, coot, drongo, marsh harrier, warbler, heron and many more. The best time to visit is between November and February.
Entry Point: NDA Road, near Bharat Electronics.

Shops

F-Cube
A lifestyle store with interesting artifacts, gift articles and knick-knacks for the house.
Shirine Garden, ITI Road,
Aundh, Pune 411007
Tel: 5898018/4024488
Closed on Monday

Banjaras
Offers a colourful range of ready-to-wear clothing for men and women. Also have tailoring facilities.
E 1 Chaitraban Residency,
ITI Road Sarjaa Restaurant
Lane, Aundh, Pune 411007
Tel: 25881844

Dass Electric Trading
A reputed showroom for branded electronics and home appliances.
Sanghvi Nagar,
D.P. Road, Near Bremen
Chowk, Aundh,
Pune 411007
Tel: 56092480/81/82

Plugin
One of the city's largest consumer durable chains, it also has branches in Camp, Tilak Road and Satara Road.
D. P. Rd, Sanghvi Nagar,
Aundh, Pune 411007
Tel: 30939299

Sony World
The electronics giant has a spacious showroom stocking the latest plasma televisions, cell phones and camcorders.
Equity Tower, D.P. Road,
Sanghvi Nagar, Aundh,
Pune 411007
Tel: 56005336/37
Closed on Monday

Samsung Digital Home
For gadget geeks, this electronics showroom stocks a vast range of Samsung products.

Plot no 8, Sanghvi,
D. P. Road, Parihar Chowk,
Aundh, Pune 411007
Tel: 56096890 / 56091376/7
Closed on Monday

Ozone
A landmark in Aundh, Ozone houses a departmental store, a gift and household accessories store, a furnishings section, a sweet shop, a cafe and restaurant.
92, Anand Park,
ITI Rd, Aundh,
Pune 411007 Tel: 56022555

Petsworld
An exclusive pet store stocking accessories and pet food. They also have a branch on Karve Road.
ITI Road, Aundh,
Pune 411007 Tel: 25897321

Natekar Sports
This is a fine outlet for sports goods and accessories and stocks all popular brands. Chaitraban Residency, Sarjaa Restaurant Lane, Aundh, Pune 411007
Tel: 25885556

Restaurants

Polka Dots
A popular multi-cuisine restaurant, Polka Dots attracts customers from

across the city. Also offers a range of mouthwatering desserts.
D. P. Road, Aundh,
Pune 411007 Tel: 56212241

Garden Court
Situated in the hills of Pashan, Garden Court is popular for its ambience and its diverse menu.
NDA Road, Chandni Chowk,
Kothrud, Pune 411029
Tel: 25283502 / 25280001

Ambrosia
Located on the outskirts of the city, the sprawling Ambrosia was one of the first restaurants in the area and continues to flourish.
S no 38/2, Bavdhan Khurd,
Tal Mulshi, Pune 411021
Tel: 22951023 / 22951571

Banjara Hills
Another hilltop restaurant, Banjara Hills offers a great meal in well-appointed surroundings.
S No 20/4/B Bavdhan Khurd,
NDA Road, Chandni Chowk,
Pune 411021
Tel: 22951019 / 22951560

Up and Above
An open air bar and grill restaurant with a wonderful view and relaxing surroundings

'Rambaugh', S No. 75,
Chandni Chowk, Kothrud,
Pune 411029
Tel:22953272 / 9371060746

Oasis
A multi-cuisine restaurant and bar, it is the ideal place to chill out with family and friends.
Sr. No. 104/5/1 Warje, NDA Road, Pune 411029
Tel: 25286276 / 5135 / 6422

Rajwada

A multi-cuisine restaurant with indoor and outdoor seating. Plenty of room for kids to run free.
15/A Kale Park,
Baner Road,
Baner 411045
Tel:25885885 / 1881

Shiv Chhatrapati Sports Complex : Built for the National Games in 1993, the sprawling complex has been selected as the venue for the third Commonwealth Youth Games (CYG) to be held in October 2008 Balewadi, Dehu Road-Katraj Bypass.

Green Park
Once a modest little eatery, it has transformed into a plush entity with indoor and outdoor seating, and a multifarious menu.
14/B, Kale Park,
Baner Road, Baner,
Pune 411045
Tel:25886265

Sarjaa
Aundh's first multi-cuisine restaurant, it continues to be a favourite with many.
ITI Road, Aundh
Pune 411007
Tel: 25886177/25880666

Kobe
Serves an interesting range of steaming hot sizzlers and snack options.
ITI Road, Aundh
Pune 411007
Tel: 25887576/77

Wazwaan
A multi-cuisine restaurant, it specialises in Kashmiri fare such as *seekh* and *shammi kababs, tabak maaz* and *kormas.*
Baner Road, Baner,
Pune 411045
Tel: 27292422

Clubs

Pancard Clubs
Spread across 15 acres on a hillside, it offers modern amenities inlcuding a sports centre, amphitheatre, landscaped gardens, kid's park, discotheque and go-karting. It also features Area 51, 'India's first revolving private entertainment lounge'. The club is open to members only.
Baner Hills, Baner Village.
Pune 411045
Tel: 27290182/83

Anandban Club
A family club with a swimming pool, tennis courts and gymnasium.
Anand Park, ITI Rd,
Aundh, Pune 411007
Tel: 25884455

Salons

Salon Headlines
Anand Park, ITI Road,
Aundh, Pune 411007
Tel: 27298586

Bellezza
Solaris Health Club,
ITI Road, Aundh,
Pune 411007
Tel: 25893565/25887464

Beauty in Toto
Shanker Smriti Apartments,
Near Ozone, Anand Park,
ITI Road, Aundh,
Pune 411007
Tel: 56611791

Hospitals

Aundh Chest Hospital

Aundh Camp, Aundh,
Pune 411027 Tel: 27280237

Kotbagi Hospital
163 D.P. Road, Aundh,
Pune 411007 Tel: 25882770

Medipoint Hospital
Aundh-Baner Boundary,
D.P. Road, Pune 411007
Tel: 27297337/27297688

Lifeline
157, Near Union Bank of India, 'Legacy', D.P. Road,
Aundh, Pune 411007
Tel: 25882053 / 25896942
9am-9pm

Health Clubs

Solaris Fitness Club
Supreme Center, ITI Road,
Aundh, Pune 411007
Tel:25893565/25887464

Callipygian Fitness Inc.
D. P. Road, Aundh,
Pune 411007 Tel: 25896195

Indiana Health Club
Baner Road, Baner,
Pune 411045 Tel: 27291620

Mobius Fitness
Opposite Kundan Garden Mangal Karyalaya, Baner Road, Pune 411045
Tel: 27292354/66242551

Sanjay Health Club
Sanjay Residency, Someshwar Wadi Corner, Baner Road, Pune 411045
Tel: 25889072

Smitz
Sukhwani Prestige, Near Ramnagar Colony, Near Hotel Saffron, Bavdhan, Pune 411021
Tel: 9890434123, 32600006

Banks and ATMs

ICICI ATM
Sudhanam, Plot No 4, Baner Road, Sakal Nagar, Aundh, Pune 411007

HDFC ATM
Pushak, 90 Anand Park, ITI Road, Aundh, Pune 411007

CASP Bhuban Plot No. 3 132/2 Pashan, Baner Link Road, Pune 411007

Sudhanam, Plot No 4, Baner Road, Sakal Nagar, Aundh Pune 411007

Citibank ATM
37 Patil Complex, Spicer College Road, Aundh, Pune 411007

Dena Bank
26, Niyoshi Park 2, Aundh, Pune 411007
Tel: 25880515

Saraswat Bank ATM
Yogita Park, Opp. ITI, ITI Road, Pune 411007

HDFC Bank
Royal Residency, Aundh Road, Aundh, Pune 411007
Tel: 25690126 / 25690752

ICICI Bank
S No 132/2, Gulmohar Pk, ITI Rd, Aundh, Pune 411007
Tel: 25890902 / 25889640

Saraswat Bank
Yashwantrao Chavan, Baner Rd, Aundh, Pune 411007
Tel:25662949

The Cosmos Co-Op Bank
1a/132, Dhanshree Apts, Aundh, Pune 411007
Tel: 25880242

Bank of Maharashtra
Shakun Apt, Sanghvi Ngr, Aundh, Pune 411007
Tel: 25883886/ 25883886

State Bank Of India
Baner Rd, Aundh, Pune 411007
Tel: 25887817

Places of Interest

Mulshi
The drive to Mulshi Dam offers stunning views and the opportunity to stop at several quaint eateries on the way. An hour's drive from the city, the Mulshi area is a picnicker's delight.

Aundh and its environs which are lush with trees and vegetation and dotted by water bodies, make it a perfect winter retreat for a wide spectrum of migratory birds.

PUNE
CENTRAL
Provogue Surfing
Classics
rovogue
Hutch
The Fall Collection
SALE

Bund Garden - Koregaon Park

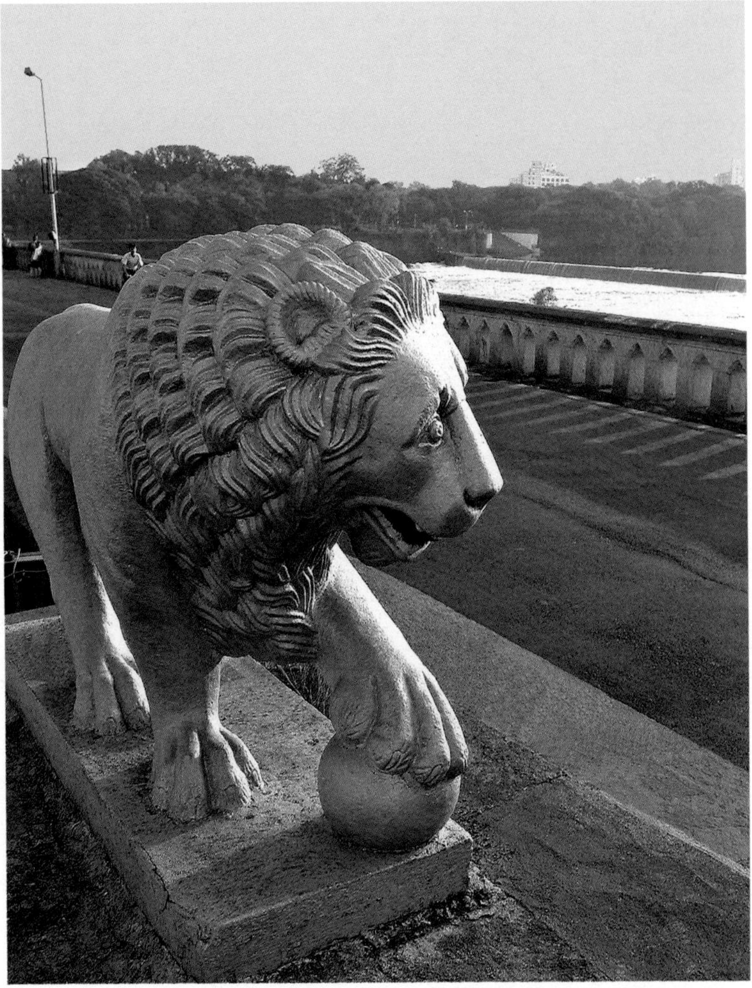

The quiet, upmarket residential localities of Boat Club Road and Koregaon Park have developed into fashionable hubs with the city's finest restaurants, nightclubs, shops, boutiques, and hotels. People from all over the world travel to Koregaon Park to visit the Osho International Meditation Resort, set up by controversial spiritual leader Rajneesh. Also in the vicinity is the bustling Station area, where two of Pune's finest hospitals are located.

Prominent Localities

Koregaon Park
An upmarket residential area, now boasting innumerable trendy boutiques and restaurants.

Boat Club Road
Another fashionable residential area lined with boutiques, shops and eateries.

Mundhwa
A rapidly developing area, now considered an extension of Koregaon Park.

Tadiwala Road
A crowded locality near the Pune Station, housing the Railway quarters.

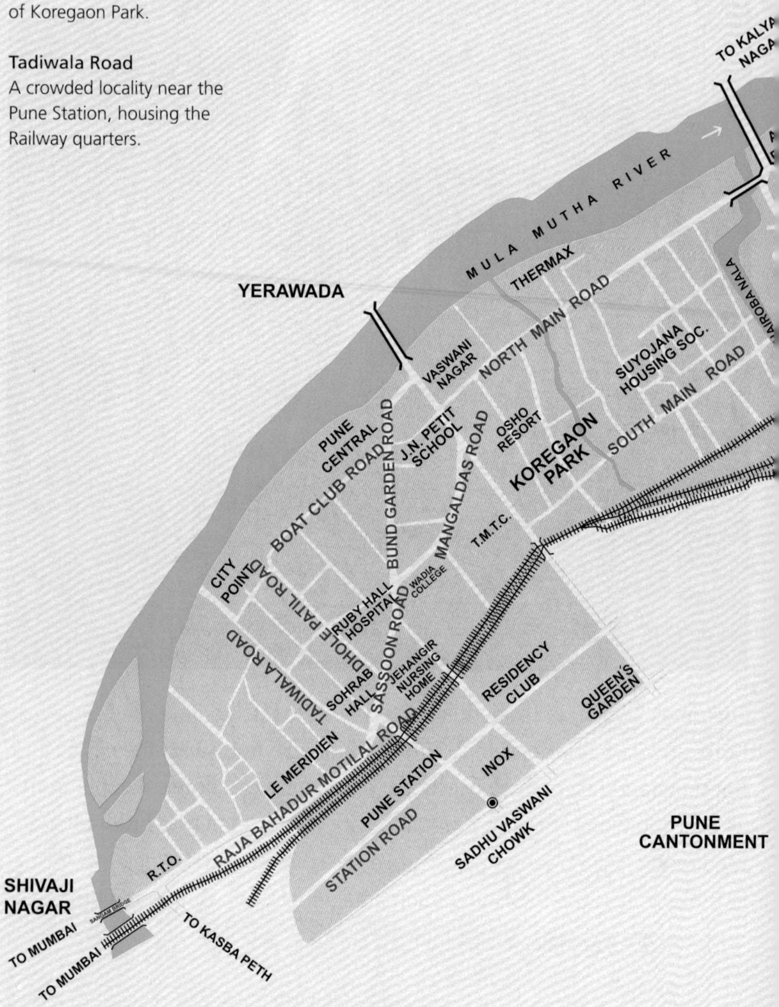

Bund Garden - Koregaon Park

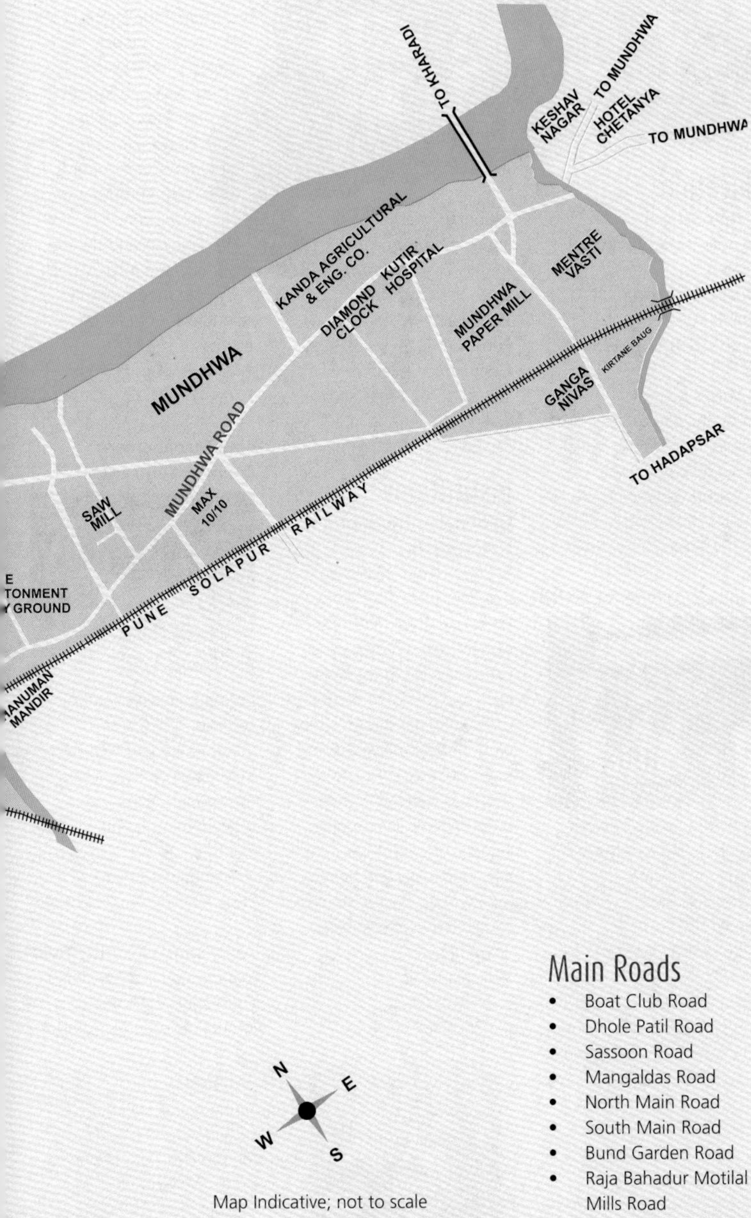

Map Indicative; not to scale

Main Roads

- Boat Club Road
- Dhole Patil Road
- Sassoon Road
- Mangaldas Road
- North Main Road
- South Main Road
- Bund Garden Road
- Raja Bahadur Motilal Mills Road

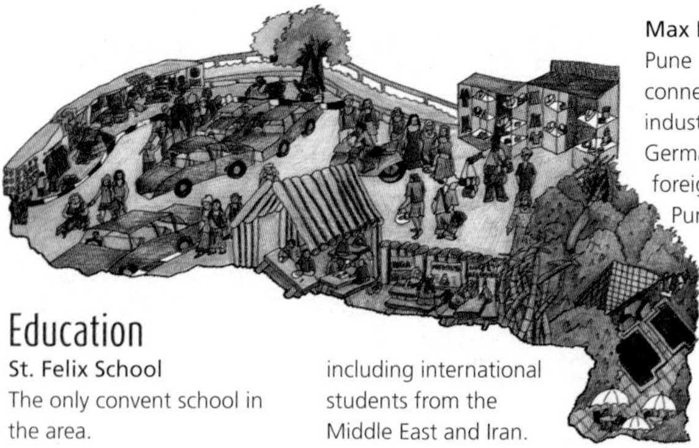

Education

St. Felix School
The only convent school in the area.
4 Boat Club Road,
Pune 411001
Tel: 26128693 / 26123616

St. Mira's School
Run by the Sadhu Vaswani Mission, it is popular with the Sindhi community.
10, Sadhu Vaswani Road,
Pune 411001
Tel: 26127841

St. Mira's College for Girls

Run by the Sadhu Vaswani Mission, it is the only all-girls college in the area.
6 Koregaon Park,
Pune 411001
Tel: 26138604 / 26124846

Wadia College
Started in 1932 with around 250 students, it has grown into one of the leading educational institutions in the city. It offers graduate courses in commerce (Ness Wadia College), science and arts (Nowrosjee Wadia College) and engineering (Cusrow Wadia College). The 16-acre campus is buzzing with students from multi-cultural backgrounds, including international students from the Middle East and Iran.
E-19, V. K. Jog Path,
Bund Garden Road,
Pune 411001
Commerce College
Tel: 26127024 Arts and Science College
Tel: 26122944

Institutions

National Institute of Naturopathy
Set up in 1986, this is an excellent place for those seeking natural methods of treatment. They have an exhaustive list of therapies including mud and magnetic therapy, spinal spray, asthma bath, underwater pressure massage, etc. Their health shop has over 100 varieties of food items like organic jaggery, unpolished rice, neti pot, mudpacks and health books. Yoga classes are also conducted here regularly.
'Bapu Bhavan',
Tadiwala Road,
Pune 411001
Tel: 26059682/3/4

Max Mueller Bhavan
Pune has a strong German connection, culturally, industrially and linguistically. German is a popular foreign language in Pune and is taught at the Max Mueller Bhavan. It is also an important cultural centre promoting music concerts, film festivals and theatre performances. Check out their monthly calendar for details on events.
14/3 B, Boat Club Road,
Pune 411001 Tel: 26131340

Tata Management Training Centre (TMTC)

Located amidst beautiful settings, TMTC was inaugurated by J.R.D. Tata in 1966 Since then it has evolved into a leading management training institute.
1, Mangaldas Road,
Pune 411001 Tel: 26139246

Army Sports Institute (ASI)
Inaugurated in 2005, it is considered to be one of Asia's finest sports institutes.

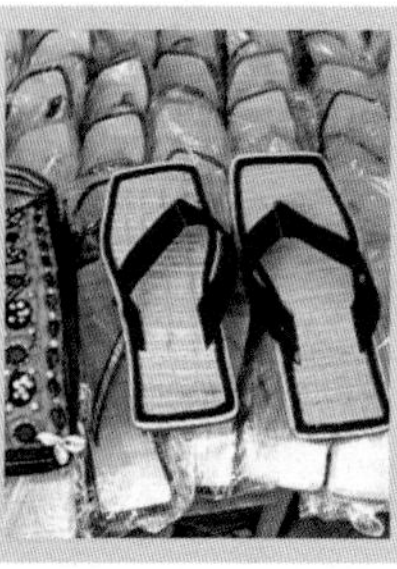

Osho slippers
These bright colored, comfortable slip-ons sold outside the Osho Commune are a rage. Made from natural grass and cloth and embellished with beads and sequins they are also known as chatai chappals.

Equipped with all modern training facilities and an Olympic size ground and pool, it has been set up to train and coach sportsmen from the Armed Forces.
Mundhwa Road, Koregaon Park Annexe,
Pune 411001 Tel: 26102926

Railway Station

Pune Railway Station

This is Pune's main railway terminus. It is abuzz with activity almost 24 hours and is surrounded by low-priced lodges and hotels. The Pune-Mumbai Taxi Stand is close by. The 24-hr café Comesum in the station premises is very popular with travellers and others seeking a late night meal.
Station Road, Pune 411001
Tel: 26126575 / 131

Govt. Offices

Road Transport Office (RTO)

This office conducts driving tests, issues driving licenses and permits for vehicles. It has an extension on Alandi Road.
Raja Bahadur Mills Road,
Sangam Bridge,
Pune 411001
Tel: 26120808 / 26051840

Customs and Central Excise Office

An important government office for collection of taxes and revenues.
41-A, ICE House,
Sassoon Road,
Pune 411001
Tel: 26050793

Curio Shops

Check out these charming shops selling metal curios and other mystic knickknacks like lucky gems, therapeutic stones, meditation bells, etc.
North Main Road,
Koregaon Park,
Pune 411001

Botanical Survey of India (BSI)

The BSI shifted to these verdant premises in 1958 It is the head office of the western circle and has under its jurisdiction several states including Goa and Karnataka. It conducts research and works for the ecological development of the region.
7th Western Circle,
Koregaon Road,
Pune 411001 Tel: 26141491

Gardens

Bund Garden

So named because it is built alongside a mini-dam (bund), the garden serves as a verdant oasis in this busy locality. It features a children's section and a well-maintained jogging track, and draws a large number of people in the evenings. At one time students from the Blind School would perform in the band stand in Bund Garden.
Bund Garden Road,
Pune 411001

Osho Teerth Nullah Park

The 12-acre Nullah Park is one of the most scenic areas in the city. Once a garbage dump, it was painstakingly converted into a beautifully landscaped green zone by Osho disciples, and features an array of exotic plants, trees and flowers, and Japanese style bridges. The Park is open to the public from 6-11am and 4-8pm.
Koregaon Park,
Pune 411001 Tel: 66019999
(Osho Meditation Resort)

Shops

Either Or

An ethnic haven, it features an assortment of clothes for men and women, jewellery, scarves, bags, and shoes.
Ground Floor, Sohrab Hall, Sassoon Road,
Pune 411001 Tel: 26050225

More Mischief

A designer showroom for men with some trendy Indo-American outfits on their racks.

34/35 Sohrab Hall, Opp Jehangir Nursing Home, Sassoon Road,
Pune 411001 Tel: 26059393

Crossword

This is the booklover's paradise.It also has a toy section and a music department. This is one of the largest Crossword outlets in the city.
Sohrab Hall, 1st Floor, Junction of RBM - Connaught Road, Behind Pune Railway Station,
Pune 411001
Tel: 26059600 / 1 / 2 / 3

Fabindia

The store stocks a cool range of trendy cotton ensembles for both men and women. Their ethnic accessories and household linen sections are also extremely popular.
Sakar-10, Opp Jehangir Nursing Home, Sassoon Road, Pune 411001
Tel: 26124820 / 26124832

Magna Book Gallery and Nutrition Centre

A recent introduction to Pune, it stocks an assortment of books with amazing prices. The Nutrition Centre stocks health food items, sugar-free chocolates, herbal creams, lotions, soaps and other cosmetics.
Graphicon Arcade, Opp Jehangir Nursing Home, Sassoon Road, Pune 411001
Tel: 56271681 / 56271682

Nature's Bounty

A house of natural products, health foods, aromatherapy oils, herbal cosmetics, low fat anytime snacks, etc. It also has an oxygen bar, proclaimed to be the first of its kind in the city
G, 11/6 Liberty 11, North Main Road, Koregaon Park,
Pune 411001 Tel: 26114627

This 'n' That

This small place is known for assorted ethnic and western wear, accessories and gift articles. Also has an outlet on NIBM Road, Kondhwa
Shop No. 2 Phase 2, Liberty Society, North Main Road, Koregaon Park,
Pune 411001
Tel: 26055146

Max Super Market

Spread over 30,000 sq ft, this is an excellent one-stop shop for groceries, vegetables, clothes and other household items.
Survey No. 179/1 Mundhwa Ghorpadi Road, Koregaon Park Annexe, Pune 411001
Tel: 66260343

Pune Central Mall

Spread over 1,60,000 sq. ft. on five floors, it has already become a popular landmark for the trendy and fashion conscious.
256, Koncord Towers, Boat Club Road, Bund Garden.
Pune 411001 Tel: 56099000

Restaurants/Cafés

German Bakery

A popular hangout for foreign visitors to the Osho

Sabby's Tattoo Studio

The first and most popular tattoo studio in Pune. Rates: Minimum Rs. 1,500 for an inch design.
A7, Ashiyana Park, 1st Floor, North Main Road, Koregaon Park,
Pune 411001
Tel: 9823176464 / 9890464681

Commune, it serves an interesting range of snacks.
291, Vaswani Nagar, North Main Road,
Pune 411001 Tel: 26136532

Hot Breads

Stocks a great variety of confectionery items.
1A/1B Gera Sterling, North Main Road, Koregaon Park,
Pune 411001
Tel: 26133757 / 26054307

Sweet Chariot Cafe

Try out this modish café with mouth-watering snacks and pastries.
Mit Corner, North Main Road, Koregaon Park,
Pune 411001 Tel: 26113363

Just Baked

A delicious range of baked goods and appetizing snacks.
198/3, Chandrakant Chambers, Dhole Patil Road,
Pune 411001
Tel: 26123296 / 26127278

Night Club

The oldest nightclub in Pune, Ten Downing Street is popularly known as TDS.
2nd Floor Gera Plaza, Boat Club Road,
Pune 411001 Tel: 26128343

ABC Farms

A landmark in the area, this two-and-a-half acre garden complex houses some of the classiest restaurants in town, and boasts some of the finest music. ABC Farms set up its first restaurant, Sangamitra, in 1994 Today, this complex is home to seven restaurants and a dairy parlor.

1) Swiss Cheese Garden: Swiss food (fondue, rosti, raclette)
2) Shisha Café: Iranian food, hookahs and jazz nights
3) Soul: Italian, with a live band
4) Olas: Mediterranean, live band (Thursday)
5) House of Chi: Chinese
6) Curve: Vegetarian
7) Golconda: Hyderabadi

North Main Road, Koregaon Park, Pune 411001
Tel: 25123220, 26876555

Riverview

A popular haunt with couples, it serves Indian cuisine, but the primary attraction here is its location on the banks of the river.
81/82 North Main Road, Koregaon Park Extension, (towards Mundhwa)
Pune 411001 Tel: 26811335

Koyla

Serves authentic Hyderabadi food, though the over-the-top décor can be quite distracting. They also have a branch on FC Road.
Hermes Vishal Bldg, Mira Nagar Corner, North Main Road, Pune 411001
Tel: 26120102

Mad House Grill

Serves continental cuisine, and some great steak options.
Lane No 6, Pingle Corner, Koregaon Park,
Pune 411001 Tel: 26124779

Spice Garden

Popular for its Mario Miranda murals and candle-lit dinners, Spice Garden specializes in Indian, Mediterranean, Parsi, Chinese and Mangalorean cuisines.
Akshay Complex,
Dhole Patil Road,
Behind Zamus,
Pune 411001
Tel: 26138941 / 26052637

Kapila Kebabs

A roadside shack, Kapila is the most popular place in town for kebabs rolls.
Bank of Maharashtra Compound,
Next to Kapila Hotel,
Dhole Patil Road,
Pune 411001

La Pizzeria

A very popular restaurant for its delectable Italian fare, La Pizzeria serves only vegetarian food.
Srimaan Hotel, 361/5B Bund Garden Road, Pune 411001
Tel: 26122369

Arthur's Theme

Excellent French food served in quiet, elegant surroundings.
Vrindavan Apartments, Off North Main Road, Koregaon Park, Pune 411001
Tel: 26132710/24032710

Indyaki

Serves North Indian food, and popularized the teppanyaki concept of dining.
South Main Road, Koregaon Park, Pune 411001
Tel:26055116/26055118

La Dolce Vita

A fine dining restaurant serving authentic Italian food.
City Point, Boat Club Road, Pune
411001
Tel: 26145555

Mainland China

One of Pune's first authentic Chinese restaurants.
Ground Floor, City point, Boat Club Road, Pune 411001 Tel: 66013030

Malaka Spice

An eclectic mix of Chinese, Malaysian and Thai food.
Vrindavan Apartments, Off North Main Road, Koregaon Park, Pune 411001
Tel: 26136293

Salons

Gazelle

Started in 1982, it is one of the popular salons in Pune. It is advisable to take a prior appointment, since they have a full schedule, particularly over weekends.
Block A, 1st Floor, Mayfair Towers, Dhole Patil Road, Pune 411001
Tel: 26120526/26128307

Multiplex

Inox

A great place for a family outing – take in a movie, do some shopping and indulge at the McDonalds outlet!
Bund Garden Road, Opp. Council Hall, Pune 411001
Tel: 26111010

Hospitals

Ruby Hall Clinic

Set up in 1959 by Dr. K. B. Grant, this 500-bed hospital is one of the biggest hospitals in the city. It has

a full spectrum of services in clinical and surgical care, as well as a wide range of outpatient services.
40, Sassoon Road,
Pune 411001
Tel: 26123391/ 2 / 9890300507

Inlaks and Budhrani Hospital

In 1989, the Sadhu Vaswani Mission set up a state-of-the-art 150-bed multi-disciplined general hospital. Together with the adjoining Budhrani Cancer Institute, it is counted among the top hospitals of Pune.
Lane 1, North Main Road, Koregaon Park,
Pune 411001 Tel: 26129080

Jehangir Hospital & Medical Centre

One of the leading hospitals of the city. In 1998, the hospital tied up with Apollo Hospitals

Group for expansion and modernization of its existing set-up.
32, Sassoon Road,
Pune 411001
Tel: 26050550/26122551

Bridges

Fitzgerald Bridge
This bridge connects Bund Garden to the Yerawada and Kalyani Nagar sections of the city.

Kalyani Nagar bridge
This bridge connecting Koregaon Park and Kalyani Nagar has drastically reduced the travelling distance between these two areas.

Major Hotels

Taj Blue Diamond
11, Koregaon Park,
Pune 411001 Tel: 26125555

Le Meridien
Raja Bahadur Mill Road,
Pune 411001 Tel: 26050505

Sun n Sand
262 Bund Garden Road,
Pune 411 001
Tel: 26137777

Central Park Hotel
Opp Council Hall, Bund Garden Road, Pune 411001
Tel: 26054000

Clubs

Royal Connaught Boat Club
One of the oldest clubs in the city, scenically located along the banks of the river.
7/8 Boat Club Road,
Pune 411001
Tel: 26113512 / 13 / 14

The Residency Club
One of the newer clubs in the city, it is very popular for its central location.
3 Queens Garden Rd,
Next to Wadia College,
Pune 411001 Tel: 26362226

Banks and ATMs

IDBI Bank ATM
Bund Garden Road, Near Mangaldas Road Police Chowky, Pune 411001

Bank of Baroda ATM
Wadia College Campus,
Bund Garden Road,
Pune 411001

ICICI Bank (ATM)
A Wing Shangrila Gardens,
Bund Garden Road,
Pune 411001
Tel: 26128248/49

H.D.F.C Bank (ATM)
9/2 Kalpataru Gardens, Boat Club Road, Opp. Narangi Baug Society,
Pune 411001 Tel: 26430266

UTI Bank (ATM)
Ashoka Galaxy, Dhole Patil Road, Next to Kanbay,
Pune 411001
Tel: 24016270/71

H.S.B.C Bank (ATM)
Amar Avinash Corporate City, Survey No. 111, Bund Garden Road, Pune 411001
Tel: 56028585

State Bank of India (ATM)
Dhole Patil Road,
Next T.C.I., Pune 411001
Tel: 26167965

Bank of India (ATM)
Next to Hero Honda Showroom, Koregaon Road,
Pune 411001
Tel: 26748017

Bank of Maharastra
1741, Dhole Patil Road,
Hotel Kapila Compound,
Pune 411001
Tel: 26141881/8

Oriental Bank Of Commerce ATM
198 Dhole Patil Road,
Next To Maitreya Travel, Pune 411001
Tel: 25670693/94

Development Credit Bank
Runwal Regency,
Sadhu Vaswani Road, Opp. Sadhu Vaswani Mission,
Pune 411001
Tel: 26122466

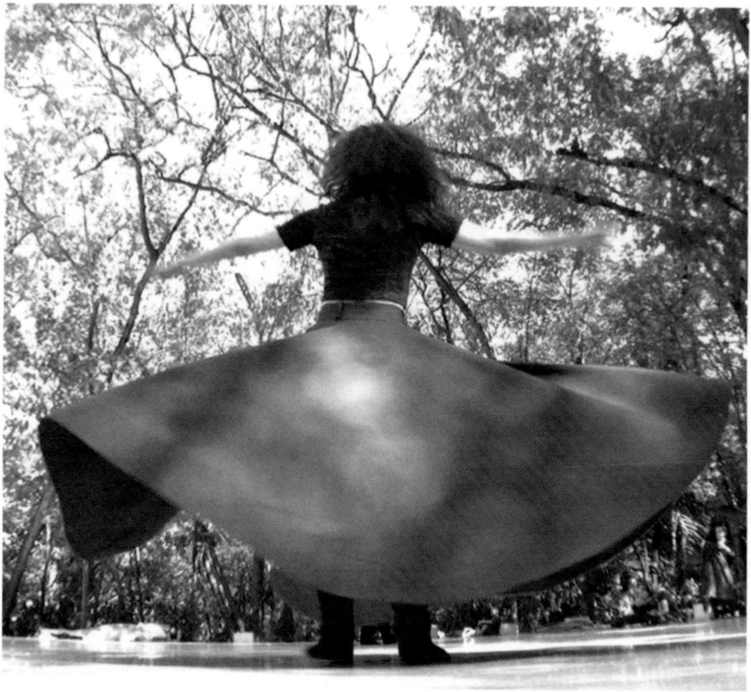

Osho International Meditation Resort

17 Koregaon Park, Pune 411001 Tel: 56019900

Once known as the Rajneesh Ashram, this is one of the main tourist attractions in Pune. The lush 40-acre campus, with lush foliage, white marble pathways, elegant black buildings, an Olympic-size swimming pool, a massive open-air stage, and cafes and restaurants provides a calming retreat even for the casual visitor.

The controversial avant-garde spiritual movement promoting meditation and uninhibited expression of body and mind was started in 1974 by Rajneesh, who later came to be known as Osho. When he passed away in 1990, the Osho Commune began to be promoted as an International Mediation Resort and continues to be patronized by a large number of foreigners. More than two lakh people from over 100 countries come to the resort every year to de-stress and rejuvenate themselves.

Meditation

The Osho Resort has devised over 50 different types of meditations, including Dynamic Meditation, Kundalini Meditation, Gourishankar Meditation, Nadabramha Meditation and many others. The striking black pyramid-shaped auditorium that can accommodate 5,000 people was the talk of the town when it was constructed. Other activities include the current western therapy approaches, the healing arts of East and West, creative arts, martial arts, esoteric sciences, tantra, zen and Sufism. The maroon-robed Oshoites are free to choose and pick their own programmes that range

from one-day events to three-month professional training modules. The Meditation Resort has a vast collection of books authored by Osho and also tapes of his discourses.

Accommodation/Tariff

The Resort has a guesthouse of 60 air-conditioned rooms built on the lines of a five star deluxe hotel, with a tariff of approximately Rs. 3,000 per night per room in peak season (winter). Other visitors rent out apartments in the Koregaon Park area. An AIDS test is compulsory for registration at the Resort. The testing facility is available on campus.

Visitors

Though you cannot enter the Osho International Meditation Resort without permission, you can avail of their 20-min guided tours.
Visitor's Timings: 9 am-1 pm and 2 pm-4 pm.
Tickets: Rs.10 per head.

Central Pune

Central Pune is the heart of the city, not just geographically, but culturally and historically as well. It was here that Shivaji spent his childhood and where the Peshwas were based. Although modern buildings are making an appearance, the City (as this area is popularly known) has still retained its old-world charm. Almost every alternate building has a historical tale attached to it. The imposing structure of Shaniwarwada, the palace of the Peshwas, has become synonymous with the identity of old Pune. The unique and traditional *wadas* (residential complexes) are a must-see for architecture buffs. Temples large and small can be found in almost all lanes in the various *peths* (areas). Atop a small hill is the Parvati Temple that gives a panoramic view of the city. This part of Pune is a shoppers' delight and includes the historic Tulshibaug market and Laxmi Road. The famous Raja Dinkar Kelkar Museum is also situated here.

Prominent Localities

Kasba Peth
The Kasba Ganpati temple, the presiding deity of the city, is located here, as are Shaniwarwada and Lal Mahal, the replica of Shivaji's residence.

Bhawani Peth
This narrow-laned area is known for the Marwari and Gujarati wholesale traders of wheat, sugar, rice, pulses and jaggery.

Raviwar Peth
Several of the wholesale hardware markets are located here.

Sadashiv Peth
Considered the heart of traditional Pune. Tilak Road, once a residential road, and today one of the longest commercial roads in the city, passes through here.

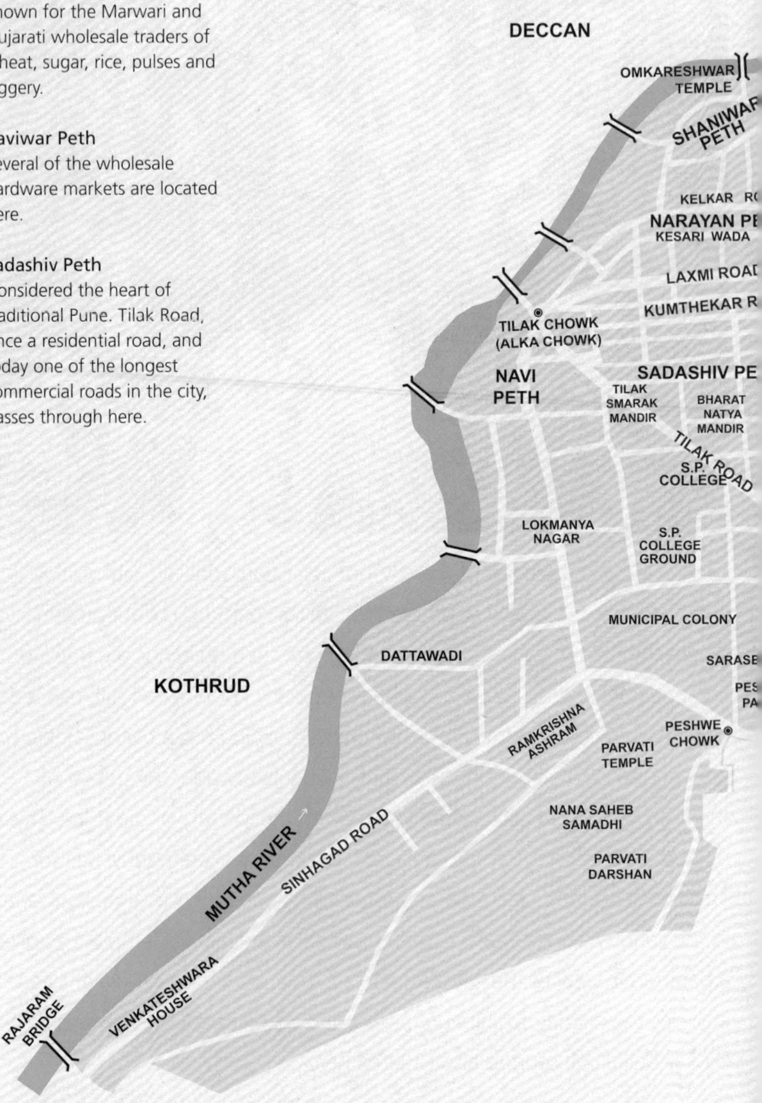

Central Pune

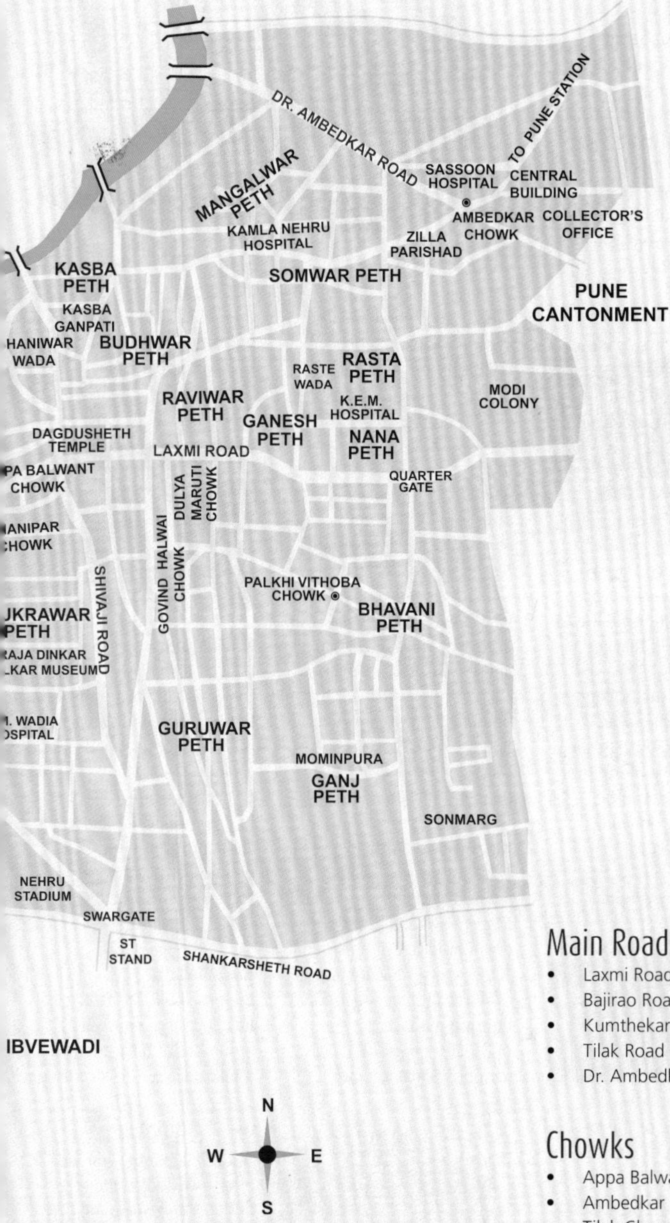

Map Indicative; not to scale

Main Roads

- Laxmi Road
- Bajirao Road
- Kumthekar Road
- Tilak Road
- Dr. Ambedkar Road

Chowks

- Appa Balwant Chowk
- Ambedkar Chowk
- Tilak Chowk (Alka Chowk)

Historic Sites

Tucked away in the hustle bustle of the lanes and by-lanes you'll discover the fascinating legacy of the Peshwas, dominated by wadas and temples. Lack of space and growing families has resulted in many *wadas* giving way to more modern structures. Many are now in a rundown state but there are still some which stand in all their old glory.

Lal Mahal

The Lal Mahal which means 'the red colored palace' is the place where Shivaji and his mother Jijabai stayed during his childhood. It was built by Shivaji's teacher Dadaji Kondev. While the original structure no longer remains, a replica was built which now houses a museum on the life of the great Maratha warrior.
Near Jijamata Udhyan, Kasba Peth, Pune 411011

Vishrambaug Wada

This three-storied *wada* was the home of the last Peshwa, Bajirao II (1775-1851). The 260 ft long and 815 ft broad *teen-chowki wada* is a combination of beautiful columns and balconies with detailed designs in the *suru* (cypress) form. It houses a museum detailing the history of the city.
Opp. Bank Of Maharastra, Bajirao Road, Sadashiv Peth, Pune 411030 Tel: 24457750

Kesari Wada

Built by the Gaikwads during the Peshwa rule, this *wada* gained historical importance after freedom fighter Lokmanya Tilak started the *Kesari* newspaper from here. Today, the *wada* continues to house the offices of *Kesari*, mementos of Tilak, and the first Indian National Flag unfurled by freedom fighter Madam Cama.
568 N. C. Kelkar Road, Narayan Peth, Pune 411030 Tel: 24459051

Mazumdar Wada

This 234-year-old wada is associated with the Mazumdar family, an eminent family of musicians. Today, it is a treasure house of music and architecture, housing manuscripts of 35,000 *bandishen* (compositions), *ghazals, tappas* and *thumris* in 175 *ragas*. (Not open to the public without prior permission.)
Mazumdar Path, Near Shaniwarwada, Shaniwar Peth, Pune 411030

Nana Wada

Built by Nana Phadnavis, the chief administrator of the Peshwas, the *wada* is known for its wooden ceilings, railings and *chhatris* (canopies). Today, a section of it is used for a school and some government offices.
Behind Shaniwarwada, Next to Sakal Office, Budhwar Peth,Pune 411002

Raste Wada

Built by the Raste family, it has two large courtyards, a number of halls and a music gallery. The facade

What is a Wada?

Traditional timber-framed brick dwellings popular during the Peshwa regime that were built around one or two central courtyards with beautiful façades, balconies and windows.

has traces of Rajasthani architecture. Rasta Peth, Near Apollo Theatre, Pune 4110011 Tel. 26055603

Tulshibaug Temple & Complex

The third Peshwa, Balaji Bajirao built this beautiful complex and named it after the *tulshi* (basil) gardens that once flourished here. The most striking feature is its tall shikhar (spire) that stands at an impressive height of 140 ft. The main temple here is dedicated

to Lord Rama, and there are two smaller temples of Ganpati and Mahadev. Shree Ram Sansthan Trust, 1225, Tulsibaug, Budhwar Peth, Pune 411002

Jogeshwari Temple

This temple is dedicated to the goddess Jogeshwari who is regarded as the main goddess of the city. An annual fair takes place in the area around the temple during the Navratri period just before the festival of Dussehra.
Near Appa Balwant Chowk, Budhwar Peth, Pune 411002

Parvati Temple

Located on top of a hill, this temple was built by Nanasaheb Peshwa in 1749 The complex has several small temples dedicated to Parvati, Vishnu, Karthikeyan and Ganesh and attracts huge crowds once a year on Kartik Purnima. There is also a museum housing possessions of the Peshwas. Parvati Hill, Pune 411030 Tel: 24443520

Khunya Murlidhar Temple

Built by a famous merchant of the Peshwa period in 1797, this temple has a marble idol of Radha and Krishna. The plot to assassinate Governor Rand was hatched here and accounts for the temple's unusual name (*Khunya* means murderous). Sadashiv Peth, Pune 411030

Trishund Ganapati Temple

The temple got its unusual name from the three trunks

(trishund) of the Ganpati idol. The elaborately carved exterior, with human and animal figures and four columns, makes it particularly eye-catching. 139, Somwar Peth, Near Kamala Nehru Hospital, Pune 411011

Omkareshwar Temple

Built on the banks of the Mutha River, this 250-year-old temple dedicated to Lord Shiva is known for its massive stone structure that survived the floods caused by the breaching of Panshet Dam in 1961
Omkareshwar Chowk, Near Vishnukrupa Hall, Shaniwar Peth, Pune 411030

Belbaug Temple

This is a Vishnu temple built in 1765 by Nana Phadnavis. Shivaji Road, Budhwar Peth, Pune 411002

Places of Interest

Raja Dinkar Kelkar Museum

This museum houses the priceless personal collection of one man, Dr Dinkar Kelkar, who collected over 20,000 precious artifacts and items of everyday-use from various corners of India. A replica of the stunning Mastani Mahal

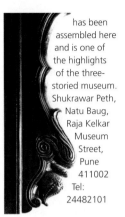

has been assembled here and is one of the highlights of the three-storied museum.
Shukrawar Peth, Natu Baug, Raja Kelkar Museum Street, Pune 411002
Tel: 24482101

Mahatma Phule Mandai (Market)
Once the main wholesale vegetable market in the city, it is named after the great social reformer Mahatma Jyotiba Phule. This beautiful neo-Gothic colonial stone structure skillfully harmonizes utility with architectural uniqueness. There are over 500 stalls selling fruits and vegetables. The market is a sight to behold at five in the morning when vendors come in hordes to stock their rekdi four-wheeled carts. You can get everything from paan leaves, flowers and puja items to clothes, bangles, and baskets – all at an excellent rate.
Shukrawar Peth,
Pune 411002

Tilak Smarak Mandir
This is a memorial dedicated to great freedom fighter and social reformer Lokmanya Bal Gangadhar Tilak. It houses a museum devoted to the life and times of Tilak and an auditorium for cultural programs. The Tilak Smarak Hall, rented out for a good part of the year, is popular for its varied handicraft exhibitions and sales.
1651, Tilak Road,
Near S.P. College,
Sadashiv Peth,
Pune 411030
Tel: 24334004 / 24339005

Places of worship

Dagdusheth Halwai Ganpati Mandir
A relatively new temple, it houses a Ganpati idol adorned with gold. It attracts a huge number of devotees especially during the ten-day Ganesh festival. The trust that runs the temple is believed to be the wealthiest in the city.
250 Budhwar Peth, Shivaji Road, Pune 411002
Tel: 24479222 / 24452049

Goadiji Parasnath Temple
This is one of the oldest and largest Jain temples of the city. Built during the Peshwa period, it was reconstructed several decades ago in marble and sandstone. Known for its architectural splendor, with intricate carvings and designs, it has over hundred idols of the 24 Jain *tirthankars.*
203 Bhawani Peth,
Nehru Road, Pune 411042
Tel: 26451756

Dhakata Sheikh Salla Dargah
Situated on the banks of the Mutha river it the heart of the old city this dargah is approximately 700 years old.
Kasta Peth, Near Kumbhar Ves Chowk, Pune 411001.

Auditorium

Bharat Natya Mandir
One of the oldest auditoriums in Pune, Marathi plays and cultural programs are regularly staged here. The prestigious inter-collegiate Marathi

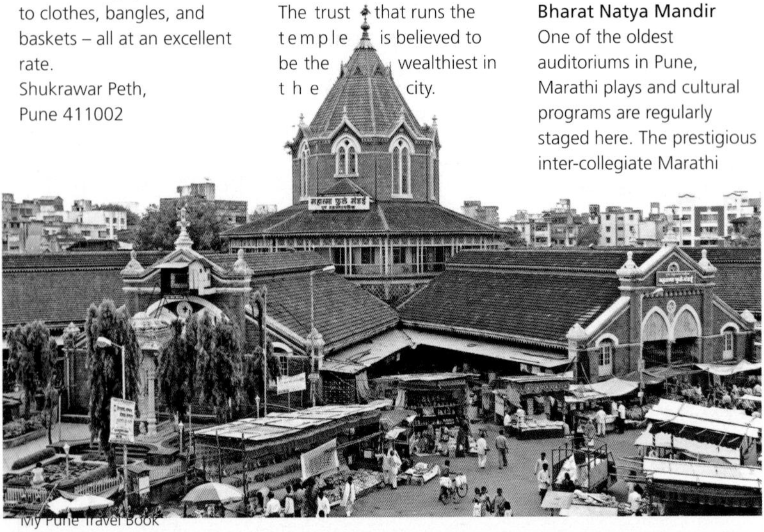

theatre festival Purushottam Karandak is held here annually.
1320, Sadashiv Peth,
Pune 411030 Tel: 24471614

Sudarshan Rangmanch
Run by the Maharashtra Cultural Centre, Sudarshan Rangmanch is a very active cultural centre. The premises comprise a theatre where many music, dance and theatre performances are held and an art gallery where painters from all over the country display their work.
421/422, Shaniwar Peth,
Pune 411030 Tel: 24490188

Libraries

Bharat Itihas Samshodhak Mandal
Next to the Bharat Natya Mandir is a nationally renowned historical research institute. It was set up in 1910 and has over 15 lakh documents, 1,200 medieval miniature paintings, 18,000 books, ancient coins, sculptures, and manuscripts.
1321 Sadashiv Peth, Next to Bharat Natya Mandir,
Pune 411030 Tel: 24472581

Nagar Vachan Mandir
This is one of the oldest libraries of the city.
At one time, particularly during the independence movement, it was a celebrated meeting place for scholars and thinkers and has witnessed many intellectual soirees.
181, Laxmi Road,
Budhwar Peth,
Pune 411002 Tel: 24450526

Sahitya Parishad Library
C/o Sahitya Parishad, Tilak Road, Sadashiv Peth,
Pune 411030 Tel: 24475963

Appa Balwant Chowk (ABC)
The area around this square in Budhwar Peth is a hub for textbooks, test papers, and stationery.
Budhwar Peth,
Pune 411002

Education

Jnana Prabodhini Trust
Set up by noted educationist Dr. V. V. Pendse in 1962, the Jnyan Prabodhini Trust has grown into a large and unique organization today with multiple schools, and

research centres.
Jnana Prabodhini Trust,
510, Sadashiv Peth,
Pune 411030 Tel: 24477691

S.P. College
The Sir Parshurambhau College for Arts and Science is the oldest college in the area.
Tilak Road, Sadashiv Peth,
Pune 411030
Tel: 24321462 / 24332479

St. Helena's School
One of the oldest girls' schools in Pune, it was started by Suzy Sorabjee. Centrally located at the meeting point of the cantonment area and the city, it was started to encourage parents to send their daughters to school.
8, Sorabji Road. Near GPO,
Pune 411001
Tel: 26126796

Abhinav Kala Mahavidyalya
This is one of the premier colleges in the city for commercial and fine arts and many famous artists have graduated from its portals.
2043, Sadashiv Peth,
Tilak Road,
Pune 411030
Tel: 24335428 / 24320599

National Institute of Virology (NIV)
The NIV is one of the major institutes of the Indian Council of Medical Research. It was set up in 1952 for investigating arthropod borne viruses. It is also the national monitoring centre for influenza, Japanese encephalitis, rotavirus, measles and hepatitis. The Institute offers a PG course in virology recognized by the University of Pune.
20-A, Dr. Ambedkar Road,
Post Box No.11,
Pune 411001
Tel: 26127301 / 26124386

Gardens

Sarasbaug
The sprawling park was created around the Ganesh temple that was originally located in the middle of a small pond. The temple is locally known as talayatla ganpati (talé meaning pond). Located near the foothills of Parvati, it is a popular evening spot.
2170, Sadashiv Peth, Near Peshwe Park, Pune 411030
Tel: 24332388

Pu La Deshpande Park
This spectacular garden, spread over 10 acres, is built like a Japanese garden. It is also called the Pune-Okayama Friendship Garden. Inaugurated in February 2006, it has become one of the most popular gardens of

the city.
Next to Parvati Water Works, Sinhagad Road, Pune 411030

Shopping Areas

Laxmi Road
One of Pune's oldest and busiest shopping streets, it runs through the central part of Pune right up to the

cantonment area. Offers a wide selection of traditional Maharashtrian saris, clothes and jewelry. This road extends from Tilak Chowk (Alka) to Phule Chowk (Quarter Gate).

Tulsibaug
A huge open market place packed with hawkers selling everything from household articles and accessories, to baubles and traditional souvenirs.
Next to Bank of Maharahtra, Janamangal Branch, Bajirao Road, Pune 411030

H.V. Mehendale
This 128-year old shop for musical instruments is one of the best in the city. It stocks everything from guitars and keyboards to tablas and harmoniums, all reasonably priced.
Budhwar Peth, Pune 411002
Tel: 24456665

Parking Places

The Municipal Corporation has built two main parking lots in the City. One is near the Mahatma Phule Markat (Mandai), while the other is off Laxmi Road near the Patrya Maruti Temple.

Aryan Cinema, Opp. Mandai Police Chowky, Shukrawar Peth, Pune 411002

Hamalwada, Off Laxmi Road. Narayan Peth, Pune 411030

Restaurants

Jana Seva
A typical Maharashtrian

Swargate Bus Stand

One of the busiest bus stands in Pune, it is the nodal point for the arrival and departure of thousands of buses from outside the city, especially those arriving from the south. At Tilak Road-Shankarsheth Road Junction, Pune 411037 Tel: 24441591

eatery, Jana Seva is a simple place that serves traditional snacks like *sabudana wadas, pohe* and *piyush,* a lemon-yellow sweet drink. Catering to the office going crowd, Jana Seva has a special menu on days of fasting.
Near Gokhale Hall,
Laxmi Road, Pune 411030
Tel: 24453118

Poona Guest House
Typical Maharashtrian snacks are available here.
100, Budhwar Peth, Laxmi Road, Pune 411002
Tel: 24455679

Durvankur Restaurant
Offers a blend of Gujarati, Maharashtrian and Marwari fare. A thali is priced at Rs. 60
Hatti Ganpati Chowk,
Tilak Road,

Sadashiv Peth,
Pune 411030
Tel: 24474438 / 24467067

Bedekar Missal
This small eating joint is one of the most famous for the famed Puneri *missal.* You will see a hoard of shoppers from Laxmi Road queuing up for a taste of the missal that has retained its taste through the years.
Next to Sathe Gadi karkhana, Below Purandare Classes, Narayan Peth,
Pune 411030

Sujata Mastani
Famous for its rich mastani, Sujata cold drink house is the favourite hang out of college students in central Pune.
1260, Sadashiv Peth,
Nimbalkar Talim Chowk,
Pune 411030
Tel: 24474641

Kawre Ice-cream
The perfect stop for refreshments in between a hectic shopping spree, Kawre's has a range of delicious ice-creams, mastanis, and faloodas.
89 Budhwar Peth,
Laxmi Road, Pune
Tel: 24455764

Movie Theatres

The City has several old single-screen theatres popular with students for their inexpensive ticket rates.

Vijay Chitramandir
310, Laxmi Road,
Pune 411030 Tel: 24454830

Alka Theatre
81 Tilak Road, Navi Peth,
Pune 411030
Tel: 24333038

Neelayam
Parvati, Near Peshwe Park,
Sadashiv Peth,
Pune 411030
Tel: 24335301

Apollo Theatre
549, Rasta Peth,
Pune 411011
Tel: 26120550

Prabhat Talkies Pvt ltd
681, Budhwar Peth,
Near Appa Balwant Chowk,
Bajirao Road,
Pune 411002
Tel: 24458856 / 24454841

Stadiums/Grounds

Baburao Sanas Athletic Ground
Built by the government in 2005 at a cost of Rs. 35 crore, this ground is known for its 400-metre synthetic track laid as per international standards.
Near Sarasbaug,
Sadashiv Peth,
Pune 411030

Nehru Stadium
This is the city's main cricket ground.
Tilak Road, Sadashiv Peth,
Pune 411030
Tel: 24440641 / 24444739

Hospitals

Sassoon Hospital
Built in 1867, the hospital building has a Gothic style structure and is listed as a heritage complex.
Near Pune Railway Station, Dr Ambedkar Road, Pune 411001 Tel: 26128000

Kamla Nehru Hospital
33 Mangalwar Peth, Pune 411011
Tel: 26121202

KEM Hospital
Sardar Moodliar Road, Rasta Peth, Pune 411011
Tel: 26125600

N. M. Wadia Hospital
283 Shukrawar Peth, Near Telephone Bhawan, Pune 411002
Tel: 24479502

Poona Hospital & Research Centre
27, Sadashiv Peth, Near Alka Theatre, Pune 411030 Tel: 24331706

Bridges

Several bridges cross the river Mutha to connect the old city with newer areas.

Sambhaji Bridge (Lakdi Pul)
It connects two of the busiest commercial areas of Pune, Laxmi Road and Deccan. Built out of wood by Peshwa Balaji Bajirao, it was and is still known as Lakdi Pul, even though, the British rebuilt the bridge in brick and stone in 1840

Shivaji Bridge
This bridge connects the area near the Pune Municipal Corporation building to the Shaniwarwada area.

Banks and ATMs

SBI ATM
307, Narayan Peth, Pune 411030
1001, Budhwar Peth, Pune 411002

Citi Bank ATM
Shop No.4, Nikhil Pride, Near Bajirao-Tilak Road Junction, Pune 411030

HDFC ATM
Sanas Plaza, Near Telephone Exchange, Bajirao Road, Pune 411030

999, A/2 Dwarka, Phatak Baug Society, Near Mahatre Bridge, Pune 411030

Bank of India ATM
Global Trade Centre, Rambaug Colony, Shop No. 1, L.B.S. Marg, Navi Peth, Pune 411030

UTI ATM
564/B, 2/3 Ramanbaug School, Near Omkareshwar,Shaniwar Peth, Pune 411030

Foyer of Global Trade Centre, Rambaug Colony, L.B.S. Marg, Pune 411030

ICICI ATM
1322, Sadashiv Peth, Near Bharat Natya Mandir Pune 411030

199, Narayan Peth, Laxmi Road, Pune 411030

501, Ajanta Complex, Near KEM Hospital, Rasta Peth, Pune 411011

State Bank India (ATM)
Tilak Road, Pune 411030
Tel: 24330900 / 24320151
Budhwar Peth, Pune 411002
Tel: 24476793, 24472043

HDFC Bank (ATM)
Aditi Apartments, 344/1, Narayan Peth, Near Modi Ganpati, Off Laxmi Road, Pune 411030
Tel: 24431041 / 42 / 44

Canara Bank (ATM)
Perugate Lane Road, Behind Bharat Natya Mandir, Sadashiv Peth, Pune 411030
Tel: 24452828

Bank of Baroda (ATM)
Sanas Plaza, Shukrawar Peth, Subhas Nagar, Bajirao Road, Pune 411030
Tel: 24472112
1786, Sadashiv Peth, Pune Vidyarthee Gruha Building, Pune 411030

Bank of India
Ravi Building, 8/2, Sadashiv Peth, Near Alka Talkies, Lal Bahadur Shastri Road, Pune 411030
Tel: 24471348

Union Bank of India
Parwani Estate, 289/3, Jawaharlal Nehru Road, Bhawani Peth, Pune 411042
Tel: 24655032 / 26450287

Dena Bank
New Timber Market, Jawaharlal Nehru Road, Ramani Building, Near Jain Temple, Pune 411042
Tel: 26455640

Bank Of Maharashtra
Bajirao Road, Opp. Vishrambaug Wada, Shukrawar Peth, Pune 411002
Tel: 24454479

Punjab National Bank
564, Nana Peth, Pune 411002
Tel: 26135279

Peths of Pune

The small geographical and administrative segments or wards of the city set-up by the Peshwas were called peths. They were self-sufficient units with their own temple and market and characterized by narrow pathways and lanes (ali) and single-storied dwellings. Each peth had its own characteristics defined by its residents and the business activities conducted there. Not all of the 18 original peths exist today, and many of the others are seeing a gradual transformation.

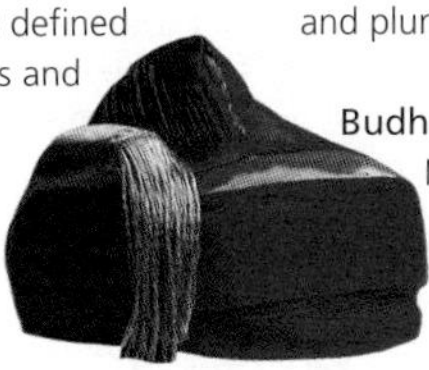

Kasba Peth

The core of the city, it was developed as a residential and business area by the Peshwas because of its proximity to Shaniwarwada, Lal Mahal and the Omkareshwar temple. The earliest settlers were a mix of the Marathas, shimpis (tailors), kumbhars (potters) and tambats (coppersmiths).

Sadashiv Peth

Originally home to Brahmins in the service of the Peshwas; they served as the fountainhead for political activism, social service, education, music and arts.

Raviwar Peth

Bohri Ali (lane) has developed over the years into one of the most popular hardware markets in Pune. The place is buzzing with carpenters, contractors and plumbers.

Budhwar Peth

More than 400 wholesalers and retailers dealing in all electronic items are based here. Budhwar Peth has gained notoriety as the 'red light' area of the city.

Guruwar Peth

Bhandi Ali, the market for traditional kitchenware, is situated here.

Nana Peth

Specializes in selling auto spare parts and draws vehicle enthusiasts from across the city.

Mangalwar Peth

This crowded and traditional area of the city has recently undergone a transformation. It also has a significant auto spare parts market.

Bhawani Peth

Apart from a large timber market, the area houses the famous Bhawani Mata Mandir as well as the Palkhi Vithoba Mandir.

Somwar Peth

One of the older peths, it houses several temples from the Peshwa era, including the Mali Maharaj Mandir and the Nageshwar Temple. The imposing Zilla Parishad (district administration) building is also situated in this area.

The 18 original peths and the year they were established:

Kasba Peth	–	1300
Shaniwar Peth	–	1610
Raviwar Peth	–	1610
Somwar Peth	–	1610
Mangalwar Peth	–	1663
Budhwar Peth	–	1703
Shukrawar Peth	–	1734
Guruwar Peth	–	1750
Nihal Peth	–	1755
Ganesh Peth	–	1755
Narayan Peth	–	1761
Bhawani Peth	–	1767
Muzzafarganj Peth	–	1768
Sadashiv Peth	–	1769
Ghorpade Peth	–	1781
Rasta Peth	–	1783
Nana Peth	–	1789
Ganj Peth	–	1789

Source: Centre For Development, Studies and Activities, Pune 1991

Shaniwarwada

Shaniwarwada is Pune's most famous monument. Built by Peshwa Thorla Bajirao I in 1730, it served as the palace and seat of political power for all the eight Peshwas who succeeded him. Pre-Independence, Shaniwarwada served as an edifice of inspiration and valor for many freedom fighters. Post-Independence, it provided an ideal platform for politicians and orators. Today, it has become a coveted cultural dais for the city and many plays and music programs are performed against its majestic backdrop. Located in the centre of the city, this palace fort serves as the starting point for most tourists who want to explore Pune.

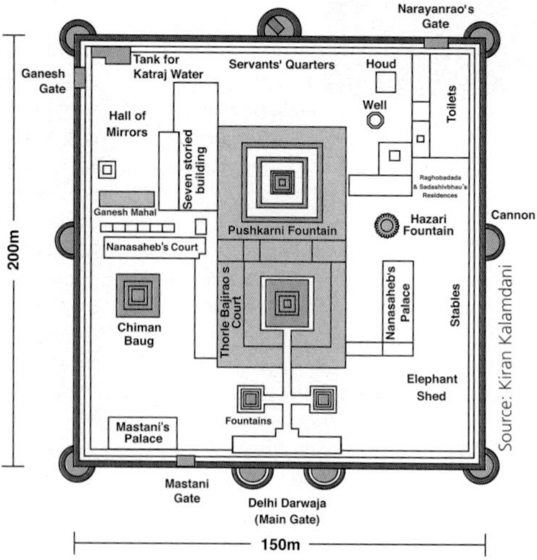

Ground Plan of Shaniwarwada

Name

'Wada' is an individual or group of dwellings in a complex. 'Shaniwar' means Saturday in Marathi. The monument was named Shaniwarwada since the construction started on Saturday.

Construction

The foundation stone of Shaniwarwada was laid by Peshwa Bajirao I on January 10, 1730 The monument was completed in 1732 Bajirao built a magnificent two-storied wada around two courtyards, with exquisite fountains, regal halls and gardens. Particularly striking was the 16-petal lotus shaped fountain called the Hazaari Kaaranje (fountain of a thousand jets). Successive Peshwas made several additions including the fortification walls with bastions and gates.

Ravaged by Fire

In 1828, a mysterious fire gutted the Peshwa palace. Unfortunately, all that remains today is the stone plinth of the massive structure (spread over 625 acres) and the bastioned walls.

Section drawing of Thorle Bajirao's Residence & Office Source: Kiran Kalamdani

Gates

The Shaniwarwada has five gate (darwajas):

1) Dilli Darwaja:
The principal gate from where the Peshwas went out for their military campaigns.

2) Ganesh Darwaja:
Located near, and facing, the Ganesh temple.

3) Jambhul/Narayan/ Natakshala Darwaja:
Used by actors and entertainers

4) Mastani Darwaja:
Used by Bajirao's mistress, Mastani.

5) Khidki Darwaja:
A window and small gate stood here originally. Also called the *Kavathi Darwaja* because there used to be a *kavathi* tree here.

Facade of Ganesh Rang Mahal

Source: Kiran Kalamdani

Mastani
She was the beautiful mistress of Bajirao, who had a palace built for her in the northeastern corner of Shaniwarwada.

Souvenirs
Warsaa, the souvenir shop on the premises, sells t-shirts and mementoes commemorating Shaniwarwada and other local monuments.

For Your Information
Location: Kasba Peth
Timings: 8 am – 6 pm. Open all days of the week.
Tickets: Adults: Rs. 5; free entry for children below 15 years.
Entry fee for Foreigners: Rs. 100 or $2
Sound and Light Show:
Timings: 730 pm - Marathi; 830 pm - English
Guides available at the entrance.

Deccan - Shivajinagar

The area around Deccan Gymkhana was one of the first to develop outside the old city across the River Mutha on its western bank. This area grew rapidly after the great flood of 1961. Today it is considered the student nucleus of the city. Almost everything here is associated with students – from paying guest accommodation and hostels, to cyber cafes, low-cost eateries, canteens, trendy bistros, and shops.

In many ways this area reflects the multi-dimensional personality of Pune with its deep-rooted tradition, growing modernity, campus ethos, culture and affinity for sports. The oldest structure of the city, the Pataleshwar Caves complex, is located on Jungli Maharaj Road, while the offices of All India Radio, the Meteorological office and the State Education Board office are in Shivajinagar. The region's biggest convention centre is under construction on Senapati Bapat Road.

Prominent Localities

Model Colony

A prestigious old residential locality where the Pune Municipal Commissioner resides. The world famous Iyengar Yoga Institute is also located here.

Fergusson College Road

Considered the nerve centre of this area, it the location of educational institutes like Fergusson College and Gokhale Institute of Economics. It also boasts several restaurants and cafés frequented by the student population.

Law College Road

The road takes its name from the prestigious ILS Law College, considered one of the best in the country. Sharing the green environs at the foot of the hill is the Film and Television Institute of India (FTII).

Bhandarkar Road

The large residential bungalows on this tree-lined road have made way for modern glass and concrete structures housing banks and business offices.

Patrakar Nagar

This area adjacent to the forested Bhamburda Hill is home to media persons, Vikhe Patil School, and Alliance Française de Poona.

Jungli Maharaj Road

A commercial hub, this busy road is a melange of offices, glitzy stores and innumerable eateries and takes its name from a *sadhu* called Jungli Maharaj who lived at a *mandir* on this road.

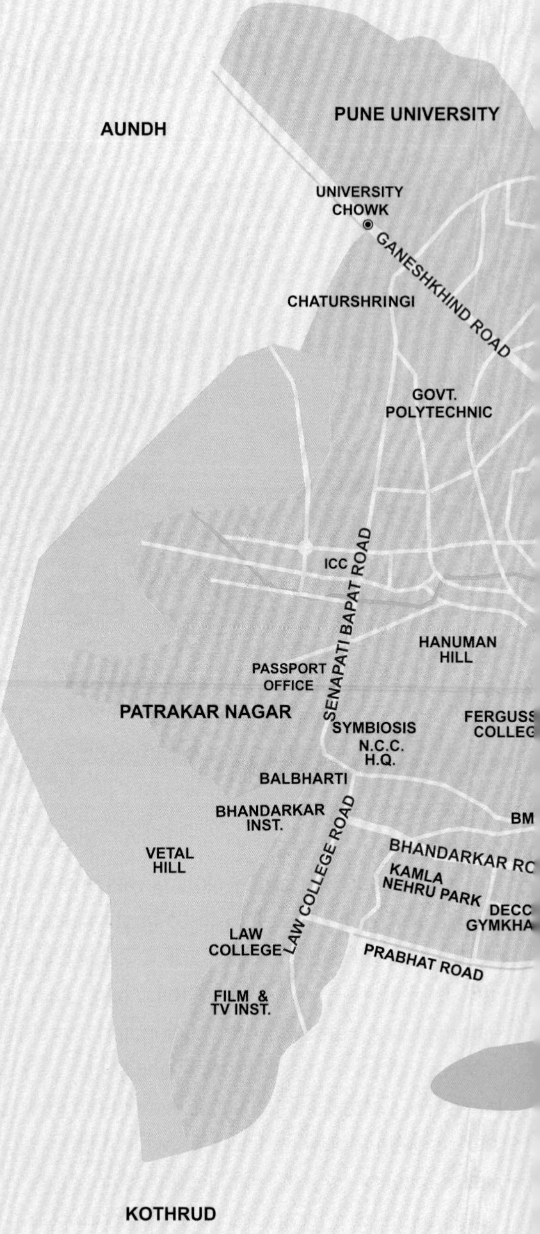

Deccan - Shivajinagar

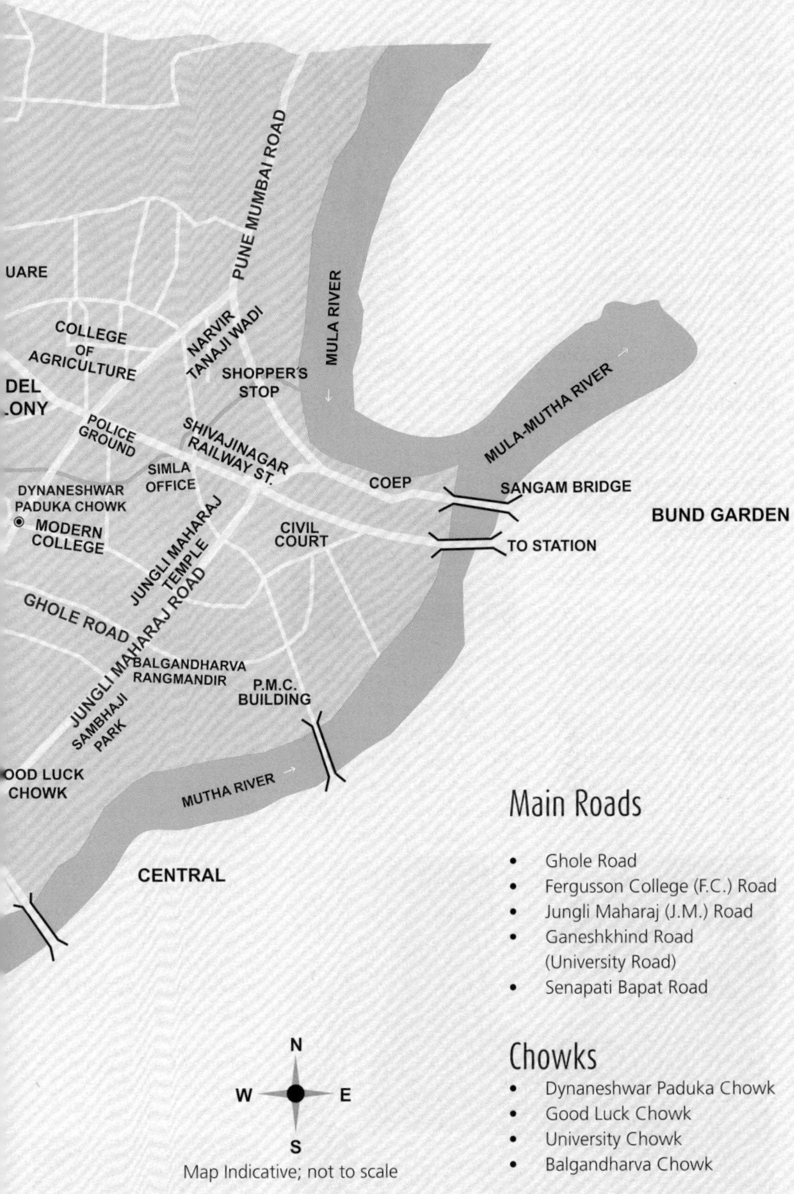

Map Indicative; not to scale

Main Roads

- Ghole Road
- Fergusson College (F.C.) Road
- Jungli Maharaj (J.M.) Road
- Ganeshkhind Road (University Road)
- Senapati Bapat Road

Chowks

- Dynaneshwar Paduka Chowk
- Good Luck Chowk
- University Chowk
- Balgandharva Chowk

Education

Symbiosis School
A part of the Symbiosis family, this increasingly popular school has a consistently good academic record.
Lane No 15, Prabhat Road.
Pune 411004 Tel: 25665935

Vikhe Patil Memorial School
Offers a balanced education with emphasis on both academics and extracurricular activities.
Senapati Bapat Road,
Patrakar Nagar,
Pune 411016 Tel: 25660550

Bharatiya Vidya Bhavan
Part of a national educational group, they also have a special centre to promote scientific temper among children.
407/408 Senapati Bapat Road, Pune 411016
Tel: 25653413

Kamayani School for Mentally Challenged Children
One of the earliest schools for mentally challenged children in the city, it offers training in various skills like knitting, pottery, mat making and other income generating activities.
270, B1 Gokhale Nagar,
Pune 411016 Tel: 25651588

Fergusson College
Named after Sir James Fergusson, it was started in1885 by social reformers Lokmanya Tilak and Gopal Ganesh Agarkar. It spreads over 108 acres and is flanked by two sports

grounds and the Hanuman Tekdi. The college ranks among the top ten colleges in India for Arts and Science. The colonial buildings and amphitheater have been used as locations for several films including Richard Attenborough's *Gandhi.*
Fergusson College Road,
Pune 411004 Tel: 25654212

Symbiosis Group of Institutions
Founded by Dr. S. B. Majumdar, Symbiosis is a comprehensive world of academics, right from KG to PG. Offering courses in law, computer science, information technology and ign communication, the most well-known degree of the institution is its MBA that attracts students from all over the world.
Senapati Bapat Road,
Pune 411004
Tel: 25676875 / 25676876

Indian Law Society (ILS) Law College
Ranked as the best college for law by *India Today* in its 2004-2005 survey, ILS Law College was founded in 1923. It trains over 1,600 students from across the country and abroad. Its library has been rated as one of India's best and has a rich collection of 45,000 books, periodicals and journals.
ILS Law College,
Law College Road,
Pune 411004
Tel: 25678678/ 25656775
Email:ilslaw@vsnl.com

College of Agriculture
One of the first five agriculture colleges

established in India, it is set in a beautiful campus. The main building of the college has a striking dome and entrance hall. The college has a huge collection of books, journals, research theses, and newsletters of Indian and foreign origin. It has also been used as a location for several films.
Ganeshkhind Road, Shivajinagar, Pune 411005
Tel: 25537889 / 25537038

College of Engineering, Pune (COEP)

Set up in 1854, COEP offers undergraduate and post-graduate courses in various streams of engineering. The institute has to its credit many outstanding engineers like Bharat Ratna Sir M. Visvesvaraya. COEP is also famous for its Boat Club and the annual regatta event.
Wellesley Road, Shivajinagar, Pune 411005
Tel: 25507214

Gokhale Institute of Politics and Economics

It offers post graduation in economics. This college is also home to the historic Servants of India Society memorial.
846, BMCC Road, Shivajinagar, Pune 411004
Tel: 25654288 / 25654289

Brihan Maharashtra College of Commerce (BMCC)

Founded in 1943 by the Deccan Education Society, BMCC is a reputed commerce college which also offers foundation courses in Chartered Accountancy and related subjects.
Off Fergusson College Road, Pune 411004 Tel: 25654943

Alliance Française de Poona

French language courses are conducted here. They also have a branch in Camp.
Indo-French Cultural Centre, 270-D, Patrakar Nagar Road, Pune 411016 Tel: 25657848

Institutions

University of Pune (UoP)

Established in 1948, the University of Pune is an internationally renowned centre for research and teaching. Built in the Italian Gothic style with a 40m high tower, the imposing main building used to be the residence of the Governor of Bombay Presidency during the British Raj. The University campus houses several distinguished institutes.
Ganeshkhind Road, Pune 411007
Tel: 25601191, Vice Chancellor
PRO: 25693868
www.unipune.ernet.in

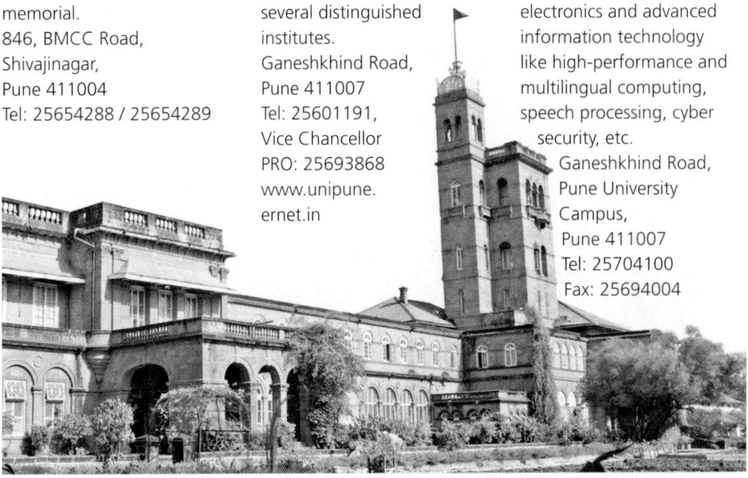

Inter-University Centre for Astronomy and Astrophysics (IUCCA)

Set up in 1988 by the University Grants Commission, under the leadership of nationally renowned scientist, Dr. Jayant Narlikar, IUCCA is a centre for training, research and development in astronomy and astrophysics. The institute conducts specialized workshops, symposiums, and exhibitions throughout the year.
Post Bag 4, Ganeshkhind, Pune University Campus, Pune 411007 Tel: 25604100
Fax: 25604699
E-mail: webm@iucaa.ernet.in

Centre for Development of Advanced Computing (C-DAC)

C-DAC built the first supercomputer in India. It is involved in the design and development of electronics and advanced information technology like high-performance and multilingual computing, speech processing, cyber security, etc.
Ganeshkhind Road, Pune University Campus, Pune 411007
Tel: 25704100
Fax: 25694004

Bhandarkar Oriental Research Institute (BORI)

Founded in 1917 in commemoration of Ramakrishna Gopal Bhandarkar, one of India's foremost pioneers of scientific orientology, BORI is a treasure trove of thousands of rare manuscripts, ancient books and texts.
812, Shivajinagar,
Pune 411004 Tel: 2656932
www.bori.ac.in

National Centre for Radio Astrophysics (NCRA)

This prestigious centre for Natural Sciences was set up in 1989 It set up the Giant Meterwave Radio Telescope, the world's largest radio telescope.
Tata Institute of Fundamental Research,
Pune University Campus,
Post Bag 3, Ganeshkhind,
Pune 411007
Tel: 25697107
www.ncra.tifr.res.in

Ramamani Iyengar Memorial Yoga Institute

Founded by Yogacharya BKS Iyenger, the institute draws yoga enthusiasts from across the globe. His dynamic Iyengar style of yoga is practiced across 300 centres worldwide. Followers include violin maestro Yehudi Menuhin, J.Krishnamurti and the Queen Mother of Belgium. Books, publications, cassettes and CD-Roms are also available for sale at the institute.
1107, B/1 Hare Krishna Mandir Road, Model Colony,
Shivajinagar,
Pune 411015 Tel: 5656134
www.bksiyengar.com

National Film Archive of India (NFAI)

This institute preserves the heritage of Indian cinema by safeguarding movie prints and promoting Indian films nationally and internationally. NFAI also conducts a film appreciation course much sought after by film fans.
P.O. Box No. 810,
Law College Road,
Pune 411004 Tel: 25652259

Indian Meteorological Department

With offices in a striking colonial structure, this government body studies weather phenomena and makes meteorological observations and forecasts. It is only open to the public on World Meteorological Day (23rd March). This department was shifted to Pune from Simla and even today is still known as 'Simla Office'.
'Simla Office', Ganeshkhind Road Shivajinagar,
Pune 411005
Tel: 25535211
www.imdpune.org

Landmarks

Pune Municipal Corporation (PMC)

This is the headquarters

Film & Television Institute of India (FTII)

A world-renowned institute that imparts training in all aspects of filmmaking. It has produced some of the finest professionals in the Indian film industry such as Shabana Azmi, Naseeruddin Shah, Om Puri and Subhash Ghai.
Law College Road, Pune 411004
Tel: 25431817 / 25433016

of the civic authorities of the city.
Shivajinagar, Pune 411005
Tel: 25501000

District and Sessions Court
A magnificent stone structure built by the British as a judicial complex in the early 1920s.
Shivajinagar, Pune 411005
Tel: 25539985 / 25539355

Criminal Investigation Department (CID)
The CID headquarters of Maharashtra undertakes important investigative matters related to the entire state. It has an impressive fingerprint, handwriting and photographic bureau, and a well known dog-training centre.
Near Sangam Bridge, Old Mumbai-Pune Highway, Shivajinagar,
Pune 411005
Tel: 25511443

International Convention Centre (ICC)
This impressive Rs. 350-crore project is being developed to house a world class convention centre equipped with exhibition facilities, trade towers, a commercial complex and conference halls.
403-A, Senapati Bapat Road, Pune 411016
Tel: 25679072 / 3
www.iccpune.org

The Passport Office
The Regional Passport Office at Senapati Bapat Road issues new passports and renews existing passports.
Sheti Mahamandal Building, Opposite Symbiosis Institute, Senapati Bapat Road,
Pune 411016
Tel: 25679962

Libraries

British Council Library
One of the oldest and most sought after libraries in the city, the BCL has a huge collection of books for adults and children. They also have a good stock of DVDs. You have to be a member to avail of its facilities. BCL offers guidance to students on scholarships and opportunities to study in the UK.
917/1,
F. C. Road,
Pune 411004
Tel: 25654351 / 25654352
bl.pune@in.britishcouncil.org

Jagtap Library
One of the oldest libraries in the area, it stocks a vast collection of English and Marathi books and periodicals.
Model Colony,
Shivajinagar,
Pune 411015

Gardens

Most public gardens are closed in the afternoons, but come alive in the evenings with hawkers, balloon sellers, horse rides and lots of food stalls.

Chitaranjan Vatika
Model Colony,
Shivajinagar, Pune 411015

Kamala Nehru Park
Bhandarkar Road,
Pune 411004

Sambhaji Park
J. M. Road, Pune 411005

Model Colony Natural Reserve Lake
Model Colony,
Shivajinagar,
Pune 411015

Hills

The lungs of Pune, the *tekdis* (hills) in the area draw a large number of people in the mornings and evenings. The hillsides have been greened through the efforts of citizens and attract a number of exotic birds.

Vetal Tekdi
Behind Law College

Hanuman Tekdi
Behind Fergusson College

Auditorium

Balgandharva Rangmandir
Named after eminent theatre artiste Bal Gandharva, it has a seating capacity of 990 people and regularly stages plays, music and dance performances.

There is an art gallery on the premises. Next to Sambhaji Park, J. M. Road,
Pune 411005
Tel: 25532959

Museum

Mahatma Phule Museum
This museum, started in 1890, displays a range of industrial and agricultural products, and handicraft articles.
1203, Ghole Road, Shivajinagar, Pune 411004
Tel: 25532750

Art Gallery

Indiaart Gallery
The Indiaart Gallery holds art exhibitions throughout the year, apart from workshops in pottery, calligraphy and cartoon making. It also has a branch in Aundh.
Kala Chhaya Campus, Opp Vikhe Patil School, Patrakar Nagar, Senapati Bapat Road, Pune 411016 Tel: 25662854

Places of Worship

Pataleshwar Caves
This 8th century rock-cut cave temple, reminiscent of the famous Ellora rock temple, was built during the time of the Rashtrakutas, the earliest rulers of Pune. Hewn out of a single rock, the temple is dedicated to Lord Shiva. In front of the cave is a circular *nandi mandapa* (pavilion) supported by thick, smooth stone pillars. The temple draws flocks of devotees on Mahashivratri (February-March).
Jungli Maharaj Road,
Pune 411005

Jungli Maharaj Temple
Adjacent to the Pataleshwar Caves is the temple dedicated to the Hindu ascetic Jungli Maharaj, and it is from here that Jungli Maharaj (J.M.) Road gets its name.
Jungli Maharaj Road,
Pune 411005

Chaturshringi Temple
Dedicated to Goddess Amba (Durga), the Chaturshringi temple situated on a hilltop bustles with activity during the nine-day festival of Navaratri (September-October).
Senapati Bapat Road,
Pune 411016
Tel: 25639032

Shops

Handmade Paper Institute
This institute was set up in 1940. Besides manufacturing a variety of handmade paper, it also stocks diaries, bags, and paper for sale.
K.B. Joshi Road,
Agriculture College Compound,
Shivajinagar, Pune 411005
Tel: 25337383 / 25538838

Kalakriti
Offers a dazzling array of artifacts, particularly wooden *jharokas, hookahs,* large chests, brass and copper items.
50/ A, Shop No. 3,
Bhandarkar Road,
Pune 411004
Tel: 25450760

Shopper's Stop
A popular fashion and lifestyle store. It also has a branch in Camp.
B Wing Godrej Eternia BLdg, Mumbai-Pune Road, Wakdewadi, Shivajinagar,
Pune 411005
Tel: 66014959

P.Y. Vaidya
A general store that attracts many customers for its Maharashtrian *masalas,* chutneys and other assorted food items.
917/19 F. C. Road,
Pune 411004
Tel: 25654819

Chitale Bandhu
Pune's most well-known sweet shop, it stocks everything from milk products like *shrikhand* to savories like *bakarwadis.* It has only two outlets at Deccan Gymkhana and Bajirao Road.
759/51 F. C. Road,
Pune 411004 Tel: 25674214

Restaurants/Cafés

Radhika
Run by an enterprising young couple, it offers a range of authentic Bengali food and sweetmeats.
Senapati Bapat Road,
Pune 411016

Vaishali
A landmark in the area, it serves the best South Indian snacks in the city and is patronized by people of all ages.
1218/1 F. C. Road,
Shivajinagar, Pune 411004
Tel: 25531244

Good Luck
A popular Irani eatery known for its *biryani* and *bun-muska* (butter) with tea. It has a loyal clientele that has been frequenting the place for decades.
Goodluck Chowk,
F. C. Road, Deccan Gymkhana,
Pune 411004
Tel: 25676893

Appa's Canteen
This canteen has been serving Punekars delicious snacks like *Sabudana Khichdi Kakdi,* and *Upeet* since 1945 Run by the Bhatt family, the canteen has been frequented by many stalwarts of Indian sports like Sunil Gavaskar, Nana Joshi and many more.
Next to the Billiards Department, Deccan Gymkhana, Shivajinagar,
Pune 411004

Kobe
Part of a Mumbai-based chain of sizzler restaurants, it draws many customers even in a predominantly vegetarian area.
Shop No 1-2-3, Business Guild, Law College Road,
Near IMD Search Institute,
Pune 411004
Tel: 25455001

Poona Coffee House
Another landmark, it was the one-time favourite of Infosys head N R Narayana Murthy, and his wife Sudha.
J. M. Road,
Deccan Gymkhana,
Pune 411005
Tel: 25531256 / 25531970

Movie Theatre

E-Square
Since it opened, it has become a bustling entertainment zone with a multiplex, hotel (Gordon House), restaurant (All Stir Fry), pub (Not Just Jazz by the Bay), food court and shopping mall.
132 University Road,
Pune 411016 Tel: 56044141
www.e-squareindia.com

Mangala
A popular multi-screen theatre, favourite of Hindi film buffs.
111, Shivajinagar,
Pune 411005
Tel: 25533468
www.clicktickets.com

Hotels

Oakwood
Good Luck Square,
Bhandarkar Road, Deccan
Gymkhana, Pune 411004
Tel: 25670011
tghotels@hotmail.com

Gordon House Hotel
132A/2A, University Road,
Ganeshkhind, Pune 411016
Tel: 66044100
e-square@e-squareindia.com

Best Western Pride Hotel
5 University Road,
Shivajinagar, Pune 411005
Tel: 25534567
pune@pridegroup.net

Centurion Hotel Quality Inn
10/1A, Ganeshkhind Road,
Opp Akashvani Bhawan,
Shivajinagar,
Pune 411005
Tel: 25510600

Hotel Coronet
1205/4, Apte Road, Deccan
Gymkhana, Pune 411004
Tel: 25530300

Salons

Gazelle
A renowned unisex salon, Gazelle also has massage facilities, which you can avail only by prior appointment.
Bhandarkar Institute Road,
Deccan Gymkhana,
Pune 411004
Tel: 25650788

Papillon
A well-equipped salon with trained personnel, Papillon is quite well known in this area.
Bhandarkar Institute Road,
Pune 411004 Tel: 25673994

Sheela's
A unisex salon equipped to do a complete makeover Sheela's also has a branch at Koregaon Park.
Shop No 26, Sagar Arcade,
F.C. Road, Pune 411004
Tel: 25539581 / 25510435

Techni Art
This salon is popular with the student community.
5 Rachna House, 1st Floor,
Near Sagar Arcade,
F.C. Road, Pune 411004
Tel: 25532540

Clubs

PYC Gymkhana
A well-equipped sports club, PYC boasts a football ground, basketball courts, a swimming pool, indoor badminton courts, and table tennis and squash facilities. The recently renovated premises also incorporate a restaurant and clubhouse.
766 Bhandarkar Institute
Road, Deccan Gymkhana,
Pune 411004
Tel: 25121894 / 25663007

Hospitals

Sancheti Institute For Orthopaedics And Rehabilitation
Set up in 1972 by Padmashree Dr. K. H. Sancheti, this is one of the largest orthopaedic Hospitals in South East Asia.
16, Shivajinagar, Pune 411005
Tel: 25533333 / 25536666

Prayag Hospital
1247, Deccan Gymkhana,
Pune 411004 Tel: 25532812

Ratna Memorial Hospital
968, Senapati Bapat Road,
Pune 411016
Tel: 25651037 / 25657564

Hardikar Hospital
1160/61 Ganeshkhind Road,
Shivajinagar,
Pune 411005
Tel: 25535326 / 25530027

Deendayal Hospital
926, F.C. Road,
Shivajinagar,
Pune 411004
Tel: 25652497 / 25651613

Joshi Hospital
778 Shivajinagar, Kamla
Nehru Park, Pune 411004
Tel: 25672565 / 25672563

Bus Stands

PMT Bus Stand
J.M. Road,
Near Deccan Gymkhana,
Pune 411005
Tel: 24440417

PMT Bus Stand
Near Pune Municipal
Corporation Building,
Shivajinagar,
Pune 411005
Tel: 24440417

Shivajinagar ST Stand
Shivajinagar, Pune 411005
Tel: 25536970

Railway Station

Shivajinagar Railway Station
Shivajinagar,
Pune 411005
Tel: 25536092

Bridge

Sangam Bridge
Built at the confluence of the Mula and Mutha rivers at Shivajinagar, the Sangam Bridge is an important link between the two sides of the city.

Banks and ATMs

SBI ATM
Survey No. 93/13 Plot No. 8,
Senapati Bapat Road,
Pune 411027

HDFC ATM
Ashish Apartment, Plot No
5, Senapati Bapat Road,
Pune 411016

Law College Raod,
Opp. Bhandarkar Institute,
Pune 411004

Citibank ATM
Chaturshringi Chowk,
Ganeshkhind Road,
Pune 411007

Shoppers Stop,
Pune-Mumbai Road,
Wakdewadi,
Pune 411005

ICICI ATM
Opp. Manoj Gore Hospital,
Law College Road,
Pune 411004

1240 A, Next to
Shreyas Hotel,
Apte Road,
Shivajinagar,
Pune 411004

UTI ATM
Shop No. 2, Vrindavan,
Opp Toyota Showroom,
Model Colony, Pune 411016

Shop No. 5, 775/3,
Sunrise Appts,
Opp Kamala Nehru Park,
Shivajinagar, Pune 411004

State Bank of India (ATM)
University Road, Veer
Chaphekar Chowk, Opp
Police Ground, Pune 411016
Tel: 25652932

1st Floor, Kumar
Renaissance,
J.M. Road, Pune 411005
Tel: 255338033 / 25532389

Pune-Mumbai Road,
Near Bhandari Auto,
Wakdewadi, Pune 411005
Tel: 25816647

Bank of India (ATM)
Opp Hotel Kamat, J.M Road,
Shivajinagar, Pune 411005
Tel: 25532014

1201/C F.C.Road, Tukaram
Paduka Chowk,
Pune 411004
Pune: 25532073

36/1, Preet Chambers,
Pune-Mumbai Road,
Wakdewadi, Shivajinagar,
Pune 411005
Tel: 25511691

Bank of Maharashtra (ATM)
1183-A F.C. Road, Sadashiv
Vilas Building, Shivajinagar,
Pune 411005
Tel: 25535056

Near Modern Café, Jungli
Maharaj Road, Shivajinagar,
Pune 411005
Tel: 25536800 / 25521008

UTI Bank (ATM)
Sterling Plaza 1262/B, J. M.
Road, Ground Floor, Deccan
Gymkhana Pune 411005
Tel: 56012695 / 56015723

ICICI Bank (ATM)
870 /1, Suma House,
Bhandarkar Road,
Opp Spencer's Daily,
Pune 411004
Tel: 56049500

Bank Of Baroda
Opp. D.S.Kulkarani Co,
1303, Shivajinagar,
Pune 411005 Tel: 25533935

Deccan Gymkhana

The oldest sports club in Pune, with well maintained facilities for cricket, basketball, tennis, and table tennis. It also provides access to Tilak Tank, the recently renovated Olympic size swimming pool.

Several national and international sportsmen began their careers here including tennis players Nandan Bal, Sandeep Kirtane, Nitin Kirtane and Radhika Tulpule, and cricketers like D.B.Deodhar, Nana Joshi, Kamal Bhandarkar.

759/2, Shivajinagar,
Pune 411004
Tel: 25670217 / 25663861

WELCOME TO
THE OXYGEN ZONE
MAGARPATTA
CITY
MAGARPATTA CITY
HON. SHRI SHARADRAOJI PAWAR
SHRI VILASRAO DESHMUKH
SHRI CHHAGANRAO BHUJBAL
SHRI PADAMSINGH PATIL
SHRI VIJAYSINGH MOHITE PATIL
SHRI JAYANTRAO PATIL
SHRI AJIT PAWAR
SHRI DILIP WALSE PATIL
SHRI VASANT CHAVAN
SHRI BALASAHEB SHIVARKAR
SHRI DATTATRAYA GAIKWAD
A PROJECT BY
MAGARPATTA TOWNSHIP DEVELOPMENT AND CONSTRUCTION COMPANY LIMITED

Hadapsar - Solapur Bazaar

Hadapsar is located at the eastern end of Pune, and can be accessed via the busy Pune-Solapur highway. The creation of the Hadapsar Industrial Estate by the government in the 1960s led to tremendous growth in the area. Prominent companies like Serum Institute of India, Honeywell, Industrial Automation Ltd. TCS, Gits Food Products Pvt.Ltd., and Pravin Masale have set up office here. The area is also emerging as an important IT hub after the establishment of Magarpatta City, a unique, self-sufficient IT township complete with plush apartments, offices, clubs, school and restaurants. Hadapsar is also known for its paragliding club.

Prominent Localities

Vitthal Nagar
A small, thinly populated area located on the eastern periphery of Pune.

Mohammedwadi
This is where the famous H.V. Desai Eye Hospital is located.

Hadapsar Industrial Estate
Developed by MIDC, it is the location of a number of prominent industries including Kirloskar Pneumatic Co. Ltd, and Honeywell Industrial Automation Ltd.

Fatima Nagar
A residential area, which has recently seen significant commercial activity.

Hadapsar Bazaar
A crowded market area crammed with shops and small eateries.

Sopan Baug
An upmarket residential area, marked by plush homes.

St. Patrick's Town
One of the oldest bungalow societies in the area, a majority of the inhabitants are Catholics.

Ghorpadi
Once a small village, it subsequently became part of the cantonment area and has a mix of old army quarters and modern construction.

Hadapsar - Solapur Bazaar

TO KHARADI
AILWAY
TO SOLAPUR
MUNDHWA KHARADI ROAD
AGARPATTA CITY
RIGHT BANK CANAL
TO MANJRI
PUNE SOLAPUR ROAD
HADAPSAR GAOTHAN
OCTROI NAKA
IBM
TO SOLAPUR
PUNE-SASWAD ROAD
DAPSAR USTRIAL ZONE
PUNE - KOLHAPUR RAILWAY
HADAPSAR FLYING CLUB
TO SASWAD
TO MIRAJ
HAMMED WADI GAOTHAN
N
W
E
S
Main Roads
Saswad Road
Mundhwa Kharadi Road
Pune-Solapur Road
B. T. Kawade Road
Map Indicative; not to scale

Industries

Serum Institute of India
Founded by the Poonawalla family in 1966, the Serum Institute of India started out by making tetanus antitoxins. Today it is the largest exporter of vaccines and immuno-biologicals in the country, and the world's largest manufacturer of the measles vaccine, better known as the DTP vaccine. The family's stud farm, one of the largest in the country, is also located in Hadapsar.
212/2, Hadapsar,
Off Soli Poonawalla Road,
Pune 411042
Tel: 26993990 / 3921

Tata Research Development & Design Centre (TRDDC)
Established in 1981, TRDDC conducts research in cutting edge technology, tools and engineering techniques, and develops intellectual property for commercial projects all over the world.
54/B Hadapsar Industrial Estate, Pune 411 013
Tel: 56042333

Gits Food Products Pvt. Ltd.
Founded as a small family enterprise in 1963, Gits is at the forefront of the instant food revolution in India. The company manufactures and exports a vast range of Indian snacks like *idlis, dhoklas,* and *gulab jamuns*.
Hadapsar Industrial Estate,
Pune 411013 Tel: 26870008

Baker's Basket

Pune's leading bakery chain with seven outlets in the city has a state-of-the-art factory in the Hadapsar Industrial Estate.
Inn Venue Hospitality Mgmt Pvt Ltd. 32/A Hadapsar Industrial Estate, Hadapsar
Pune 411013
Tel: 26875050

Defense Centre

Army School of Physical Training (ASPT)
Established in 1947, the school conducts 36 physical training and sports coaching courses for selected candidates from all ranks of the Army, students from the police, and para-military forces. It also provides basic training in sports and games and accepts enrolments from neighbouring foreign countries like Sri Lanka, Bhutan, Nepal and Maldives.
Ramtekdi Hadapsar
Pune 411028
Tel: 26873522

Education

Annasaheb Magar Mahavidyalaya
This college has a full-fledged faculty for arts, science and commerce.
Hadapsar, Pune 411028
Tel. 26990376

Sadhana Vidyalaya
Located amidst a large residential settlement, this was one of the earliest schools of the area.
Hadapsar,
Pune 411028
Tel: 26999871

Magarpatta City

Inaugurated in 2001, this mega township has become a coveted business and residential address. Leading MNCs like Aviva, EDS, EXL, Sybase, and Amdocs have set up shop here. The township has about 120 acres of green cover, with 32,000 trees and 20 lakh sq. ft. of lawns. Amenities include a golf course, aqua sports centre, sports complex, school and restaurants. Off Pune Solapur Highway, Hadapsar, Pune 411028 Tel: 26823900/1/2

Restaurants

Courtyard Greenview
A secluded and spacious eatery with a relaxed ambience. It has a comfortable lounge bar and the restaurant offers a mix of Indian, Thai, Italian and continental cuisine. It also has conference facilities.
Pune-Solapur Road

Deccan Harvest
A popular multi-cuisine outdoor restaurant.
143 Magarpatta City, Off Pune-Solapur Highway, Hadapsar Pune 411028
Tel: 26824142

Shops

Big Bazaar
Part of a national chain of superstores, it stocks a wide variety of items at bargain prices.
Fun and Shop Bldg. Solapur Road, Himalaya House Area, Fatima Nagar, Pune 411040 Tel: 66420500

Hadapsar Flying Club

Run by the civil aviation department of the central government, the Hadapsar Flying Club offers gliding opportunities for licensed pilots, hobby flyers and gliding enthusiasts. Equipped with a fleet of Super Blaniks and several imported gliders from the Czech Republic, it is open five days a week from Sunday to Thursday. Near Gadital Bridge, Saswad Road, Hadapsar Pune 411028 Tel: 26992048/26991012

Krome Planet Furniture
One of the biggest furniture outlets in the city, it stocks a wide range of Indian and imported furniture.
Amar Manor, 32/3, Pune

Solapur Road, St. Patricks Town Corner, Opp ASPT, Pune 411013
Tel: 26815052/ 53

Movie Theatre

Vaibhav
This is the only theatre in the area and attracts large crowds, especially after its recent renovation.
Pune Solapur Road, Hadapsar, Pune 411028
Tel: 26870211

Places of Interest

Rajbaug
Legendary Hindi filmmaker Raj Kapoor had a beautiful farm called Rajbaug at Loni where he shot films such as Satyam Shivam Sundaram. The farm was recently handed over to the MIT educational trust, which has set up a design academy and international school on the premises.

Bharatiya Agro Industries Foundation (BAIF)
Set up by Manibhai Desai in 1967 at Urulikanchan, this is a unique rural integration and development centre that conducts multidisciplinary programmes and activities to help farmers and local villagers become self-sufficient. It is recognised as a leading research institute and has received several awards for its pioneering role in rural development.
Urulikachan, District
Pune 412202
Tel: 26926448

Nisargopachar Ashram
This Naturopathy Centre was also started by Manibhai Desai. The ashram implements a treatment process that involves the use of the five basic elements of nature, namely earth, water, fire, air and sunlight. The centre has also has accommodation facilities.
'Nisargopachar Gramsudhar Trust' Urulikachan, District
Pune 412202
Tel: 26926298

Sanskruti
Sanskruti is a garden-restaurant spread over 4 acres with an ample play area and a host of activities like bangle making, *mehendi,* pottery, live folk music and dances. It serves authentic Gujarati and Rajasthani meals.
Opp. Indian Oil Corporation,
Solapur Highway,
Loni-Kalbhor, Pune 412201
Tel: 26915156/7/8

Banks and ATMs

Citibank ATM
Bhosale Arcade, Near Nokia Centre, Pune-Solapur Road,
Hadapsar, Pune 411028

SBI ATM
Survey No. 153/1-A/1-A/1,
Pune-Solapur Road,
Pune 411028

Magar Petroleum,
Mundhwa - Hadapsar Road,
Opp. Magarpatta City,
Pune 411028

HDFC ATM
Opp. AICT,
Pune Solapur Road,
Hadapsar, Pune 411028

ICICI ATM
Serum Institute,
Pooonawala Group,
Survey No.223 / 5 - A / 2 / 2,
Hadapsar,
Pune 411028

UTI ATM
Shop No 9,
Vaibhav Cinema Complex,
Pune-Solapur Road,
Hadapsar,
Pune 411013

Bank of Maharashtra
Near Overbridge,
Pune Solapur Road,
Hadapsar,
Pune 411028

Bank of India
Hadapsar Industrial Estate,
Post Bag No. 1,
Hadapsar,
Pune 411013

Getaways

Bhigwan Lake
Situated on the outskirts of a small village less than 100 km from Hadapsar, the lake attracts a number of migratory birds during winter such as brahminy ducks, coots, lapwings, stilts, and ibis. It is considered to be one of the largest breeding places of painted storks in Maharashtra.

Khadki

The cantonment of Khadki (formerly Kirkee) was developed under the British. Several key defense establishments are located here and of the 3,000-acre area, only 121 acres is notified as civilian area. The momentous Battle of Khadki that brought an end to the glorious Peshwa regime and established the British rule in 1817 was fought here. Khadki is also known as a bastion for hockey, as it has produced many national stalwarts like Baburao Narasappa Nimal, Joseph Phillips and Dhanraj Pillay. What distinguishes Khadki from the other parts of Pune are its wide roads, quiet avenues, leafy environs, low-rise buildings and abundance of colonial bungalows that house army officers.

Prominent Localities

Range Hills
A residential area packed with families working in the defense sector.

Khadki Bazaar
A lively, bustling market place that attracts locals and neighboring villagers in large numbers.

Bombay Sappers
Maintained by the engineering department of the Armed Forces, this is one of the most beautiful and best kept areas of Khadki.

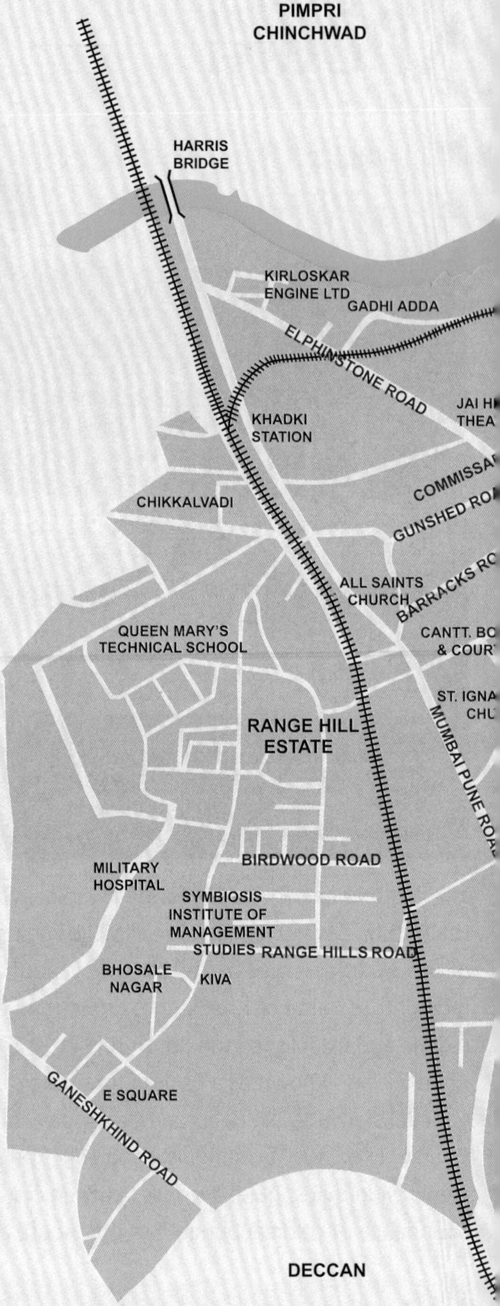

Khadki

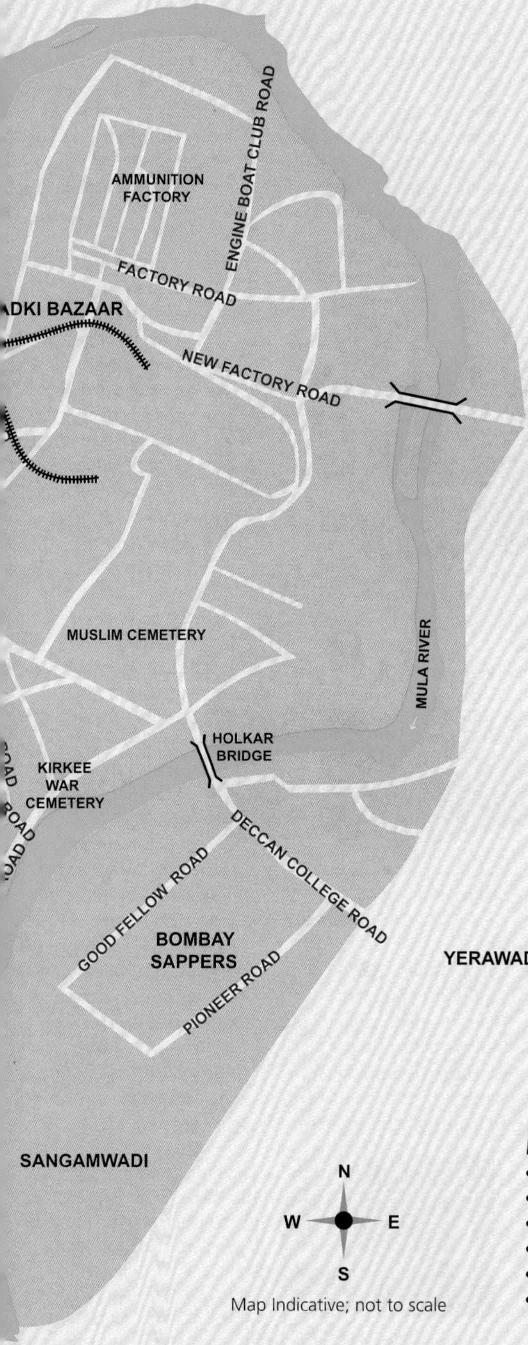

Map Indicative; not to scale

Main Roads

- Mula Road
- Factory Road
- Elphinstone Road
- Range Hills Road
- Mumbai Pune Road
- Laxmanrao Kirloskar Road

Landmarks

Bombay Sappers Association (BSA)

In 1837 the Bombay Engineer Group (BEG) was shifted to the eastern bank of the river Mula. The term 'sappers' commonly refers to military engineers engaged in tasks such as building bridges and fortifications. The Bombay Sappers have the unique distinction of winning the Victoria Cross, the Param Vir Chakra and the Ashok Chakra.
HQ BEG & Centre,
Khadki,
Pune 411003
Tel: 26682171
Email: bsaKhadki@vsnl.net

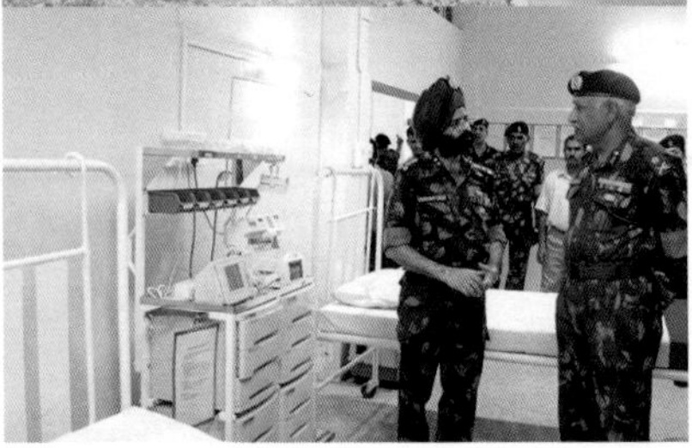

College of Military Engineering (CME)

CME provides technical training and engineering support to the Armed Forces. It has a wide spectrum of faculties ranging from combat to civil, electrical and mechanical engineering. Three lakes in the premises attract a host of migratory bird. The college sailing club is very active. All officers are required to cycle to their offices or classes once a week in an effort to maintain a clean environment.
CPO, Bombay-Pune Road,
Khadki, Pune 411031
Tel: 27145194

Paraplegic Rehabilitation Centre (PRC)

Set-up in 1974, this was the first rehabilitation centre of its kind in India to cater to 100% disabled-ex-servicemen from all over the country. Workshops are held regularly for all inmates. Some have become successful Mouth and Foot Artists and many of them are excellent sportsmen who have won medals in paraplegic events.
Park Road, Near Durgamata Mandir, Khadki,
Pune 411020 Tel: 25820505

Queen Mary's Technical School for Disabled

This is the only institute in the country that imparts ITI recognized vocational training to disabled soldiers and army officers and their dependents.
Park Road, Khadki,
Pune 411020
Tel: 25816779

Military Hospital

The Military Hospital Khadki, is a premier orthopaedic institution and caters to soldiers who have suffered war casualties. The specialized departments here are the orthopaedic centre, spinal cord centre and joint replacement centre.
Near CME Workshop,
Range Hills Road,
Khadki Cantonment,
Pune 411020
Tel: 26363901 / 25803169

Kirkee War Cemetery

This is one of the most beautiful spots in Pune. Maintained by the Commonwealth War Graves Commission, here lie 1,576 graves of British and Indian soldiers who died during the World Wars. The garden surrounding the graves is very attractive with brightly colored bougainvillea canopies and callistemon (bottlebrush) trees.
Timings: 8 am - 4 pm.
Mula Road, Khadki,
Pune 411003
Tel : 25814462

Khadki Bazaar

This is an old, colorful and famous market. It is known for its cluster of saree shops that stock the popular bastas - the pack of sarees and dress materials bought during weddings to be given as customary gifts to family members. The Bazaar also has a large number of jewelers.
Elphinstone Road, Khadki, Pune-411 003

Places of Worship

All Saints Church

Built in 1869, this small church has beautiful stained glass windows believed to be imported from Belgium. Services are held in English, Marathi and Malayalam.

Elphinstone Road, Opposite Khadki Business Centre, Khadki, Pune 411003
Tel: 25813969

St. Ignatius Church

Also built by the British, this century-old church still attracts a fair number of worshippers.
General Thimaya Road, Bombay-Pune Road, Khadki, Pune 411003 Tel: 25817179

Kali Bari Durga Temple

Constructed by the local Bengali community, the Kali Bari temple attracts a large number of devotees during the Durga pooja festivities.
254B Park Road, Near Khadki Station,
Pune 411020 Tel: 25693533

Gurudwara Shri Gurusingh Sabha

Devotees gather here in large numbers to attend the religious discourses, especially on Sundays.
Elphinstone Road, Khadki Bazaar, Khadki,
Pune 411003
Tel: 25822732

Bridge

Holkar Bridge

Over 150 years old, the bridge links the western part of the city with the other side of the river.

Movie Theatre

Jaihind

This is a small, old theatre in need of maintenance. Since it is the only one in the locality, it is still operational.
Pune –Mumbai Highway, Near Khadki Railway Station,
Khadki, Pune 411003
Tel: 25817741

Education

St. Joseph's Convent Girls High School

A well-established school in Khadki, it has classes from Lower KG to the 10th.
36 Burr Road, Khadki, and Pune 411003 Tel: 25813325

St. Joseph's Boys High School

Affiliated to the SSC board this is a very sought after school for boys.
36, Burr Road, Khadki,
Pune 411003
Tel: 25818041

St. Thomas Public School

Started by missionaries this co-education school is affiliated to the SSC board.
Swastik Road, Behind Railway Station, Khadki,
Pune 411003 Tel: 25815304

All Saints High School

This SSC board school is run by the trust of the All Saints Church.
Church Road, Khadki,
Pune 411003
Tel: 25813969

Symbiosis Institute of Management Studies (SIMS)

This premier management institute is set amidst verdant surroundings.
It offers a range of management programmes with specializations in marketing, finance,

operations, IT and International Business.
Plot No. 6, Opposite EME Workshop, Range Hills Road, Khadki Cantonment
Pune 411020
Tel: 30213200
www.sims.edu

Tikaram Jagannath (TJ) College

A college affiliated to the University of Pune offering arts, commerce and science disciplines.
491, Elphinstone Road, Khadki,
Pune 411003
Tel: 25811491/8246

Restaurants & Pubs

Kiva
An intimate little lounge bar done up in Mexican-Indian style and offering a range of exotic cocktails.
Symphony C Building, Range Hills Road, Bhosale Nagar, Khadki, Pune 411020 Tel: 25538339

Royal Symphony Hotel Pvt. Ltd.
A popular multi-cuisine restaurant, one of the few in the area.
210/ A, Opp Kumar Vastu, Range Hills Road, Pune 411016 Tel: 25539061

Railway Station

Khadki Railway Station
Travellers heading for Aundh, Pashan, Pune University and neighboring areas will find Khadki and Shivajinagar railway stations most convenient, though not all trains stop at Khadki.
Elphinstone Road, Khadki, Pune 411003 Tel: 2581.6658

Banks and ATMs

HDFC ATM
Opp Kirloskar Oil Engines Ltd, Khadki, Pune 411003

UTI ATM
Kohinoor Plaza, Near Business Centre, Khadki Bazaar, Khadki Pune 411003
High Explosives Factory, Khadki Pune 411003

ICICI ATM
Soap Factory, Ammunition Factory, Khadki, Pune 411003

Cosmos Bank ATM
Kohinoor Plaza, Near Bus Stand, Khadki Bazaar, Khadki Pune 411003

Cosmos Bank Ltd
Elphinstone Road, Bopodi, Pune 411003

State Bank of India
Cantonment Area, Khadki, Pune 411003 Tel: 25813381

Punjab National Bank
4 Khadki Business Centre, Khadki Bazaar, Khadki Pune 411003 Tel: 25817963

Bank of Maharashtra
Deepshri Building 156, Old Bazaar, Khadki Pune 411003 Tel: 26697570

Kondhwa - Wanowrie - Bibvewadi

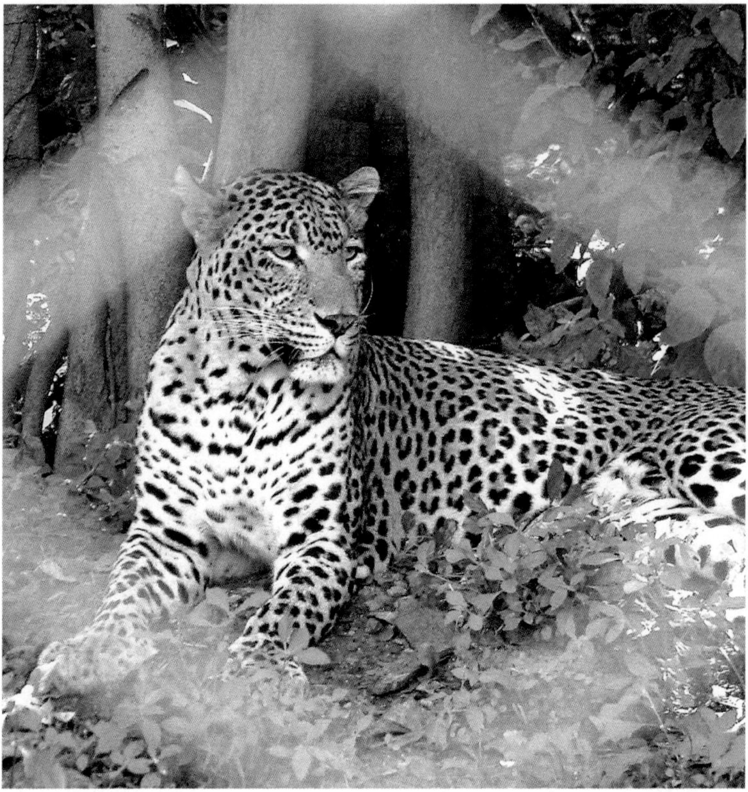

At the southern end of the city, Kondhwa, Wanowrie and Bibvewadi have developed into important residential areas over the last two decades. One of the first housing societies to be constructed in Kondhwa was Salunke Vihar, exclusively for retired defense personnel. Now several stylish residential complexes have been built here and in the adjoining Wanowrie area. A number of major educational institutions are also located here, the oldest being the National Institute of Bank Management (NIBM). The development of deemed university Bharati Vidyapeeth in Bibvewadi has seen a tremendous influx of students into the area.

Prominent Localities

Kondhwa
A growing residential locality with large complexes, it has recently seen the establishment of several educational institutions.

Lulla Nagar
Once an upmarket residential locality marked by bungalows, it is now being taken over by several high-rise monoliths.

Wanowrie
A largely well-planned area, it is attracting a significant cosmopolitan population that has recently moved to the city.

Fakhri Hills
A significant section of Pune's Bohri community has relocated to luxurious houses in this area.

Salisbury Park
A prime residential area, this is the location of Mira Society, Pune's oldest housing society.

Mukund Nagar
The Tilak Maharashtra Vidyapeeth is located in this basically residential area.

Gultekdi
The area is dominated by Market Yard, Pune's wholesale vegetable, fruit, flower and grain market.

Katraj
Pune's Government Milk Dairy, the zoo and snake park can be found here.

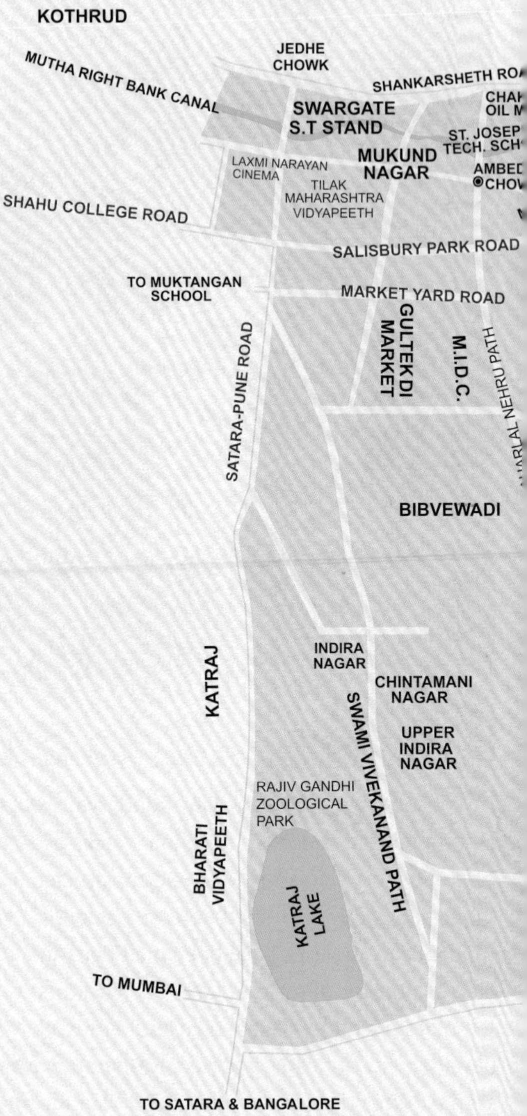

Kondhwa - Wanowrie - Bibvewadi

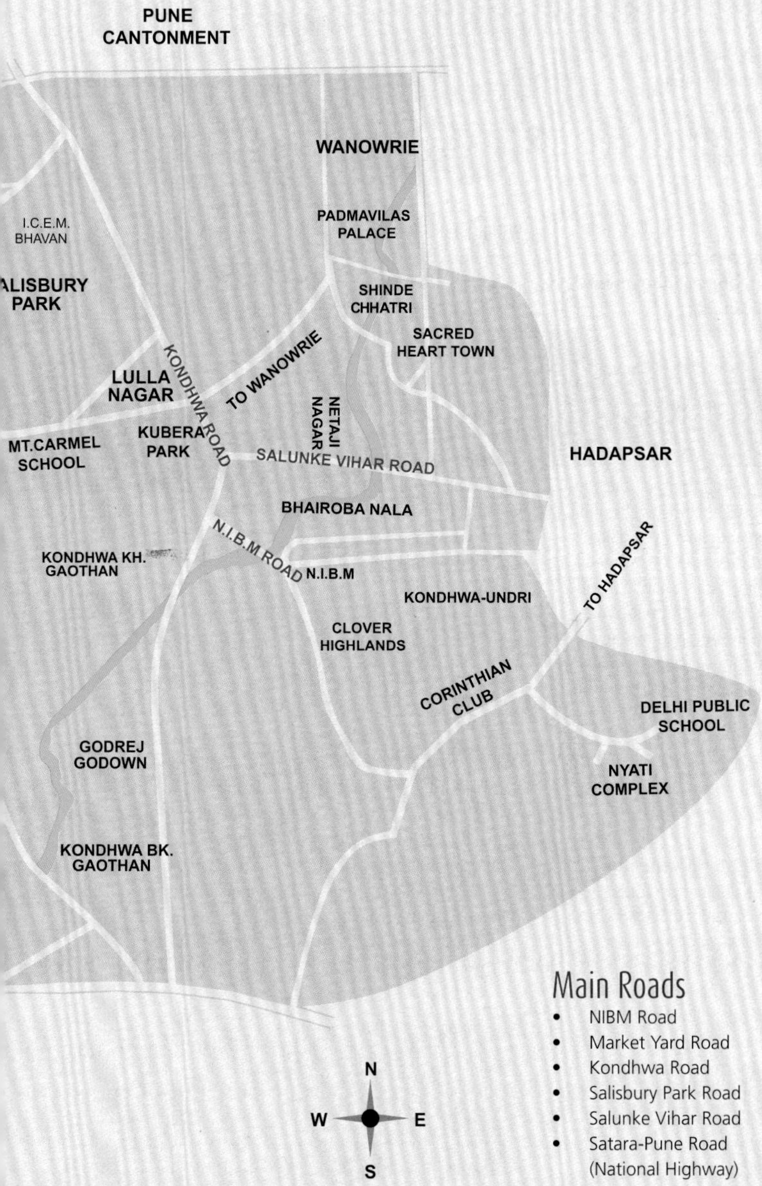

Map Indicative; not to scale

Main Roads

- NIBM Road
- Market Yard Road
- Kondhwa Road
- Salisbury Park Road
- Salunke Vihar Road
- Satara-Pune Road (National Highway)

Education

Vishwakarma Institute of Technology (VIT)

Established in 1984, VIT offers undergraduate and postgraduate courses in engineering.
666, Upper Indiranagar, Bibvewadi, Pune 411037
Tel: 24281594 www.vit.edu

National Institute of Banking Management (NIBM)

NIBM is a premier institute for research, training and consultancy in the field of banking and finance in India. Established in 1969 by the Reserve Bank of India, it has complete residential and educational facilities. The Institute also publishes books, journals, reports and research papers.
Kondhwa Khurd, NIBM P.O., Pune 411048 Tel: 26833080
www.nibmindia.org

Bharati Vidyapeeth

This deemed University offers degrees in Arts, Science, Commerce, Medicine, Dentistry, Ayurveda, Homeopathy, Nursing, Engineering, Architecture and Hotel Management. It also has a Pharmacy and Management College at Paud Road.
Katraj-Dhankawadi Campus, Pune Satara Road, Pune 411043
Tel: 24362516
www.bharatividyapeeth.edu

Tilak Maharashtra Vidyapeeth

Established in 1921, the Tilak Maharashtra Vidyapeeth was set up as a memorial to Lokmanya Tilak. Its Open Education Centre offers a Bachelor's degree of Arts (BA) in social sciences through correspondence.
Vidyapeeth Bhavan, Gultekdi, Pune 411037
Tel: 24461856/24467888
Fax: 24466068

Delhi Public School (DPS)

Part of the Delhi-based chain of schools, it follows the CBSE Board pattern.
Nyati County, Vill: Mohammadwadi, Kondhwa, Pune 411028
Tel: 26970418
www.dpsfamily.org

Billabong High School

Started in 2006 by educationist Lina Ashar of the Kangaroo Kids School, it follows the Australian methods of teaching. It has ICSE and IGCSE syllabi and is the first centrally air-conditioned school of the city.
Dorabjee Paradise, Corinthian Club Road, Extn. NIBM, Pune 411048
Tel: 39525552

Gardens

Gool Poonawalla Jogging Park

One of Pune's best maintained and scrupulously clean parks, it is popular with the fitness conscious and others looking for a relaxing environment.
Salisbury Park, Pune 411037

Jagtap Nursery

One of Pune's most popular nurseries, it is a one-stop shop for plants and gardening accessories.
3, Phayre Road, Near Golibar Maidan, Behind S.M. Joshi Hindi High School, Pune 411040
Tel: 26363432

Mahadji Shinde Chhatri

Located in Wanowrie, it was built in memory of the great Maratha general Mahadji Shinde, and has a mixture of Peshwa, European and Rajasthani styles of architecture. Construction was started in 1830 and completed in 1910.
Survey No, 75, Wanowrie, Pune 411040 Tel: 26852141

Housing Societies

Ganga Satellite
Near Shinde Chhatri,
Wanowrie, Pune 411040
Tel: 26803456

Clover Village
Survey No. 66/ 67,
Wanowrie, Pune 411040

Clover Highlands
25/1 To 4, off NIBM Road,
Kondhwa Khurd,
Pune 411048

Sacred Heart Town
Wanowrie, Pune 411040

Libraries

P40 Library
A well stocked neighbourhood library with a range of English fiction and non-fiction books and magazines.
Opp. Salunke Vihar, Salunke Vihar Road, Pune 411040
Tel: 56217560

Friends Library
A good collection of novels and magazines for booklovers in the area.
Salunke Vihar, Crystal Castle Building, Shop No 2,
Pune 411040
Tel: 26855124

Shopping Malls

TruMart
Konark Indrayu,
Off NIBM Road,
Kondhwa Khurd,
Pune 411048 Tel: 26800112

Rajiv Gandhi Zoological Park

This well-maintained zoo is a big attraction for children. The Katraj Snake Park housed here is one of its kind in the country and has more than 150 different types of snakes.
Opp. Katraj Dairy,
Pune-Satara Highway,
Pune 411043 Tel: 24370747

Mantra Magic
Clover Linkfield Plaza, Near Clover Village, Salunke Vihar Road, Pune 411040

KK Bazaar
Wing B, K.K. Bolsar Market, Pune Satara Road Dhankawadi, Pune 411043
Tel: 66500444 /9371003457

Vishal Mega Mart
B Wing KP City Mall, Wanowrie Road, Fatima Nagar, Pune 411040
Tel: 26822337/ 38

Club

Corinthian Club
Built in the Greco-Egyptian style and spread over a acres of lush surroundings, it plays host to the city's most high-profile Holi bashes, Diwali parties, Dandiya get-togethers, fashion shows, product launches and corporate meets.
Off NIBM Road,
Nyati County South,
Pune 411028
Tel: 26970900

Restaurants

Baan Thai
This small restaurant specialises in Thai and Chinese cuisine.
Kubera Colony, Bakers Point, NIBM Road, Pune 411048
Tel: 32911907 / 3294007

Kimling

Located on the first floor of the snazzy Gera Junction, it offers an appetizing Chinese meal.
Shop No 1, Gera Junction, Kondhwa Road, Lulla Nagar, Pune 411040 Tel: 32931635

Foodies
A small modest eatery that draws crowds for its succulent *kathi kebabs* and rolls.
Shop No 2, Bakers Point, NIBM Road, Kubera Colony, Pune 411048 Tel: 26832729

ZK's
Cricket star Zaheer Khan's multi-cuisine restaurant and lounge bar is a gastronomic delight, and draws a large number of fans.
301/302 Winner Court, Kondhwa Road, Lulla Nagar, Pune 411040 Tel: 26834455

Southern Spice
If you are looking out for some authentic South Indian coastal seafood, this is where your search ends.
Brahma Majestic, Shop No. 11, NIBM Road, Pune 411048 Tel: 26805080

The Terrace
For good tandoori food and al fresco dining, head towards The Terrace.
Brahma Majestic, Shop No. 11, NIBM Road, Pune 411048 Tel: 26805080

Hospitals

Noble Hospital

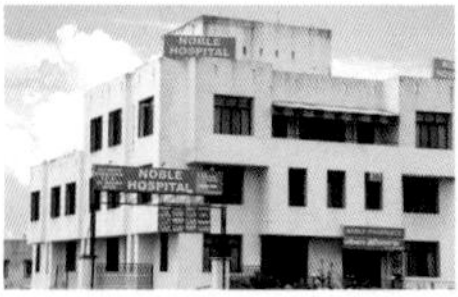

Near Fakhri Hills, Kondhwa Road, Kondhwa, Pune 411040 Tel: 24003201

Shanti Diagnostic and Polyclinic
Sukhsagar Nagar, Pune 411046 Tel: 56784077

Saisneh Hospital and Dignostic Centre
Pune-Satara Road, Near PMT Depot, Katraj, Pune 411046
Tel: 26959208 / 308
www.saisneh.com

Pawar Hospital
49/22, Balaji Nagar, Behind Ellora Palace, Dhankawadi, Pune 411043
Tel: 24372008 / 24373196

Banks and ATMs

State Bank of India ATM
Survey No. 65 Kedari Nagar, Wanowrie, Pune 411040

Pune-Satara Road, Dhankawadi, Pune 411043

ICICI Bank ATM
Sacred Heart Town, Shop No 1, Wanowrie, Pune 411040

Ruhi Apartments, Salunke Vihar Rd, Kondhwa Khurd, Pune 411048

HDFC ATM
Sacred Heart Town, Shop No. 11, Wanowrie, Pune 411040

Ashoka Clover, Pune-Satara Road, Pune 411009

Bank of Maharashtra ATM
Indira Nagar Wasahat, Bibvewadi, Pune 411037

Bibvewadi Katraj Road, Near Rajarshi Shahu Bank, Pune 411037

Citibank ATM
Sacred Heart Town Shop No 15, Wanowrie, Pune 411040

UTI ATM
Bharati Vihar, Bharati Vidyapeeth, Katraj, Pune 411046

Pune-Satara Road, Bio Bhavan, Opp. City Pride, Pune 411009

Bank of Maharashtra (ATM)
Poonam Plaza, Survey No.694/2 Plot No-12, Market Yard, Pune 411037
Tel: 24264474

Tilak Maharashtra Vidyapeeth Campus, Gultekdi, Pune 411037
Tel: 24352273

Bibvewadi Road, Renuka Building, Bibvewadi, Pune 411037 Tel: 24212071

ICICI Bank (ATM)
Somshank Chambers, Survey No. 46, Plot-1, Pune-Satara Road, Pune 411009

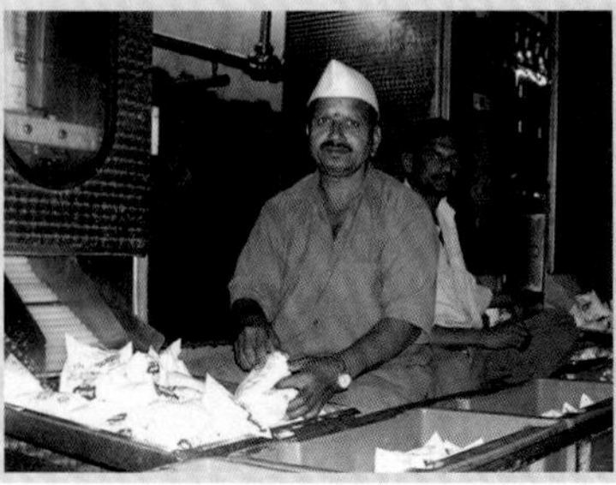

Katraj Dairy

The Katraj Dairy is a district level cooperative organisation registered in 1960. Today it delivers about 2 lakh 40 thousand liters of milk to the city daily. Its products range from milk, cream and *ghee* to *lassi*, milk powder and ice cream.
Pune Zilla Sahakari Doodh Utpadak Sangh Maryadit, Pune Satara Road, Katraj, Pune 411046 Tel: 24367946

UTI Bank (ATM)
Plot No 75/2/2, B Building
No 7, Sacred Heart Town,
Wanowrie, Pune 411040
Tel: 26853817 / 18

HDFC Bank
3/4, Mayurpankh
Apartments, Next to Konark
Complex, Pune 411048
Tel: 26930917

49/1 Pune-Satara Road,
Aranyeshwar Corner,
Sahakar Nagar,
Pune 411009
Tel: 24224332

State Bank of India (ATM)
Pune-Satara Road,
Dhankawadi,
Pune 411043
Tel: 24367521 / 22

Oriental Bank of Commerce (ATM)
49, Commercial Complex,
Sacred Heart Town,
Wanowrie,
Pune 411040
Tel: 26852014 / 26852655

4-5, C-2 Bramha Estate,
NIBM Road, Kondhwa
Khurd, Pune 411048
Tel: 26837526 / 27

Market Yard

The wholesale vegetable and fruit market of the city. Market Yard is bustling with activity right through the wee hours of the morning until late hours of the night. In the late evening animals can be seen feeding on the left-over ensuring that nothing goes waste!

Bank Of India
Anchor House, 9 Sawhany
Sujan Park, Wanowrie,
Kondhwa Road,
Pune 411040
Tel: 26830037/ 26831054

Shop No. 4, Wonder City,
Pune-Mumbai Bypass
Highway, Katraj,
Pune 411046

Central Bank Of India
Pune-Satara Road, Bio
Bhavan, Aranyeshwar,
Pune 411043
Tel: 24223765

Bank Of Baroda
20 Omkar Jyoti Niwas
Adarsh Nagar, Market Yard
Rd, Pune 411037
Tel: 24266143

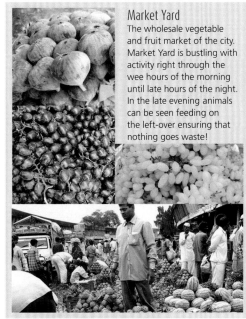

Kothrud - Erandwane - Warje

The vast Erandwane area encompasses Karve Road and all its offshoots on both sides, and stretches up to Kothrud. Just a few decades back, Kothrud was a far-flung, underdeveloped, sparsely populated area of Pune, but in recent years, it has earned the distinction of being the 'fastest growing suburb in Asia'. The area is teeming with new residential complexes, restaurants, educational institutes and cyber cafes.

Adjoining Kothrud is the suburb of Warje. One of the fringe villages incorporated into the Pune Municipal Corporation in 1997, only mere traces of the old village remain today. Rapid development has taken place in the area due to its proximity to the industrial township of Pirangut and accessibility to Hinjewadi's IT Park via the Pune Dehu Road Bypass. However there are still extensive stretches of green cover here under the protection of the Government's forest department.

Prominent Localities

Prabhat Road

An upmarket residential area, comprising 15 lanes, some of which still feature the rambling old bungalows of yore.

Kothrud

This is a largely Maharashtrian dominated residential area and is popular with the traditional Punekar who has moved out of the old city.

Karve Nagar

Named after social reformer Maharshi Dhondo Keshav Karve, there are several educational institutions here.

Warje-Malwadi

Once a village, the area is now an upcoming residential locality witnessing significant construction activity.

Paud Road

This locality is home to the Maharashtra Institute of Technology (MIT) campus and has several large housing societies. Pune's first flyover, connecting Karve Road to Paud Road was inaugurated here in 1998.

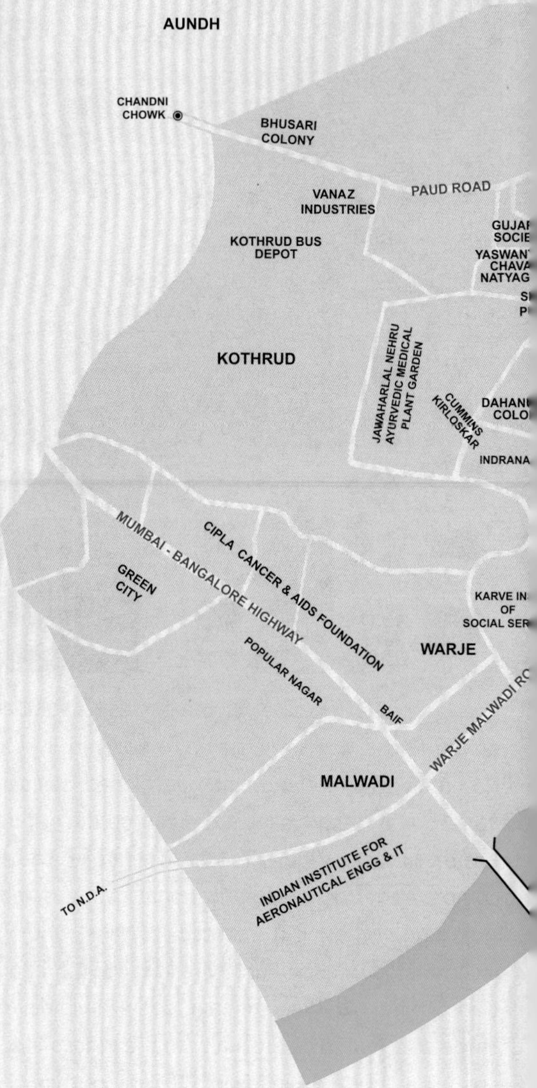

Kothrud - Erandwane - Warje

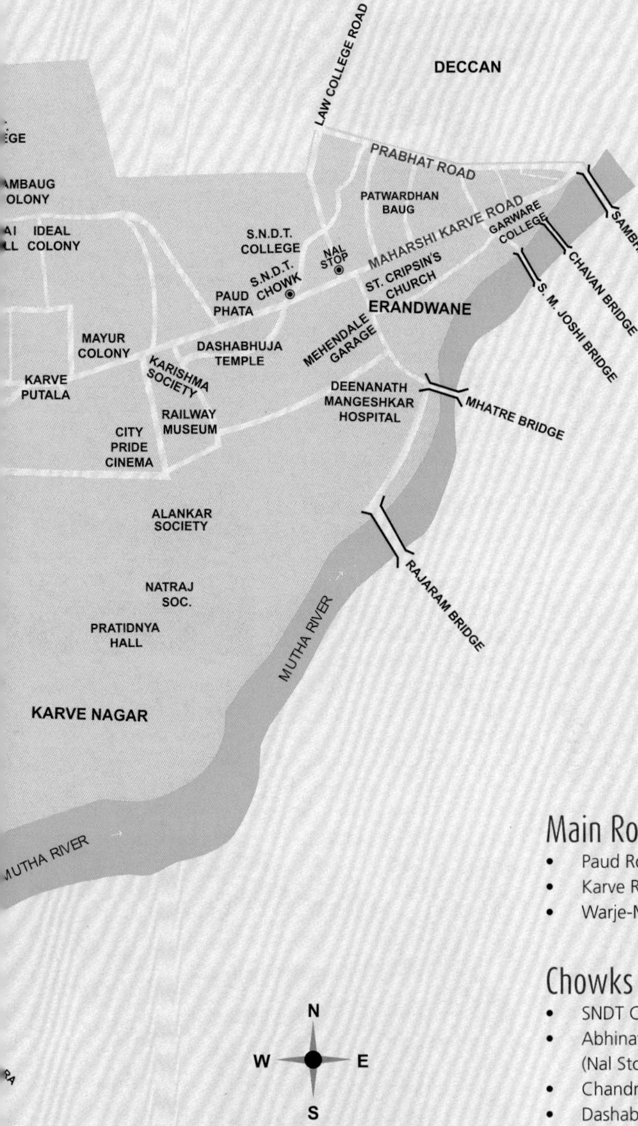

Map Indicative; not to scale

Main Roads

- Paud Road
- Karve Road
- Warje-Malwadi Road

Chowks

- SNDT Chowk
- Abhinav Chowk (Nal Stop)
- Chandni Chowk
- Dashabhuja Ganpati Chowk

Education

P. Jog High School
This school has both English and Marathi medium sections.
Beside UTI Bank, Mayur Colony, Kothrud,
Pune 411029 Tel: 25431065

MES Bal Shikshan Mandir
A co-educational school, Bal Shikshan Mandir is a branch of the MES Garware School on Karve Road.
131, Mayur Colony,
Kothrud, Pune 411029
Tel: 25435260 / 25435733

Dr. Kalmadi Shamrao High School
Started by educationist Dr. Kalmadi Shamrao, this school has a reputation for imparting quality education.
Dr Ketkar Marg, 36
Erandwane, Pune 411004
Tel: 25434300/3136

Millennium National School
Founded in 2000 by Dr.Pathak, Millennium has become popular for its unique blend of academics and co-curricular activities.
18, Hill Side, Karve Nagar,
Pune 4110052 Tel: 5436239

Abhinav Vidyalaya High School
A co-educational school, Abhinav has an excellent academic record and is one of the most sought after schools of the area.
Karve Road, Nal Stop, Pune
411004 Tel: 25442812

New India English School
This co-ed SSC school has a primary and secondary section and is run by the very famous Raja Shree Shivraya Pratishthan which also runs other schools in the area.
Kothrud,
Pune 411038.
Tel: 25280291

Rosary International School
A well-established institution, Rosary has schools across the city.
Madhav Baug Shiv Tirth Nagar, Paud Road, Kothrud,
Pune 411038
Tel: 25410446

107/108 Katraj Dehu Road
Bypass, Warje, Pune 411052

SNDT College
Started by renowned educationist Maharshi Dhondo Keshav Karve with merely five students, SNDT has grown today into a premier university with excellent higher education opportunities for women.
Maharishi Karve, Vidya Vihar,
Karve Road,
Pune 411038
Tel: 25420528

MIT College
Established in 1983, MIT was among the first engineering colleges in the private sector in Maharashtra. It was set up under the Maharashtra Academy of Engineering and Education Research (MAEER) and offers multiple courses in both undergraduate and postgraduate disciplines.
S.No.124, Paud Road,
Kothrud, Pune 411038
Tel: 25431795/ 25432767
Fax: 25442770
Email: info@mitpune.com

Abasaheb Garware College

A landmark in this area, the college has arts, science and commerce sections.
Karve Road,
Pune 411004
Tel: 25450796

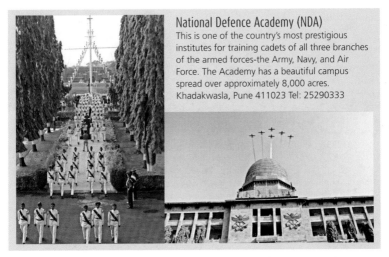

National Defence Academy (NDA)

This is one of the country's most prestigious institutes for training cadets of all three branches of the armed forces-the Army, Navy, and Air Force. The Academy has a beautiful campus spread over approximately 8,000 acres.
Khadakwasla, Pune 411023 Tel: 25290333

Cummins College of Engineering for Women
Set up in Karvenagar in 1991, it is the first engineering college in the country exclusively for women.
Karve Nagar, Pune 411052
Tel: 25467210

School of Fashion Technology (SOFT)
In 1998 Maharshi Karve Stree Shikshan Sanstha came together with National Institute of Fashion Technology (NIFT) and Ministry of Textiles (Govt of India) to create SOFT. The college offers graduate and postgraduate programs in fashion and textile design as well as apparel production and merchandise management.
Near Cummins Engineering College, Karve Nagar,
Pune 411052
Tel: 25444328 /25442782
Email: softpune@vsnl.net

Indian Institute for Aeronautical Engineering & Information Technology
Founded in 2001, this institute trains students for aeronautical science and aircraft engineering.
140/6, Near Warje Chowk,
NDA Road,
Warje Malwadi,
Pune 411052
Tel: 25292151 /4197 /4347
Email: enquiry@iiaeit.org

Vedacharya Ghaisas Guruji Ved Pathshala (Ved Bhavan)
Founded by Vedmurti Vinayak Hari Ghaisas, Ved Bhavan conducts studies of Vedas. Various eminent sages like the Shankaracharyas of Shingeri have visited the campus. There is also a famous and revered Siddhi Vinayak temple in the campus.
Chandini Chowk,
Pune 411021
Tel: 25282568

Theatre/Museums

Yashwantrao Chavan Natyagruha

This 900-seat auditorium has fulfilled a long held demand for Marathi theatre lovers in the Kothrud area.
Karve Road, Karve Putla,
Throat Udyan, Pune 411038
Tel: 25395232

Joshi's Museum of Miniature Railways
Formally opened in 1998, it is the collection and work of B. S. Joshi, an engineer who spent nearly 40 years on the project. A 20 minute

program transports you to an imaginary city controlled by over 1,000 wires and featuring 65 signals, lampposts, flyovers, toy trains, circus, swimming pools and other captivating features. 17/1 b/2 G A Kulkarni Road, Near Sangam Press, Karve Road
Pune 411038
Tel: 25435378

Kshipra Sahniwas Hall
An important cultural centre, it holds regular performances.
Kshipra Sahniwas Society, Karve Nagar,
Pune 411052
Tel: 25440120

Gandhi Bhavan
This centre dedicated to Mahatma Gandhi has a gallery of rare photographs tracing the life of the Father of the Nation. It also has exhibits on low-cost energy saving devices used in agriculture, like biogas plants, and easy-to-make greenhouses.
Near Kirloskar Cummins, Kothrud, Pune 411038
Tel: 25385091 10 am-5 pm

Gardens

Major Tathawade Udyan
Named in memory of the martyr, this garden is a favourite with residents in the locality.
Opposit Tol Hospital,
Karve Nagar, Pune 411052

Smriti Van
This lush area was once a barren hill until a voluntary group called Nisarga Sevak initiated a unique afforestation project where people were invited to plant trees in memory of their loved ones. The concept is now being duplicated at the former Kothrud Garbage Depot which is being developed as a garden by the Pune Municipal Corporation.
Behind Kirloskar Cummins Factory, Karve Nagar,
Pune 411052

Places of Worship

Dashabhuja Ganapati Temple
This 300-year old temple, situated at the busy junction of Karve Road and Paud Road, is said to have been received by one of the

Peshwas as a wedding gift.
Paud Phata, Karve Road,
Pune 411029 Tel: 25434353

Mrityunjayeshwar Mandir
Dedicated to Lord Shiva, this temple dates back to the time of the Peshwas
Kothrud, Karve Road,
Pune 411029
Tel: 25430992

St. Crispin's Church

A heritage structure, this 100-year-old church was the only Protestant church outside the cantonment area. Near Sharda Centre, Karve Road,
Pune 411004 Tel: 25456979

Vitthal Mandir
Rajaram Bridge, Kothrud,
Pune 411052

Health Clubs

Chaitanya Health Club
One of the first health clubs to open in this locality, it boasts an excellent swimming pool and holds competitive swimming programs.
Rambaug Colony,
Paud Road, Pune 411038
Tel: 25460799/ 25455197

Solaris
This is a multi-activity sports club, with a 250-meter roller skating track, jogging track, four synthetic tennis courts, swimming pool, squash court, three badminton courts, 10 table tennis tables, a 22-feet high rock climbing wall, 11-station adventure sport facility, a vintage car and bike museum and a mini-movie theatre.
Mayur Colony, Kothrud, Pune 411029 Tel: 25468778

Choice Health Club
Popular with children engaging in their first swimming lessons.
Survey No 127/1
A3 Karve Road,
Kothrud,
Pune 411038
Tel: 25434191

Shopping

Karve Road
A popular shopping area offering a variety of apparel, jewelry, furnishings and hardware. Among the prominent showrooms here are Ranka Jewellers, Rajmal Lakhichand Jewellers, Kasat Saris and Alurkar Music House.

Paud Road
Several inner city shops have opened up branches here, such as P.N. Gadgil Jewellers. Brands such as Raymonds and Megamart also have outlets here.

Gitai Shopping Mall
One of the first shopping malls in the locality.
Ideal Colony, Near Anand Nagar, Paud Road, Kothrud, Pune 411029
Tel: 25455767/ 25455768

Multiplex

City Pride
A recent addition to Pune's series of multiplexes it has three screens, a gaming arcade and a food court.
Karve Road, Erandwane, Pune 411038
Tel: 25458875 / 76

Restaurants/Cafés

Chinese Room Oriental

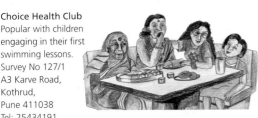

One of Pune's first authentic Chinese restaurants, it is very popular with people living in the area.
17A 4/5 Erandwane, Continental Chambers, Karve Road, Pune 411004
Tel: 25441179

Kimaya
This middle-range vegetarian restaurant, with a pleasant sit-out, serves both snacks and meals.
127, Karve Road, Kothrud, Pune 411029
Tel: 56007852

Durga
A popular student hangout, they whip up the most outstanding cold coffee in town. Also try their delicious *pav bhaji, bhurji pav* and *masala pav.*
Malti Complex, Off Paud Road, Near MIT College, Pune 411038 Tel: 25450565

Mirch Masala
An Indian restaurant serving primarily North Indian food.
Amruta Heights, Swarnabaug Colony, Near Dahanukar Colony, Karve Road, Pune 411029 Tel: 25463949

Hotels

Hotel President
34/11, Erandawane, Prabhat Road, Lane No 8, Behind Kohinoor Mangal Karalaya, Pune 411004 Tel: 25431797
www.hotelpresidentpune.com

Hotel Senator
This is a clean and comfortable three-star hotel.
54, Lokmanya Colony, Opp Vanaz Factory, Pune 411038
Tel: 25399999

Hospitals

Deenanath Mangeshkar Hospital
Legendary playback singer Lata Mangeshkar started this multi-specialty, state-of-the-art hospital in memory

Paud Flyover

In 1998 Pune's first flyover was inaugurated at Dashabhuja Ganpati Chowk (Paud Phata) Karve Road.

of her late father. Spread over six acres, it commenced operations in 2001.
Erandwane, Near Mhatre Bridge, Pune 411004
Tel: 256023900/256023027

Jog Hospital
46/2b/2, Paud Road,
Pune 411038 Tel: 25889234

Krishna Hospital
2 Anjanwel, Prashant Society, Paud Road, Pune 411038 Tel: 25460625

Sahyadri Hospital
A super specialty 150-bed hospital that opened in 2004.
30/ C Karve Road,
Opp Garware College,
Erandwane, Pune 411004
Tel: 25443000 Website: www.sahyadrigroup.com

Cipla Cancer and AIDS Foundation
A Palliative Care Centre for incurable cancer patients, it is located in scenic surroundings.
Survey No. 118/1 Bangalore Highway,
Opp Popular Nagar,
Pune 411029
Tel: 25231131

Bus Stand

The Kothrud Bus Depot is an important junction from where you can get buses to all parts of the city.

Bridges

Mhatre Bridge
Built across the Mutha River, it connects Erandawane to Navi Peth.

Banks and ATMs

UTI Bank ATM
Next to Santosh Hall,
Sinhagad Road,
Pune 411052

Plot no 57,
Mayur Colony,
Kothrud,
Pune 411029
Ganga Vishnu Heights, Somnath Path, Karve Road, Pune 411032

Lunawat Complex, Paud Road, Kothrud,
Pune 411038

State Bank of India ATM
Deenanath Mangeshkar Hospital, Erandwane,
Near Mahatre Bridge,
Pune 411004

Plot No. 860/b-29/1-2,
Vibhas Gandhi Nagar,
Kothrud
Pune 411038

Survey No. 121/122, Near Anandnagar,
Pune 411052

HDFC Bank ATM
Swayamsiddha Society, Near More Vidyalay,
Paud Road, Kothrud,
Pune 411038

Plot No. 58/59, Mayur Colony, Kothrud,
Pune 411029

ICICI Bank ATM
Mohite Twin Towers,
Next to Jagtap Hospital,
Anand Nagar, Pune 411052

Damodar Villa Survey No. 311/312, Kothrud,
Pune 411038

Saikunj Plot no. 11,
Paud Road, Kothrud,
Pune 411038

Citibank ATM
Ramkrishna Complex,
Paud Road, Kothrud,
Pune 411038

Suvarna Complex, Survey No. 155, Karve Road,
Pune 411038

State Bank of India
Opp S.N.D.T. College, Karve Road, Erandwane,
Pune 411004
Tel: 25421029

Hingane Khurd Branch,
Singhgad Road,
Pune 411052

HDFC Bank Ltd.
Netrali Apartments, Law College Road, Erandwane,
Pune 411004 Tel: 25121444
Other Branch: 25121580

ICICI Bank Ltd.
76/41, Shantisheela, Law College Road, Erandwane,
Pune 411004 Tel: 25435967

Bank of Maharashtra
Indrapuri Society,
Ganesh Nagar,
Karve Nagar,
Pune 411052
Tel: 25466365

Bank of India
133/1, Geetanjali, Shriman Society, Karve Nagar,
Pune 411052
Tel: 25452912
Branch at Warje: 25235864

Bank of Baroda
LBS Road Branch Off Singhgad Road,
Bank of India Colony,
Pune 411030
Tel: 24332238

United Western Bank Ltd
34/12, Shweta Aptsritage,
Karve Nagar,
Pune 411052
Tel: 25422484

The Cosmos Co-Op Bank Ltd.
Swastikshree Mega, Karve Nagar,
Pune 411052
Tel: 25435310
Branch at Kakade City, Warje.

Getaways

Khadakwasla Lake

It is one of the most beautiful lakes near Pune and a popular picnic spot. About seven kilometers from Warje, it is famous for its picturesque and scenic surroundings. The adjacent Peacock Bay with its dry deciduous forest attracts a variety of woodland birds like shrikes, tree pies, warblers, and peacocks. The Khadakwasla Dam, built across the Mutha River, and its tributary Ambi, is one of the three major dams that provide water to Pune.

Smart

Pimpri-Chinchwad

In the early sixties, Pimpri and Chinchwad were villages on the outskirts of Pune. Their transformation into a full-fledged township, collectively known as Pimpri-Chinchwad, took place after the Maharashtra Industrial Development Corporation (MIDC) set up an industrial zone in the area. Within a decade over 1,000 industrial units have sprung up, among them some of the leading companies of the country such as Tata Motors Ltd., Bajaj Auto Ltd., SKF, Philips, Sandvik Asia and Daimler Chrysler India Pvt. Ltd.

The Pimpri-Chinchwad Municipal Corporation (PCMC) was once the richest municipal council in Asia. The area is also an important religious and historical centre and boasts more than 100 beautifully landscaped public gardens.

Prominent Localities

Pradhikaran-Nigdi
The most urbanized area of Pimpri-Chinchwad, it has shopping complexes, institutes, restaurants, hospitals, well-developed roads and some beautiful bungalows.

Pimpri
Pimpri is the main industrial hub. A large Sindhi community resides here.

Chinchwad
Several references to the village of Chinchwad can be found in documents relating to the time of Shivaji and the Peshwas. Narrow roads and old wadas share space with burgeoning new development.

MIDC-Bhosari
The largest and most populated area under the PCMC. While MIDC has developed as an organized industrial zone, Bhosari has a large network of small-scale industries.

Other Prominent Localities

- Yeshwant Nagar
- Vallabh Nagar
- Nehru Nagar
- Hindustan Antibiotics Quarters Colony
- Sant Tukaram Nagar
- Pimpri Station
- Chinchwad Station

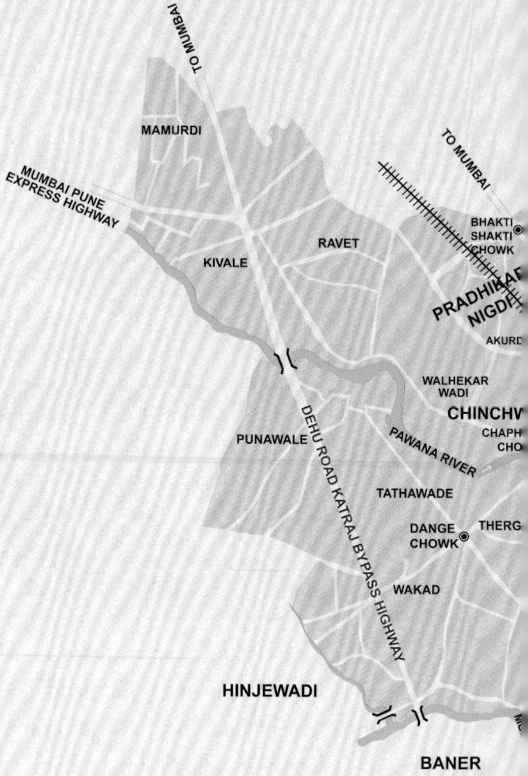

Pimpri-Chinchwad

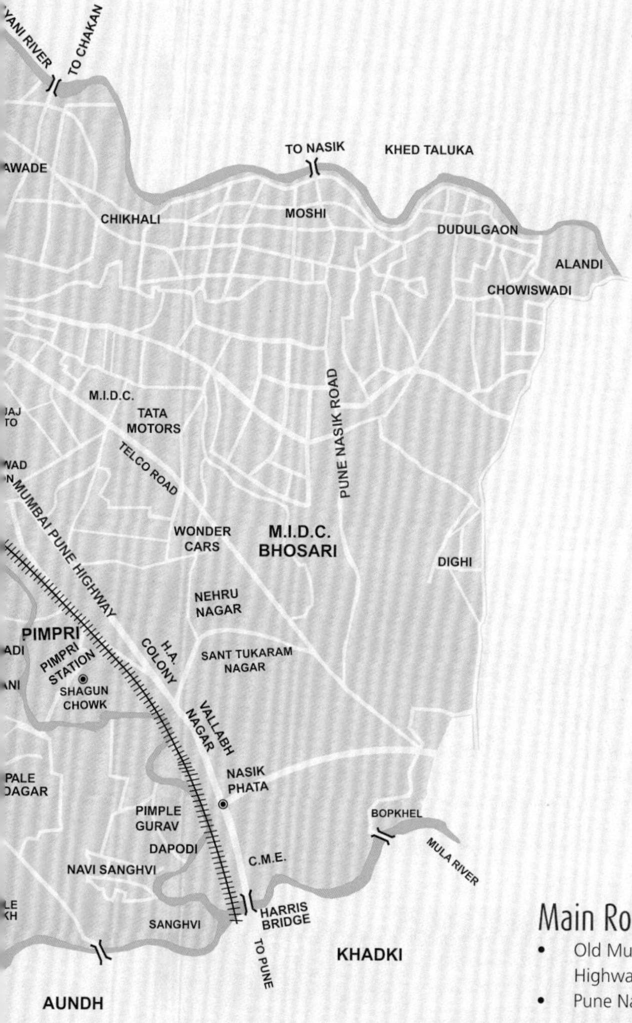

Map Indicative; not to scale

Main Roads

- Old Mumbai-Pune Highway
- Pune Nashik Highway

Chowks

- Nasik Phata
- Bhakti Shakti Chowk
- Chaphekar Chowk
- Dange Chowk
- Shagun Chowk

Industries

Encouraged by liberal laws and subsidized rates, a slew of companies set up shop on the special estates developed by the MIDC. The Pimpri-Chinchwad Industrial Estate is home to more than 4,000 industrial units in the large, medium and small sectors.

Some of the prominent companies:

Tata Motors Ltd.
www.tatamotors.com

Force Motors Ltd.
www.forcemotors.com

Sandvik Asia Ltd.
www.sandvik.com

Forbes Marshall Pvt. Ltd.
www.forbesmarshall-inc.com

Phillips India Ltd.
www.india.philips.com

Bajaj Auto Ltd.
www.bajajauto.com

Daimler Chrysler India Pvt. Ltd.
www.mercedes-benz.co.in

Kinetic Engineering Ltd.
www.kineticindia.com

Alfa Laval (India) Ltd.
www.alfalaval.com

Indian Card Clothing Co. Ltd.
www.cardindia.com

Hindustan Antibiotics Ltd.
www.hindantibiotics.com

SKF Bearings India Ltd.
www.skf.com

Pudumjee Pulp & Paper Mills Ltd. www.pudumjee.com

Gardens

Rajarshi Shahu Udyan

This is a beautiful garden spread over six acres. The colourful water fountains add to its beauty in the evening.
Shahu Nagar, Chinchwad, Pune 411019

Yashwantrao Chavan Rose Garden

A Kashmir-style garden devoted to the propagation and conservation of rose plants. There are 60 varieties of roses here and also a mini train for children.
T Block, MIDC, Bhosari, Pune 411026

Poly House Project

A novel project designed to teach school children about floriculture and impart new techniques to farmers and upcoming floriculturists.
Talawade Gairan, Dehu-Alandi Road, PCMC, Pune 411025

Bahinabai Choudhary Zoological Park

There are over 150 birds, reptiles and animals here. The main aim of this zoo is to undertake captive breeding programs of endangered species.
Vrindavan Society, PCMC, Chinchwad, Pune 411019
Tel: 27496036
Entry Ticket: Rs.5

Bhosari Lake

This lake abounds in fish, birds, turtles and water plants. A beautifully designed octagonal meditation hall has been built at its centre.
Bhosari, PCMC, Pune 411039

Durgadevi Hill Park

Often called a mini hill station, it offers a panoramic view of the city and has over 1,70,000 trees.
An eye-catching Nature Clock near the entrance welcomes visitors.
Pune-Mumbai Highway, Nigdi, Pune 411044

Environment Heritage Park

This garden has brought together varied ecosystems like equatorial semi-green, deciduous, medicinal and wetland to portray the

environmental diversity of the region.
T Block, MIDC, Bhosari, Pune 411026

Bhakti-Shakti Statue Park
Statutes of Maratha King Shivaji Maharaj, and Sant Tukaram, one of the greatest saints of the region, can be seen in this beautifully landscaped garden.
Near Jakat Naka, Mumbai-Pune Road, Near PCMC Building, Nigdi, Pune 411044

Appu Ghar Amusement Park
(Indira Gandhi Udyan)
This park is designed like the Appu Ghar in Delhi and has various rides and games. The rustic ambience makes for an excellent getaway for the whole family. Entry tickets are priced at Rs. 5 per head.
Indira Gandhi Udyan, Pimpri Chinchwad Muncipal Corporation Sector 23, Nigdi, Pune 411044
Tel: 27854040

PCMC Garden Department: 27121791

Sai Udyan - Butterfly Park

The main attraction of this garden is the section developed for the conservation and display of various types of butterflies found in the Western Ghats.
Vrindavan Society, PCMC, Chinchwad, Pune 411019

Dolphin Water Park
A popular haunt for children and families, it is a fun place to spend the day.
Pradhikarn, Pimpri Chinchwad Municipal Corporation, Nigdi, Pune 411044
Tel: 66303433 / 890037435

Heritage Sites

Chaphekar Wada and Chaphekar Smarak
In the history of revolutionaries of India, the martyrdom of the three Chaphekar Brothers stands out prominently. Recently, Chaphekar Wada underwent a facelift and now houses a museum with paintings about the freedom struggle.
Pagechil Talim Road, Chinchwad, Pune 411033
Tel: 27441218

Morya Gosavi Temple
This beautiful temple is the pride of Chinchwad. Situated on the banks of the river Pavana, the temple and its surroundings, especially the ghats behind it, are very scenic and provide a peaceful sanctuary. It is named after Moraya Gosavi, who is believed to have found the Ganesh idol in the nearby Morgaon village and consecrated it here. Thousands of devotees flock to the temple for the annual festival held every year in the Hindu month of Shravan (August-September).
Mangal Murti Wada, Ahead of Chaphekar Chowk, Chinchwadgaon, Pune 411033
Tel: 27453138 / 3123

Institutions

Dr. D. Y. Patil Group of Institutes

This group has a network of colleges and institutes covering everything from arts, commerce, science, engineering, pharmacy, catering and architecture, medicine to nursing and midwifery. The also have a number of schools, all based in this area.
Sant Tukaram Nagar, Opp. H.A. Company, Pimpri, Pune 411018 Tel: 27421095
www.dypatil.com

Pimpri-Chinchwad College of Engineering
Set up in 1990 under the Pimpri Chinchwad Education Trust, this college offers degrees in the various streams of engineering.
Anandibag, Opp Beck Company, Nehru Nagar Road, Pimpri, Pune 411018
Tel: 27653168 / 27653166
www.pccoepune.com

Manghalmal Udharam College of Commerce

Run by the Jai Hind Sindhu Education Trust this is one of the most eminent Commerce colleges in the area and is renowned for its high standard of education.
Pimpri, Pune 411017
Tel: 27413943

Maharashtra Academy of Engineering

Located on the bank of the Indrayani River, this institute is well known for its technical education.
Dehu Phata, Kelgaon, Alandi Dehu Road, Pune 412105
Tel: 27185857 / 5514 / 6416
www.mitpune.org/mae

National AIDS Research Institute

Established in 1992 NARI, as it is known, is involved in research to detemine the dynamics of the HIV virus and how it can be controlled. NARI runs seven clinics in different parts of the city which provide counseling and are equipped HIV and AIDS testing centres.
73, G- Block, MIDC, Bhosari, Pune 411026 Tel: 27121342
www.nari-icmr.res.in

Schools

St Ursula's High School

A convent school run by missionaries, it is co-educational and is affiliated to the SSC board.
Post office, Akurdi,
Pune 411035Tel: 27652669

Judson High School

One of the popular schools of this area Judson High is a co-ed school that is affiliated to the SSC board.
Near Pimpri Station, Pimpri, Pune 411018 Tel: 27475736

Jnana Parbodhini Secondary School

A branch of the renowned Jnana Parbodhini school in the city, this school has both Marathi and English mediums of education.
Pimpri- Chinchwad Municipal Corportation, Pradhikaran, Nigdi, Pune 411044
Tel: 27654380

H. A. Secondary School

This co-ed school has both English and Marathi mediums

of education.
Hindustan Antibiotic Colony, Pimpri, Pune 411018
Tel: 27423110

Jai Hind High School

One of the most sought after schools in this area, this co-ed SSC school is run by the Jai Hind Sindhu Education Trust.
Pimpri, Pune 411017
Tel: 27415273

Shopping Centres

Kohinoor Arcade

A one stop shopping spot, stocking everything from clothes and jewelry to electronic consumer goods.
Nigdi Chowk, Nigdi, Pune 411031
(Next to the new flyover)

Pimpri Market

This busy market has a number of stores selling good quality clothing at very reasonable rates.
Behind Pimpri Station, Shagun Chowk, Pimprigaon, Pimpri 411018

Mega Mart

This recently opened store stocks a range of reasonably priced branded wear and attracts hundreds of shoppers everyday.
Opposite PCMC Building, Mumbai-Pune Highway, Pimpri, Pune 411018
Tel: 27292880

Restaurants

Golden Palms

A pleasant restaurant serving a wide variety of vegetarian and non-vegetarian food.
The Moghlai dishes are recommended.
Barber Complex, Pune-Mumbai Road, Near Octroi Naka, Nigdi Pune 411044
Tel: 27640868

Mayur

The perfect place to go if you feel like eating a

Gujarati thali.
Opposite Jayshree Talkies, Chinchwad, Pune 411019
Tel: 27476999 / 27472071

Hotel Bhola

A very popular restaurant of the area Bhola serves excellent thalis and other vegetarian food.
Block D-2, Plot No 64, Telco Road, MIDC, Chinchwad, Pune 411018
Tel: 27462847 / 66114023

Vrindavan
From South Indian snacks to excellent Chinese food, it offers all.
Kohinoor Marvel, Near Bhakti-Shakti Garden, Nigdi Pune 411044 Tel: 27471110

Hotels

Panchsheel Hotel
Popular with business travellers and ideal for conferences, the hotel is well-appointed. Its restaurant attracts several locals drawn to the scrumptious fare.
C32, Near MIDC Office, Chinchwad, Pune 411019 Tel: 27472012

Hotel Kalasagar
Offers a sizeable conference room, A/C and Non A/C rooms, and a good restaurant. A good choice if you want to be in close proximity to the Industrial estate.
Near Old Pune- Mumbai Highway, Near Vallabhnagar, Pimpri, Pune 411034
Pimpri Tel: 27125901

Hotel Emerald Park
Has clean comfortable rooms and a good restaurant.
P 63, D 1 Block, MIDC, Chinchwad, Pune 411019
Tel: 27477468 / 27477469

Hospitals

Niramaya Hospital
A multi specialty hospital with an efficient Emergency Centre. Near Post Office, Behind Jayhind Petrol Pump, Chinchwad station, Pune 411033 Tel: 27441860

Lokmanya Hospital
A well equipped hospital with specialist doctors.
Lokmanya Medical Foundation, Near Chinchwad Station, Chinchwad, Pune 411033
Tel: 27456496

Padmashri D.Y. Patil Hospital
Part of the D.Y. Patil foundation that also runs a medical college in the area.
D.Y. Patil Medical College and Hospital, Mahesh Nagar, Mumbai Pune Highway, Pimpri, Pune 411018
Tel: 27420605

Talera Hospital (Blood Bank)
Equipped with an ICU and expert doctors, this is one of the reputed hospitals in the area. Chaphekar Chowk, Chinchwad, Pune 411033
Tel: 27610054

Movie Theatres

Fame Jai Ganesh Multiplex
With a seating capacity of 1,100, this three-screen completely air-conditioned multiplex is the first of its kind in the Pimpri-Chinchwad area.
Off Mumbai Pune Highway, Chinchwad, Pune 411019 Tel: 27442744
The area also has several single-screen theatres that sell tickets at very affordable rates.

Vishal Chitra Mandir
206/1 By Road Pimpri, Pimpri 411018
Tel: 27470440

Jayashree Talkies
Pune Mumbai Highway, Chinchwad, Pune 411019
Tel: 27473494

Ashoka Chitra Mandir
Pimprigaon, Pimpri 411018
Tel: 27460908

Delux Cinema
469, Pimpri, Pune 411017 Tel: 27454304

Libraries

Abhinav Vachanalaya and Library
1147/1, Vijaynagar,
Kalewadi, Pune 411033
Tel: 27612374

Public Library
P.C.M.C Bhavan, Pimpri,
Pune 411018 Tel: 27477777

Banks and ATMs

Citibank ATM
Lakshmi Complex, 240/A1, Mumbai-Pune Road,
Chinchwad Pune 411019

Bank of India ATM
P.F., Post Bag No. 1101,
Pimpri, Pune 411018

SBI ATMs
Jai Hind Service Station,
Bharat Petroleum Dealer,
Pimpri, Pune 411018

Pradhikaran, Nigdi,
Pune 411031

Opp. Gadgil Jewelers,
Chinchwad , Pune 411031

H.D.F.C. Housing Complex,
Chinchwad, Pune 411019

ICICI ATMs
Ground Floor, Shop No. 3,
Gokhale Plaza, Chinchwad,
Pune 411033

MIDC Electronic Sadan
No.2, Creche Building,
Bhosari, Pune 411026

HDFC ATMs
Plot No. 1, Sector - 27 A,
Pradhikaran , Nigdi,
Pune 411044

Shop No. 4, Kapote
Shyama Regency, Opp.
TELCO, Tanajinagar,
Chinchwad, Pune
411033

UTI ATMs
MIDC Bhosari, Century
Enka, Pune 411026
Shagun Chowk, Pimpri
Bazaar, Pimpri, Pune 411017

HDFC Bank (ATM)
Kamala Crossroads, Wing-A,
Finolex Chowk, Opp PCMC
Office, Pimpri, Mumbai -
Pune Road, Pune 411017
Tel: 27425702 / 04

ICICI Bank (ATM)
Shop No. 3-8, Ground Floor,
F - Wing, Premier Plaza, Old
Mumbai - Pune Highway,
Chinchwad,
Pune 411019
Tel: 27484420

UTI Bank (ATM)
"Balwant", Chaphekar
Chowk, Station Road, Near
Post Office, Chinchwad
Gaon, Pimpri-Chinchwad
Pune 411033
Tel: 27442506 / 27442505

Bank of India
C-8, Mumbai-Pune Road,
Chinchwad,
Pune 411019
Tel: 27481754

State Bank of India
Industrial Finance Branch
Pimpri. Mumbai-Pune Road,
Kasarwadi,
Pune 411018
Tel: 27124555 / 27125244 /
27125764

Bank of Baroda
PCMC Compound, Pimpri,
Pune 411018
Tel: 27420639
Zonal Office,
Olympic House,
Pimpri, Pune 411018
Tel: 27420840

Bank of Maharashtra
24/385, PCNTD,
Akurdi, Pune 411035
Tel: 27658250

Canara Bank
Pimpri Station Road,
Pimpri, Pune 411018
Tel: 27425880

Central Bank of India
Pimpri Station Road,
Pimpri,
Pune 411018
Tel: 27472827

Centurion Bank Ltd
Mumbai-Pune Road,
Pimpri, Pune 411018
Tel: 27426001

Pune Cantonment

The Cantonment area, popularly called Camp, is one of the most vibrant and cosmopolitan localities of Pune. The British set up base in Pune in 1817 after they defeated the Peshwas at the Battle of Kirkee. The initial idea was to develop the city as the monsoon capital but it soon developed into a typical 19th century army town and gradually grew into a permanent military settlement. Post Independence, the Indian Army established the headquarters of the Southern Command here. The army presence has given the area an ambience of its own. Its wide tree-lined roads, colonial bungalows and buildings, gothic churches, schools and sprawling clubs set this area apart from the old city.

Prominent Localities

M.G. Road and Surroundings

Mahatma Gandhi Road, popularly called Main Street, is the commercial nerve centre of this area. Main Street is flanked by Dr. Coyaji Road (East Street) on one side, while on the other side are a series of small connecting streets such as Centre Street and Taboot Street.

Shivaji Market

Beyond Centre Street is a grand old stone building housing the cantonment area's vegetable and fish market. Opposite the market is St. Xavier's Church, one of the oldest Catholic churches in Pune.

Pul Gate

To one end of Main Street is Pul Gate, once the entry to this part of the city.

Queen's Garden

An Army residential area, with several Government buildings like the Council Hall in the vicinity.

Empress Garden

The impressive Race Course, which dominates the area, lies right next to the sprawling botanical garden known as Empress Garden.

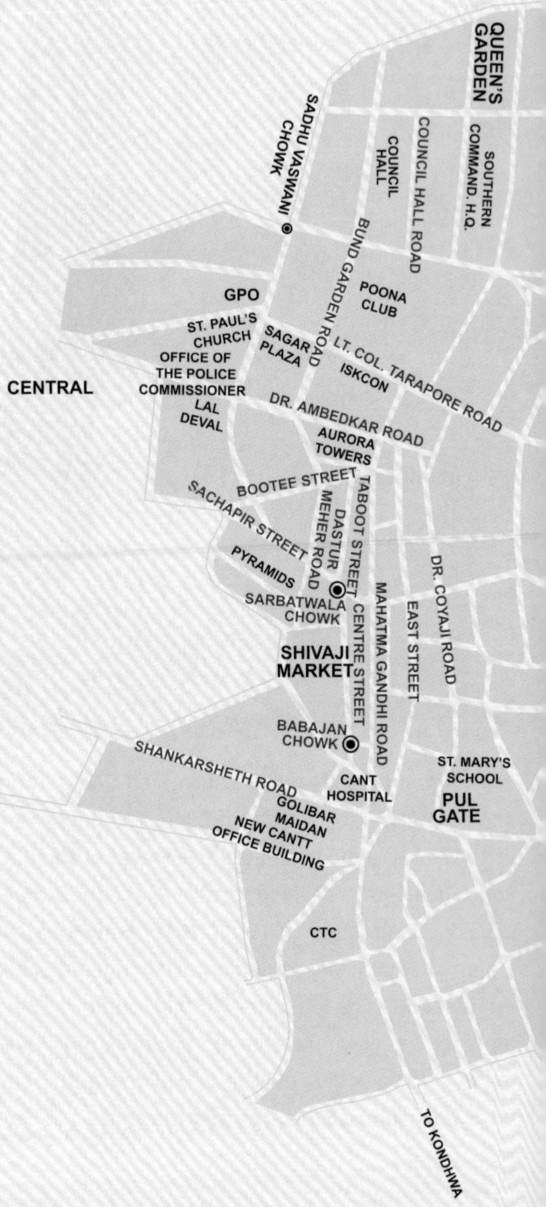

Pune Cantonment

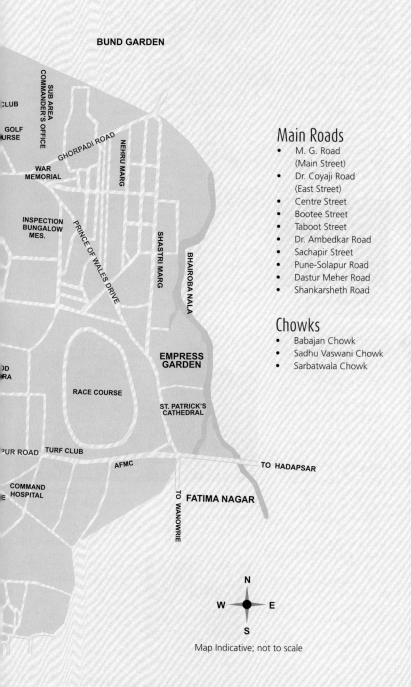

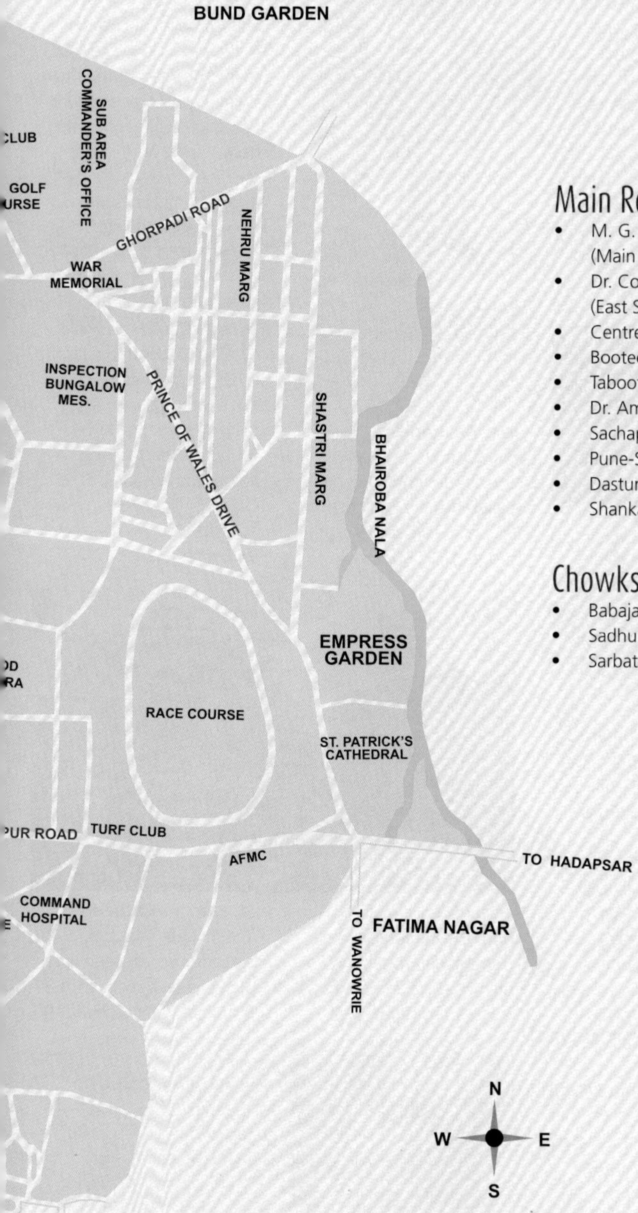

Map Indicative; not to scale

Main Roads

- M. G. Road (Main Street)
- Dr. Coyaji Road (East Street)
- Centre Street
- Bootee Street
- Taboot Street
- Dr. Ambedkar Road
- Sachapir Street
- Pune-Solapur Road
- Dastur Meher Road
- Shankarsheth Road

Chowks

- Babajan Chowk
- Sadhu Vaswani Chowk
- Sarbatwala Chowk

Landmarks

Armed Forces Medical College (AFMC)
Spread over 250 acres, the AFMC is one of the country's premier medical colleges, offering a vast range of specialist and super specialist disciplines. The unique AFMC health museum is the largest of its kind in South East Asia. The campus has been declared a bicycle-only zone in an effort to reduce pollution.
Pune-Solapur Road,
Camp, Pune 411040
Tel: 26811205 / 26306010

Command Hospital
This is the largest military hospital in Pune, catering to Armed Forces personnel. All major facilities are available here. They also have some beds for civilians.
Southern Command,
Wanowrie, Pune 411040
Tel: 26306138 / 196

Cardio Thoracic Centre (CTC)
A special unit of the Command Hospital, it provides both medical and surgical treatment for cardiac and respiratory disorders.
Golibar Maidan,
Pune 411040 Tel: 26306178

Artificial Limb Centre (ALC)
This was set up to meet the prosthetic needs of disabled personnel of the Armed Forces. Comprehensive care for the disabled is provided below one roof at ALC. Since 1951 these facilities have been extended to civilians also.
Southern Command,
Wanowrie,
Pune 411040 Tel: 26306191

War Memorial
The 50-ft high elegant column designed and built by the Military Engineering Service is engraved with the names of 1,080 post Independence martyrs from the defense services from Maharashtra. The memorial was unveiled on August 15, 1998.

Prince of Wales Drive,
RSI Golf Course,
Pune 411001

Places of Worship

St. Xavier's Church
This Catholic Church is one of the oldest in the city. Of special interest are the huge stained glass windows with panels depicting incidents from the life of St Francis Xavier.
2007, St. Vincent's Street,
Opp. Shivaji Market,
Pune 411001 Tel: 26356776

St. Paul's Church
St Paul's Church was built circa 1870. Located near the GPO, the striking building has a rounded apse and a tall octagonal bell tower.
2 Church Road, Behind
Police Commissioner's
Office, Near G.P.O,
Pune 411001
Tel: 26120757

St. Patrick's Cathedral
The majestic structure of the cathedral can be seen from afar. The residence of the Bishop of Pune is adjacent

M. G. Road

Mahatma Gandhi Road or Main Street is a popular shopping street with trendy showrooms, stores and eateries. On weekends, it is converted into a festive 'walking plaza'. MG Road also recently became the first Wi-Fi enabled area in the city.

to the cathedral.
1-B Prince of Wales Drive,
Near Race Course,
Pune 411001 Tel: 26332329

Holywood Gurudwara

Originally built as a dance hall by the British, it was later reconstructed into the Gurudwara Guru Nanak Darbar.
Gurudwara Road,
Near Race Course, Camp,
Pune 411001 Tel: 26360919

Hanuman Temple

This small and old Hanuman temple on Centre Street is a landmark and attracts a continuous stream of devotees.
Shree Astha Siddhi Hanuman Mandir, 343 Sachapir Street Camp,
Pune 411001
Tel: 26340047 / 26340027

Ohel David Synagogue (Lal Deval)

An attractive red brick-and-stone building, this synagogue was built by Sir David Sassoon in 1867 when the Jews moved to Pune to work for the British. Another synagogue is located in Rasta Peth.
Dr. Ambedkar Road, Camp,
Pune 411001

Hare Krishna Temple (ISKCON)

The ISKCON Temple, like its branches in other parts of the country, is a large religious and cultural centre. Regular *kirtans* and other programmes are held here.
Lt. Col. Tarapore Road,
Next to Dastur Primary School, Camp,
Pune 411001
Tel: 26331044

Vasupujya Swami Jain Temple

A beautiful, ornate temple in the heart of Camp.
657 Jain Mandir Path,
Sachapir Street,
Camp, Pune 411001

Sir J.J. Agiary (FireTemple)

Only Zoroastrians can enter the fire temple, built by Sir Jamsetjee Jejeebhoy in 1844.
826, Dastur Meher Road,
Opp. J.J. Garden, Camp,
Pune 411001 Tel: 26135514

Clubs

The Royal Western India Turf Club

Adjoining the Pune Race Course, the colonial style club house has excellent accommodation facilities for its members, and is usually packed during the racing season. On regular days you'll see people jogging, walking or exercising along the racecourse.
1, Solapur Road,
Race Course, Pune 411001
Tel: 26362666

Poona Club

The Poona Club was started in 1882 with the amalgamation of the Poona Gymkhana and the Lloyd Polo Club. Having established a legacy of sports, the Poona Club today provides a number of excellent services for games like tennis, squash, golf and billiards.
6, Bund Garden Road,
Pune 411001 Tel: 26360083

Rajendra Singhji Institute (RSI)

This is a club exclusively for Defense officers, and boasts several amenities including a sprawling golf course.
Ashoka Marg, Near Circuit House, Pune 411001
Tel: 26361105

The Ladies Club

3 Lt. Col. Tarapore Road,
Camp, Pune 411001
Tel: 26362674

Poona Parsi Gymkhana

33, Off Kahun Road, Near Kendriya Vidyalaya,
Pune 411001 Tel: 26361206

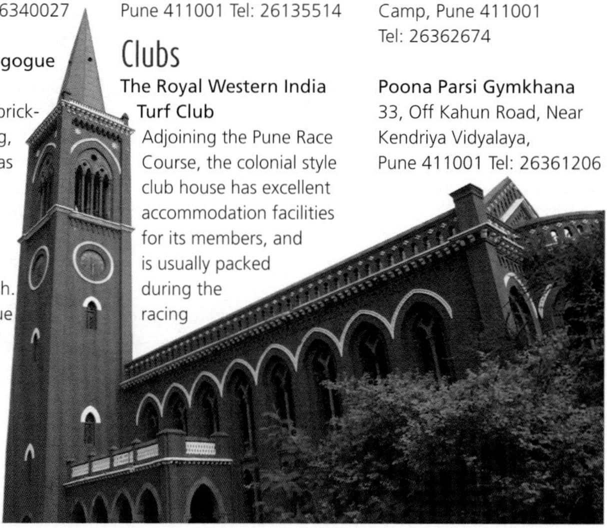

Horse Racing

The Pune horse racing scenario comes alive in the monsoon. Hundreds of racing enthusiasts from Mumbai and other prominent race centres descend on the city on race weekends during the season from mid-July to end-October.
Most popular races: Independence Day Trophy, S A. Poonawalla Million, RWITC Invitational Trophy
Tote: Over Rs. 4 crore

Schools

Camp has several missionary schools that were set up to cater to the European, Anglo-Indian and Christian communities. They are famous for their old, colonial buildings and sprawling grounds.

St. Mary's High School
Established in 1866 as a girls' school, it is today one of the premier schools of the city. A boys' section was started some years back. It is affiliated to the ICSE Board, New Delhi.
5-B,General Bhagat Singh Marg, Camp, Pune 411001
Tel: 26156282

The Bishop's School
This all-boys school was set up in 1864. It recently opened a co-ed branch in Kalyani Nagar. It is affiliated to the ICSE Board, New Delhi.
5-A, General Bhagat Singh Marg, Camp,
Pune 411001.
Tel: 26360437/ 26330261

St. Vincent's School
Founded in 1867 by the Jesuits, it is considered, one of the best boys schools in Pune.
St. Vincent's Street, Near Shivaji Market, Camp, Pune 411001
Tel: 26352135

Sardar Dastur Group of Schools

Established in 1893 as a school for Parsi girls, it later opened its doors to all communities. Today there are a group of schools under the Sardar Dastur banner.
Trust Office, 2, Lt. Col. Tarapore Road,
Camp, Pune 411001
Tel: 6362630

St. Anne's School
Located near St. Vincent's School, this convent school is exclusively for girls.
Convent Street, Camp,
Pune 411001
Tel: 27690519

Hutchings High School
A popular co-ed school, it is affiliated to the ICSE Board, New Delhi.
7, Phayre Road,
Pune 411040
Tel: 26352764

Library

Edward Albert Library
Built in 1881, this colonial building with its wide porches and spacious verandas provides ample room for leisurely reading. The façade of the building is plain, but it has beautiful woodwork inside. The quiet ambience of its reading rooms attracts many students.
East Street, Camp,
Pune 411001

Landmarks

Police Commissioner's Office
The Police Commissioner's office is an important hub for journalists, politicians and other important bureaucrats. Besides the Commissioner, the senior officers in charge of crime and civil law also have offices in the complex.
2, Sadhu Vaswani Road, Next to GPO, Camp,
Pune 411001 Tel: 26125396 / 26208371 Ext: 201

Pune Archives (Peshwe Daftar)
It has over four crore original documents, some dating back to the 16th century, preserved

West End Theatre

One of the oldest cinema houses in the Camp area, and the only one with a soda fountain, it acquired its new avatar about a decade back.
9, Dr. Ambedkar Road, Camp,
Pune 411001 Tel: 56031447

in 39,000 cloth bundles. There are letters written by Shivaji's grandson, maps of the Maratha empire, land records of the Peshwa period, diplomatic treaties, balance sheets, and detailed papers of individual fields and plots that are of immense historical importance. The Archives continue to be a treasure house for historians and researchers.
Bund Garden Road,
Opp. Council Hall,
Pune 411001 Tel: 26127307

General Post Office (GPO)

The General Post Office is listed among the best colonial structures in the city. In the garden, dominated by a huge banyan tree, you can still see three large boulders known as *hathi dagads* (elephant stones), once used to tether elephants that carried the mail.
Sadhu Vaswani Road, Pune 411001
Tel: 26125516

Council Hall
In 1870 engineer Colonel Melliss chalked out the plans for this Venetian Gothic structure. The Council Hall was the venue for the ball held in honour of Queen Victoria's son in 1886, and witnessed several magnificent balls in later years. Today it houses the office of the Divisional Commissioner.
Bund Garden Road,
Pune 411001 Tel: 26361353

Zero Stone
This is an important landmark of Pune as all city distances are measured from here.

Circuit House
This is the State government guesthouse. A new Circuit House was recently constructed across the road from the old one.
18, Queen's Garden,
Ashoka Marg, Solapur Road,
Pune 411001
Tel: 26361802/ 26361803

Land Records Museum
Set up in 2004 by the Pune Municipal Corporation, the museum is the first of its kind in the country and displays a detailed history of the system of land records.

Timings: 4 pm-6 pm.
213, New Admin Building,
Opp. Council Hall,
Pune 411001 Tel: 26050006

Gardens
Empress Garden
Set up in 1830 and spread over 60 acres, this is one of the most beautiful gardens in the city. Besides being a rich repository of rare plant species like baobab, cannonball, bauhinia climber (believed to be more than a century old), it is also a popular spot with children and adults. The annual plant and flower exhibition held here is an important botanical event.
Prince of Wales Drive, Near Race Course, Camp,
Pune 411001
Tel: 26361840 / 26331193

Rani Laxmibai Udyan
Located on the busy junction of East Street and M.G. Road, this Park is packed with children and families in the evenings.
Off M.G. Road,
Bata Chowk, Camp,
Pune 411001.

J. J. Garden
Tucked behind Aurora Towers, this beautiful garden with fountains is the perfect place to take a break from the hustle and bustle of the city.
Dastur Meher Road,
Behind Aurora Towers,
Camp,
Pune 411001

Shopping Areas
Shivaji Market
Built in 1885 to cater to the Cantonment and Civil Lines population as well as military officers and troops, the Shivaji Market is spread over 4,734.9 sq. m. and is

constructed in the Victorian Gothic style with Islamic and Maratha motifs. The market has a strict segregation of vegetable, fruit, mutton, beef, chicken and fish sections.
Gaffer Street,
Sharbatwalla Chowk,
Pune 411001

Main Street
A shopper's paradise, it houses a number of arcades and malls, in addition to branded stores and other small shops.
M.G.Road,
Pune 411001

Fashion Street
This popular shopping zone was created between Main Street and East Street to accommodate hawkers. It has over 400 stalls selling goods at bargain prices.
End of M. G. Road,
Near Grand Darbar,
East Street, Camp,
Pune 411001

Stores

Dorabjee's
This 95-year-old departmental store is an institution of the city. Families have shopped here for generations. It is famous for its imported stock of sauces, meats, cheese, chocolates, biscuits, etc.
1-B Dr. Ambedkar Road,
Pune 411001
Tel: 26052882/83

Kayani Bakery
Famous for its delicious Shrewsbury Biscuits tourists seldom leave without a packet.
East Street, Pune 411001
Tel: 26360517

Royal Bakery
Well known for its delectable cakes and melt in the mouth *batasa* (butter) biscuits.
200, M. G. Road, Camp,
Pune 411001
Tel: 26345251

Budhani Wafers
Reputed to sell the crispiest wafers in town in various flavours.
682, Taboot Street,
Pune 411001.
Tel: 26134118/26131264

Chandan
This compact grocery store set up in 1948 sells a wide range of niche items like Kolkata jaggery, Amristsar *papad,* Punjabi *wadi* and other special items.
217/218, M.G. Road,
Camp, Pune 411001
Tel: 26342063

Bombay Store
This was one of Pune's first high-end lifestyle stores. It stocks a wide range of aromatic candles, beauty products, showpieces, jewelry, fabric, clothes, hand made paper, table and kitchen ware, bed and bath linen, and all things made in India.
M. G. Road, Pune 411001
Tel: 26131891/26131067

Poona Drug Store
Housed in a heritage building, this 100-year-old shop is one of the landmarks on M.G. Road.
M.G. Road, Pune 411001
Tel: 26130913

Pantaloons
This popular factory outlet stocking apparel and accessories is housed in an elegant two-storied colonial house.
3 Castellino Road, Off East Street, Camp, Pune 411001
Tel: 26330467/ 26363430

Haji A Gani Hiroli
Located in a narrow lane, this old shop with an interesting multi-chamber layout has a huge stock of traditional Poona saris, salwar suits and fabrics.
Centre Street, Camp,
Pune 411001 Tel: 26340994

Sudhan Jewellers
This store has a range of exquisite gems, silver and gold jewellery, in both ethnic and contemporary designs.
Wonderland Building,
M. G. Road 7, Pune 411001.
Tel: 26133378

New Kashmir Stores
A treasure trove of ethnic Kashmiri artefacts, this store stocks exquisitely carved wooden boxes, tables,

etc. They have a range of beautifully embroidered shawls and kurtas and some exclusive jewellery.
323, M. G. Road,
Pune 411001 Tel: 26138436

Malls

Pyramid
1978 Convent Street, Camp,
Pune 411001
Tel:1600-1199-11 (Toll Free)

Nucleus
1 Church Road, Opp.
Commissioner's Office,
Camp, Pune 411001
Tel: 26120790/ 56096262

Restaurants and Cafes

Kwality
The 60-year old restaurant serving north Indian fare is very popular with families.
6, East Street, Camp,
Pune 411001
Tel: 26360629

Mayur
A place to get traditional Gujarati food served in an Indian plate *'thali'*.
East Street, Pune 411001
Tel: 26130909

Chung Fa
Started in 1970, this is one of the oldest Chinese restaurants of Pune. Film star Raj Kapoor used to frequent this place.
2435, East Street,
Pune 411001
Tel: 26136678

Dorabjee
A specialty restaurant serving authentic Parsi fare.
845 Dastur Meher Road, Camp,
Pune 411001
Tel: 26145955

Pasteur
An assortment of cakes and pastries, cookies and ice creams form the menu at Pasteur.
6 M.G. Road,
Opp. Bombay Store,
Pune 411001
Tel: 26137848

Marz-O-Rin

Centrally located, this fast food joint is famous for its beverages and sandwiches.
Bakthiar Plaza, MG Road,
Pune 411001
Tel: 26130774 / 26136690

Hotels

Aurora Towers
This is a four-star hotel in the locality. Its attractive in-house lounge bar, Aqua, is always packed in the evenings with a mix of executives, collegians and foreigners.
9, Dr. Ambedkar Road,
Pune 411001
Tel:26131818.

Sagar Plaza
This 76-room four-star hotel is convenient to access from the railway station and airport.
1, Bund Garden Road,
Pune 411001
Tel: 26122622/12/23
Fax : 26122633

Banks And ATMs

ICICI ATM
Kalpataru Arcade,
8 M. G. Road, Pune 411001

Indian Overseas Bank
7, Wonderland Building,
M.G. Road, Pune 411001
Tel: 26130998/ 26139007

UTI Bank ATM
287 A M.G. Road, Opp.
Bata Showroom,
Pune 411001

Bank of Maharashtra
Vardhaman Building,
Shankar Sheth Road,
Pune 411042 Tel: 26451940

HDFC Bank (ATM)
K. P Housing Society Ltd.
General Thimayya Road,
East Street, Pune 411001
Tel: 26430266

State Bank of India
Poona College Campus,
Golibar Maidan, Pune
411001 Tel: 26349116/ 14

UTI Bank (ATM)
Parmar House, 2413, East Street, Gen. Thimayya Road,
Camp, Pune 411001
Tel: 26330611/ 51/ 65

Punjab National Bank
Aurora Towers Ground Floor,
Camp, Pune 411001
Tel: 26137627

Bank of India
8/A, Dr. Coyaji Road,
Post Box No. 56,
Pune 411001
Tel: 26360713/14

मध्यवर्ती कारागृह
187
येरवडा पुणे

Yerawada - Nagar Road

Just across the Bund Garden Bridge is the area known as Yerawada, known across the country for its jail! Till a decade or so ago Nagar Road, as the Pune-Ahmednagar Road is commonly called, went past Yerawada and through a thinly populated area famous only for the Aga Khan Palace where Mahatma Gandhi was imprisoned by the British.

Over the last few years this area has undergone a radical transformation with the development of localities like Kalyani Nagar and Viman Nagar. A significant BPO/IT belt is building up along the Kalyani Nagar-Viman Nagar-Kharadi stretch with state-of-the-art IT parks and shiny glass and chrome buildings taking the place of farmland.

Prominent Localities

Yerawada
Apart from the Central Jail, it also houses a sprawling golf course.

Kalyani Nagar
Named after Pune's premier industrialist Neelkanth Kalyani who resides here, this upmarket locality attracts many new migrants to the city. A large number of restaurant and entertainment options can be found here.

Viman Nagar
A large residential township with well developed markets and other amenities.

Lohegaon
Site of the Air Force Base, it is also the location of the civil airport. The large open spaces are rapidly filling up with construction activity.

Kharadi
Once farmland, this area is developing into an IT hub and several massive townships are coming up.

Vadgaon Sheri
A BPO and semi-industrial belt that is slowly gaining importance as a residential neighbourhood.

Vishrantwadi
This is an upcoming residential area with huge townships and societies.

Yerawada - Nagar Road

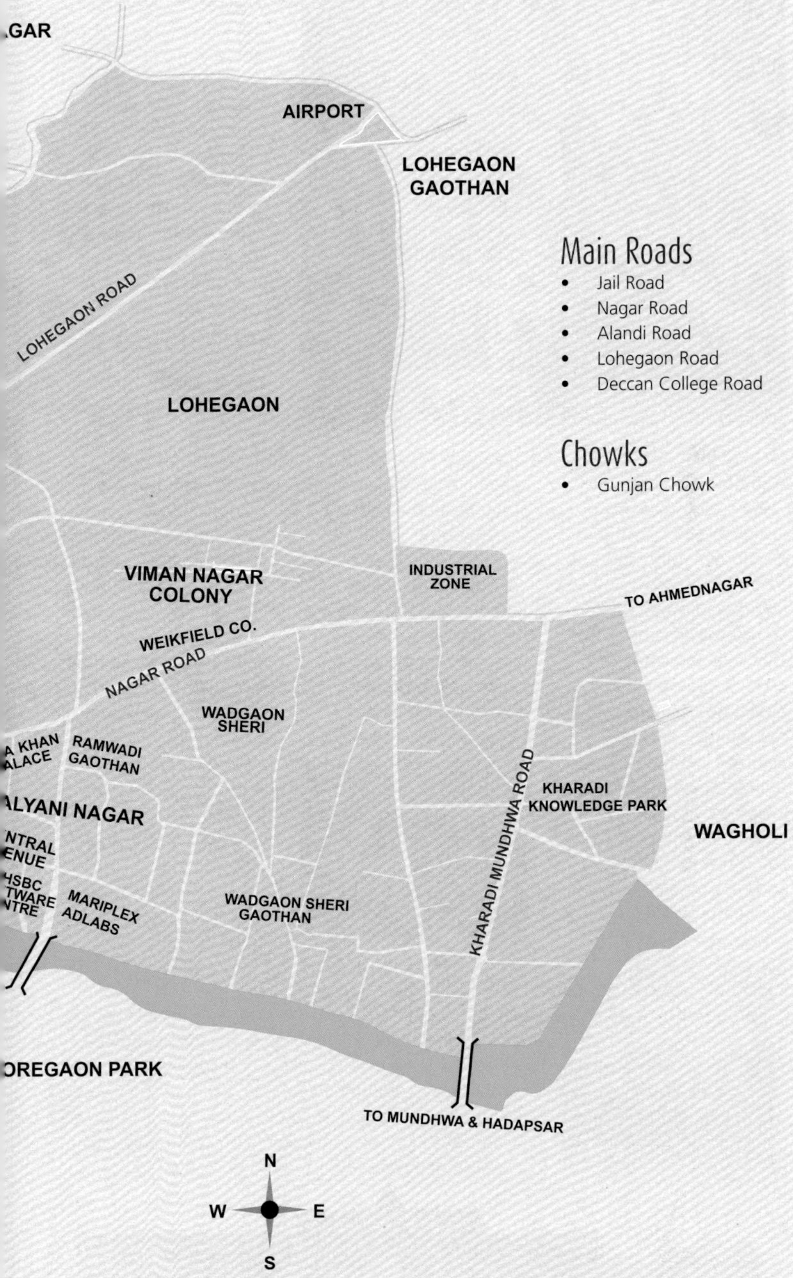

Main Roads

- Jail Road
- Nagar Road
- Alandi Road
- Lohegaon Road
- Deccan College Road

Chowks

- Gunjan Chowk

Map Indicative; not to scale

Historical Sites

Aga Khan Palace

This is where Mahatma Gandhi, his wife Kasturba Gandhi and his trusted follower and private secretary Mahadev Desai were detained during the Quit India Movement in 1942 The palace ground has marble memorials to Kasturba Gandhi and Mahadev Desai, both of whom passed away here. The museum recreates glimpses of the Independence struggle and has preserved various personal belongings of Gandhiji.

Open from 9 am-530 pm.
Gandhi National Memorial,
Nagar Road, Pune 411006
Tel: 26680250 / 1834

Central Jail

Built around 1870, it was here that Mahatma Gandhi was imprisoned during the independence struggle and started the *harijan* (untouchables) movement.

A Gandhi *sthan* (place) has been created inside the jail and some of the relics of his time, and the cell in which he spent his days, have been preserved. Since Gandhi's time, several hardened criminals have been lodged at the prison, and some of them have met a gory fate. Visitors are not allowed entry into the prison without permission.
Central Building 1,
Yerawada Prision, Jail Road,
Yerawada
Pune 411006
Tel: 26696115 / 26696707

Institutions

Jail Officers Training School

Set up in 1955, this institute trains officers in correctional administration and prison management. It also trains newly recruited guards and non-commissioned officers.
Near Central Jail,
Jail Road, Yerawada,
Pune 411006
Tel: 26692417

Education

Symbiosis International School

This international school with an IB programme is part of the Symbiosis

Deccan College (PG and Research Institute)

This is the alma mater of India's eminent leaders like Lokmanya Tilak, R. G. Bhandarkar,

Gurudev R. D. Ranade and R. N. Dandekar. Deccan College is hailed as one of the oldest and best institutes in the country for post-graduate studies and research, particularly in the fields of Indology, anthropology, and archaeology. It is housed in an attractive colonial monument built in 1868 in the neo-Gothic style. Yerawada, Pune 411006 Tel: 26693794

Source: Heritage Cell, PMC

Education Society.
Viman Nagar, Pune 411014
Tel: 26634550

Bishop's School

Started in 2004, this is the co-ed branch of the well-known Bishop's School for boys in Camp.
Plot No. 78, Yerawada,
Near Pepsi Godown,
Kalyani Nagar, Pune 411006
Tel: 56212204 / 56212205

Erin Nagarvala High School
Started by late Dr. (Mrs.) Erin Nagarvala and her husband Nosh Nagarvala, this is one of the earliest schools in the locality. It is actively involved in the social and civic issues of the locality.
12, Kalyani Nagar,
Pune 411006 Tel: 26681166

The Lexicon International School
Spread over lush green acres on the Pune-Ahmednagar highway, this international co-ed school is equipped with state-of-the-art infrastructure and amenities for overall development of the child. It also has boarding facilities.
Lexicon Estate, G No. 726,
Wagholi, Pune-Nagar Road,
Pune 412207
Tel: 27051818
www.lexicon.edu.in

International School of Business & Media (ISBM)
The institute specialises in marketing, finance, HRD, industrial relations and media-related disciplines like advertising, public relations, corporate communications, journalism and TV production.
Ashoka Plaza, S. No 32/2,
Next to Weikfield Company,
Nagar Road,
Pune 411014
Tel: 26633444 / 46
www.isbm.ac.in

Symbiosis Centre of Design
Established under the aegis of Symbiosis International Educational Centre, it offers Bachelor's courses in communication, product, and fashion design. It also has a Bachelor's programme in fashion communication and fine arts.
Next to Weikfield,
Viman Nagar, Pune 411014
Tel: 26634547 / 48
www.symbiosisdesign.ac.in

Landmarks

Weikfield Products Co. (I) Pvt. Ltd.
Started in 1956 to manufacture custard powder and corn flour, today the company is associated with a wide range of processed food products including chutneys and sauces and is a leading exporter of processed foods from India.
Weikfield Estate,
Nagar Road,
Pune 411014
Tel: 26633111/2
www.weikfield.com

Library

The Reading Habit
Opened in 2005, this spacious library stocks a wide range of books from bestsellers to books on health, fitness, IT, travel, and self-help.
No 7, Parsun Plaza,
Viman Nagar, Pune
Tel: 56619521

Lohegaon Airport

It is one of the few airports in the country to serve both as a civilian airport and military air base. On December 12, 2005, the first international flights to Dubai and Singapore were inaugurated. Lohegaon, Pune
Tel: 26612598 / 26689433

P-40
Part of a chain of libraries, it houses a diverse selection of English books and magazines.
Gera Landmark, Next to ICICI Bank, Kalyani Nagar, Pune 411014

Shopping Centres

Nilgiriwalas Mega Shoppe
This customer-friendly departmental store is well-stocked with grocery and household knick-knacks.
Blue Hills Society, Nagar Road, Pune 411014
Tel: 26690364

Ishanya Design Mall
This is one of India's first niche malls, dedicated to design shops for building exteriors and interiors.
Opp. Golf Course, Shastri Nagar, Yerawada, Pune 411006 Tel: 66458000

Clubs & Parks

Pune Golf Course

One of the finest golf courses in the country, it has 18 holes and a yardage of 6198/5488. It hosts some major golfing tournaments round the year, including the prestigious Maharashtra Amateur Open.
Airport Road, Yerawada, Pune 411006 Tel: 26689351

Baron's Health Club
Located conveniently within Kalyani Nagar, this club has a gym and pool among other facilities.
Opposite Jogger's Park, Kalyani Nagar, Pune 411014

Jogger's Park
Built as a result of the initiative of the residents of the area, this well-laid out park has a jogging track and is very popular with people of all ages.
Opp. Baron's Health Club, Kalyani Nagar, Pune 411014

Places of Worship

Parnakuti Temple
This temple dedicated to Lord Shiva is located on top of a small hill, near the Bund Garden Bridge.
Yerawada, Pune 411006

Restaurants

Soho
The atmosphere in this lounge bar cum restaurant, built in a converted barn, is very congenial. Advance reservation is recommended.
Behind Ramvadi Octroi Post, Next to Bishop School, Kalyani Nagar, Pune 411014 Tel: 26681987

Polka Dots
Serves excellent continental food.
Metro Traders, Behind Ramvadi Octroi Post, Next to Bishops School, Kalyani Nagar, Pune 411014
Tel: 56611739

The Ship
Offers good food, wine and an appropriately nautical ambience.
First Floor, Forteleza, Above Megamart, Kalyani Nagar, Pune 411006
Tel: 26608777

Saat Handi
For Avadhi, Punjabi and Kashmiri cuisine. Try out their Kashmiri *roganjosh, ghost narangi, kofta-e-naaz* or *paneer pasanda.*
12, Landmark Garden, Kalyani Nagar, Pune 411001
Tel: 26612934 / 26612935

The Bounty
Offers a wide variety of sizzlers and makes a great venue for a cozy dinner with friends and family.
Landmark Garden, Kalyani Nagar, Pune 411001
Tel: 26613360 / 26611758

Kremes n Krusts
A small café serving mouth-watering truffle cakes, pastries, breads and sandwiches.
Shop No.6, Landmark Garden, Kalyani Nagar, Pune 411006 Tel: 26615730

Multiplex/Movie Theatre

Mariplex Gold Adlabs
With four movie screens, a lavish food court, and a string of upmarket boutiques and stores, Gold Adlabs serves as a one-stop

IT Hub
Some of the biggest names in the IT and ITES industry are located in Kalyani Nagar, Vadgaon Sheri and Kharadi. Among them are Mphasis, Cybage, WNS, Parametric Technologies Corp (PTC), HSBC, and EXL Services.

location for food and fun. Outlets include Subway, McDonald's, Café Coffee Day, New Yorker, Crossworld and Archies. The House of Horrors (5-min walk through a haunted house) is a novel attraction here.
Mariplex Mall, Marigold Complex, Kalyani Nagar, Pune 411006 Tel: 56096464

Gunjan
A single-screen theatre located next to the Talera Ford showroom at Yerawada.
Airport Road, Yerawada, Pune 411006
Tel: 26694484

Hospitals

Yerawada Mental Hospital
Run by the Central Government, the Yerawada Mental Hospital includes a rehabilitation centre for addicts, an asylum for the mentally challenged and a half way home for people with mental disabilities like schizophrenia.
Nagar Road, Opp. Yerawada Jail, Pune 411006 Tel: 26692543

Kataria Hospital
A small private hospital.
Nagar Road, Yerawada, Pune 411006
Tel: 26697183

Banks and ATMs

HDFC ATM
Hermes Heritage, Shop No. 1, Kalyani Nagar, Pune 411006

Niyati Business Park, Wadgaon Sheri, Near Kalyani Nagar, Pune 411006

UTI ATM
Shop No 8, Amrut Park CHS, Kalyani Nagar, Pune 411006

Shop No 1, Viman Prestige, Viman Nagar, Pune 411014

Opp. Ventura Marisoft, Near Gold Adlabs, Kalyani Nagar, Pune 411014

Citibank ATM
Shop No 6, Amrut Park Co-operative Soc. Ltd., T. P. Scheme Area, Kalyani Nagar, Yerawada, Pune 411006

ICICI ATM
Shop No 3, G-Mart, Gera Harmony, Next to Spencer's Daily, Kalyani Nagar, Pune 411014

Shalimar Triumph, Plot No. 72, Viman Nagar, Pune 411014

State Bank of India ATM
Pune, 9 Brd Extention Counter, Pune-Nagar Road, Pune 411014

Union Bank ATM
Central Avenue, Opp Preet Mandir, Kalyani Nagar, Pune 411006

HDFC BANK (ATM)
78 Kalyani Nagar, Bishop's Co-ed. School Campus, Near Pepsi Godown, Pune 411016
Tel: 26616501 / 2

UTI Bank (ATM)
Marigold Premises, Ground Floor, Survey No. 15, Vadgaonsheri, Pune 411014

IDBI BANK (ATM)
Plot 128, Ground Floor, Blue Hills, Nagar Road, Pune 411014
Tel: 26612039

Bank of Maharashtra
Kalyani Nagar, Pune 411006 Tel: 27033498

Agrasen Urban Co-Operative Bank
P.S. Plaza Complex, Yerawada, Pune 411006 Tel: 26692296

Pune for Travellers

- Where to Stay • Where to Eat • Where to Party • Where to Shop
- Entertainment, *Art and Culture, Films, Heritage Sites*
- Adventure Activities • Picnic Spots • Children's Special
- Pilgrim Centres

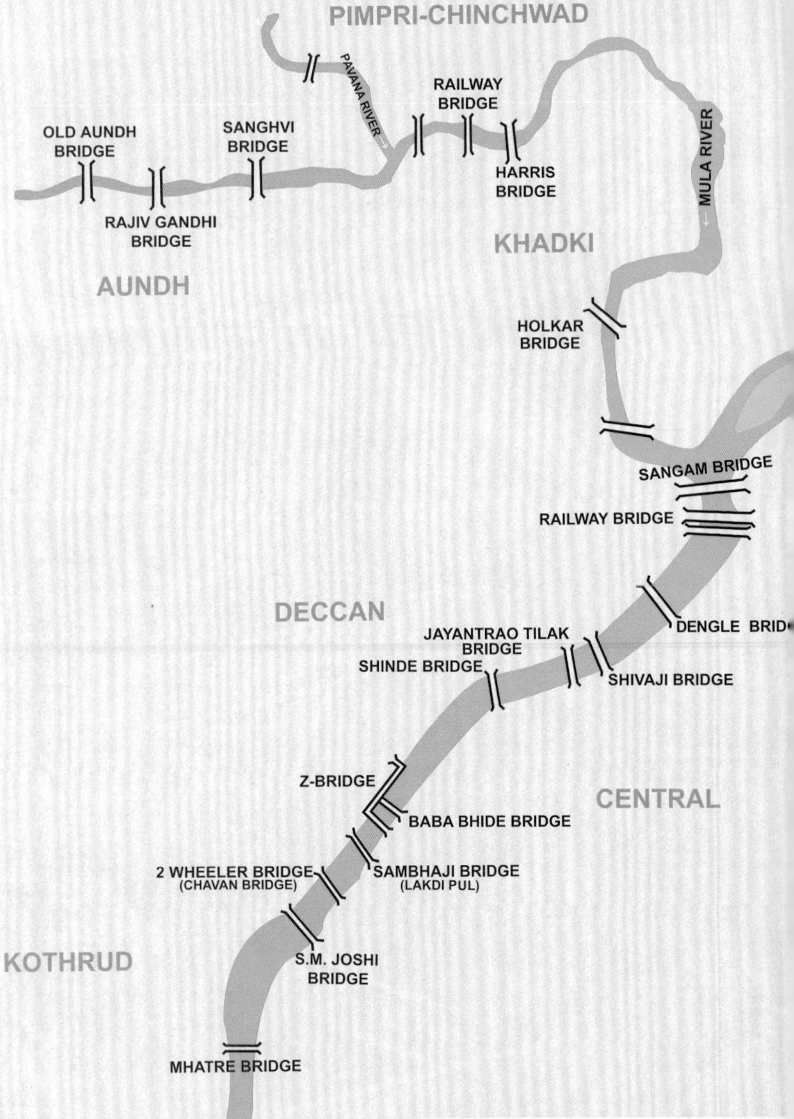

Map Indicative; not to scale

Sambhaji Bridge (Lakdi Pul) and Z Bridge

Bridges in Pune City

Baba Bhide Bridge and Z Bridge

:zgerald Bridge

Harris Bridge

vaji Bridge (Nava Pul)

Jayantrao Tilak Bridge

17th PUNE INTERNATIONAL MARATHON 200
START
START

कलोपासक पुणे
आयोजित

Where to Stay

Pune has all types of accommodation for every kind of traveller and to suit every budget. Visitors have a choice of five star hotels, service apartments, mid-range and economy hotels, hostels, and inexpensive lodges.

Where to Look

A number of five star hotels like the Taj Blue Diamond, Le Meridien and Sun-n-Sand can be found in the Bund Garden area. The Best Western Pride Hotel and the Gordon House Hotel are located on the west side of the city on Ganeshkhind Road.

Business hotels such as Central Park, Coronet and Centurion are gaining popularity as the number of business travellers to the city rises. Not as high priced as the five star hotels, they are centrally located and offer a range of amenities.

Mid-range hotels can be found in the Deccan Gymkhana and Pune station areas. Modest hostelries and boarding houses can be found across the city.

Paying guest (PG) accommodation is available throughout the city, particularly in areas like Deccan Gymkhana, Kothrud, Kondhwa, Kalyani Nagar and Koregaon Park.

Hotel Grading and Facilities

Hotels can be classified into five different star categories, with five star hotels at the top end of the spectrum The standard of a hotel and the facilities it offers depends on its rating. Five star hotels are high-priced, fully air-conditioned, and equipped with a swimming pool, gymnasium, in-house restaurants, etc. Three star hotels will have fewer

facilities, but many of them boast 'five star service at three star prices'.

Most hotels have a TV, telephone, and laundry service.

Hotel Rates and Discounts

Hotels give discounts for group/corporate bookings or regular guests. Some even offer seasonal or weekday discounts. Hotel tariffs do not include meals. Check-in and check out time for most hotels is noon.

Approximate Room Tariff Range

Note: Service Tax between 3-15% is applicable on all room tariffs

Five Star : Rs. 5,000-15,000
Four Star : Rs. 3,000-7,000
Three Star : Rs. 3,000-5,000
Two Star : Rs. 700-1,500
One Star : Rs. 500-800

Extra Costs

Many other conveniences are provided by hotels – most of which come at a price.

Hotels charge steep rates for long distance telephone calls or other business utilities (internet, fax, etc). Snacks and drinks consumed from the mini-bar in the room cost extra. Sometimes rooms with a view are priced higher.

Advance Booking

Most hotels have a round the clock booking service. It is advisable that you make prior bookings, or rooms in the hotel of your choice may not be available. Hotels

are full throughout the year, with 60% of the guests being corporates. There is a rush of visitors during festivals, especially the 12-day Ganeshotsav (August-September), and in winter. Confirm your reservation before arriving at the hotel. Notify the hotel in case you are delayed so that they retain your booking. Most hotels do not charge cancellation fees if you cancel your booking a day in advance. Retention fees are charged in case of a 'no show'.
Most of the hotels listed below have been approved and graded by the Federation of Hotel and Restaurant Associations of India and been classified according to their star rating.

Five Star Deluxe

Le Meridien

Built in traditional Rajasthani style, this hotel offers unprecedented luxury. It has 179 rooms including a Presidential suite and 20 deluxe suites. It has some excellent restaurants, among them Spice Island (Thai and Chinese), La Brasserie (multi-cuisine), Chingari (North Indian), Entresol Bar (rooftop bar adjacent to swimming pool), Tea Lounge (for English tea and pastries) and Scream (a discotheque).
Room Tariff:
Rs. 7,500 – 13,000
Raja Bahadur Mill Road,
Pune 411 001
Tel: 26050505 / 26122000
Fax: 26050506 / 26050525
Website: www.pune.lemeridien.com
Email: sales@lemeridien.com

Sun-n-Sand

This five-star hotel has 115 well-appointed rooms and suites, which include an exclusive business centre. It houses three restaurants offering Indian and international cuisine, a lounge bar, a health club, a swimming pool, and business centres.
Room Tariff:
Rs. 7,000-13,000
262 Bund Garden Road,
Pune 411001
Tel: 26137777
Fax: 26134747
Email: sales@sunnsandpune.com

Taj Blue Diamond

The oldest five star hotel in Pune, it has 108 plush rooms including 11 suites, eight banquet halls with capacity of up to 200 persons, and an open banquet area for up to 600 persons. The Mystic Masala restaurant specializes in Indian cuisine while Whispering Bamboo offers Thai and Chinese cuisine. The hotel also has a 24-hour coffee shop and Casabella, the Anglo-Saxon poolside bar.
The exclusive nightclub Club Polaris is open for members and for in-house guests only.
Room Tariff:
Rs. 6,500-15,000
11, Koregaon Road,
Pune 411001
Tel: 56025555
Fax: 56027755
Email: bluediamond.pune@tajhotels.com / bdresv.pune@tajhotels.com

Best Western Pride Hotel
This centrally located hotel has a total of 111 rooms and attracts a number of business clients. It has two restaurants, Puran da Dhaba and Golden Arch, a coffee shop Café Valentino and a restobar, Xstasy.
Room Tariff:
Rs. 5,950-10,500
5, University Road,
Shivajinagar,
Pune 411005
Tel: 25534567
Fax: 25533228
Email: pune@pridegroup.net

Gordon House Hotel
This recently opened hotel has 30 elegantly furnished boutique rooms spread over four floors. The rooms have different themes and have imaginative names such as English Country, Don's Den, and Zen & Now. The hotel also has conference facilities, and guests have access to All Stir Fry (oriental restaurant) and Not Just Jazz by the Bay, a nightclub.
Room Tariff:
Rs. 5,500-12,000
132A/2A, University Road,
Ganeshkhind, Pune 411016
Tel: 66044100
Email: e-square@e-squareindia.com

Four Star

Central Park Hotel
Conveniently located near Camp, Koregaon Park and the INOX multiplex, this hotel has 69 deluxe rooms.
Room Tariff: Rs. 5,000-8,000
Opp. Council Hall, Bund Garden Road,
Pune 411001
Tel: 26054000
Fax: 26050211
Email: centralpark@vsnl.net

Kohinoor Executive
Situated near the shopping and business areas of the city, the hotel has 60 rooms and two suites.
Room Tariff:
Rs. 2,200-3,300
Apte Road, Deccan
Gymkhana,
Pune 411004
Tel: 25532000 / 25531811
Fax: 25532447

Centurion Hotel Quality Inn
This newly built boutique hotel has convenient access to the busy Pimpri-Chinchwad industrial belt, Hinjewadi and other commercial districts. It has 54 rooms.
Room Tariff: Rs. 3,000-4,500
10/1A, Ganeshkhind Road,
Opp Akashvani Bhawan,
Shivajinagar,
Pune 411005
Tel: 25510600

Oakwood
This business hotel has 45 elegant rooms and a well-equipped business centre.
Room Tariff:
Rs. 2,300-4,000
Bhandarkar Road, Deccan
Gymkhana,
Pune 411004
Tel: 25670011
Fax: 25676699
Email: tghotels@hotmail.com

Sagar Plaza
Situated in the cantonment area, this 76-room hotel is barely a kilometer away from the railway station and 15 minutes from the airport.
Room Tariff: Rs. 4,000-9,000
1, Bund Garden Road,
Pune 411001
Tel: 26122622 / 12 / 23
Fax: 26122633
Email: tsp@sarovarparkplaza.com

Aurora Towers
Within walking distance of M.G. Road, this 69-room hotel is a popular landmark in Camp. Room Tariff: Rs. 4,500-8,500
9, Dr. Ambedkar Road, Pune 411001
Tel: 26131818
Email: hotelaurora@usa.net

Hotel Regency
This hotel has 44 aesthetically designed and well-equipped rooms. The 24-hour coffee shop, restaurant and bar - The Derby - serves an array of specialties.
Room Tariff: Rs. 3,500-8,000
192, Dhole Patil Road, Pune 411001 Tel: 56033611

Heritage Hotels

Sunderban
Located in the scenic Koregaon Park area, it has 50 rooms and a beautiful garden. It is the only hotel adjacent to the famous Osho Meditation Resort. Availability of rooms can be difficult during the monsoons or winter.
Room Tariff: Rs. 3,000-4,000
19, Koregaon Park, Next to Osho International Meditation Resort, Pune 411001
Tel: 26124949
Fax: 26123535
Email: tghotels@hotmail.com

Three Star

The President Hotel
Located in a primarily residential area, it provides easy access to commercial hubs in the city.
Room Tariff: Rs. 2,600-5,000
34/11, Erandawane, Prabhat Road, Lane No. 8, Behind Kohinoor Mangal Karalaya, Pune 411004
Tel: 25431797 / 66031797
Website: www.hotelpresidentpune.com

Hotel Woodland
This hotel is comfortable, clean and centrally located.
Room Tariff: Rs. 2,900-5,000
Sadhu Vaswani Circle, Near Pune Railway Station, Pune 411001
Tel: 26126161 / 26136161
Email: info@tghotels.com

Hotel Ashish Plaza
Located opposite Fergusson College, it has 35 rooms and one suite.
Room Tariff: Rs. 2,200-5,000
1198, Shivajinagar, F. C. Road, Pune 411004
Tel: 25536541/42

Hotel Coronet
One of a range of mid-size business hotels, it is simple and well-appointed.
Room Tariff: Rs. 2,500-5,000
1205/4, Apte Road, Deccan Gymkhana, Pune 411004 Tel: 25530300

Two Star

Hotel Nandanvan
Room Tariff: Rs. 650-950
1212/A, Shivajinagar, Apte Road, Pune 411004
Tel: 25531111

Hotel Meru
Room Tariff: Rs. 500-1,190
Ladkat Wadi Road, Off Dhole Patil Road, Pune 411001 Tel: 26123939
Fax: 26119494 Email: tghotels@hotmail.com

Hotel Srimaan
Room Tariff: Rs. 995-1,595
361/5A, Bund Garden Road, Pune 411001
Tel: 26133535/26122369
Email: srimaan@vsnl.com

One Star

Hotel Homeland
Room Tariff: Rs. 550-800
18, Wilson Garden, Near Pune Railway Station, Pune 411001 Tel: 26127659

Hotel Ashiyana
Room Tariff: Rs. 575-900
1198 Shivajinagar,
F. C. Road, Pune 411004
Tel: 25538011

Hotel Shalimar
Room Tariff: Rs. 260-400
12/A, Sadhu Vaswani Road,
Pune 411001 Tel: 26129191

Others

Seasons, an Apartment Hotel
Managed by the famous Orchid group of hotels, Mumbai, the hotel offers a choice of executive apartments, studio apartments, one bedroom and two bedroom apartments. It also has a sports bar, all day world cuisine restaurant, and café on the premises.
Room Tariff:
Rs. 4,500 to 9,500
128/2 Sanewadi, Aundh,
Pune 411007 Tel: 40009999
Fax: 40009888
Email: info@seasonsaundh.com

Pichola Hotel
This is convenient if you have work in the Pimpri-Chinchwad industrial belt or at the IT Park at Hinjewadi. They serve pure vegetarian Gujarati, Punjabi and South Indian food.
Room Tariff:
Rs. 1,100-2,600
55/2, Ganeshkhind Road, (Raj Bhavan Road), Aundh,
Pune 411007 Tel: 25885695
Email: hotelpichola@ip.eth.net

Hotel Shreyas
Situated in the city centre, it has 48 rooms, and serves typical Maharashtrian vegetarian fare.
Room Tariff: Rs. 855-980
1242/B, Apte Road,
Deccan Gymkhana,
Pune 411004 Tel: 25532023
Fax: 25536908

Service Apartments

Service apartments are ideal for corporate employees, expatriates on transfer and families on extended stay as they blend the conveniences of home and hotel perfectly.

Seasons Service Apartments
This was the first service apartment complex in the city. It offers elegantly furnished one or two bedroom apartments with all modern amenities.
Trinity Court, Off South Main Road, Koregaon Park,
Pune 411001
Tel: 26140130

Bel Air Suites and Service Apartments
The two bedroom suites are priced at over Rs. 5,000/day, inclusive of continental breakfast, housekeeping services, 24-hour security and airport and railway pick up with prior notice.
333, Koregaon Park, Off North Main Road,
Near Cosmos Bank,
Pune 411001
Tel: 30523333 / 30524431

Hostels

Hostels are mostly concentrated in and around the education hub of Deccan-Kothrud.

Sharda Niketan Girls Hostel
Spread over a two-acre campus, it has a health club, swimming pool and library, and can accommodate 276 students. The rooms are spacious and comfortable with attached bathrooms. Hostel fee per annum is Rs.15,000 for Maharashtrians and Rs. 25,000 for non-Maharashtrians (inclusive of meals).
30/2B Karve Nagar,
Pune 411052
Tel: 25444319

R. K. Khadilkar Girls Hostel
The hostel can accommodate 90 girls (three to a room). Annual fees amount to Rs. 17,000.
79-B/2, Corner of 15th Lane,
Prabhat Road,
Pune 411004
Tel: 25658252

Saheli Home Ladies Hostel
This hostel has a capacity of 60 students, two or five girls to a room. The monthly fee is Rs. 2,500 excluding food.
Near Cummins College of Engineering, Karve Nagar,
Pune 411038
Tel: 25422514

Baramati Boys Hostel
This plush hostel for boys can accommodate 250 students. Hostel fee per annum is Rs.22,000 inclusive of meals. Admissions start in June.
270/C, Gokhale Nagar,
Pune 411004
Tel: 25658686 / 25659191

Youth Centres

YMCA
Offers standard, reasonably priced accommodation. The a/c double rooms are priced at Rs. 900 and non-a/c room at Rs. 600 per day with breakfast included. Advance reservation is recommended.
382, New Rasta Peth,
Quarter Gate,
Pune 411011
Tel: 26134842 / 26131338
Race Course
Tel: 26360504

YWCA
5 Gurudwara Road,
Pune 411001
Tel: 26360300

Don Bosco Youth Centre
4 Koregaon Road,
P.O Box No 216,
Pune GPO,
Pune 411001
Tel: 26122813

Paying Guest (PG) Accommodation
Paying guest accommodation is scattered throughout the city, and sought by students, IT/ BPO employees and long staying visitors to the Osho Resort and the Iyengar Yoga Institute. In areas like Senapati Bapat Road, PG accommodation on a sharing basis is usually available for approximately Rs. 2,000 per month. In areas like Aundh, which are closer to the University and

Spicer College, the rates vary between Rs. 1,800-2,000 per month. Koregaon Park mostly attracts foreigners. Kondhwa and Kalyani Nagar are convenient for BPO employees working in the area. Basic amenities are provided in PG accommodation. Cooking facilities are not usually available. Breakfast may or may not be included in the fee.

Bakarwadi

Snacks

Laddu

Paan Mithai

Where to Eat

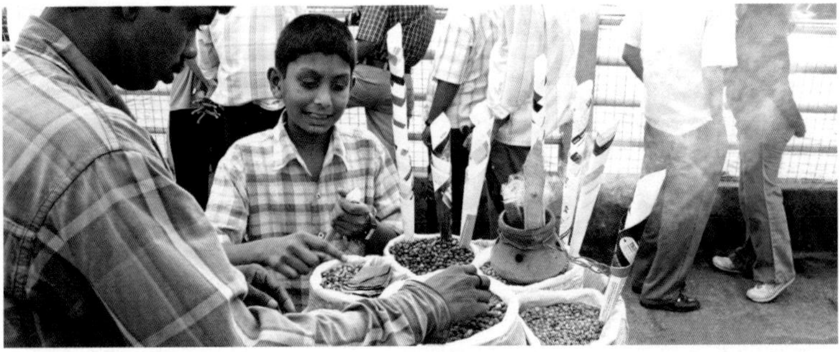

Puneites love to eat out as is amply evident from the range of culinary delights available at eateries ranging from small shacks to specialty restaurants and plush outlets at star hotels. Pune caters to every taste and budget, and offers a choice of regional Indian cuisine in addition to several global options. Whether you're seeking wholesome South Indian vegetarian food or Japanese sushi, you won't have to travel very far for it.

Location

Pune is dotted with eateries, and as each new area develops, a host of eating places springs up. The two main food avenues however are Jungli Maharaj (J.M.) Road for traditional vegetarian Indian food and budget eating; and Koregaon Park for a more high priced international range. Some fine garden restaurants are located just a few miles out of the city, and those in the Chandni Chowk area also offer spectacular views.

Timings

All South Indian eateries are open for breakfast, and serve favourites such as steaming hot *idlis* and *dosas*. A traditional Maharashtrian breakfast of *kaande pohe*, or *missal pav* is served at many small eateries, especially in the inner city. For *brun maska* and *chai* head for an Irani restaurant located on prominent street corners. Coffee shops in star hotels serve an extensive breakfast buffet. Lunch is served anytime between 11 am to 3 pm, and is a busy time for mid-priced eateries that cater to office crowds. Dinner starts at 7 pm and the last order is taken by 11 pm. Most restaurants down their shutters by midnight.

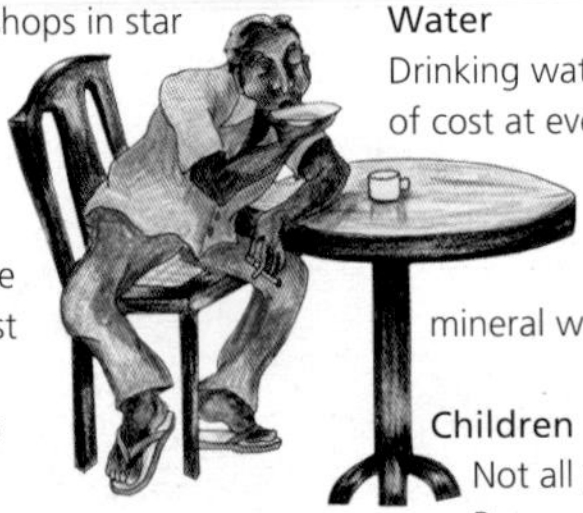

Alcohol

The legal drinking age in India is 21, and applies for entry into pubs, lounge bars and discotheques. Most good restaurants stock both domestic and imported spirits. Wine is being increasingly served at upmarket restaurants – try out some good Indian wines from the Sula and Indage vineyards located near Pune.

Did you know?
Jungli Maharaj Road is believed to have the highest density of eateries on any road in any city in India.

Water

Drinking water is served free of cost at every restaurant. Most eating places also sell bottles of mineral water.

Children

Not all restaurants in Pune are child-friendly. Some open-air restaurants have a designated play area for children, while a few others offer a high-chair facility for toddlers.

Toilets

Most restaurants have a washroom facility.

Tips and Taxes

How much you tip the waiters is a matter of choice. The norm is to leave 10% of the bill value, but anything is appreciated at the small eateries. A value added tax, (VAT) is charged at most of the mid- and high-end restaurants.

Restaurants

These restaurants have been chosen across a wide range to reflect the richness and range of the Puneri platter.

Budget Bites

The eateries listed here offer some of the best traditional fare at reasonable prices. Meals for two persons generally cost under Rs.100

Manmeet

Specializes in North Indian *chaat* items such as *bhel puri, paani puri,* and *aloo chaat*. Both branches are usually packed in the evening.
Near Sant Tukaram Paduka Chowk, Fergusson Road, Pune 411004
Tel: 30940450.
Ganpati Chowk, Dhole Patil Road, Pune 411001 Tel: 30940451

Vaishali

Almost fifty years old, this South Indian (Udipi) restaurant was the first of its kind in the locality and rapidly gained popularity for its good food and cheerful ambience. Over the decades, Vaishali has become an institution, firmly embedded in the nostalgic memories of Puneites who have moved away. Apart from South Indian favourites, it also serves items such as the popular SPDP (sev potato dahi puri).
1218/1, Fergusson College Road, Pune 411004
Tel: 25531244

Roopali

A sister concern of Vaishali, Roopali is a favourite haunt for journalists, office goers and other regulars. Along with the South Indian specialties, it also offers South Indian *thalis* (complete pre-plated meals).
Fergusson College Road, Pune 411004
Tel: 23352951

Good Luck

A typical Irani restaurant, it attracts people who like their typical *bun-maska-chai* or *kheema-bun*.
Goodluck Chowk, Deccan Gymkhana,
Pune 411004 Tel: 25676893

Radhika

Drop in for an evening snack or brunch at Radhika. Juice, coffee, *masala-pav* and other simple snacks feature on the menu card.

For vegetarians

All South Indian or Udipi restaurants in the city serve pure vegetarian food prepared fresh every day.

927, Sanas Memories, F.C. Road, Pune 411004
Tel: 25664393

Kamat

A large South Indian restaurant with extensive seating, it is a favourite with students and office-goers.
Kamat Building, Kothrud, Pune 411038
Tel: 66012233

Shiv Sagar

Their specialty is South Indian food with a twist, such as the popular Chinese *dosa*. Patrons swear by the *pav-bhaji* served here.
J. M. Road, Opp Sambhaji Park, Shivajinagar, Pune 411005
Tel: 25532179

Poona Coffee House

A landmark in the area, the restaurant serves a mix of sandwiches, North Indian delicacies and desserts.
Opp. PMT Bus Depot, Deccan Gymkhana, J.M. Road, Pune 411005
Tel: 25531256 / 25531970

Coffee House

One of the swankier South Indian restaurants in the city,

it also serves North Indian fare and is popular with office-goers in the Camp area. Try their *rawa dosas* and *uttappas*.
2 A, Dr. Ambedkar Road,
Pune 411001
Tel: 26130716 / 1282

Faaso's
Named after an African country, this small eatery offers a range of reasonably priced wraps in egg, vegetable, chicken and mutton variations.
Shop No. 1, Aditya Classic,
Baner Road,
Pune 411045 Tel: 27293940
Kothrud Branch: Near Chaitanya Health Club,
Ideal Colony, Paud Road,
Kothrud, Pune 411038
Branch also at Fatimanagar

Kapila Kebabs
Located at a street corner, this tiny eatery is only open in the evening when it draws droves of customers eager to taste its famous chicken *kebab* rolls.
Bank of Maharashtra Compound,
Next to Kapila Hotel, Dhole Patil Road,
Pune 411001

Thalis

A *thali* (large steel plate) meal is a typically Indian experience. It usually involves unlimited helpings of a dozen or more items, and you have to be alert because sometimes the food is served faster than you can eat it!

Shabree
Its rustic setting is a perfect backdrop for the typical vegetarian Maharashtrian cuisine served here. Also on

the premises is Sharvaree, which serves a varied breakfast buffet, and other Maharashtrian snacks.
Next to Tukaram Mandir,
F.C Road, Shivajinagar,
Pune 411004 Tel: 25531511

Rasoi Dining Hall
Located in the heart of the city, it serves authentic vegetarian Maharashtrian food.
Laxmi Madhav Apartment,
324, Shaniwar Peth,
Pune 411030 Tel: 24453066

Sahare Dining Hall
This spacious and clean eatery serves delicious Gujarati and Rajasthani *thalis*. It also offers the option of an onion- and garlic-free Jain thali.
5, Sadhu Vaswani Road,
Opp. GPO,
Pune 411001 Tel: 26126138

Mayur
Serves authentic Gujarati food and is usually filled to capacity.
East Street, Camp,
Pune 411001 Tel: 26130909

Shreyas
Serves typical Maharashtrian fare such as *varan-bhat, puranpoli, aamras,* etc.
1242-B Apte Road,
Deccan Gymkhana,
Pune 411004
Tel: 25531963

Jana Seva
A simple place that serves some of the city's best *sabudana wadas, pohe* and *piyush,* a lemon-yellow sweet drink. Catering mainly to office-goers, they have a special menu on days of fasting.
Near Gokhale Hall,
Laxmi Road, Pune 411030.
Tel: 24453118

Durvankur
A mix of Gujarati, Maharashtrian, and Rajasthani fare, priced reasonably.
Hatti Ganpati Chowk,
Tilak Road, Sadashiv Peth,
Pune 411030 Tel: 24474438

Regional Fare

Indian cuisine varies from region to region. Here are some restaurants that serve food from different parts of the country.

Lucknowi

Nawab
Feast on some royal Avadhi preparations here like the Galawati Kebab, Kakori *Kebab, Murgh Mussalam,* and *fragrant biryanis.*
San Mahu Complex, Bund Garden Road, Pune 411001
Tel: 6202475 / 26054274

Kashmiri

North West Frontier
An excusive Kashmiri eatery, try their *Tabak Maaz* (fried lamb ribs), *Gushtaba, Aab Aosht* and other tender meat delicacies.
Uttam Tower,
Opp. Aga Khan Palace,
Nagar Road, Pune 411014
Tel: 56619300 / 56619301

Wazwaan
Offers a range of Kashmiri dishes, such as *Tabak Maaz* and *kormas,* in a Kashmiri ambience.
Primrose Mall S No. 76/3,
Baner Road, Baner,
Pune 411045 Tel: 27292422

Hyderabadi

Golconda
For typical Hyderabadi fare, in a restful open-air ambience. Don't miss the *Pathar Kabab.*
ABC Farms, North Main Road, Koregaon Park,
Pune 411001 Tel: 26817415

Koyla
The colorful décor is a little overwhelming, but the food is worth a try.
Opp. Police Grounds,
Fergusson College Road,
Pune 411004 Tel: 26120102

Branch at North Main Road,
Koregaon Park,
Pune 411001

Malvani / Konkani

Malvani Gajali
The name comes from Malvan, a small village on the Konkan coast. Malvani food is a complex combination of spices, coconut, and meat or sea food. Some great food served in a rustic ambience.
Krida Nagar Road, Baner,
Pune 411045 Tel: 27291667

Mahesh Lunch Home
A branch of the famous Mumbai eatery, it serves a range of coastal preparations.
18 Dr. Ambedkar Road,
Pune 411001
Tel: 26133091

Coconut Grove
A great selection of coastal cuisine, and ideal for sea-food lovers.
Near Ambedkar Bhavan,
Mangalwar Peth, Maldhaka,
Pune 411002
Tel: 26053981 / 26053982

Punjabi

Chaitanya
A popular student hangout, it serves a reasonably priced vegetarian Punjabi meal and a range of *parathas*.
1199/b Chanakyapuri Apts,
Next to Hotel Ashish Plaza,
F. C. Raod, Pune 411004
Tel: 25520945
Branches at Dhole Patil Road and Paud Road

Only Parathas
A *paratha* paradise, with more than 250 vegetarian varieties on offer - from the traditional *aloo* and *gobi* to the unconventional baby corn-mushroom.
G4 Metropole Complex,
Bund Garden Road,
Next to INOX
Pune 411001
Tel: 26051834 / 35

The Great Punjab
Well appointed and spacious, it serves traditional Punjabi fare cooked to perfection.
5, Jewel Tower, Lane 5,
Off North Main Road,

Koregaon Park,
Pune 411001
Tel: 26145060 / 30932023

Puran da Dhaba
The Punjabi *dhaba* experience with live *geet* and *ghazals* in a rustic village ambience.
The Pride Hotel, 5, University Road, Shivajinagar,
Pune 411005 Tel: 25534567

Rajasthani

Chokhi Dhani
For the traditional flavours of Rajasthan, drive to this village resort and savour *Gatte ki Sabji, Kadi Besani, Pakori, Kachori* or opt for the Rajasthani *thali.*
Ganga Retreat Countryside,
Opp Pune Nagar Highway,
Near Ramwadi Octroi Post,
Wagholi, Pune 411007
Tel: 27051032

Rutugandh
For a hugely satisfying meal of rich, mouth watering Rajasthani fare, head for this popular eatery.
638 J.M. Road, Near Z Bridge, Decaan Gymkhana,
Pune 411004
Tel: 25536560 / 66029201

Bengali

Radhika
Authentic home-cooked Bengali food, ranging from Mutton *Kosha* to Mustard Fish. Typical Bengali sweetmeats such as *Kheer-kadam* and *Rasgollas* are also available.
Senapati Bapat Road,
Pune 411016

Restaurants with a View

Garden Court
Situated in the scenic Pashan hills, this multi-cuisine restaurant is popular with families and couples looking for a romantic getaway.
76/2, Pashan-NDA Road,
Chandni Chowk,
Pune 411021 Tel: 25283502

Riverview
On the banks of the Mula River, it is popular as much for its scenic location, as its wide and varied menu. The sea food is particularly recommended.
81/82 North Main Road,
Koregaon Park Extension,
Pune 411001
Tel: 26811335 / 6

Ambrosia
Spread across a hillside on the outskirts of the city, Ambrosia is child-friendly and offers many options for people seeking a different dining experience.
Survey No 38/2,
Bavdhan Khurd,
Pune 411029
Tel: 22951023 / 22951571

Mini Cafés

Marz-O-Rin
Their sandwiches and rolls have been a favourite of generations of M.G. Road shoppers. Also serves cold coffee, milkshakes, juices, burgers, etc.
Bakthiar Plaza,
6 M.G. Road, Pune 411001
Tel: 26130774 / 26136690

German Bakery
An eclectic selection of salads, imported cheese, soya delicacies, hummus sandwiches, Spanish omelets, and more. Popular with tourists and college students.
291, Vaswani Nagar,
North Main Road,
Pune 411001
Tel: 26136532

Just Baked
A collection of sinful chocolate cakes, tarts, mousses, cheesecakes,

cookies and sandwiches layered with mayonnaise and cheese. An open kitchen allows you to watch the bakers at work.
198/3, Chandrakant Chambers,
Dhole Patil Road,
Pune 411001
Tel: 26123296 / 26127278

Flapjack
Serves irresistible crepes, desserts, cookies and pastries.
Central Park Hotel,
Bund Garden Road,
Pune 411001 Tel: 26054000

Sweet Chariot
This hip café, which has outlets in Hyderabad, Bangalore and Chennai, has a range of delectable snacks including quiches, burgers, pizzas, puffs and desserts.
Mit Corner, North Main Road, Koregaon Park,
Pune 411001
Tel: 26113363

Hot Breads
A one-stop shop for freshly baked bread including mixed grain and whole wheat varieties. Also serve a range of mouth-watering pastries and croissants.
1A/1B Gera Sterling, North Main Road, Koregaon Park,
Pune 411001
Tel: 26133757 / 26054307

Dorabjee Cafetaria
A truly value-for-money range of desserts and snacks ranging from samosas and sandwiches to quiche and puffs.
Outside Dorabjee Departmental Store,
Dr. Ambedkar Road,
Pune 411001
Tel: 26052882 / 83 / 84

World Cuisine

Pune has an exciting and impressive range of restaurants serving international cuisine.

Italian

La Pizzeria
Serves authentic vegetarian pastas and pizzas, and is a favourite of many.
Srimaan Hotel, 361/5B
Bund Garden Road,
Pune 411001
Tel: 26122369

La Dolce Vita
Exclusive Italian cuisine served in an elegantly appointed space. Also stocks an impressive range of wines.
City Point, Boat Club Road,
Pune 411001 Tel: 26145555

Lebanese

Flags
Pegged as a world cuisine restaurant, Flags is popular for its Lebanese food.
G2, Metropole Complex,
Bund Garden Road,
Next to INOX,
Pune 411001
Tel: 26141617 / 18

Hitebar
The succulent *shawarma* dished out by their kitchen is the best in town.
Office No. 2,
Kumar Corner, Convent Street,
Pune 411001
Tel: 26334080

Wanowrie Branch:
9850495030

South East Asian

Whispering Bamboos
Situated in the Taj Blue Diamond, this swanky eatery serves up some impressive Thai and Chinese food in discreetly elegant surroundings.
Taj Blue Diamond, 11
Koregaon Park,
Pune 411001 Tel: 24025555

Malaka Spice
Specializes in Thai, Malaysian and other South East Asian delicacies. Attractive indoor and outdoor seating arrangement. Has a permanent display of paintings by local artists.
Vrindavan Apartments, Off North Main Road,
Koregaon Park,
Pune 411001 Tel: 26136293

Silk Route
A subtly designed multi-level restaurant serving a wide range of exotic oriental and South East Asian dishes. Try the sushi.
357/1, Lane No 6,
Pingle Corner,
Koregaon Park, Pune
411001
Tel: 26135793

All Stir Fry
The wok counter allows you to choose your ingredients and sauces from a vast assortment, which a chef will then toss together for you. The *a la carte* menu features several other

interesting options. The dim sums are recommended.
Gordon House Hotel, E-Square, Ganeshkhind Road, Pune 411016
Tel: 66044100

Chinese

Mainland China
One of a national chain of restaurants, Mainland China is particularly well known for its executive lunch, and is a favourite with office-goers in the area.
Ground Floor, City point, Dhole Patil Road, Near Akshay Complex, Pune 411001 Tel: 66013030

Chinese Room
One of Pune's oldest Chinese restaurants, it has maintained its standards and remains popular with many regulars.
2434, East Street, Pune 411001
Tel: 26131336 / 26145613

Swiss

Swiss Cheese Garden
A lively atmosphere and rustic ambience sets apart the Swiss Cheese Garden from other restaurants. Try the cheese fondue for a truly Swiss experience.
ABC Farms, North Main Road, Koregaon Park, Pune 411001
Tel: 26817413

French

Arthur's Theme
Rated as one of the best restaurants of the city, it rustles up some of the most mouth-watering and authentic French fare. Try their fish croquettes, or traditional French onion soup or just pick your favourite from the menu.
Vrindavan Apts, Off North Main Road, Koregaon Park, Pune 411001 Tel: 26132710

Iranian

Shisha Café
Low cots, Persian food, dim lighting and the exotic aroma of hookahs makes this a very popular place, especially on Fridays when a live band serenades diners. The café also opens for breakfast at 10 am. Try the Zereshk Polo, Cranberry Rice, and Chello Fesenjan.
ABC Farms, North Main Road, Koregaon Park, Pune 411001 Tel: 56202674

Blue Nile
One of the oldest Irani restaurants in town, its biryani is very famous.
4, Bund Garden Road, Opposite Poona Club, Pune 411001 Tel: 26125238

Pizzas

Pizza Express
Unlike other pizza places, this one is quiet and spacious and also offers a selection of salads and pastas.
Ground Floor, Sohrab Hall, Sassoon Road, Pune 411001
Tel: 26059001 / 2

Pizza Corner
This international pizza chain chose Pune for its first outlet in western India. The menu offers a wide range of pizzas, soups, salads, appetizers, pastas, bakes, deserts and beverages.
1st Floor, The Hub, North Main Road, Koregaon Park, Pune 411001
Tel: 26055511

You will find branches of Smokin' Joe's, Domino's Pizza, and Pizza Hut in most prominent areas across the city. All of them offer home delivery facilities.

Sizzlers

The Place Touche
Clover Centre, Dr. Ambedkar Road, Next to West End Theatre, Pune 411001
Tel: 26134632

The Bounty
Landmark Garden,
Kalyani Nagar,
Pune 411006
Tel: 26613360

Zamu's
189, Nirmal Building,
Dhole Patil Road,
Pune 411001 Tel: 26123610

Yoko
G-3, 5th avenue,
Dhole Patil Road,
Pune 411001 Tel: 30908165

Kobe
Abhinav Sankul, Pushpak
Park Corner, ITI Road,
Aundh, Pune 411027
Tel: 25887576/77
Branch: Law College Road

Local Delights

1 **Puranpoli**
Flatbread stuffed with a sweet mixture of jaggery and pulses.

2 **Varan Bhaat**
Lentil soup eaten with steamed rice and served with clarified butter.

3 **Masale Bhat**
Spicy rice dish with vegetables.

4 **Pithla Bhakri**
Thick flatbread made of different cereals, and eaten with a preparation made from gram flour.

5 **Amti**
Spicy lentil soup.

6 **Matki Usal**
Sprouted green gram

7 **Misal**
Spicy mixture of sprouted green gram, gravy, onions, tomatoes and crispies.

8 **Thalipeeth**
Flatbread made of cereals.

9 **Chirote**
Crispy sweetmeat resembling a pinwheel.

10. **Ukadiche Modak**
Steamed rice flour dumplings stuffed with coconut; popular during the Ganesh festival.

11 **Sabudana Khichdi**
Sago preparation.

12 **Poha**
Flattened rice tempered with onions, potatoes and spices.

What is mastani?

A rich milkshake-ice cream-dry fruit combination, named after the infamous mistress of Peshwa Bajirao I.

Paan

A betel nut leaf stuffed with tobacco or other sweet fillings, *paan* is a very popular Indian after-dinner option, and plentifully available at street corners and outside restaurants. Pappu, an air-conditioned *paan* parlour with branches across the city, serves 60 varieties of *paan* in stlye!

Pappu Paan
Poonam Apartment,
Bibvewadi-KondhwaRoad,
Pune 411040 Tel: 24260401

Branches: Portico on J.M.Road, Ashish Plaza on F.C. Road and Hotel Sarjaa in Aundh.

Chandini Paan Shop
Outside Sagar
Plaza Hotel, Pune 411001

Shaukeen
Nal Stop, Karve Road,
Pune 411004

Puran Poli

Varan Bhat

Paan

Dosa

Thalipeeth

Modak

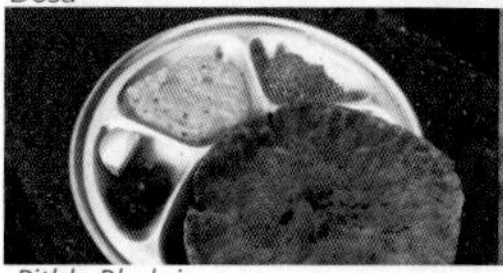

Pithla Bhakri

Khichadi

Bhajji

Where to Party

Puneites love to party. The growing number of pubs, clubs, lounge bars and discotheques testifies to the lively night life, which attracts students, young BPO workers, IT and other professionals, foreign visitors and even nearby Mumbaikars. Just as Pune works hard during the day, it truly rocks at night.

Discos/Pubs/Lounge Bars

The discos, pubs and lounge bars of Pune are trendy, hip and happening. They offer varied options to eat, drink, socialize or just hang out.
Timings: Most of them are open from 9 pm to about 1.30-2.00 am.
Cover Charge: Rs. 200-600 (per person)

Thousand Oaks
An intimate pub setting that often features live acts. The attractive open air seating area is dimly lit and ideal for those wishing for a quieter evening.
2417, East Street,
Pune 411001 Tel: 26343194

Fire and Ice
Unarguably the largest dance floor in Pune, this one is for youngsters seeking loud music and a rocking time.
Metro Traders Compound,
Behind Ramvadi Octroi Post,
Next to Bishop's School,
Kalyani Nagar,
Pune 411014
Tel: 26695861 / 26615056

Soho's
A refurbished barn serves as the bar area, while the outdoor seating is lit by gently swaying lanterns that create a wonderful ambience. The food is recommended.
Behind Ramvadi Octroi Post,
Next to Bishop's School,
Kalyani Nagar,
Pune 411014 Tel: 26681987

Nirvana
A spacious lounge area, offset by a noisy, crowded bar.
Ground Floor Metropole Building, Bund Garden Road, Next to INOX,
Pune 411001
Tel: 66024733 / 66025733

Ten Downing Street (TDS)
Designed as a typical English pub, it also has an exclusive dance floor on the upper level.
2nd Floor Gera Plaza,
Boat Club Road,
Pune 411001
Tel: 26128343

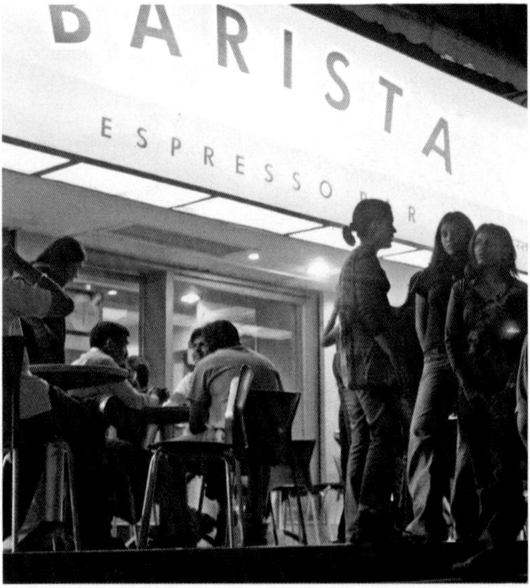

Kiva
A cozy little place with Mexican Indian overtones. Plays great retro music and serves interesting cocktails.
Symphony C Building, Range Hills Road, Bhosale Nagar, Pune 411020.
Tel: 25538339

Scream
One of the most popular discotheques in the city, Scream has a huge dance floor and hosts some very happening parties.
Le Meridien Hotel, Raja Bhadur Mills Road, Pune 411001
Tel: 26050505

Lush
One of the latest additions to the list of pubs in Pune, Lush has great music and a very classy crowd.
Shop 14-19, City Tower Building, Dhole Patil Road, Pune 411001

Sphinx
There are three distinct sections here: the bar, the lounge-restaurant and the dance floor, all connected to each other.
Plot No 396/398 Sphinx House, South Main Road, Greenfield Park, Koregaon Park, Pune 411001
Tel: 9823322111 / 30583338

Club Polaris
The nightclub at the Taj Blue Diamond is pretty exclusive. Entry is reserved for members and hotel guests.
Hotel Taj Blue Diamond, Koregaon Park, Pune 411001
Tel: 26125555

Zanzibar
A great place to hang out with friends over exotic drinks and appetizing snacks.
Central Park Hotel, Bund Garden Road, Pune 411001
Tel: 26054000

Xtasy
Larger than most other pubs in the city, Xtasy is the perfect place to chill out after a day's work.
Best Western Pride Hotel, 5 University Road, Shivajinagar, Pune 411005
Tel: 25534567

> **Nightspots Tally**
> The city has 19 pubs and discotheques. Mumbaikars make up more than 50 % of the weekend crowd here.

Aqua Lounge
Strikingly done up in shades of blue and wood, it has a mid-size dance floor and well stocked bar.
Aurora Towers, 9, Dr. Ambedkar Road, Pune 411001
Tel: 26131818

Leather Lounge
A comfortable blend of the rustic and contemporary, Leather Lounge is a great place to chill out in especially in the early part of the evening.
9-20 321A Amba Commercial Complex, M. G. Road, Pune 411001
Tel: 66012013 / 11 / 12

Where to Shop

Pune's retail sector is witnessing tremendous growth. The influx of malls, swanky showrooms and posh departmental stores in the last decade or so has added to the vibrancy in the market and widened the choice for Puneites. However the traditional markets and bazaars nestled in narrow lanes have long fascinated shoppers and will continue to do so.

Shopping Zones

M.G. Road in Camp is one of the most popular shopping avenues in the city. Tree-lined and dotted with eateries, it's the perfect place for leisurely shopping excursions. On weekends, the whole stretch becomes a lively walking plaza.

J.M. Road and F.C. Road in the Deccan Gymkhana area reflect the changing face of Pune. A large number of showrooms and outlets of international brands are located here, apart from an astounding range of eateries.

> **Siesta Time**
> Most traditional shopkeepers in Pune still observe siesta time, and will down shutters between 1-4 pm.

Laxmi Road is the longest commercial street of Pune and has the biggest cluster of shops selling traditional saris, clothes and jewellery.

North Main Road and Dhole Patil Road in the Koregaon Park-Bund Garden area are famous for their designer boutiques, high-end showrooms and exquisite restaurants.

Tulsibaug
situated off Laxmi Road, is a narrow, crowded market lane. In the compound of the temple situated here, you will find many small shops selling traditional and contemporary brassware.

Timings
Most departmental stores and malls are open for business seven days a week from 10.30 am to 9 pm.

Sunday is shutters down for over 60 % of the older shops in most areas. Shops in the inner city and Deccan Gymkhana area remain closed on Monday.

Sales and Discounts
Sales are generally coordinated with major festivals. The peak period is around the Hindu festival of Diwali (October-November) and at the end of summer and winter. This is when a large number of shops, including malls, give discounts and float exciting offers and schemes. Clearance sales usually take place at the start of the monsoon.

Bargaining
Bargaining is common, especially at small stores, outlets and roadside stalls. If skillfully handled, prices can sometimes be halved.

Pune has an amazing variety of stores, ranging from small bargain shops to exclusive boutiques and fabulous malls. We even have our very own flea market!

Apparel and Accessories

FabIndia
An attractive range of trendy cotton and silk Indian wear for men, women and children. They also have a large linen and furnishings section.
Sakar-10, Opp Jehangir Nursing Home, Sassoon Road, Pune 411001
Tel: 26124820 / 26124832,
Branch at ITI Road, Aundh.

Either Or
This is the place for ethnic-contemporary wear, artifacts, bags, funky jewellery, and other knick-knacks. Also check out their eco-friendly books and stationery.
Sohrab Hall, 21,
Sassoon Road,
Pune 411001
Tel: 26050225

Bombay Store
A diverse collection of household products, clothes, jewellery, leather goods and stationery. 322 M.G. Road, Pune 411001 Tel: 26131067

Babe
This small boutique stocks a range of svelte Indian and western wear. Also offers tailoring facilties.
6, M .G. Road, Camp,
Pune 411001 Tel: 26135239

Burgundy
For exquisite hand embroidered outfits and designer wear.
1st Floor, Prem's Restaurant, Opp. SBI Bank, North Main Road, Koregaon Park,
Pune 411001 Tel: 56096571

Bottoms Up

A small but hip collection of reasonably priced shoes and clothes.
Sagar Arcade, F.C. Road,
Pune 411004

Jai Hind Collections
An exclusive store for men, with a huge range of Indian and western wear.
Kunte Chowk, Laxmi Road,
Pune 411030 Tel: 24450105

Just Casuals
An affordable selection of trousers, capris, colourful tops, t-shirts, skirts - just about everything that collegians or young working people can think off.
Shop No 13 Tulsidas Apts, Dastur Meher Road, Camp,
Pune 411001
Tel: 26125018 / 26125645
Branches at Bhandarkar Road, and Koregaon Park.

More Mischief
This is an upscale, designer showroom for formal men's wear ranging from traditional richly embroidered *sherwanis* to contemporary flawlessly cut Armani suits.
34/35 Sohrab Hall, Opp Jehangir Nursing Home, Sassoon Road,
Pune 411001
Tel: 26059393

Westside
Part of a national chain of stores featuring a selection of clothes and accessories for men, women and children, in addition to home accessories.
Kakade Magnum Mall,
Dr. Ambedkar Road,
Pune 411001
Tel: 26119920

Cotton World Corp
Features a wide range of formal and casual western outfits in cotton.
Laxmi Sadan,
J. M. Road,
Pune 411004
Tel: 24030313

Gold Shops
at Sonya Maruti Chowk, Budhwar Peth are famous for traditional Maharashtrian ornaments. Other famous jewellers include Ranka Jewellers (Kothrud & Laxmi Road), Waman Hari Pethe (F.C. Road) and Ashtekar Jewellers (Laxmi Road).

Foreign Brands
Popular foreign brands such as Benetton, Levis, Nike, Adidas and Reebok are available at malls and stand alone stores across the city.

Jewellery

P.N. Gadgil
One of the largest jewellery stores in the city, stocking traditional and modern designs in gold, silver, diamonds and semi-precious stones, in addition to gift items in silver.
PNG House, Laxmi Road, Pune 411030
Tel: 24435001
Branches at Paud Road: 25464726, Camp: 26052424, Chinchwad: 27443444

Sudhan
For authentic silver jewellery and a wide range of precious and semi-precious stones. Wonderland, M.G. Road,
Pune 411001
Tel: 26133378

Para Amor
Designer jewellery boutique with an exquisite collection of contemporary and traditional Indian styles.
5 Sohrab Hall,
Sassoon Road,
Pune 411001Tel: 2605969

Footwear

Shoe World
A large shoe shop with a wide range of footwear for men and women. The company develops its own style and designs.
Next to PMT Stand, J.M. Road, Deccan,
Pune 411005
Tel:26348891

Stout Footwear
One of the oldest dealers of traditional *kolhapuri chappals* and *mojris.*
349, Centre Street,
Pune 411001 Tel: 26340189

Several national brands like Metro, Regal, Shoebox have stores on M.G. Road and other prominent shopping areas.

Children

Butterfly
This 1,500 sq ft shop is exclusively for children up to the age of 14 years. Stocks clothes, accessories, toys, games, prams, cribs, chairs and other baby stuff.
689, Narayanpeth,
Bajirao Road,
Pune 411030 Tel: 24458343

Bonsai
Exclusively for children, it stocks the gamut from clothes and toys to candy and accessories.
ITI Road, Next to Ozone, Aundh,
Pune 411007
Tel: 25896647

Toy World
This store has it all from board games to prams, and Barbie dolls to Nintendos.
60, M.G. Road,
Pune 411001
Tel: 26342022

Kheliya
Well stocked with puzzles, games, slides, prams and tricycles.
42 Krishnaprasad Society, Rambaug Colony, Near Bedekar Mandir, Paud Road,
Pune 411038
Tel: 25459003
Branch at Narayan Peth
Tel: 24450547

World of Toys
A one-stop shop for toys ranging from board games, electronic games, CDs, posters, puzzles, books and stationery.
2417/A, Exhibition Road, East Street,
Pune 411001
Tel: 26341534

Interiors

Sanskriti Arts
Check out this store for some unusual curios sourced from different villages around India - wooden seed sprinklers, spice boxes, candle stands, frames, brass idols, lamps, vases, side tables, coffee tables, and paintings.

Sapphire Apartments,
EP No 347, Near Pizza Hut,
Koregaon Park,
Pune 411001 Tel: 26139933

Just Antiques
Specializes in antique-finish furniture and objets d'art.
Ganga Commerce, Lane No 5, Hoganas Compound, North Main Road, Koregaon Park,
Pune 411001
Tel: 9890032531 / 9370146186

Contemporary Arts and Crafts
A branch of the popular high-end Mumbai store, it stocks lovely artifacts and gift items.
Sohrab Hall, Sassoon Road,
Pune 411001 Tel: 26051177

Om to Home and More
Started by Bollywood star Rati Agnihotri, this signature store has a designer clothesline and accessories for the home.
Virwani Plaza, East Street,
Pune 411001 Tel: 26332038

Books

Crossword
This large and well-appointed bookstore also stocks music, movies, and stationery. It has branches across the city and small outlets in multiplexes and superstores.
Sohrab Hall, 1st Floor, Junction of RBM - Connaught Road, Behind Pune Railway Station,
Pune 411001 Tel: 26059600
Branches at
J.M. Road Tel: 25537005,
Aundh Tel: 24028013 and
Senapati Bapat Road.

Manneys
This is one of the oldest and most popular bookshops in the city, and stores a wide range of books.
Clover Centre,
Dr. Ambedkar Road, Camp,
Pune 411001 Tel: 26131683

Popular Book Store
Well known in the Deccan Gymkhana area, it also stocks a range of toys and other items.
Popular Book Store, Next to Garware Bridge, F. C. Road,
Pune 411004 Tel: 25671737

Parking

Malls and large stores normally have their own parking arrangements, although valet service is not common. At other places, you will have to park on the road. Pay and park services are available on some major roads. Vehicles, if wrongly parked, will be towed away.

Stationery

Venus Traders
A plush and extremely well stocked stationery super store, first of its kind in the city.
1226/1, Off F. C. Road, Near Roopali Hotel, Pune 411004
Tel: 25535757
Branch: Nucleus Mall,
Opp. Pune GPO,
Pune 411001

Music

Planet M
An affiliate of the *Times of India* newspaper, Planet M has a wide range of music and accessories, and has small outlets at malls and superstores.
Above Dorabjee's Departmental Store,
Dr. Ambedkar Road, Camp,
Pune 411001 Tel: 26141707
Branch at Pune Central Bund Garden Road.

Music World
Music lovers will find some great bargains here in addition to a vast repertoire of new releases.
Nucleus Mall,
Opp GPO, Camp,
Pune 411001
Tel: 26140467

Alurkar Music House
One of the oldest family-run music shops in the city, it stocks a good range of Indian classical music. Tickets for the Sawai Gandharva festival are available here.
4 Swapna Nagri,
Karve Road,
Pune 411004 Tel: 25440662

Sports

Champion Sports
Spread over two floors, this popular store stocks the best brands in sports equipment and gear.
759/52 Deccan Gymkhana,
F. C. Road,
Pune 411004
Tel: 25674534

Sports & More
A good one-stop shop for sports and accessories.
C-1, Chinar Building,
Floriana Estate, Kalyani Nagar, Pune 411006
Tel: 27036577

Natekar Sports
Run by former Davis Cupper, Gaurav Natekar, the store stocks top of the line sports goods and accessories.
Chaitraban Residency, Sarja Restaurant Lane,
Aundh, Pune 411007
Tel: 25885556

Assorted Shopping

Hong Kong Lane
This narrow, congested lane is extremely popular with collegians on the look out for junk jewellery, trendy belts and rings, shoes, bags, garments, and even bestsellers – all available at discounted rates.
Opp. Deccan Bus Stand, J.M. Road.
Pune 411004

Juna Bazaar
Held every Sunday and Wednesday from 9 am to 3 pm, this is Pune's famous flea market. You'll get everything here, from old silk saris, Lee Cooper jeans, Hitkari crockery, and door hinges to antiques, ancient coins, and tools. It offers the best bargains in town and is frequented by foreigners, students and shoppers looking for great deals.
Vir Santaji Ghorpade Road, near Maldhaka Chowk.

Tulsibaug
This is a fascinating market comprising narrow lanes packed with stalls and small road-side vendors that sell everything from jewellery and hair accessories to clothes, household utensils and souvenirs.
Next to Bank of Maharashtra,
Janamangal Branch,
Bajirao Road.

Dorabjee's
One of Pune's oldest and finest departmental stores, it stocks everything from fresh veggies, to cereals, food grains, a range of household products, imported cheese, and cold cuts. There is a well-stocked cafeteria and wine shop on the premises.
1-B Dr. Ambedkar Road,
Pune 411001 Tel: 26052882

Famous Food Shops

Royal Bakery
Possibly the oldest bakery in town, their bread, biscuits and cakes are renowned throughout the city and outside it. Try their famous wine biscuits.
200, M. G. Road, Camp,
Pune 411001
Tel: 26345251

Kayani Bakery
The Shrewsbury biscuits from this celebrated bakery are much sought after by visitors to the city. They also

Pune's Best Buys

- Puneri Sari
- Osho Chappals
- Nose Ring *(natha)*
- *Parkar-polka* (traditional skirt-blouse)
- Shrewsbury biscuits and *Bakarwadi*

374 Bhawani Peth, Opp Bhawani Mata Temple Pune 411042 Tel: 26454561

Malls

There are nearly two dozen superstores, malls, and hypermarkets in Pune, and several more in the pipeline. The total retail area in Pune is expected to touch nearly 4,000,000 sq. ft. by end-2007

stock a range of cakes and melt-in-the-mouth biscuits.
East Street, Pune 411001
Tel: 26360517

Chitale Bandhu
The crisp *bakarwadis* from Chitale Bandhu disappear off the shelves with amazing speed, and are on the visitor's must-buy list. They also are famous for their wide range of sweets.
777 Sadashiv Peth, Opp Bank of Maharshtra, Near Vishrambaug Wada, off Bajirao Road,
Pune 411030.
Tel: 24473208
Branch at: Deccan Gymkhana

Laxminarayan Chiwda
Now available across the globe, this spicy rice flake mixture is typically Puneri and makes a good gift for friends back home.

Malls and Supermarkets

Pune Central
256, Koncord Towers,
Boat Club Road,
Bund Garden.
Pune 411001
Tel: 56099000

Pyramid
1978 Convent Street,
Camp, Pune 411001
Tel: 1600-1199-11
(Toll Free No)

Nucleus
1, Church Road, Opp Police Commissioner's
Office,
Pune - 411001
Tel: 26120790

Mariplex
Survey No 15, Wadgaon Sheri,
Kalyani Nagar,
Pune 411014
Tel: 56092698 / 99

KK Bazaar
Wing B, K K Bolsar market
Pune Satara Road,
Dhankawadi,
Pune 411043
Tel: 66500444 /
9371003457
Branch at Sachapir Street.

Big Bazaar
Fun and Shop Bldg.
Solapur Road, Himalaya House Area
Fatima Nagar, Pune 411040.
Tel: 66420500 / 5608 / 3025

Spencer's Daily
Survey No 161/2/2
D. P. Road
Aundh, Pune 411007
Tel: 25880938
Branches: Kothrud,
Bhandarkar Rd,
Paud Rd, Wanowrie.

TruMart
Abhijeet Court
Bhandarkar Road
Pune 411004
Tel: 25659627
Branches can be found accross the city.

Entertainment

Art and Culture

Pune is the cultural hub of the region and has a strong foundation of music, dance, theatre and literature. It is home to several well-known artistes and patrons throng the various festivals and concerts held at venues ranging from private homes to auditoria and historic monuments. Book readings and choir recitals are as popular as theatre festivals and dance performances, and the visitor to the city is bound to find some activity to interest him. Just check out the daily newspapers to find out what's on.

Theatre

Marathi theatre, which has its roots in the city, is the most reputed in India. Ranging from *natyasangeet* (musicals) to comedy and drama, the productions are professionally produced and feature actors and performers of high caliber. Some of the country's finest actors began their careers at the city's Theatre Academy, or have been discovered at the Purushottam Karandak, the popular inter-collegiate drama competition.

English theatre is in its infancy but amateur drama groups put up several productions during the year. Gujarati, especially Parsi, theatre also has many fans in Pune.

Plays are regularly staged at auditoria like Bal Gandharva Rang Mandir (built in memory of *natyasangeet* icon Bal Gandharva), Bharat Natya Mandir, Tilak Smarak Mandir, Nehru Memorial Hall, and Yashwant Rao Chavan auditorium.

Dance

Pune's artistic milieu draws exponents of various Indian dance forms such as Kathak, Bharatnatyam and Odissi. Danseuses such as Rohini Bhate, Prabha Marathe, Sucheta Bhide-Chaphekar and Yogini Gandhi conduct classes attended by students from across the country and abroad.

Music

Legendary Hindustani classical vocalist Pt. Bhimsen Joshi and sitar maestro Ustad Usman Khan are among the many talented musicians who live in Pune. Featuring prominently on the Indian classical music calendar of the country is the Sawai Gandharva festival, held in Pune every year in December. Apart from attracting performances by eminent artistes from all over the country, the festival is also a prestigious platform for upcoming singers and musicians.

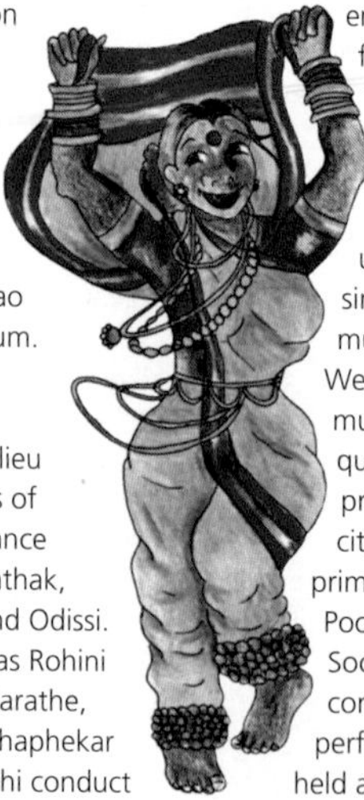

Western classical music also has a quiet but growing presence in the city promoted primarily by the Poona Music Society. Several concerts and solo performances are held at the Mazda Hall in Dastur School and the Gulati Hall at St. Vincent's School. The Pune Jazz Club is doing a commendable job of promoting jazz, and often organizes live shows at

A surprising number of well-known theatre personalities such as Dr. Shriram Lagoo, Dr. Jabbar Patel and Dr. Mohan Agashe are alumni of Pune's B.J. Medical College.

restaurants and other venues in the city. Outstanding examples of fusion music come out of the Osho International Meditation Resort, where the intermingling of cultures and nationalities lends itself to some creative wizardry. Several restaurants, such as Soul and Shisha Café at ABC Farms, feature bands playing New Age and alternative music, apart from other popular live acts. Music is also a passion with the youth of Pune, and several rock bands have originated in local garages and outhouses.

Art

Pune is not a major art market but it has produced some renowned painters such as Subhash Awchat and Sujata Bajaj. In recent years a number of art galleries have opened their doors to connoisseurs and are doing their bit to promote upcoming artists and sculptors. Art shows and related activities are held at Balgandharva Rang Mandir, Sudarshan Art Gallery, Art2Day, Vaishwik Art Environment and Indiaart. Small galleries have also sprung up in some banks, restaurants, multiplexes and at the airport.

Auditoria

Bal Gandharva
Next to Sambhaji Park,
J. M. Road, Pune 411005
Tel: 25532959

Bharat Natya Mandir
Sadashiv Peth,
Pune 411030 Tel: 24471614

Nehru Memorial Hall
Dr. Ambedkar Road,
Pune 411001
Tel: 26128560 / 8558

Tilak Smarak Mandir
Tilak Road, Pune 411030.
Tel: 24339920 / 24334004

Yashwant Rao Chavan Auditorium
Karve Road, Karve Putla
Thorat Udyan,
Pune 411038 Tel: 25395232

Sawai Gandharva Auditorium
Opp. Police Grounds,
University Road,
Shivajinagar, Pune 411005
Tel: 25535570

Music Societies

Poona Music Society
C/o Atur India Foundation
Atur Chambers
6th Floor 2/A
Dr. Ambedkar Road,
Pune 411001
Contact Benifer Battiwala
Tel: 26131713 / 12
www.punemusicsociety.com

Pune Jazz Club
Meetings held every third Sunday of the month from 11 am-1 pm at Max Mueller Bhavan,
Boat Club Road,
Pune 411001
Tel: 26131340

Concert Halls

Mazda Hall
Dastur School Campus
2 Lt. Col Tarapore Road,
Opp Ladies Club,
Pune 411001
Tel: 26362634

Gulati Hall
St Vincent's School Campus
Pune 411001
Tel: 26352135

Restaurants with live Bands

Shisha Café
ABC Farms,
Mundhwa Road,
Koregaon Park,
Pune 411001
Tel: 56202674

Soul
ABC Farms,
Mundhwa Road,
Koregaon Park,
Pune 411001
Tel: 56206997

Art Galleries

Balgandharva Art Gallery
Next to Sambhaji Park,
J. M. Road,
Pune 411005 Tel: 25532959

Sudarshan Art Gallery
421/422,
Shaniwar Peth,
Pune 411030
Tel: 24490188

Art 2 Day
Tilak Road,
Hirabaug, Shukrawar Peth,
Pune 411002 Tel: 24452706

Vaishwik Art Environment
Survey No 246,
House No 1982
Saket Society, D P Road,
Aundh Pune 411007
Tel: 27298182

Indiaart
Kala Chhaya Campus
Opp Vikhe Patil School,
Patrakar Nagar,
Senapati Bapat Road,
Pune 411016
Tel: 25662854

Films

Pune has played a central role in the growth and development of Indian cinema. From the legendary contribution of Prabhat Studios to the world-class grooming of future filmmakers at the Film and Television Institute of India, the city has been at the vanguard of film production in India. Pune also hosts two international film festivals attended by a large number of film buffs: the Asian Film Festival, and the Pune International Film Festival held in January every year.

Film and Television Institute of India (FTII)
FTII is a landmark of Pune. One of the most eminent film schools in Asia, it conducts courses in all disciplines of the film industry including editing, music, screenplay and cinematography. Its halls and auditoriums have been the training ground for some of the country's most accomplished actors, directors and technicians. FTII was formed in 1962, after the historic Prabhat Films Studio pulled down its shutters. The huge 'Wisdom' tree near the auditorium has witnessed passionate debates and discussions on films and filmmakers and symbolically reflects the growth of FTII.
FTII, Law College Road,
Pune 411004
Tel: 25431817/25433016/

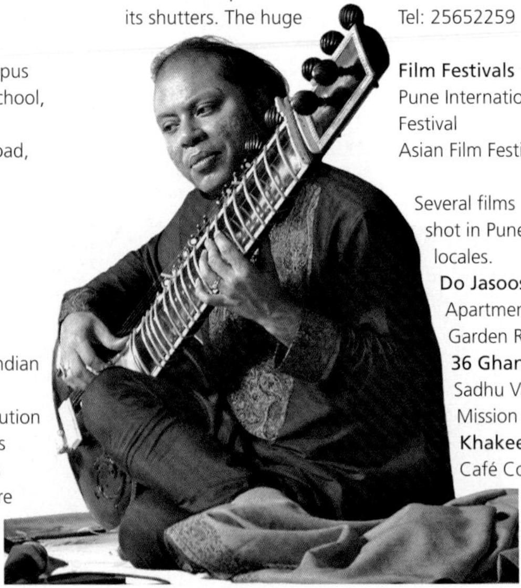

National Film Archives of India (NFAI)
Films get made, are seen and most often, forgotten. Not at the NFAI. Situated across the road from the FTII, the NFAI has the prime responsibility of preserving the cinematic heritage of India and other countries as well. Its vaults are a treasure house of more than 16,000 classics bought from across the world. For researchers and film fanatics, its library is like a pilgrimage to the land of information and knowledge. The NFAI also plays an active role in the dissemination of film culture through film appreciation courses and film festivals.
NFAI, Law College Road,
Pune 411004
Tel: 25652259

Film Festivals In Pune
Pune International Film Festival
Asian Film Festival

Several films have been shot in Pune at these locales.
Do Jasoos: Five Star Apartments on Bund Garden Road
36 Ghante: Near Sadhu Vaswani Mission
Khakee: Outside Café Coffee Day on East Street
Munnabhai MBBS: Agriculture College at Shivajinagar
Majorsaab: National Defence Academy
The Legend of Bhagat Singh: Fergusson College and Edward Library on East Street

Marathi Cinema

Pune has always been the fountainhead of Marathi cinema - from the days of filmmakers like S. Fatehlal, V. Damle, V. Shantaram, S. Kulkarni, and Baburao Pai who made renowned films like *Amrit Manthan, Manoos,* and *Sant Tukaram;* to contemporary legends like Amol Palekar, Jabbar Patel, Sumitra Bhave and Sunil Sukhtankar who have made award winning films like *Anaahat, Doghi, Vaastupurush,* and *Devrai.* Marathi cinema found global recognition when Sandeep Sawant's *Shwaas* received an Oscar nomination in 2004

Pune's Multiplexes

Inox
Bund Garden Road,
Opp. Council Hall,
Pune 411001 Tel: 26111010

E-square
132 University Road,
Pune 411016 Tel: 56044141

Gold Adlabs
Survey No 15,
Wadgaon Sheri,
Kalyani Nagar,
Pune 411014
Tel: 56096464 / 565

City Pride
Satara Road,
Pune 411009
Tel: 24212355 / 24213291

City Pride
Karve Road, Erandwane,
Pune 411038
Tel: 25458875 / 76

Fame Jai Ganesh
Off Pune – Mumbai
Highway, Akurdi,
Pune 411035 Tel: 27442744

Heritage Tours

A city with millennia of history behind it, Pune is dotted with ancient and beautiful heritage buildings be they houses, temples or libraries. Built across a large span of time, each of these structures is a reflection of the society, culture, technology and style prevalent at the time of its construction.

INTACH Pune has created a set of maps that show specific routes on which one can see these heritage buildings that are part of Pune's cityscape. These maps are available at Warsaa the heritage store at the Shaniwarwada.

Central Pune
It is suggested that you walk your way through these tours, as the distances are short and it is difficult to drive through the narrow lanes in this area. The places mentioned are all very famous and anyone you ask will be able to give you directions and guide you to the monuments.

Exploring Shaniwar and Kasba Peth
Excluding the time you spend at each site the suggested walk through this area will take you about 45 minutes.
You can start the tour at Shaniwarwada which is a very important monument of the city and also has parking facilities. The next stop is the Amruteshwar Mandir followed by Nana Wada, and then the temple of Kasba Ganpati, who is the presiding deity of the city. Mazumdar Wada comes next; followed by a walk through Tambat Ali, the precinct of the age old, yet renowned copper craft.

Shukrawar Peth
The walking time for this tour is approximately 35 minutes.
Begin at the Mahatma Jyotiba Phule Mandai, the main vegetable market in Pune around which you will find ample parking space. Move on to the Burud Ali, where you can see bamboo craftsmen at work. The next stop on the route is the Rameshwar Mandir followed by Tulsibaug where one can see quaint bronze curios on sale. Vishrambaug Wada, comes next followed by the Nagar Vachan Mandir and Belbaug Mandir.

Cantonment
This area was created by the British and is thus dominated by western styles of architecture. This area is

vast and spread out, parking is available at most of the sites and you can drive your way through these tours.

Upper Cantonment

The travelling time for this tour would be about 15 minutes.
St. Paul's Church is the first stop on this tour followed by the General Post Office which was built in the Palladian architecture style. The next site is the Peshwe Daftar or the Pune Archives which houses more than four crore original documents, some dating back to the 16th century. The Council Hall situated opposite the Peshwe Daftar followed by the Ohel David Synagagoe are the other monuments on this route.

Lower Cantonment

Driving time on this tour is approximately 40 minutes. You begin at the Shivaji Market Precinct situated at the heart of Cantonment and move further in to explore the actual Shivaji Market complex and the St. Xaviers church situated opposite each other. Next you visit Main Street, (M.G. Road) an important street for shoppers dotted with quaint buildings from a different era. You can then take a leisurely drive through East Street, Kahun Road, Napier Road, Right Flank Road and Prince of Wales Drive, which will help you get a fairly good picture of Colonial Pune.

INTACH Pune

The Indian National Trust for Art and Cultural Heritage (INTACH) was founded

in 1984 in New Delhi due to the urgent need for documentation and preservation of India's vast heritage. The organization works through its various local chapters such as the Pune Chapter (1986) made up entirely of local residents. Over the years the Pune Chapter has been working to document, preserve, promote and develop awareness of the city's considerable Built, Cultural and Natural Heritage.
For Pune's Built Heritage INTACH has been bringing out publications highlighting the City's heritage structures dating from Shivaji's times to the British Period, and helping in their restoration. It has brought to light unheralded monuments dating back to 1000 BC in the PCMC area and has with Deccan College pushed back the age of the city to 200 BC through findings of an archaeological excavation under Kasba Peth.

Pune is rich in art, craft and cultural heritage. Recognising this, Pune chapter has been trying to document and promote activities such as the Tambat, (copper-bronze metalwork) tradition by helping the craftsmen design new products, improve efficiency, and market their wares.
In 2004 'Warsaa – The Heritage Shop' was opened jointly with the PMC to sell local handicrafts in the premises of Shaniwarwada.
For the third thrust area Natural Heritage, the Chapter has joined hands with many other NGOs, and the PMC and PCMC to develop a cheap and effective method for treating water pollution. It has also been active through its members in dealing with issues such as air pollution, garbage and preserving bio-diversity.

Adventure Activities

The hills, valleys and rivers surrounding Pune provide ideal opportunities for adrenalin-pumping adventure sports like paragliding, horse riding, rafting and rappelling.

Paragliding

The Hadapsar Flying Club, located in an eastern suburb of the city, conducts paragliding courses for beginners. You can also drive 50 kms out of the city to Kamshet where professionals will familiarize you with the equipment and ground handling, and guide your first solo flight.

Organizations that conduct paragliding classes:

Hadapsar Flying Club
Near Gadital Bridge,
Saswad Road,
Hadapsar, Pune 4110 28
Tel: 26992048 / 26991012

Wings and Flights
Tupe Nagar, Malwadi,
Near Sadhana High School,
Hadapsar, Pune 411028
Tel: 9371033226 /
9822023790

Temple Pilots
C25, Kamdhenu Ridhhi,
Mahatma Society,
Kothrud,
Pune 411038
Location: Kamshet
Tel: 9823384654 /
9822433052
Approx. charges: Rs. 8500 for the beginner's course. (3 days)

Nirvana Adventures
2A, Takshila Appts,
Tagore Rd, Santacruz,
Mumbai 400054
Tel: 9323708809
Branch: Kamshet
Approx. charges: Rs 1500 for 10-15 min tandem flights (a pilot flying with a passenger).

Rafting/Canoeing/Kayaking

The best place to engage in these exhilarating water sports is at the Kundalika River near Pune.

Wild Country Learning
Flat No 101
Lords Manor,
49 Sahaney
Sujan Park
Lulla Nagar
Kondhwa,
Pune 411040.
Tel: 9890190406 /
9422506288
Location: Kundalika River,
Approx. charges: Rs. 1,500 for one session (1 day)

Mercury Himalayan Explorations
Mercury Travels Limited,
C-3, 1st Floor, Shardaram Park,
37 Sassoon Road,
Pune 411001
Tel: 24030712 / 26131349

Windsurfing

The Khadakvasla Lake, about 20 kms southwest of Pune on the Pune-Sinhghad Road, is the ideal location for windsurfing.

Pune District Sailing Association
5 Parisar, 109/1-2 Thorat Colony, Opp old Karnataka High School, Off Prabhat Road
Pune 411004
Tel: 9371036316
Conducts sailing at

Paragliding Paradise

Kamshet is one of the most popular destinations for paragliding in Maharashtra. Situated at an altitude of 670m. on the Pune-Mumbai route, it can be reached by road. Local trains from Pune to Lonavala also halt at Kamshet.

Kundalika River

Located about 100 kms west of Pune, this scenic river flows through thick forests below the Mulshi and Bhira dams.

Khadakwasla Lake on weekends
Khadakwasla Lake lies about 20 km south-west of Pune on the Pune-Sinhghad Road

Panshet Water Sports
The Maharashtra Tourism Development Centre (MTDC) conducts various water sport activities in the picturesque area between the Panshet and Varasgaon dams,

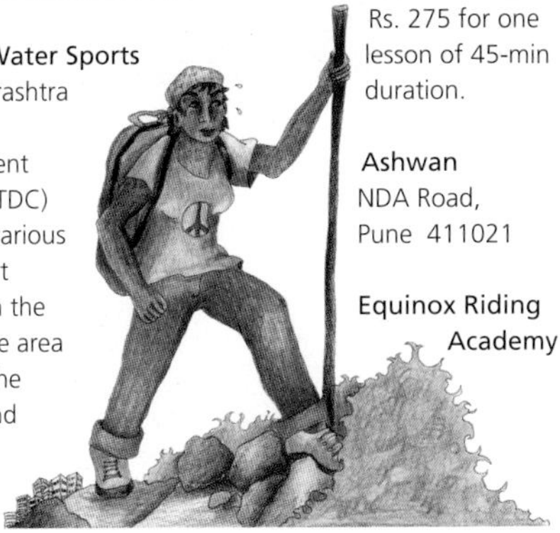

approximately 40 kms southwest of Pune. Visitors to the aqua sports centre have the option of trying out speedboats, water scooters, kayaks, and windsurfing.

Horse Riding

Pune's strong links with the Army makes horse riding a prominent sport in the city. Several private riding schools regularly conduct classes and camps for different levels of expertise.

Japalouppe Equestrian Centre
Somatne Phata,
Talegaon Dabhade
Tel: 9890920183 / 9823258952
Approx Charges: Rs. 275 for one lesson of 45-min duration.

Ashwan
NDA Road,
Pune 411021

Equinox Riding Academy
Shantai Farms,
Survey No. 274,
Wakad-Aundh Main Road,
Pune 411057
Tel: 9850825047

Rappelling

Steeped in history, the many forts around Pune are also popular rappelling sites. Several trekking organizations conduct rappelling training at these points.

Yuvashakti
388 Narayan Peth,
Pune 411030.
Timings:
10 am-12noon
& 6-8 pm
Tel: 24456696
Approx Charges:
Rs. 100
for one training session.

Wild Country Learning
Flat No 101 Lords Manor,
49, Sahaney Sujan Park,
Lulla Nagar Kondhwa,
Pune 411040
Tel: 9422506288

Enduro

An extremely popular adventure race held in February every year. Participating teams have to trek and cycle across the Sahyadri ranges, cross rivers, build rafts and engage in archery contests, before touching the finishing line. Organized by the National Education Foundation, Enduro attracts over 50 teams and a large number of spectators.
Tel: 48359/9823044181
Website: www.enduro3com

Picnic Spots

There are loads of exciting places around Pune worth exploring. Puneites miss no opportunity to get their share of fun, thrill and adventure at these breathtaking locales. Areas around the city offer several opportunities for nature trails, trekking, bird watching and other outdoor activities.

Trekking

Favourite trekking destinations include temples and the over 200 forts around Pune. Most of the popular forts can be accessed from the old Mumbai-Pune highway. State Transport (ST) buses or local trains will take you to the nearest village or railhead. While some treks are easy, others can be formidable. In the rains the climb can get slippery and muddy, and solo treks are not recommended.
Best Season: June to September and November to February

Forts		Distance in Kms
Sinhagad	–	25
Rajmachi	–	56
Tikona	–	62
Korigad	–	75
Shivneri	–	92
Raigad	–	155
Harishchandragad	–	191
Pratapgad	–	140
Lohagad	–	52
Visapur	–	52
Rajgad	–	85
Sudhagad	–	123
Purandar	–	32
Torana	–	50

Popular Forts

Sinhagad
Located at a height of 1,400m this is one of the most popular and accessible forts around Pune city. Legend has it that Maratha king Shivaji's general Tanaji Malsure scaled the steepest side of the cliff with the help of ropes and a giant monitor lizard. He successfully recaptured the fort but lost his life.
A grieving Shivaji lamented, *"Gad aala pan sinh gela"*

- the fort *(gad)* is won but the lion *(sinh)* is gone.
How to get there : Buses ply from Swargate bus stand to the base of Sinhagad. By car you take the Khadakwasla-Donje road; after crossing Donje village, turn towards the road leading to Golewadi Marg.

Harishchandragad
This fort provides for a fantastic, though challenging climb particularly during the monsoons when it is misty and wet, and breathtakingly verdant. In summers, Harishchandragad is dry, barren and burnt.
How to get there : On the Pune-Nashik road turn off at Aale Phata-the road leads to Aurkuni, at the base of Harishchandragad.

Korigad
At a height of 930m, Korigad overlooks the picturesque Amby Valley, the famous Sahara Housing Project. Atop this fort is the Korlaidevi temple and a lake that fills up during the monsoons, making it an ideal location to take a refreshing dip.
How to get there: Drive down to Amby Valley in Lonavala. The trek

to Korigad begins at Ambavane village.

Tikona

One of the smaller forts conquered by Shivaji, Tikona is flanked by Lohagad to the north, the Pavana Lake to the west and Korigad to the southwest. It isn't a very tough trek and once on top, the breeze and panoramic view make it worth the climb.

How to get there: From Pune you take the Paud Road towards Lonavala. On the way is Tikona Peth, the base of Tikona.

Shivneri

This is the fort where Shivaji was born. The entire Sahyadri range can be viewed from the fort. The serene Shiv-kunj temple and metal sculptures are the other attractions here.

How to get there : Located on the Pune-Nashik Road. Head towards Junnar on the Pune-Nashik highway. On crossing Junnar village, take the dirt track to the Shivneri fort, which can be seen in the distance.

Rajmachi

A very popular getaway during the monsoons, it is surrounded by deep valleys on three sides and a lush green forest on the other. It offers an adventure packed trek including a stream crossing and steep climbing. People also trek to the nearby Sanjeevani and Shrivardhan forts.

How to get there: Take the local train to Lonavala. Once there head back towards Tungarli village. Alternatively take the Lonavala exit off the Pune-Mumbai expressway. Just before you enter the town the road turns off towards Tungarli village. Cars must be parked here in the village.

Pratapgad

A winding road leads up to Pratapgad from Mahabaleshwar. The fort is famous for its statue of Shivaji and the Bhavani Mata temple, which draws many devotees during the Navratri festival. While the lush Konkan stretches in one direction, the hill station of Mahabaleshwar lies in the other.

How to get there: Located on the Pune-Satara road, Pratapgad is 20 kms from the hill station of Mahabaleshwar.

Raigad

Located at a height of 915m, it is a tough climb to the fort, but visitors can avail of the ropeway that takes one directly to the top. Also known as Durgadeshwar, the fort has great historic significance. Shivaji's coronation took place here and the great king also breathed his last here.

How to get there : Take the Bhor-Varandha ghat towards Mahad. The road from Mahad leading towards Panvel also breaks off to head towards Raigad.

Duke's Nose

When you travel along the Pune-Mumbai Expressway, you'll see a distinctively shaped rock just before Lonavala, known as Duke's Nose. So named because it resembled the nose of the Duke of Wellington, it is a very popular trekking destination. You can trek up one evening, camp overnight and enjoy a picture postcard sunrise next morning.

How to get there: Take a local train to Lonavala and

walk along the railway track towards Khandala. Turn right at the temple near the station. Or drive down to Khandala and park at the railway station. The trek begins here.

Trekking Organizations

Pugmarks Holidays
595, Deccan Gymkhana, Nandadeep Building, Behind Sai Petrol Pump,
Pune 411004 Tel: 56014112 / 56014113
www.pugmarksholidays.com

Yuvashakti
388 Narayan Peth,
Pune 411030
Tel: 24456696
Timings:10 am-12 & 6-8 pm

Foliage
203, Maharkar Chambers, Karve Road Kothrud,
Pune 411038
Tel: 56032406

Zhep
20/60 Vijaya Nagar Colony, Sadashiv Peth, Behind S.P. College, Pune 411030.
Tel: 24335723

Nature Walks
A-10, Ashok Kiran Society, Ashok Path Lane, Off Law College Road
Pune 411004
Tel: 25465648

Caves

Karla Caves
Built in the 2nd century BC, the main attraction of these Buddhist caves is the massive *chaitya* or prayer hall that is 45 m long, 15 m wide and 16 m high. The 37 delicately carved pillars leading up to the monastery look stunning. A steep 350-step climb (183m) leads to the caves. Also take in the Bhaja and Bedsa caves nearby where some fine looking stupas from the Satavahana period have been unearthed.
How to get there: Located 40 km from Pune on the Pune-Mumbai road. Take a State Transport bus or hire a private taxi up to the Karla caves.

Beaches

While Pune is land bound, several secluded and serene beaches are located just a few hours away.

Diveagar
Clean and not yet commercialized, the beach is located in the picturesque Konkan. Surrounded by rustic homes and coconut plantations it makes a lovely idyll for someone seeking a silent holiday. A gold Ganapati idol was unearthed in the area. Distance from Pune: 65 km
How to get there: ST buses ply from Swargate to Diveagar. If you intend to drive down, go through Tamhini *ghat* and carry on to Mhasala via Mandgaon and take the diversion to Diveagar.

Shrivardhan
This coastal village with wide stretches of pristine beach provides a tranquil getaway. There are several rock formations in Shrivardhan worth seeing. Or you could just go beach hopping to the nearby and equally beautiful Harihareshwar 5 km away. Distance from Pune: 170 kms
How to get there: You would have to drive down via Tamhini, Mandgaon and Mhasala and take the diversion to Shrivardhan.

Alibaug
A popular beach resort, Alibaug is located midway between Mumbai and Pune. A number of shacks and restaurants along the beach cater to the needs of foreigners and locals alike. Surrounded by mango orchards, Alibaug is good destination during the hot mango season. Distance from Pune: 150 km

How to get there: Take the Khopoli exit off the Pune-Mumbai Expressway and head towards Pen. From there take the Mumbai-Goa highway and exit at Wadkhal. Alibaug is 30 km from Wadkhal.

Other Places of Interest

Tamhini

The small forest of Tamhini is paradise for nature lovers. Tamhini is widely considered a 'sacred grove'. The villagers believe that the forest has a life and is sacred and must be worshipped. Little streams flow between the roots and rocks spread throughout the forest and the entire picture reflects the symbiotic relationship of nature.

Distance from Pune: 40 kms

How to get there: There are buses from Swargate to Tamhini village from where you can take a jeep up to the Vanzai temple. By car drive down towards the Mulshi dam, where the road diverts to the right towards Tamhini.

Bhimashankar

A prominent religious destination, the Bhimashanakar temple houses one of the five *jyotirlingas* in Maharashtra. It is also popular with trekkers and naturalists. The Shekharu, a giant squirrel (almost the size of a tomcat) dwells in the coppices of the Bhimashakar forest, which is now protected as a national park. Local guides conduct nature walks through the forest and evening trails are especially popular. Trekkers begin their journey at Karjat village, from where it is a rigorous four-hour climb though streams and thickets of the jungle.

Distance from Pune: 120 kms

How to get there : Buses ply from Shivajinagar to Bhimashankar. Alternatively, drive down towards Nashik and turn off the highway at Manchar to head towards Bhimashankar. Trekkers can take a train to Karjat and then a bus to Khandas from where the trek starts.

Thoseghar Waterfalls

Thoseghar is famous for its high waterfalls. The sound of water gushing down into the deep valley below, the aroma of *kanda-bhajji* (onion fritters) and hot *elaichi* (cardamom) tea makes this destination an ideal picnic spot especially during monsoons.

Distance from Pune: 137 km

How to get there : Located on the Pune-Satara Road. Drive down to Satara (113 km) from where you head towards the base of Sajjangad. Thoseghar waterfalls are 13 km from here.

Nature Trails

A sprawling retreat set in lush green farmland and equipped with tree houses, rocky trails, a natural pool, and an impressive menagerie. Regular children's camps are conducted here during the summer vacation. The farm is also open for day-trips on Sundays after prior booking. For a lazy afternoon and farm fresh food call 9822966111

Distance from Pune: 20 kms

How to get there : Catch a bus from Pune Station up to Murunji, and take a six-seater to Nature Trails, which is well marked by signboards. If driving, head past Hinjewadi and turn

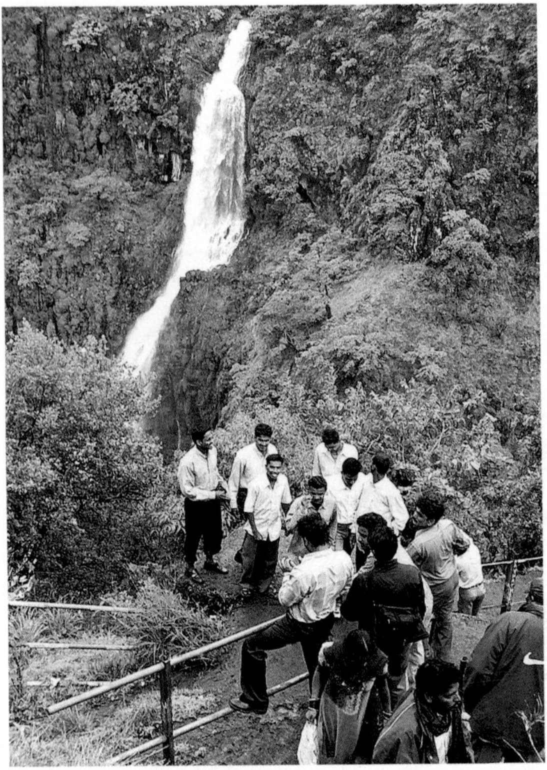

right to Marunji village. At the village turn right on to a dirt track that leads to Nature Trails – just follow the signboards.

Japalouppe Equestrian Centre
Located at Talegaon, not too far away from Pune, the Japalouppe Equestrian Centre is primarily a riding school. It also makes a great getaway during winters and early or late monsoons. A totally rustic experience, with limited hot water, no air conditioners and tents to camp in, Japalouppe makes an out-of-the-book setting for painters, poets, philosophers and animal lovers. Call 9823258952 for bookings.
Distance from Pune: 35 kms
How to get there : Catch local train from Pune Station/ Shivajinagar to Begdewadi. Japalouppe is a 15 min walk from this station. If driving, take the Pune-Mumbai highway, and look out for the Japalouppe Signboard once you near Talegaon.

Hill Stations

Mahabaleshwar
This is one of the most beautiful hill stations of Maharashtra. It is extremely popular with families, honeymooners and youngsters. Even though it has fallen prey to commercialization, it still provides a cool, comforting escape from hectic schedules.
Distance from Pune: 120 km
How to get there : Located on the Pune - Satara Road. Buses ply from Shivajinagar and Pune Station to Mahabaleswar everyday.

Matheran
Situated on a hilltop at an altitude of 800 m, this is the country's only eco-sensitive hill station. Cars are not allowed into Matheran beyond a certain point, and visitors have to walk, take a hand-drawn rickshaw or depend on horses for conveyance. Matheran offers stunning views but may be too crowded in the summer and winter for a really pleasant stay.
Distance from Pune: 150 km
How to get there: Take the Khopoli exit off the Pune-Mumbai expressway and continue on the old Pune-Mumbai highway. Turn right at Chowk towards Karjat. At Karjat Phata turn left to Neral. Matheran is about 21 km from Neral.

Lonavala-Khandala
These twin hill resorts are famous for their scenic beauty and pleasant climate. Located between Mumbai and Pune, at a distance of 5 km from each other, they are popular weekend retreats.
How to get there: Take the local train to Lonavala from Pune. Or drive up along the Pune-Mumbai expressway.

Children's Special

Pune can be a fun place for children. With its beautiful gardens and parks, historic monuments and museums, nature trails and scenic picnic spots, there's plenty to keep a child amused and interested.

Museums

Joshi's Museum of Miniature Railways

A miniature fantasy world of trains, cars, people, parks, bridges, and swimming pools awaits the visitor at this popular museum. The 20-minute programme held every Saturday and Sunday is unique and will keep both children and adults riveted. Special shows can be organized for weekdays with prior booking. Check timings for Marathi and English commentary.
17/1 b/2 G A Kulkarni Road, Near Sangam Press, Kothrud, Pune 411038
Tel: 25435378

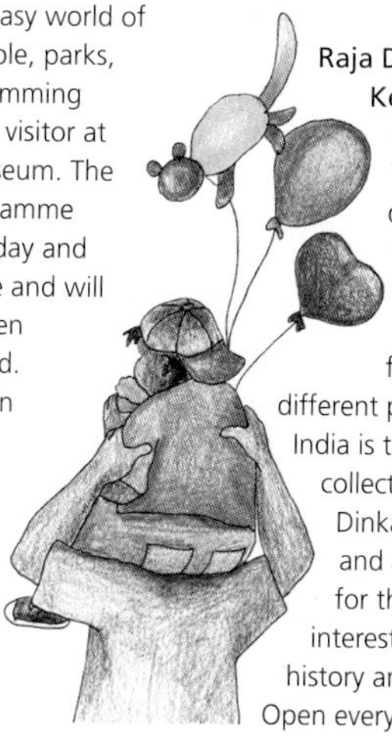

Tribal Cultural Museum

An intriguing journey into the life and times of tribals. On display are handcrafted items like combs, utensils, ornaments, and musical instruments in addition to life-size tribal market tableaux. The Museum is open every day from 10 am to 530 pm. Closed every second and fourth weekend of the month and on government holidays.
28 Queen's Garden Road, Pune 411001
Tel: 26362071

Raja Dinkar Kelkar Museum

This delightful treasure house of antiques from different parts of India is the personal collection of Raja Dinkar Kelkar, and a must-see for the visitor interested in history and culture. Open every day from 10 am to 5 pm. Closed on government holidays.
1378 Shukrawar Peth, Natu Baug, Raja Kelkar Museum Street, Pune 411002
Tel: 24482101

Historical Visits

Aga Khan Palace

The 'Father of the Nation' Mahatma Gandhi and his wife Kasturba were imprisoned here by the British during the 1942 Quit India Movement. The photographic display and Gandhiji's memorabilia throw light on an important slice of history. Open from 9 am to 545 pm.
Gandhi National Memorial, Nagar Road. Pune 411006
Tel: 26680250 /1834

Shaniwarwada

Synonymous with the city and symbolic of Pune, Shaniwarwada was the stronghold of the ruling Peshwas. Though not much is left to see, visitors can take a quick round of the palace, *nagarkhana* and garrisoned wall. Enthusiastic guides will narrate some interesting tales about life in Shaniwarwada during the heydays of the Peshwas.
Shaniwarwada, Kasba Peth, Pune 411036

Parks, Zoo and Aquarium

Jog Bird Park

Bird lovers will enjoy this exhaustive collection of native and other exotic birds like macaws, parakeets, cockatoos, vultures, eagles, etc. Open from 10 am to 1pm and 3 pm to 6 pm. You can't miss it, you'll hear the

birds a mile off!
Survey No 38/2, Bavdhan Khurd, Pune 411029

Konark Bird Park
A spacious aviary in scenic surroundings, it has a collection of over 100 exotic species of pheasants, macaws, parakeets, emus, cassowary and rhea. There is a small restaurant on the premises.
Pirangut Road, Near Chandni Chowk, Bavdhan, Pune 411044
Tel: 22951203
11 am-6 pm - Open all seven days

Osho Teerth Garden
An initiative of the Osho International Meditation Resort, this breathtaking garden features a rich variety of exotic flowers and plants. A haven of peace, it might not however be the right place for a rambunctious child!
Koregaon Park, Pune 411001 Tel: 66019999

Empress Garden
One of Pune's oldest gardens, it is a sprawling place dominated by stately trees. A popular venue for exhibitions, flower shows, and nature walks, it also has a special children's play area.
Empress Garden, Near Race Course, Camp, Pune 411001 Tel: 26361840 / 26331193

Rajiv Gandhi Zoological Park
Also known as the Katraj Zoo, this 168-acre space houses a Zoo, Snake Park, and Animal Rescue Centre. The Park was started by famous herpetologist and animal lover Neelimkumar Khaire, who holds a place in the Guinness Books of World Records for staying in an enclosure with poisonous snakes for 72 hours! Open from 10.30 am to 630 pm. Closed on Wednesday.
Opp Katraj Dairy, Pune Bangalore Highway, Pune 411043 Tel: 24370747

Aquarium
Part of the centrally located Sambhaji Park, this little aquarium has an impressive collection of fish on display.
Sambhaji Park, J. M. Road, Pune 411005 Tel: 25532514

Boating Park
Though part of a military campus, this scenic picnic spot is open to visitors seeking a boat ride, or just a place for children to run wild.
Campus of the SRP Group 2, near Army School of Physical Training (ASPT), Ramtekdi, Hadapsar, Pune 411028

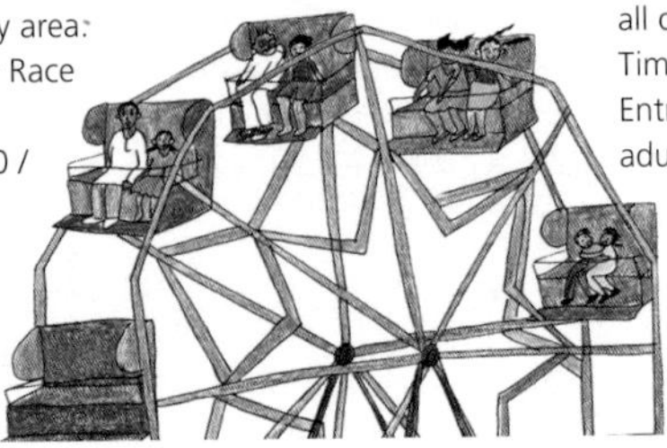

Some well-known parks

Sarasbaug
2170, Sadashiv Peth, Near Peshwe Park,
Pune 411030.
Tel: 24332388

Major Tathawade Udyan
Opp Tol Hospital, Karve Nagar, Pune 411052

Sambhaji Park
J. M. Road,
Pune 411005
Tel: 25532514 / 25338553

Kamla Nehru Park
Bhandarkar Road,
Pune 411004

P. L. Deshpande Park
Next to Parvati Water Works,
Sinhagad Road,
Pune 411030.

Peshwe Energy Park
The park offers an introduction to all forms of alternative sources of energy. Its brilliant display includes a ride in a toy train that operates on solar energy. The Park is open on all days except Wednesday.
Timings: 10 am-8 pm.
Entrance Fee: Rs. 3 for adults, Rs. 2 for children.
Add: Near Baburao Sanas Athletic Ground, Sarasbaug, Sadashiv Peth,
Pune 411030.
Tel: 24332388

Parvati Temple
A famous landmark, the Parvati temple situated on a hilltop is popular with children and adults. It involves a rigorous climb up 108 broad steps, but the view at the top is worth the effort. There is a small museum on the premises. The best time to climb up is early morning.
Parvati Hill, Pune 411030.

Amusement Parks

Diamond Water Park
Featuring several water rides, wave pools and dancing fountains, this is the ideal destination for those seeking to cool off in summer.
Formerly Splash Mountain: Water Park Road, Lohegaon, Pune 411047 Tel: 56300509

Angraaj Water Park
Modest in size, it offers a choice of water rides and pools that will delight children.
Kondhwa Budruk, Survey No 37, Kahdi Machine Chowk, Pune 411041
Tel: 26932921

Appu Ghar
One of the earliest amusement parks in the area, it is equipped with ferris wheels, merry-go-rounds, and speed rides. There are direct buses from Pune Station to Appu Ghar, located on the outskirts of the city.
Indira Gandhi Udyan, Pimpri Chinchwad Muncipal Corporation,
Sector 23, Nigdi,
Pune 411044
Tel: 27854040

Inter-University Centre for Astronomy and Astrophysics (IUCAA)
A visit to IUCAA at the University of Pune can be very rewarding, especially

for those with a scientific temperament. In-house scientists guide visitors in the use of the telescope and facilitate stargazing, especially on days when a meteor shower or eclipse is predicted. Famous toy-maker Arvind Gupta conducts regular workshops to encourage children to learn scientific principles through the medium of toys.
Campus of Pune University, Ganeshkhind Road,
Pune 411017
Tel: 25604602 / 103

Short Getaways

Sinhagad
The ancient Sinhagad fort atop a hill 25 kms from Pune is one of the most popular trekking destinations. Trekking up can be arduous however and is not recommended for small children.

Abhiruchi Village
Located 5 kms from Pune, Abhiruchi is designed like a Maharashtrian village and apart from authentic Maharashtrian food, features animal rides, mini-train rides, fruit orchards, farms, blacksmiths and potters. An entry fee of Rs. 100 for adults, and Rs. 50 for children is levied.
Bhide Baug, Sinhagad Road, Wadgaon-Budruk,
Pune 411046
Tel: 24392483

Manas Holiday Resorts
Located in picturesque surroundings, this family retreat is popular for its boating faculties and go-karting tracks.
Bhugaon, Taluka Mulshi, Paud Road,
Pune 410042
Tel: 9822657659 / 32933863

Sanskruti
This ethnic resort offers an attractive mix of art, craft, food and culture. Located 15 kms from Pune, it will appeal to children and adults. Open from 5.30 pm to 10.30 pm on weekdays; 10.30 am to 3.30 pm and 5.30 pm to 10.30 pm on Saturday and Sunday.
A cover charge of Rs.225 per adult and Rs.125 per child is levied.
Opp. Indian Oil Corporation, Solapur Highway,
Loni-Kalbhor, Hadapsar,
Pune 411201
Tel: 26915156/7/8

Pilgrim Centres

The areas around Pune abound with beautiful temples and places of religious significance worth visiting.

(Distance from Pune in kms)

Alandi	–	21
Dehu	–	24
Baneshwar	–	35
Narayanpur	–	35
Jejuri	–	38
Bhandara	–	40
Bhuleshwar	–	50
Wai	–	88
Shivthar Ghal	–	90
Sajjangad	–	123
Shri Ghorwadeshwar	–	124
Bhimashankar	–	125
Harihareshwar	–	130
Shirdi	–	183
Pandharpur	–	204

Alandi
Located on the banks of the Indrayani River, Alandi is famous for the *samadhi* and temple of saint-poet Dnyaneshwar. The town is especially crowded during the Hindu month of Ashad (June-July) when over two lakh pilgrims, especially from the *warkari* sect, walk almost 150 km (about 22 days) from Alandi to Pandharpur accompanying the sacred *palkhis* (palanquins).
Among other important sites at Alandi are the sacred wall of Dnyaneshwar and the Vitthal-Rakhumai temple.

Dehu
Located on the river Indrayani, this temple town is famous for the 17th century Marathi poet saint Sant Tukaram (1608-1650), who spent his life here. One can visit the Vithoba temple and listen to the *abhangas* (religious verses) of Sant Tukaram. Thousands of *warkaris* (devotees) converge at this holy town for Tukaram Beej (March 17), which marks the day Sant Tukaram died, and during the annual Wari before Ashadhi Ekadashi when Tukaram's *palkhi* is carried to Pandharpur.

Pandharpur
This is a prominent pilgrim centre, famous for its temple of Lord Vitthal. Thousands of devotees gather here in the festive Hindu month of Ashadhi Ekadashi (July-August).

Bhandara
Though Sant Tukuram's hometown was Dehu, he chose Bhandara as his spiritual haven and wrote many of his poems here. He was particularly drawn to the serenity of the Bhamchandra caves, a popular pilgrimage centre even today.

Shirdi
This is a very popular pilgrimage centre drawing devotees from all over the country and even from abroad. Every activity at Shirdi revolves around the vast temple complex dedicated to Sai Baba, one of Maharashtra's most revered saints. Devotees start queuing up from early morning for a *darshan*

of the life-size statue of Sai Baba. Other places of importance are the Gurusthan, the Kandoba Temple, and Shani and Narsimha Mandir.

Bhimashankar

A pilgrim paradise, Bhimashankar is known for its scenic splendor, thick forests and the beautifully carved temple of Lord Shiva that is part of the 12 *jyotirlingas* (most sacred Shiva temples) in India. On Mahashivratri day (end February), over a lakh devotees attend a special religious fair held here. Located close to the Shivneri fort, the place takes its name from the river Bhima that originates here, while Shankar is another name for Lord Shiva. The Bhimashankar Wildlife Sanctuary also attracts a number of visitors.

Harihareshwar

Popularly known as the Kashi of Southern India, the 16th century Shiva temple on the seashore houses idols of Brahma-Vishnu-Mahesh and Devi Parvati. Harihareshwar is also a popular beach resort.

Shivapur

Situated in this small town is the mausoleum of Kamar Ali Darvesh, a revered sufi saint who lived more than 500 years ago. Within the compound of this dargah is a stone weighing approximately 70 kgs. It is said that when exactly eleven men put their fingers under the stone and in unison say "Kamar Ali Darvesh", the rock rises and levitates for as long as his name is drawn out.

Sajjangad

This pilgrim centre is associated with Samarth Ramdas Swami, the spiritual guru of Chhatrapati Shivaji, who lived in Sajjangad and took *samadhi* here. The Sajjangad fort is located here and thousand of devotees attend the festivities on Das Navami day.

Shivthar Ghal

A small place, rarely mentioned on the list of 'places to see,' Shivthar Ghal is of special importance because this is where Samarth Ramdas Swami (Shivaji's guru) wrote *Dasbodh,* his famous spiritual guide. Shivthar Ghal also offers a picturesque view of the surrounding hills, waterfall and river.

Wai

Located in the Satara district on the banks of River Krishna, Wai is famous for its temples. There are seven *ghats* (mountain passes) in the region, each with one or more temples: Gangapuri, Madhi Ali, Ganapati Ali, Dharmapuri, Brahmanshahi, Ramdoh and Bhimkundan.

Baneshwar

Well known for the old but beautiful temple of Lord Shiva situated deep in the woods *(ban)*. The temple also has idols of Goddess Laxmi, Lord Vishnu and Lord Mahadeva. Also worth seeing are the five Shivlings located in a trench here. Baneshwar is a famous picnic spot with a lovely garden and waterfall.

Jejuri

The town is well-known for its Khandoba temple situated on a hill. Khandoba is the family deity of many Maharashtrians, especially the Dhangar tribe, one of the oldest in the state. Over 40,000 devotees assemble for the *jatra,* the annual fair, in November. The town of Jejuri was put on the international literary map when noted poet Arun Kolatkar wrote the book

Jejuri, which according to Salman Rushdie is "one of the great treasures of modern Indian literature".

Bhuleshwar
The Shiva temple on the hill holds special significance in Hindu mythology, because this is where Goddess Parvati danced for Lord Shiva before they were wed on Mount Kailash. Large crowds of devotees throng the temple during the Hindu month of Shravan and on Mahashivratri.

Narayanpur
The tree of Audumbar in Narayanpur, the village of Sant Changdev, is worshipped by many pilgrims. The old temple of Narayaneshwar comprises three sculptures dating from the Yadav era. The town is situated at the base of the Purandar fort.

Shri Ghorwadeshwar
This place is known for its temple and numerous caves. Archaeologists believe that these caves were built in the latter half of the 3rd century AD. Thousands of people from the neighboring villages collect here every Mahashivratri.

Ashtavinayaka

'Vinayaka' is another name for Lord Ganesha. Within a distance of 120 km from Pune lie eight idols or images of the Lord, which have been naturally formed by the forces of nature, and are collectively known as Ashtavinayaka. Every year thousands of devotees and tourists trace the route of the Ashtavinayakas, making Pune their base. State Transport buses ply to all eight locations.

Morgaon
Built in the 14th century, this temple of Mayureshwar lies on the Pune-Baramati road. One of the foremost temples of the Ashtavinayakas, the village in which it is located

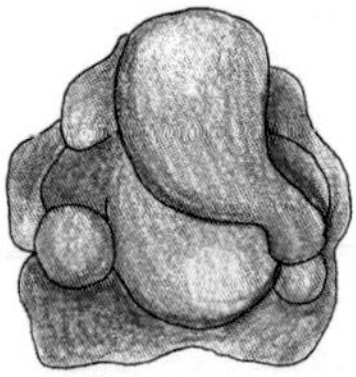

derives its name from the fact that it is shaped like a peacock; *mor* meaning peacock and *gaon* meaning village.
Distance: 56 km
How to get there: If driving, head past Hadapsar towards Loni, cross Yewat, Chauphula and Supa, before finally arriving at Morgaon.

Ranjangaon
The temple was built sometime between the ninth and tenth centuries. The idol is known as Mahaganapati/ Mahotkat because of its magnanimity, reflected in its ten trunks and twenty arms. Madhavrao Peshwa is said to have built a room in the basement of this temple to store the idol of the Lord.

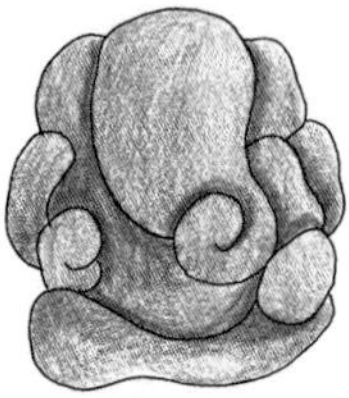

Distance: 50 km
How to get there: Take the Pune-Nagar highway and head to Shikrapur. Ranjangaon is 21 kms before Shirur.

Siddhatek
The idol here is identified as Siddhivinayak and the area near the temple was developed by queen Ahilya Bai Holkar.
Distance: 99 km on the Pune-Solapur highway.
How to get there: Located

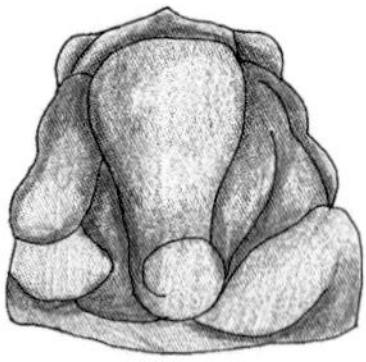

near Nagar district, it is accessible by bus or train.

Take the train to Daund or Boibel, and a bus to the temple from there.

Theur

With a wooden gathering hall dating back almost 400 years, this temple of Chintamani was built during the reign of the Peshwas.

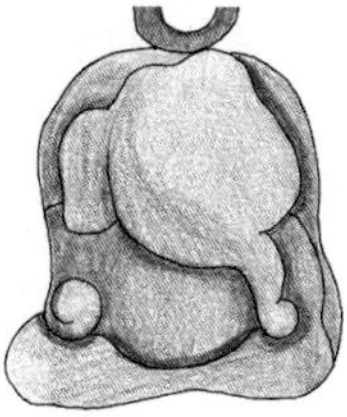

Distance: 25 km off Pune-Solapur Road

How to get there: The temple is situated near the naturopathy centre of Urli Kanchan, and can be easily accessed by State Transport buses.

Pali

Situated in the Raigad district, the bejeweled idol receives the first rays of the sun every day.

Distance: 111 kms.

How to get there: Head from Pune to Lonavala and then to Khopoli; Pali is the next village.

Mahad

Another temple situated in the Raigad district, this temple, known here as Vardavinayaka, was built in 1725 It is said that this idol

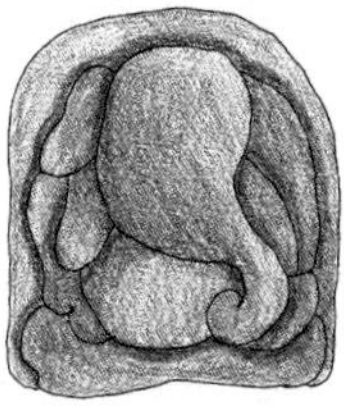

was found in a well behind the temple.

Distance: 84 km

How to get there: Off the Mumbai-Pune highway, break away at Lonavela from where you drive down towards Khopoli and then Mahad. The Konkan railway also passes the Mahad station.

Ozar

Located in the Junnar

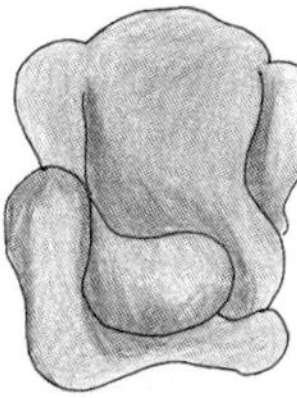

district, this is the temple of Vigneshwara, yet another name for Lord Ganesha. The gleaming diamond studded eyes of the Lord have become a big attraction here.

Distance: 85 km

How to get there: Ozar is near Narayangaon off the Pune-Nashik road.

Lenyadri

The 50 feet wide and 60 feet long hall of this Ashtavinayak temple has been naturally carved from a single rock and doesn't hold evidence of any pillars. Located on the banks of River Kukdi, one of the many stories about this

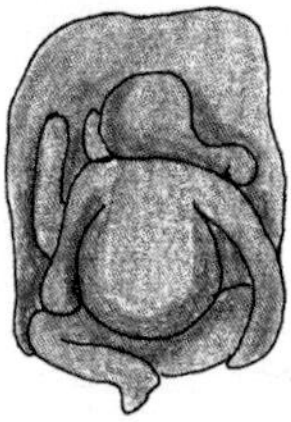

place says that goddess Parvati spent her time in penance at this temple and gave birth to lord Ganesha here.

Distance: 97 km

How to get there: Drive down the Pune-Nashik highway towards Chakan, then Rajgurunagar and Mancher. From there head towards Narayangaon via the Junnar road. Lenyadri is on the route from Narayangaon to Junnar.

Pune Essentials

When To Visit

A visit to Pune is enjoyable almost throughout the year.

Summers in Pune are hot. Most visitors keep away from the city from mid April to mid May, when the heat is at its worst. In May, day temperatures may soar to above 40° C. Streets are deserted in the afternoon – people prefer to stay indoors, or engage in short naps! The beginning of June brings in a flock of national and international students seeking college admissions.

The monsoons, spreading over four months from June to September, are a good time to visit Pune. The city gets moderate rain that transforms the landscape into vibrant shades of green. Monsoon treks to nearby forts and hills are popular at this time. The rains also herald the city's biggest and most-awaited festival, the Ganeshotsav, which takes place in late August or early September. Many visitors time their trips to the city so that they can witness the grandeur of the festival and religious fervor of the people.

In winter, from November to February, night temperatures dip to around 6° C but the days are nice and balmy. This is when the city is at its most vibrant. Several colourful exhibitions, celebrations and festivals are held, including the renowned Sawai Gandharva Festival of Indian classical music.

Tourist Offices

The Maharashtra Tourism Development Corporation (MTDC) is the only official government organization catering to the needs of tourists in Pune.

MTDC also has a counter at Pune Railway Station. Tel: 020-26689428

There are many places of interest around Pune for day trips, overnight stays and short holidays. MTDC has resorts and other accommodation at 27 destinations in Maharashtra. Contact the office for a list of relevant information.

MTDC accommodation is comfortable and clean and ranges from independent cottages and deluxe rooms to air-conditioned and non-air conditioned rooms. Room tariffs are reasonable - generally between Rs. 500 to 2,000

MTDC provides phone numbers of local tourist guides who will assist you on a guided tour of Pune city.

The Pune Municipal Transport conducts 'Pune Darshan' bus tours of the city throughout the day. To enquire about bus timings call 24440417, extension 257 (Moledina/Station Stand), and 255 (Deccan Gymkhana Stand). To hire a taxi for the tour call Pune Taximen Consumers Co-op Soc: 26121090 / 26145365

> Maharashtra Tourism Development Corporation (MTDC) 'I' Barrack (Block) Central Building, Zilla Parishad Office, Pune 410001 Tel: 26126867/26128169
> Log on to: www.mtdc.com
> Office Hours: 930 am to 500 pm

Listed below are some private tour and package holiday organizers:

Girikand Travels Pvt. Ltd.
759 / 90 B, Bhandarkar Institute Road,

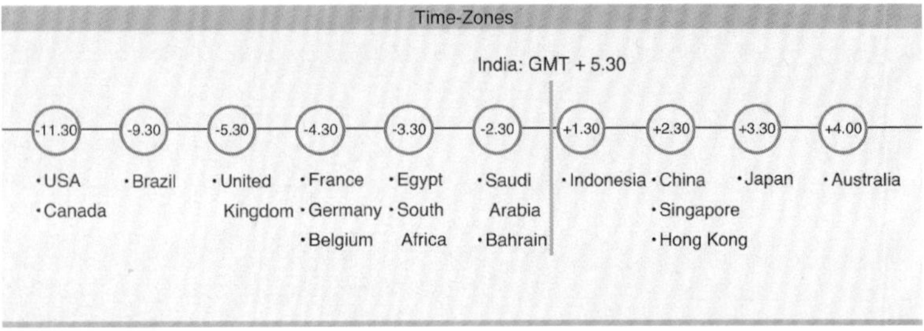

Deccan Gymkhana, Pune 411004
Tel: 2565 3570 / 2565 9970
www.girikand.com

Raj Travels
3rd floor, B-21 Mittal Court, Rasta Peth, Pune 411011
Tel: 26119043 / 53 / 26124877 / 37877
www.rajtravels.com

Prasanna Holidays and Tours Pvt. Ltd.
269 / 270, Devi Heights, Shaniwar Peth, Pune 411030 Tel: 24480228
www.prasannatours.com

Kesari Tours
Eden Hall, Near Deep Bungalow Chowk, Opp. Om Market, Shivajinagar, Pune 411016 Tel: 25661111
www.kesaritours.com

Getting Around Pune

Although Pune is a large city, there are many places of interest that are best enjoyed on foot, particularly sections of old Pune. The city's public transport (buses/trains) is not very efficient and can be difficult to use for one unaccustomed to the system. It is more convenient to use an auto-rickshaw to move around the city.

Planning Your Journey

If possible, avoid the rush hours from 830-10 am and 6-8 pm when you might get caught among commuters in traffic bottlenecks.

It is also advisable to check for local festivals and celebrations that are a regular feature of life in Pune. You might find yourself caught in a procession or very slow moving traffic.

Street Network

Prominent arterial roads include Ganeshkhind Road, Karve Road, Tilak Road, M. G. Road, Nagar Road, and Laxmi Road. A huge labyrinth of smaller lanes and by-lanes crisscrosses the city, apparently without any logic! If confused or lost, it is best to ask passersby for directions. By and large, people are helpful and will guide you correctly.

Road Discipline

Traffic in Pune can get unruly, but visitors are advised to follow common rules such as stopping at signals and zebra crossings, and overtaking from the right-hand side only.

One-way streets are common in the city and often there is a lack of appropriate signage to mark these places. If you are unfamiliar with a road, keep a watch on the direction of the traffic or ask people before venturing into it to avoid a fine.

If you need to park on the road follow the P1- P2 rule. Park on the P1 side of the road on odd dates and on the P2 side on even dates. If there are no indications or signboards, check with someone before you park your vehicle to avoid having it towed away.

Signboards

The names of areas and general directions are prominently displayed on overhead green boards near traffic lights and at regular intervals on arterial roads.

However locating street names on smaller roads in the interior may be difficult, and it would be easier and more convenient to ask someone for directions.

Walking

Not all roads in Pune have pavements and

you will find lots of people walking along the roads. Watch where you are going as roads here are not very pedestrian friendly.

On Saturday and Sunday evenings M.G. Road converts into a walking plaza, and is a fun place to visit.

Cycling

While bicycles are not as common in Pune as earlier, you will come across several cyclists on the roads. City environmentalists are trying to promote the use of cycles and a few Defence institutes like the Armed Forces Medical College have declared their campus cycle-only zones.

Auto-rickshaws

Pune boasts over 15 lakh auto-rickshaws, and they are often the most convenient mode of transport. There are authorized

auto-rickshaw stands across the city, and ideally you should hire the first rickshaw in the queue. In areas where there are no stands, just hail a passing rickshaw.

Fare is to be paid according to the meter reading, so ensure that the meter is pulled down when you step into a rickshaw. Since fares tend to change often, corresponding tariff cards are available with each rickshaw driver. Compare the meter reading to the tariff card before you pay the fare. The fare starts at Rs. 8 for the first kilometer. There is an easy way to calculate the tariff: (Meter Reading x 6) + Rs. 2 (However this is liable to change, so check the tariff card.)

If you are travelling after midnight or before 5 am an additional charge of 50% will be levied. Rickshaw drivers generally refer to this as 'half return'. A surcharge is levied for luggage exceeding 14 kilos. Prepaid auto-rickshaws are available at the Pune Railway Station and at the Airport. If you have a serious complaint against a rickshaw driver call 26120054 or report him to a nearby police station.

Six-Seaters

These are larger auto-rickshaws that can accommodate six or more passengers. Six-seaters are not allowed in many areas in the city and ply mainly on specific routes on the outskirts. They are convenient and cheap for short trips.

Hiring Vehicles

You can hire a private taxi with driver for sightseeing within Pune for approximately Rs. 800-1,000 per day. Rates vary according to the type of car and number of kilometers travelled. You can also hire these cars for outstation trips, however the charges may differ.

Two-wheelers are also available on hire for a deposit of Rs. 5,000-10,000, refunded as soon as the vehicle is returned. Rents range from between Rs. 50-80 per day.

Useful Numbers

Rent-a-Car

Pune – Mumbai Taxi Stand
Opp. Asiad Bus Stand,
Station Road,
Pune 411001 Tel: 26135784

Girikand Travels Pvt. Ltd.
759 / 90 B, Bhandarkar Institute Road,
Deccan Gymkhana, Pune 411004
Tel: 25653570 / 25659970

Hertz
B/5 Ground Floor 5th Avenue,
177/3, Dhole Patil Road,
Pune 411001 Tel: 66021818

Royal Cars
Shop No 16 Arihant Court,
481 Rasta Peth,
Behind Hotel Shantai, Pune 411011
Tel: 26127330 / 56231783

Auto Stand
Log on to http://www.punepolice.com/autostand.htm to locate an auto-rickshaw stand near you.

Visa and Passport

The Foreigners' Registration Office on Dr. Dadabhoy Naoroji Road, Mumbai handles visa extensions (maximum extension of six months).

Foreigner's Regional Registration Office (FRRO)
Annex Building,
Near Police Commissioner's Office,
Dr D. N. Road, Mumbai 400001
Phone: 022-22620446
Office Timings: 10 am-2 pm

Foreigners staying in Pune for prolonged periods should register at:

Foreigner's Registration Office
Police Commissioner's Office Premises,
2, Sadhu Vaswani Road,
Next to GPO, Camp,
Pune 411001
Tel: 26125396 / 26208371

The Regional Passport Office at Senapati Bapat Road issues new passports and renews existing passports.

The Passport Office
Sheti Mahamandal Building,
Opposite Symbiosis Institute,
Senapati Bapat Road,
Pune 411016
Tel: 25679962

Currency

The Indian units of currency are Rupees (Rs) and Paise (p).
100 Paise = One Rupee.
Coins commonly found in circulation are in denominations of 25p, 50p, Rs. 1, Rs. 2, and Rs. 5 Paper currency or notes in circulation are in denominations of Rs. 5, 10, 20, 50, 100, 500 and 1,000 The notes are fairly distinctive in varying colours and sizes that increase marginally with the denomination.

There is no limit on the amount of foreign currency or traveller's cheques that you can bring into India. Foreign exchange in cash up to US$5,000 or cash plus travelers cheques up to a value of US$10,000 can be brought into the country. Cash and traveller's cheques exceeding the above limits should be declared on arrival in India to Customs in the Currency Declaration Form (CDF).

Foreign Exchange Bureaus

Thomas Cook India Ltd
13 Thakkar House
2418, General Thimaya Road,
Camp, Pune 411001
Tel: 26330978

Chinchwad
Tel.: 27456733 / 27456734
Office Timings: Mon-Sat 930 am - 6 pm.
Sunday closed.

Centrum Forex Ltd
Office No. 108, Sohrab Hall,
Sassoon Road, Pune 411001
Tel: 26059402 / 3
Office Timings: 930 am - 6 pm.
Saturday till 200 pm. Sunday closed.

LKP Forex
4, Thakkar House, 2418, General Thimaya Road, Pune 411001 Tel: 26347041
Hinjewadi Branch: 22934871

Traveller's Cheques (TC)
Traveler's Checks can be changed at all Forex centres. They can also be directly used at most hotels and large stores. Restaurants generally do not accept TCs.

Credit Cards
Credit cards are generally accepted at stores and restaurants across the city. It is advisable however to enquire whether a particular card

Money Exchange

Money can be exchanged at all banks and most hotels in the city. There are also a number of money exchange centres and authorised Foreign Exchange (Forex) bureaus.

Most Forex dealers offer doorstep delivery of amounts of US$500 and above. However, you will need to give them your passport number and address.
1 Lakh = 100,000 1 Crore = 10,00,000

is accepted at an establishment before you make a purchase.

Automatic Teller Machines (ATMs)

ATMs of most major banks can be found in prominent residential and business areas like Camp, Deccan, Koregaon Park, Kothrud and Aundh.

ATMs of all MNC banks accept Visa and Mastercard. Instructions are in English, Hindi and Marathi. In case of any difficulty, seek the help of the attendant present.

Number of ATMs of Prominent Banks
UTI Bank: 57
ICICI Bank: 53
HDFC Bank: 40
SBI: 39
Bank of Maharashtra: 24

Communication Services

Telephones and Postal Service

The public sector company Bharat Sanchar Nigam Limited (BSNL) provides the largest network of telecommunication services in Pune. They have over 45 lakh wired landline connections in the city. Other wired landline service providers are Reliance Infocomm, Airtel and Tata Indicom.

Cellular Phones

For mobile phones Idea, Hutch, Airtel and BSNL offer GSM based network services, while Reliance and Tata Indicom offer CDMA connectivity.

Cellular phones are ubiquitous in Pune. Handsets and connections are easily available at company outlets and other big stores. Prepaid and recharge cards are available at small shops across the city. Handsets are also available on rent.

STDs/ISD Phone Centres

Private STD/ISD booths are scattered throughout the city.

New Cell Connection
Documents required: 1) Proof of identification 2) Proof of address. The minimum time required for the connection to be activated is 12 hours, though some dealers could organize it for you in less time.

They are bright yellow in colour and display the words 'STD/ISD' in bold black letters.

Most of them are open from 8 am to midnight, all seven days of the week.

International Calls

India's International Access Code – 00
India's Country Code – 91
Pune's Area Code – 20

To call a Pune landline from Mumbai or other neighboring areas in Maharashtra and Goa from a landline phone, you prefix the number with 9520

Internet Access

Cyber cafés are now found in every nook and corner of the city. Pune has one of the highest densities of cyber cafés in the country. Apart from Internet connectivity, they provide conveniences like printouts/tea/coffee for an extra charge. However, watch out for power cuts. In certain areas cyber cafés are shut on Thursdays.

Charges vary from Rs. 10 to Rs. 35 per hour depending on the quality of services and locality of the net café.

Timings: They are open from 8 am to midnight. A few are open 24 hours.

Fax

Fax or Facsimile services are available all over the city at public telephone booths or business centres. It costs approximately Rs.10 to send one page to any local number; for outstation and international faxes the rates vary according to prevailing STD and ISD rates.

Postal Services

The Postal Service in

India is run by the Indian government. Post Offices in India send and receive regular mail and parcels, offer Speed Post and Registered Post services, and also function as banks.

The minimum stamp value required on a letter or postcard is Rs. 5 If the weight of the letter or envelope exceeds 20 grams the required stamp value increases.

There is a post office in every locality in Pune. Collections from post boxes are made once or twice a day and taken to the GPO (General Post Office) where they are sorted and forwarded to their destinations.

Courier Services

Pune has a large network of courier service providers with branches across the city. Some of the prominent ones are listed below:

Courier Services:

Blue Dart
Nityanand Complex,
Shop No 9-13,
247/A, Bund Garden Road,
Pune 411001 Tel: 26120636

DHL Express (I) Pvt. Ltd
Atur House,
16 A, Dr. Ambedkar Road,
Pune 411001
Tel: 26341141 / 26137374

Desk To Desk Cargo (DTDC)
Shop No 1, Hidayatulla Complex,
Off Shankershet Road,
Bhavani Peth,
Pune 411037
Tel: 66034602 / 32501993

Aramex India Pvt. Ltd
G/5 Parmar Chambers,
Sadhu Vaswani Chowk,
Pune 411001
Tel.: 26125678 / 26114675 / 26114677
Tathawade Branch:
64100785

Toilets

Finding a public toilet in Pune can be quite difficult. In case of an emergency, try to use the restroom in the nearest hotel, restaurant, or mall, where you will find clean toilets. Most restrooms in such places feature both Indian squat type as well as Western style toilets.

While restrooms in high-end hotels are well equipped, you may not find toilet paper in restrooms belonging to small restaurants and stores. It is recommended that you equip yourself with some if you are going to wander around the city or go sightseeing.

Electricity

Electric current flows at 240 volts AC, 50 cycles per second.Wall sockets are of the two, three or five round pins variety. If your appliance plug has a different shape, you will need an adaptor. Power adaptors are available at all large stores.

Maharashtra state suffers from a severe power crisis and frequent power cuts are a common feature of life in Pune. While daily 'load shedding' has been suspended, power cuts may occur without warning. Thursday is reserved for maintenance and many areas, especially the industrial zones, may go without power on those days.

TV, Radio, Newspapers

Television

In Pune you can watch the free government run Doordarshan (DD) entertainment, sports, news and regional language channels. For a wider choice of channels, you can subscribe to cable television, which will give you access to Indian and international channels such as Star TV, Sony, Zee, BBC, Discovery, MTV, CNN, etc.

DTH or Direct to Home is also gaining popularity, wherein you buy your own dish and receiving unit and subscribe specifically to the channels you want to watch.

Most hotels subscribe to cable television.

Radio

India opened its airwaves to private radio broadcasters in the year 2000 At present you can access the following radio stations in Pune, though several more are expected soon:

Radio Mirchi

The leading private radio network in Pune, it provides daylong entertainment comprising popular Indi-pop and Hindi film music, and lively talk shows. Tune in to 939 FM.

Vividh Bharati

A popular government operated radio station, it broadcasts traditional and classical Hindi and Marathi music and songs.

Newspapers

Prominent city newspapers are published in Marathi or English but publications in other regional languages are also available. Newspapers are sold by roadside vendors or at kiosks at stations, bus stops and the airport.

English Dailies

The Times of India
The Indian Express
The Maharashtra Herald
The Economic Times

Marathi Dailies

Sakal, Kesari, Loksatta, Maharashtra Times Lokmat, Tarun Bharat, Sandhyananda, Punyanagri

Hindi Dailies

Aaj Ka Anand
Navbharat

A vast selection of other national English publications is available on the stands including newspapers like *Asian Age, Economic Times, Financial Express, Hindu Business Line* and *Business Standard;* weekly news magazines like *India Today, Outlook, The Week;* general interest magazines like *Society, Savvy, Femina, Cosmopolitan;* and niche magazines like *Car, Bike,* etc.

Measures and Weights

Metric measures and weights were uniformly introduced in transactions throughout the country by 1962

Conversion Table

Metric to Imperial

1 millimeter = 004 inch
1 centimeter = 04 inch
1 metre = 3 feet 3 inches
1 kilometer = 06 mile
1 gram = 004 ounce
1 kilogram = 22 pounds
1 liter = 18 pints

Imperial to Metric

1 inch = 254 centimeters
1 foot = 30 centimeters
1 mile = 16 kilometers
1 ounce = 28 grams
1 pound = 454 grams
1 pint = 06 liter
1 gallon = 46 liters

Laundry

If you are staying in a hotel, it is recommended that you use their laundry services to get your clothes cleaned and ironed. Small laundries and dry cleaning outlets are located in all prominent areas of the city. Some have branches across the city and offer home pick-up and delivery. Most localities have local *dhobis* or laundrymen who work in small stalls. They will collect your dirty clothes and linen, and deliver them back to you washed and ironed.

Rates: Depending on the service required, rates vary from as low as Rs.3 per garment to be ironed, up to Rs. 200 for dry cleaning.

Some laundries

Coins Drycleaners

829, Dastur Meher Road, Camp,
Pune 411001 Tel: 26055574

Several fortnightly and monthly neighbourhood newspapers are also available such as *The Puneite, Metroscan,* and *Street Guardian* among others. You can pick these up free at stores across the city. *Citadel* is a monthly city magazine that covers interesting aspects of Pune.

Dhulaai
Shop 1, Kanhiya Classic,
Narangi Baug Road, Dhole Patil Road,
Pune 411001
Tel: 26120444

Aundh Branch
E -7 Chaitraban Residency
Sarjaa Lane, Baner Road,
Pune 411007
Tel: 25885544

Kalyani Nagar Branch
102 Victorial Forteleza,
Next to Megamart, Kalyani Nagar,
Pune 411006 Tel: 32935444

Shree Nageshwara Laundry
Sane Dairy Chowk,
Bhandarkar Road,
Near Cosmos Bank,
Pune 411010 Tel: 25670835

Photography and Video

Listed below are the location and telephone numbers of some stores that provide photographic services such as developing and printing. Some also sell cameras and related equipment.

Fotofast Studio
Aurora Towers,
M.G. Road, Pune 411001
Tel: 26130727 / 26138227 / 26141587

Bund Garden Branch
Tel: 26129177,25810239
(Fotofast has a chain of outlets all over the city; call them and find one closest to you)

Camera Technic
Opp Abhinav High School
Kothrud, Pune 411038
Tel.: 56222305

Arihant Camera House
Near Krishna Hospital,
Paud Road, Pune 411038
Tel: 25467591

Jay Pee Videos
12/a, Surya Shree,
SBI Colony, Near Apsara Theatre ,
Market Yard,
Pune- 411037 Tel: 24260398

One Hour Photo
A/6, Vivekanand Park,
Ambedkar Rd,
Near Nehru Memorial Hall,
Pune 411001 Tel: 26120605

Ratanz Photo Studio
K 4, Opposite Poona Drug Store,
M. G. Road, Pune 411001
Tel: 26130808

Women Travellers

There was a time when single women travellers drew a lot of attention, especially foreigners. Though times have changed, it is better to stay on your guard. It is advisable to dress modestly in keeping with social norms. Be cautious when talking to strangers, crosscheck or verify information or look for an official source of information, and avoid lonely places after dark. Use your discretion when accepting invitations to dinners and late night outings.

Senior Citizens

While traditionally Pune is a safe city for senior citizens, it pays to be vigilant when travelling alone. Several senior citizens organisations exist in the city.
Association of Senior Citizens' Organisations of Pune (ASCOP): 24479709
All India Senior Citizens' Confederation: 25431648
Community Aid Sponsorship Programme: 24472069
Other Help Line Numbers: 26122880

Emergency Services

- Police Control Room: 26122880
- Police: 100
- Fire: 101
- Ambulance: 102

Useful Phrases and Questions

Phrases

English-Marathi

Yes **Ho**
No **Nahi**
Please **Krupaya**
Thank you **Aaabhar**
Sorry **Maaf kara**
Hello **Namaskar**
Goodbye **Aaccha**
How are you? ***Tumhi kashe aahat?***
I'm very well, thank you.
Me theek aa-he , dhanyawaad / Aabhar
Do you speak English?
Tumhi ingreji bolta ka?
I don't understand.
Mala samzhat naahi
Could you speak slowly, please?
Krupaya tumhi haloo bolu shakta ka?
Could you repeat that please?
Krupaya punha mhana
See you later
Nantar bhetu
What is your name?
Tumche naav kaay aahe?
My name is...
Majha naav ---- aahe
I don't know Marathi
Mala Marathi yet naahi

Questions

Who? ***Kon?***
What? ***Kaay?***
What is it? ***He kaay ahe?***
When? ***Kadhi / kevha?***
What time is it? ***Kiti wajle aahet?***
Where? ***Kuthe?***
Why? ***Ka?***
How? ***Kase?***
Where is this place?
Hee jaaga kuthe aahe?
Where is the railway station?
Station kuthe aahe?
Where is the tourist information office?
Paryatan vibhag kuthe aahe?
Where are the toilets?
Sandaas kuthe ahe?
Where can I find a city plan?
Shahracha nakasha kuthe milel?
Where can I change some money?
Paise kuthe badlu shakto?
I want to go (to) here
Mala ithe______ jaayacha aahe.
How far is this place?
Hi jaaga kitee door aahe?
How much?
Hyache kiti?
What are you doing?
Tumhi kaay kartay?
Is it allowed?
Hyala parvangi aahe ka?
I stay here
Me ithe rahato
To the left
Daavi kade
To the right
Uzvi kade
Straight
Saral
In front of
Samor/Pudhe
Behind
Maage
What is the time?
Kitee vazale?

Mealtimes

A meal ***Jevan***
Breakfast ***Naashta***
Have you eaten? ***Tumhi jevalat ka?***
Can I get some water, please?
Mala thoda paani milel ka?
Do you get vegetarian
non-vegetarian food here?
Ithe shakahari/maasaahari
jevan milte ka?
Vegetarian ***Shakahari***
Non – vegetarian ***Maasaahari***
Water ***Paani***
Tea ***Chaha***
Bread ***Pao***
Rice ***Bhaat***
Chapatti ***Poli***
Vegetables ***Bhaaji***
Fork ***Kata***
Spoon ***Chamacha***
Knife ***Suri***
Chicken ***Kombdee***
Fish ***Massa***
Milk ***Dudh***
Potato ***Batata***
Salad ***Koshimbir***

Emergency

Help me, please!
Krupaya mala madad kara!
I'm lost. ***Mee haravlo aahe***
Stop! ***Thamba!***

Days of the week

Day ***Divas***

Sunday **_Raviwar_**
Monday **_Somwar_**
Tuesday **_Mangalwar_**
Wednesday **_Budhwar_**
Thursday **_Guruwar_**
Friday **_Shukrawar_**
Saturday **_Shaniwar_**

Numbers

One **_Ek_**
Two **_Don_**
Three **_Teen_**
Four **_Chaar_**
Five **_Paach_**
six **_Sahaa_**
Seven **_Saat_**
Eight **_Aath_**
Nine **_Nau_**
Ten **_Dahaa_**
Hundread **_Shambhar_**
Thousand **_Hazaar_**
Ten Thousand **_Dahaa Hazaar_**
One Lac **_Laakh_**

Train Timings

Up Trains	Pune Arr.	Pune Dep.
Bangalore Mumbai Udyan Express 6530	1545	1550
Bhubaneshwar Mumbai Konark Express 1020	2345	2355
Chennai Dadar Express 2164	0215	0225
Howrah Pune Azad Hind Express 2130	0650	2125
Kanyakumari Mumbai Express 1082	0040	0050
Nizamuddin Vasco Goa Express 2780	1630	1640
Pune Ahmedabad Ahimsa Express 1096 (Wed, Fri)		1940
Pune Jammu Tawi Jhelum Express 1078	1435	
Down Trains	**Pune Arr.**	**Pune Dep.**
Ahmedabad Pune Ahimsa Express 1095 (Sun, Fri)	0445	1600
Dadar Chennai Express 2163	0110	0230
Mumbai Bangalore Udyan Express 6529	1140	1145
Mumbai Bhubaneshwar Konark Express 1019	1900	1910
Mumbai Kanyakumari Express 1081	1915	1925
Pune Howrah Azad Hind Express 2129		1825
Pune Jammu Tawi Jhelum Express 1077		1740
Vasco Nizamuddin Goa Express 2779	0405	0415
For Mumbai		
Deccan Express	Up 1008 1530	Down 1007 1110
Deccan Queen	Up 2124 0715	Down 2123 2025
Pragati Express	Up 2126 0750	Down 2125 2000
Indryani Express	Up 1022 1835	Down 1021 908
Incity Express	Up 2128 1755	Down 2127 1953
Sinhagad Express	Up 1010 0605	Down 1009 1840

Train timings are liable to change for current timings call 26136666

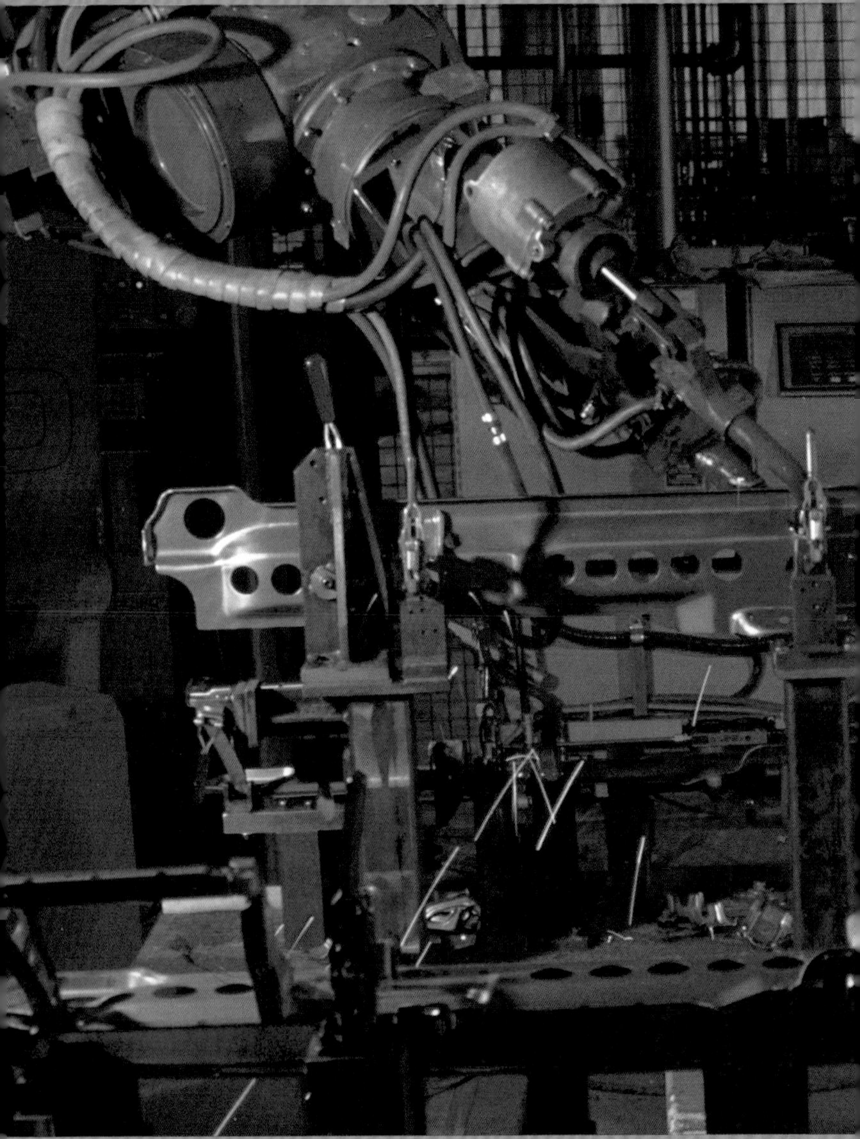

Business

- Introduction • Auto Industry • Information Technology
- Agro Industry • Biotechnology • Design • Industrial Hubs
- Setting Up Business in Pune • List of Business Associations

Introduction

From a town largely associated with culture and academics to one of the premier industrial centres of the country with a sizeable presence on the global map, Pune's commercial journey has been breathtaking.

Its historic tryst with industry started pre-Independence when the British set up factories to manufacture ammunition. In 1946 the Kirloskars, one of the city's leading industrial houses today, chose Pune to start their oil engine business. The prestigious Hindustan Antibiotics Limited, the first public sector pharmaceutical undertaking, was also established at the time.

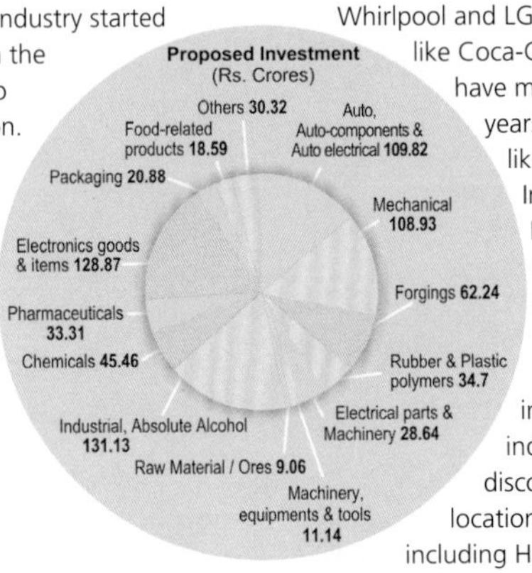

But what really changed the fortunes of the region was the formation in 1960 of a huge industrial estate at Pimpri Chinchwad near Pune by the government-backed Maharashtra Industrial Development Corporation (MIDC). The attractive business environment created by MIDC drew industry giants like the Tatas, Bajajs, Garwares and Firodias and a host of small and medium sized manufacturing and engineering units. The floodgates for rapid industrialization had been opened and huge stretches of farmland began to give way to clusters of enclosed factory campuses.

The sector that took the lead was the automobile industry. Pune developed as one of the largest automobile manufacturing centres in India, producing the entire spectrum of auto components, and was proudly billed the 'Detroit of India'. Another, more present-day industry that has catapulted the city into the global business arena is the information technology industry and its enabled services. The meteoric growth of this sector has made the city one of the most successful IT/BT centres in the country.

Strong Sectors·

- Automobiles and Auto Components·
- IT and ITES
- Biotechnology
- Agro and Food Processing
- Alcohol
- Industrial Design

In the 1990s, with globalisation becoming the new mantra, Pune began attracting its share of foreign capital especially in the information technology and engineering industries. While foreign companies like Whirlpool and LG and multinationals like Coca-Cola and Frito Lays have moved here in recent years, old establishments like Daimler Chrysler India Pvt. Ltd. and Honeywell Automation Ltd. have only got more entrenched.

The unabated rise in the number of new industrial units led to the discovery of other industrial locations around Pune city including Hadapsar, Jejuri, Mulshi, Talegaon, Ranjangaon and Hinjewadi. The vast network of educational and research institutions provided the perfect support for the growth of industries in the region.

Pune Ranks

- Seventh largest city in India
- Sixth largest metropolitan economy in India
- Highest per capita income in India

With the availability of a qualified workforce and amenable living conditions, Pune has been projected as one of the 'most suitable cities in India for doing business' and among the top 'emerging global cities' of the world.

Pune's past may be firmly rooted in culture and tradition, but industry has played a major role in propelling it into the future.

Auto Industry

The automobile industry of Pune is the flagship industry of the region and one of the largest in the country. Known as the 'Detroit of the East', the city rolls out the entire range of vehicles from rugged trucks, tractors, and three-wheeler autorickshaws to luxury passenger cars, snazzy scooters and motorbikes. It also manufactures the whole spectrum of auto components and caters to markets across the globe.

Graph indicative, not for reference
(Source: District Industries Centre, Pune)

Beginning in the 1960s, some of the world's leading auto and auto ancillary manufacturing companies have set up home in Pune. Many of them have pioneered new products and played a key role in the industrialization of the region. To Tata Motors Ltd., India's largest car manufacturer, goes the credit of manufacturing the Indica, India's first indigenously designed passenger car, many of which you will see cruising on Pune roads. Today, the Pune region accounts for more than 50% of the automobile production of India.

Major Players

- Bajaj Auto Ltd.
- Tata Motors Ltd.
- Force Motors Ltd.
- Kinetic Motor Ltd.
- Daimler Chrysler India Pvt. Ltd.
- Piaggio Vehicles
- L & T John Deere

Pune also has a very substantial presence of auto component manufacturers. Bharat Forge Ltd., for instance, is the second largest forging company in the world and India's largest exporter of auto components. Some of the other top names are Apollo Tyres, Toyota Kirloskar, Indo Schottle, Harita Grammar, Seco Tools, and Carraro. It is estimated that about 70% of the small scale and medium industries in Pune are directly dependent on the automotive sector.

Of the Rs. 800 crore invested by new players in the region between 2001 and 2005, over Rs. 400 crore was for the auto sector.

The region has developed as a key auto engineering design, product research and development centre and boasts prominent establishments like the Automotive Research Association of India, Central Institute of Road Transport, and the Vehicle Research and Development Establishment. A Rs. 68-crore Auto Cluster Development and Research Institute has been set up at Chinchwad by the Mahratta Chamber of Commerce, Industries and Agriculture (MCCIA) to enhance the global competitiveness of the auto industry in Pune.

With an excellent resource pool, technological lead, presence of major global players, and a massive consortium of small units, the auto industry in Pune is ready to zoom to the top both at home and overseas.

Information Technology

The information technology (IT) industry has made the largest contribution to the changing face of Pune, and not just through their swanky steel and glass office structures. The city is considered a leading IT destination and accounts for significant annual software exports. Over the past few years some of the world's largest names in the IT business have set up operations here.

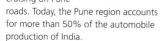

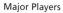

Pune's journey to becoming a leading hub for IT and allied services began in the mid 1990s, fuelled by the increasing need for software professionals in the United States of America and other world markets. The city boasts premier engineering and other educational institutions, which produced a quality, and affordable workforce, soon making it a favourite in the global IT arena.

Indian majors like Infosys, Wipro, Tata Consultancy Services, Cognizant, KPIT, Zensar Technologies, and Dishnet set up operations here and were soon joined by a stream of world giants such as IBM, Amdocs, TACO Vistion Engineering, MSC Software and Eaton Technologies.

The Maharashtra government also swung into action and began promoting the IT and IT-enabled services (ITES) sectors on a priority. It set up a Knowledge Corridor between Mumbai and Pune and the Rajiv Gandhi Infotech Park at Hinjewadi, one of the first and the largest software technology parks in the country. It also encouraged similar private initiatives.

The city has witnessing a three-digit growth in the registration of new IT firms for three successive years: 112 in 2005-06, 109 in 2004-05 and 107 in 2003-04. The enrolment of MNCs has more than doubled, with 28 software multinationals registered in 2005-06 as compared to 15 in the previous year. A large number of these companies specialize in the telecom and electronics segments.

- In 2005-06, the city registered an export turnover of Rs. 9,100 crore as against Mumbai's Rs. 7,300 crore.·
- The IT industry in Pune showed a growth of 48%, second only to Hyderabad. [Source: Software Technology Park of India (STPI)]

Top Exporters	Rs. in Crore
Infosys	1419
Tech Mahindra	832
Wipro	446
HSBC	385

The city is also experiencing a BPO-KPO boom. Both Business Process Outsourcing and Knowledge Process Outsourcing units are labour intensive and have created huge employment opportunities. In 2005-26 the total workforce employed by IT-BPO firms in Pune was over 1.5 lakh. Some of the leading names are WNS, Convergys, Phasis, EXL, Progeon, Spectramind, HSBC, Barclays and Aviva.

Eighty-three new government-approved private IT parks are coming up in Pune, the highest number among all major IT destinations in the country. [Source: STPI]

The IT-ITES sectors are concentrated in areas like Hinjewadi, Kalyani Nagar, Viman Nagar, Kharadi, Magarpatta and Aundh.

An increasing number of IT professionals are moving into the city drawn by its challenging work atmosphere and superior quality of life.

Agro Industry

Like the rest of Maharashtra state, Pune also has a significant agriculture and agro-business sector. Its central location has helped it become one of the main centres

for the agro industry, especially for food processing, floriculture, horticulture, poultry, wineries, milk and dairy products.

The food processing industry is at the forefront. The highly perishable nature of farm products has led to the emergence of hundreds of value-added industries. An estimated 2,000 primary, secondary and tertiary processing units operate in the area, making everything from pickles and pulps to sauces and squashes. Some of the leading players are Weikfield Products Co. (I) Pvt. Ltd, Gits Food Products Pvt. Ltd., and Pravin Masale.

Pune is also home to the Rs. 1,300-crore Venkateshwara Hatcheries Group, the largest fully integrated poultry group in Asia, and the country's biggest poultry exporter. Founder, late Dr. B. V. Rao, is credited with changing the face of the fledging and largely unorganised domestic

poultry industry by turning it into a highly professional dynamic industry. There are scores of small and medium sized players in the dairy and floriculture sectors. To promote the sector the government has set up a 200-hectare Floriculture Park at Talegaon, 40 km from Pune.

Foreign Players

The arrival of foreign majors gave the food industry a big shot in the arm. PepsiCo's snack food division, Frito-Lay set up a sprawling manufacturing plant at Ranjangaon. Cargill Foods, which entered with a joint venture, has today become one of the largest companies in the domestic edible oils industry. Tetra Pak, one of the world's leading food processing and packaging companies, commenced operations at Takwe near Pune in 1997 and is today the single-source supplier to all major dairy and fruit juice companies in India and 35 other countries.

Marketing Hub

Pune is also a key marketing centre for farm produce. It is surrounded by vast stretches of arable land and flourishing markets such as Mumbai, Nasik, Nagpur and Aurangabad. It also serves as a strategic conduit between northern and southern India, as yields from Hyderabad, Chennai and Bangalore all pass through Pune. The Maharashtra State Agricultural Marketing Board, an apex organisation that has done pioneering work in developing and coordinating agricultural marketing in the state, is also based in Pune.

Food Park

Pune has the distinction of setting up one of the first private food parks in India, the Chordia Food Park, spread over 100 acres in Shirwal.

Reputed Institutes

The growing potential of agro-business has led to the simultaneous growth of institutions offering related education. The College of Agriculture is one of the first five agriculture colleges established in India. Other leading institutes are Symbiosis Institute of International Business that offers a Master's Programme in Agri-Business Management, Dr. B.V. Rao Institute of Poultry Management and Technology, and Reserve Bank of India College of Agricultural Banking.

Biotechnology

Pune has become a significant centre for biotechnology because of its excellent intellectual infrastructure. The city's earliest brush with biotechnology was in 1954, with the establishment of Hindustan Antibiotics Ltd., the country's first penicillin factory, and then the largest producer of penicillin in Asia.

Since then pioneering work has been done, particularly in human health and pharmacy, by the large number of eminent establishments based in the city, among them Emcure Pharmaceuticals and Shreya Biotech. A 136-acre Biotech Park has been set up in Hinjewadi, and India's first Special Economic Zone (SEZ) for biotechnology at Hadapsar will see growing participation of private institutions and enterprises.

India's Top R & D Centres in Pune

- National Chemical Laboratory (NCL)
- National Centre for Cell Science (NCCS)
- Serum Institute of India
- Hindustan Antibiotics Ltd. (HAL)
- National Institute of Virology (NIV)
- National Aids Research Institute (NARI)
- Therapeutic Drug Monitoring Laboratory

Several other centres have given the biotech industry in Pune a major fillip with their path-breaking research and development. Among them are the Animal Diseases Investigations Laboratory, involved in the diagnosis and research of animal diseases and recognised as a reference laboratory by the Government of India; the Venkateshwara Hatcheries Group, the largest producer of poultry vaccines in India; the Bharatiya Agro Industries Foundation (BAIF) and the Vasant Dada Sugar Institute, both doing innovative work in bio-application for livestock and agriculture.

Reputed Institutes

Pune also offers an excellent opportunity for students looking for specialization in biotechnology and allied subjects. There are a number of reputed institutions like the Institute of Bioinformatics & Biotechnology (IBB), affiliated to the University of Pune; Agharkar Research Institute; Bharati Vidyapeeth's Rajiv Gandhi Institute of Information Technology and Biotechnology; and the Vidya Pratisthan's School of Biotechnology, Baramati.

> One of every two children immunized in the world is vaccinated by vaccine produced by Pune's Serum Institute of India. (Source: Serum Institute of India Ltd)

The government of Maharashtra is developing the Mumbai-Pune corridor for the biotechnology industry. With outstanding institutional support and a growing number of private players, the city is on the path to becoming one of the biotech captains of the country.

Design

Pune is rapidly developing as a prominent engineering design centre. The availability of technically qualified personnel and increasing global demand for design services has led to phenomenal growth of this sector.

Many leading companies are expanding their portfolio to include engineering design services required for mechanical, chemical and product development. An estimated 20,000 people are involved in the designing, engineering and related technology services business in the city today.

Pune is a nerve centre for automobile design and engineering. Companies like Tata Motors Ltd. have long had a tradition of research, with one of the largest R&D teams in the country working on new product development and technology upgrades. Tata Technologies provides engineering and design (E&D) services to global automotive and aerospace companies like GM, Ford, DaimlerChrysler, Toyota, Volkswagen and Honda. Tata AutoComp Systems (TACO) also has an extensive auto systems design and development base in Pune.

Cummins Research and Technology India Limited, an offshoot of power house Cummins India Ltd, is engaged in design and development work for engines, power generation sets and filtration systems. It is fitting thousands of buses in India and overseas with hybrid engines that burn liquefied-natural gas. Engineering technology company Neilsoft is providing niche services in Computer Aided Design (CAD) and Computer Aided Manufacturing (CAM). Other large companies that are developing design divisions are Bharat Forge Ltd., Atlas Copco, and Honeywell Automation India.

Foreign Players

A significant number of international names, particularly American, are zooming in on Pune to set up design centres. Emerson, a $15.6 billion US engineering and technology corporation, was the first multinational in Pune to open a design engineering centre in the city. Other American companies include Nvidia, world leaders in programmable graphics processor technologies; and Dana Inc., an auto design and engineering company. Korean behemoth LG has set up a global design centre at its Ranjangaon manufacturing complex.

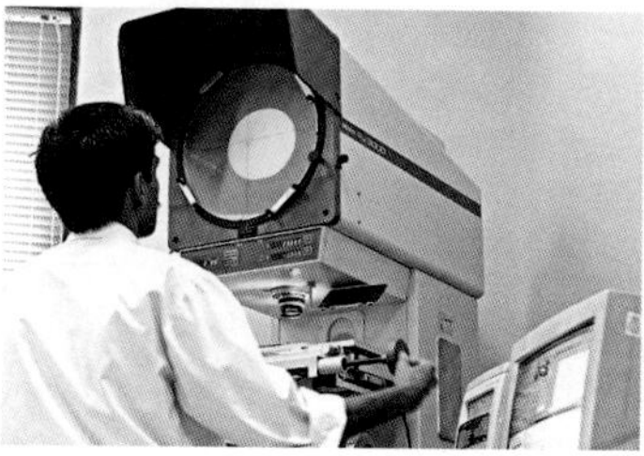

Reputed Institutes

Pune has a number of institutes providing quality education in engineering design, 3D Design and allied fields. Prominent among these is C-DAC's Advanced Computing Training School (ACTS), which offers a Diploma in VLSI Design (DVLSI) tailored to launch present and future electronic designers into the vast field of Electronic Design Automation (EDA). Symbiosis Institute of Design offers graduate programs in product design and engineering.

Industrial Hubs

When the first industrial belt was set up in Pimpri-Chinchwad in 1962, not many people were willing to lay a wager on Pune and its future prospects. However, today the city has grown beyond expectations to become one of the key industrial centres of the region. A cluster of large, flourishing industrial parks created with government and private initiatives now surrounds Pune.

Pimpri-Chinchwad

Developed by the Maharashtra Industrial Development Corporation (MIDC), this industrial belt is among the best known in India, and instrumental in putting Pune on the global industrial map. Spread over an area of over 1,200 hectares, it is now fully occupied with over 3,500 industrial units, a majority of them auto and manufacturing giants and ancillary industries.

Hinjewadi

Located near the Pune-Mumbai Expressway, this sprawling Infotech Park grabbed international attention with its futuristic concepts and state-of-the-art amenities. Spread over 590 acres, the first two phases of the Park were met with overwhelming response, drawing IT majors such as Wipro and Infosys, and dozens of BPO units. The development of Phase III and IV of the park are now underway. A Biotech Park in the same area is also being developed for the benefit of pharma and biotech companies.

Ranjangaon

Located 55 km from Pune, this area boasts the largest foreign direct investment for greenfield projects in the country, attracting an investment of a staggering Rs. 6,535 crore between 2003-2006. Companies that have set up operations here include LG Electronics India Pvt. Ltd., Swarovski India Pvt. Ltd, Whirlpool of India Ltd., Dow Corning (I) Pvt. Ltd., Pepsi's Frito Lay India, Bekaert Industries Pvt. Ltd., Anchor Daewoo Industries Ltd. and Panasonic India.

Chakan

About 30 km from Pune on the Pune-Nashik National Highway is the Chakan Industrial Park, home to auto bigwigs like Bajaj Auto Ltd., Badve Auto Components, Mahindra Automotive Steels, Minda Group, Keihin Fie, Lucas-TVS and Suprajit Engineering. An international airport is expected to come up at Chakan.

Important Hubs

Chakan - Auto
Hinjewadi - IT
Talegaon - Floriculture
Ranjangaon - White Goods
Daund - Chemical
Pimpri Chinchwad - Auto and Manufacturing

Talawade

The MIDC has recently established a 75-acre Software Technology Park at Talawade near the Pimpri Chinchwad industrial area.

Kharadi

Located on the eastern end of the city near the airport, the Kharadi Knowledge Park is spread over 30 acres and being developed as a residential-cum-commercial area.

Magarpatta

This first of its kind cyber city introduced the walk-to-work concept with homes and offices located in close proximity. Set up in Hadapsar, it is home to leading MNCs like Aviva, EDS, EXL, Sybase and Amdocs.

Talegaon

Located about 40 kms from Pune along the Mumbai-Pune Road this industrial/ floriculture park is set in scenic surroundings along the banks of the Indrayani River.

Daund

Declared a chemical zone, the Kurkumbh village and its neighboring areas in Daund taluka, about 70 kms southeast of Pune, are attracting several ethanol and industrial alcohol-producing units.

Setting Up Business in Pune

Doing business in Pune can be a rewarding proposition. The city has an impressive lineage of diverse entrepreneurship. Many ventures have grown to become national and international giants and have served as a beacon of inspiration to other start-up businesses in the region.

Setting up a business activity can be facilitated by organizations such as the Mahratta Chamber of Commerce, Industry and Agriculture (MCCIA) or the Confederation of Indian Industry (CII), Pune Regional Office. These organizations have exhaustive member-lists and profiles of their businesses and are the nodal agencies for business development in the region.

Steps necessary for setting up business in Pune depend on the kind of activity proposed. If you are planning to set up a manufacturing unit, the first step is identification and selection of product. Traditionally, the Pune business district has been the stronghold for manufacturing of auto, auto-components and auto electrical products. However industries like food processing and other agro-industries, electronic goods, pharmaceuticals, chemicals, and packaging also have a significant presence in the area.

Once the sector has been identified, some other key issues that need attention are ascertaining the status of the business (Proprietorship / Partnership / Pvt. Ltd. Company), conducting a market survey of the product, if necessary, and preparing a Project Report of the proposed activity, which is important while seeking bank finance.

According to an MCCIA study report, "When a medium or large scale unit proposing to manufacture an item that does not require compulsory licensing has to set up new operations, the unit can apply to the Secretariat of Industrial Assistance (SIA) by filing an Industrial Entrepreneur's Memorandum (IEM) application...Once the IEM application is filled with the necessary information and sent across to the SIA, provisional acknowledgement is issued to the unit. This IEM acknowledgement helps the unit to avail of finance schemes of various Financial Institutes, arrange for loans on land, raw material and other statutory clearances."

Between 2001 and 2005, 128 proposals were received from new players (medium and large scale industries) for setting up operations in Pune. Of these, 90% were from private limited companies. Nearly 5,000 SSI (small scale industry) units filed provisional SSI to set up operations in Pune. According to the IEM filing, Pune District attracted a total proposed investment of Rs. 773.09 crore from new medium and large scale manufacturing units in the same period.

After the fundamentals of the business have been established, one of the first requisites is to register the office with the Pune Municipal Corporation or the Pimpri Chinchwad Municipal Corporation under the Shops & Establishments Act. Thereafter, a plot, constructed shed, or rented premises, preferably in an industrial area, needs to be identified. New or second hand machinery needs to be purchased or hired.

Various crucial permissions need to be sought before setting up a unit:

- Maharashtra State Electricity Board (MSEB) office for power connection
- Income Tax authorities for the Permanent Account Number (PAN) & Tax Deduction Account Number (TAN)
- Central Excise Department for registration of Service Tax
- Superintendent of Sales Tax for registration under VAT
- Sales Tax Office for registration of Professional Tax for the unit and for the employees
- Regional Provident Fund Commissioner's office for Provident Fund Act Registration
- Directorate of Industrial Safety & Health for the Factories Act Registration.

Several government and other agencies provide assistance to small scale industries:

- Joint Directorate of Industries, District Industries Centre (DIC)
- Khadi and Village Industries Commission (KVIC)
- Maharashtra Small Scale Industries Development Corporation (MSSIDC)
- Maharashtra Industrial Development Corporation (MIDC)
- Western Maharashtra Development Corporation (WMDC)
- MITCON / Laghu Udyog Mitra Committee
- Maharashtra State Financial Corporation (MSFC)
- Small Industries Service Institute (SISI)
- Small Industries Development Bank of India (SIDBI)
- National Small Industries Corporation Ltd (NSIC)
- Maharashtra Pollution Control Board (MPCB)
- Chief Controller of Explosives
- Bureau of Indian Standards

In certain cases (for specific sectors, women entrepreneurs, Small and Medium Enterprises, etc.) subsidies are available from/through DIC, DC (SSI) Office, New Delhi or SIDBI. The Government of Maharashtra (under the Package Scheme of Incentives) also offers various benefits for industrial activities located in less developed areas of the region.

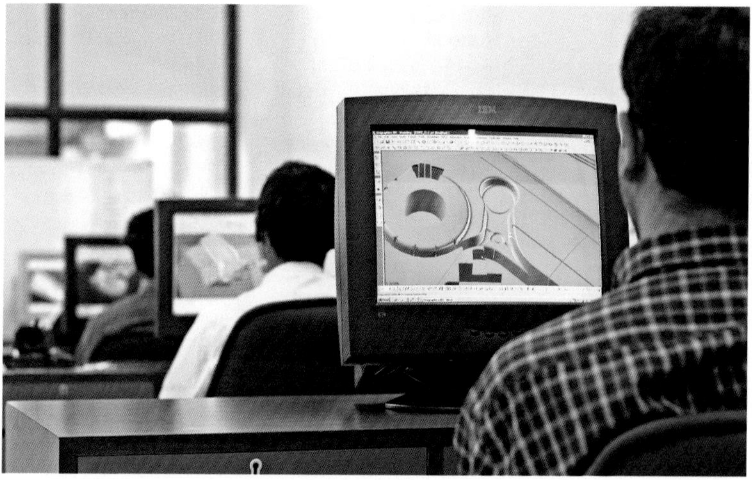

List of Some key business centres and associations in Pune

Mahratta Chamber of Commerce, Industries And Agriculture (MCCIA)
505 & 506, A & B Wing,
MCCIA Trade Tower,
International Convention Centre,
403-A, Senapati Bapat Marg,
Tel: 25709000
Email: info@mcciapune.com
Website: www.mcciapune.com

Confederation of Indian Industry (CII)
Bungalow 2,
Ganeshkhind Road,
Pune 411005
Tel: 25536159 / 25536159
Fax: 25536892
Email: ciipune@vsnl.com

Maharashtra Industrial Development Corporation (MIDC)
Jog Centre,
Bombay-Pune Road,
Wakdewadi, Pune 411005
Tel: 25813985 / 25819446
Fax: 25812975
Email: ropune@midcindia.org

Secretariat for Industrial Assistance (SIA)
Department of Industrial Development
Ministry of Industry,
Udyog Bhavan,
New Delhi 110001
Tel: 011-23011983
Fax: 011-23011770
Website: www.indmin.nic.in

Maharashtra Small Scale Industries Development Corporation (MSSIDC)
Kamala Chambers, 687,
Budhwar Peth,
Near Prabhat Talkies,
Pune 411002
Tel: 24430482 / 24495779
Fax: 24486860

Western Maharashtra Development Corporation Ltd. (WMDC)
Kubera Chambers, 2nd floor,
Dr Rajendra Prasad Road,
Shivajinagar, Pune 411005
Tel: 25533325

MITCON
Kubera Chambers,
Dr Rajendra Prasad Road,
Shivajinagar, Pune 411005
Tel: 25534322 / 25533309
Fax: 25533206
Email: mitconmail@gmail.com

Software Technology Park of India (STPI)
Kubera Chambers,
Dr Rajendra Prasad Road,
Shivajinagar, Pune 411005
Tel: 25539834
Hinjewadi: 22932644 / 22934662
Email: sttp@sttp.soft.net

Maharashtra State Financial Corporation (MSFC)
S. P. College Compound, Above Post Office,
Tilak Road, Pune 411030
Tel: 24331145 / 24331989
Fax: 24338003
Email:msfcpro@pn3.vsnl.net.in

Poona Merchants' Chamber
Vyapar Bhavan,
Near Market Yard,
Gultekadi, Pune 411037
Tel: 24271130 / 24271130
Fax: 24271150

Khadi and Village Industries Commission (KVIC)
1153, Ganeshkhind Road,
Pune 411005
Tel: 25655351/25675865
Email: cbrti@pn3.vsnl.net

Association of Women's Enterprises
Industries of Maharashtra
1 Kamal Baug Gokhale Road,
Pune

Architects Engineers & Surveyors' Association
1199/B, Shivajinagar,
Chanakyapuri,
(Y.B.C.Bldg) F.C. Road,
Pune 411004
Tel: 25510671 Fax: 25531592
Email: aesa@vsnl.net

Builders Association of India
Jackson Hut, Compound of Chief Engineer,
Rajendrasinghji Road,
Pune. Tel: 26362441
Fax: 26360934

Promoters & Builders Association of Poona
501 Mantri Terrace, Thube Park,
Shivajinagar, Pune 411005
Tel: 25510864 / 25521512
Email: pbap@vsnl.net
Website: www.pbap.org

District Industries Centre (DIC)
Agriculture College Compound,
Shivajinagar, Pune 411005
Tel: 25537541 / 25537966
Fax: 25530307 / 2553 8046
E-mail: dicmhpun@mah.nic.in

Development Commissioner (Small Scale Industries) DC (SSI)
A-Wing, 7th Floor, Nirman Bhavan, New Delhi 110011
Tel: 91-11-23022220, 23022221, 23022211, 23022209
Fax: 91-11-23068315, 23066726, 23061068
Email:dcssihq@sidomail.net
Website:www.laghu-udyog.com

Maharashtra Centre for Entrepreneurship Development (MCED)
Agriculture College,
Shivajinagar,
Pune 411005
Email: info@mced.org

Small Industries Service Institute (SISI)
Govt. of India, Ministry of SSI,
Kurla Andheri Road, Sakinaka,
Mumbai 400072
Tel: 91-22-28576090/3091/7166
Fax: 91-22-28578092
Email: smallind@vsnl.com

Small Industries Development Bank of India (SIDBI)
Pune Branch Office,
Suryakiran Hotel Building,
JC-8, First Floor,
Mumbai - Pune Road,
Chinchwad, Pune.
Tel: 27474333/27476045/27463223

National Small Industries Corporation Ltd (NSIC)
Zonal Office, Prestige Chamber,
3rd Floor,
Kalyan Street, Masjid (East)
Mumbai 400009
Tel.: 91-22-23738275, 23470272
Fax: 91-22-23741989
Email: romum@nsic.co.in

Maharashtra Pollution Control Board (MPCB)
Regional Office Pune
Jog Center, 3rd floor,
Mumbai Pune Road,
Wakdewadi, Pune 411005
Tel: 25811627/25811694
Fax: 25811701

Bureau of Indian Standards
657-660, Market Yard, Gultekdi
Pune 411037 Tel: 24274807
Email: pnbo@bis.org.in

Maharashtra State Electricity Board
Pune Urban Zone,
ADM Building, Rasta Peth,
Pune 411002
Tel: 26135740/ 25663940
Fax: 26132052

Income Tax Department, Pune Region.
12, Aayakar Bhavan,
Sadhu Vaswani Chowk,
Pune 411001
Tel : 26114236
Email: ajcitsys@mah.nic.in
Website: www.incometaxpune.mah.nic.in

Provident Fund Office
Pune Cantonment Board Building,
Golibar Mainda,
Pune 411001
E-mail: srpfpun@mah.nic.in
Tel: 26344039
Fax: 26356145

Sales Tax Department
Pune-I Division Office
Vikrikar Bhavan, Air Port Road,
Opp. Golf Court, Yerawada,
Pune 411006
Website: www.salestax.maharashtra.gov.in

Commissionrate of Central Excise
41-A, ICE House, Sassoon Road, Pune 411001
Tel: 26050793/ 26051840/ 26051602/603/604
Fax: 26051802/ 26051821
Email: cexpune@vsnl.com / cexpune@excise.nic.in

Director General of Foreign Trade
C Block, Commercial Building No.2,
Pune Municipal Transport Building, Swargate,
Pune 411037 Tel: 24441577
Fax: 0212-541577
Email: jdgft@mah.nic.in

Office of the Commissioner of Customs
ICI House: 41 A, Sassoon Road,
Opp. Wadia College,
Pune 411001
Tel: 26051852
Fax: 6051849
Email : cuspune@pn3.vsnl.net.in

Container Freight Station
B-1, F-II Plot No. 1,
Yeswant Nagar, Telco Road,
Pimpri MIDC, Pune 411018

District Consumer Dispute Redressal Forum
692, Pushpa Heights,
Bibewadi, Pune 411
Tel: 24210364/ 24217489

Office of Dy. Chief Controller of Explosives
Industrial Assurance Building,
Opp. Churchagate Station,
Fort, Mumbai 400020

Director of Industrial Safety & Health
Maharashtra Factory Inspection Office,
Commerce Centre, 5th Floor,
Tardeo-Mumbai 400034.
Tel: 24942230/ 24942231

- Anand Deshpande • Anu Aga • Arti Kirloskar • Arun Firodia
- Atul Kirloskar • B.G. Deshmukh • B.K.S. Iyengar • Christopher C. Benninger
- Dr. Charudutt Apte • Dr S.B. Mujumdar • Dr. Vasant Gowariker
- Dr. Vijay Bhatkar • Dr. Wilfried G Aulbur • Ganesh Natarajan
- Jaswinder Narang

My Pune

- Jaymala Diddee • Lila Poonawalla • N.B. Chitale • Ninad Bedekar
- Prahlad Chhabria • Pratap Pawar • Pratima Joshi • Prof. S. V. Kogekar
- Rahul Bajaj • Rati Forbes • Ravi Pandit • Sanjeev Abhyankar
- Sudhir Sharma • Sujit Patwardhan • Suresh Kalmadi
- Uday Narayanrao Borawake

Anand Deshpande

Anand Deshpande is the founder, chairman and managing director of Persistent Systems. An alumni of IIT, Kharagpur, he has been conferred with many awards and has chaired conferences organized by NASSCOM and CSI. He is also Chairman of the Computer Society of India, Pune Chapter.

How does one describe Pune? Queen of the Deccan, Oxford of the East, Cultural Capital of Maharashtra, One of Forbes' emerging global cities, a preferred IT destination and a well established manufacturing hub.

You name it, we have it and there is no place like Pune to make one's home, educate the children, build careers, enrich your life culturally and eventually call it a day and enjoy retirement in peace. And while all this is true, Puneites will also tell you that the city has undergone an incredible transformation over the last decade.

This traditional city of the Peshwas has witnessed astonishing growth. It has got a 'face change' from a 'pensioner's paradise' to a cool cosmopolitan city. Today, Pune is dotted with multiplexes, coffee shops, shopping malls and International food chains. It is slowly emerging as a city of dreams. A city where the bourgeois is given the prospect of a good life, at an affordable price. This rapid metamorphosis can largely be attributed to the onset of the IT industry in Pune.

> A recent global survey found that Pune is the place where the happiest Indians in the entire world live.

In spite of this change, the most outstanding aspect of Pune and its people is the fine balance they have maintained between modernity and their age-old rich culture and tradition. Not surprising that a recent global survey found that Pune is the place where the happiest Indians in the entire world live. The reason for this is that Pune is culturally alive. It exemplifies an indigenous culture and ethos, in which education, arts and crafts, and theatre are given due prominence. Marathi may be the city's mother tongue, but it has an ethnic mix of migrants - Parsis, Christians, Jews, Muslims, Gujaratis, South Indians, Bengalis, Punjabis, Sindhis - that have enriched the city beyond measure, giving it a warmth and vibrancy, while also giving it the cosmopolitan feel. On the whole Pune comes across as a reasonably disciplined and industrious city. Who knows where the IT revolution will take this city, but it is changing many people's lives. It is undoubtedly on the move, ready to join the global village.

Anu Aga

Anu Aga was the Chairperson of Thermax from 1996 to 2004. For leading the business turnaround of Thermax, she was honoured with the Financial Express Lifetime Achievement Award. She continues to remain an active Director of the company. An advocate of communal harmony, Mrs. Aga speaks passionately against sectarian intolerance and strengthening of secular values. She supports the work of Akanksha, an NGO that promotes education of children from slums.

For the last 35 years Pune has been my home. I grew up in Mumbai and it was there that my father first established our small family business. But as we grew and needed more space, we moved to Pune. We could not have thought of a better option - close to Mumbai, with land and skilled labour available at affordable rates. The infrastructure was quite adequate then, and to top it all, Pune had such balmy climate.

I love Pune. Though the growing city sometimes makes me uneasy, I wouldn't like to live anywhere else. I like Pune's friendly people and its cosmopolitan ethos. Like many Indian cities its streets and buildings reflect many centuries and the culture and mores of its people. Pune is a city that blends tradition and modernity.

Pune is a city that blends tradition and modernity.

To anyone new to this city I would recommend a walk around its *wadas*. They preserve the ambience of the old Pune. I cherish the memories of the several open-air concerts I attended at Shaniwarwada. Then there is the Kelkar Museum that houses a priceless collection of art objects brought together by the loving care of one man. And of course, the Rock Garden close to the Osho Ashram is not to be missed. We have the Pune University campus and the Empress Garden, benign and sad reminders of the shrinking public space that is available to us today.

One place I am very fond of is the Italian vegetarian restaurant, La Pizzeria. Though I am a non-vegetarian, I love the culinary delights offered by La Pizzeria.

Pune has the potential to grow by attracting talent and investment. Supported by its good educational and research institutes, the city has already moved beyond its traditional manufacturing base. It has emerged a major centre for IT and biotechnology industries. To realize the aspirations that many people like me have for this city, we need to take care of some of the concern areas: improve its infrastructure, especially our roads and the availability of power; and discipline our traffic so that Pune can shed its dubious reputation as the city with the highest two wheeler accidents.

I am confident that Pune can meet these challenges if our administration and civil society join hands. All of us who celebrate this city's uniqueness should work together to make this happen.

Arti Kirloskar

Having studied Graphic Art from Delhi College of Art, Arti Kirloskar subsequently did her Masters in Fine Arts. She has helped curate a number of artists' shows and has held numerous exhibitions while experimenting with design in different media such as glass, pottery and textiles. A keen lover of Indian dances she was a student of Odissi for over a decade. She enjoys trekking, and painting in her spare time. She is presently Chairperson of INTACH, Pune.

I got married and came to Pune 25 years ago from Delhi, Pune was like a hill station in those days, all green and pleasant.

In the beginning there was a feeling of cultural emptiness not because of the city environment but because of the language. But over the years I have learnt Marathi and with the language barrier reduced I can now enjoy the plays and rich cultural offerings of the city.

People in Pune are now savvy about art as an investment, and we see galleries opening all over the city. The quality of art displayed and made in the city has also greatly improved. I hope this will lead to an increased visual sensitivity in Punekars and that they will voice their disgust over some of the visual eyesores being built around the city in pretence of being 'modern'.

Punekars are broad minded, understated, educated, intelligent, well read and adventurous.

I love the simplicity of the people of Pune. The respect for the individual and for women strikes you especially when you come from the male dominated world of north India. Punekars are broad minded, understated, educated, intelligent, well read and adventurous. I enjoy the conversations and debates I have with the friends I have made here, and I learn a lot every time I interact with them.

Vetal Tekdi, and the University campus used to be my favourite places to go for a walk and enjoy the beauty of nature, but the with the development in the city I now have to move further out to Sus or all the way to Mulshi, to enjoy the same. The Pataleshwar caves however have retained their calmness even in the urban jungle.

A tour of the old city, Tulsibaug, Tambat Ali, the old temples, the lake on the outskirts of Pune, the nearby caves and the numerous places perfect for treks make the city of Pune unique. The rivers Mula and Mutha that transverse through the city give us the much-needed relief from the concrete claustrophobia creating fresh air corridors for the city.

I see Pune becoming another Mumbai. I would like to see Pune become like Rome but with the intense urbanization of the city, I feel I am fighting a losing battle. The population is becoming younger and more mobile, and values and roots seem to lose the significance they used to have.

Pune seems to be going the Bangkok way with the sky train, traffic and general chaos yet its saving grace are the beautiful people and a culture and heritage so rich its makes you proud to be a Punekar!

Arun Firodia

Chairman of Kinetic Engineering Ltd. and the Kinetic Motor Co. Ltd., Arun Firodia is a member of the Executive Committee of the Society of Indian Automobile Manufacturers, and is extremely active in social and environmental causes. He has been awarded FICCI CSR Award 2003 for Empowerment of the Physically Challenged and the NCPEDP - Shell Helen Keller Award 2004, for Employment of Disabled People.

My father Shri H K Firodia took up a job in 1950 with the S T Workshop, as a Jr. Engineer and so we moved to Pune. He bought a house on Prabhat Road, then known as Pune's Hollywood. Many film actors and actresses lived in our neighborhood. After SSC, I joined the Fergusson College, then went to IIT Powai and then to MIT (US) for my post graduation.

It was my father's dream to make two wheelers for the common man and he developed a totally indigenous design, the very popular "LUNA" which became a generic name for its class.

On my return from the US, I joined my father to start the production of this vehicle.

We found Pune to be an ideal location with its closeness to Mumbai, availability of land, water, power, technical manpower, etc. Above all Pune has beautiful climate, almost all the year round. I find it to be a most livable city.

Pune has many natural advantages. Situated amongst hills with three rivers and huge dams, it has a beautiful landscape. Known as the Oxford of the East, it has educational institutions with a rich history like Deccan College, Fergusson College, COEP, B. J. Medical, University of Pune, and SNDT Women's College. A number of Defence Establishments like NDA, CME, AIT, AFMC and IAT are also situated here along with Research Institutes like ARDE, HEMRL and NCL- all landmark institutions.

Puneites are known as a most discerning people and Pune enjoys the reputation of being an ideal test market. Whatever gets accepted in Pune is sure to find acceptance anywhere in the world!

Pune has provided India leadership in both political and social spheres, and is unique in its cultural prowess.

Pune has provided India, leadership in both political and social spheres, and is unique in its cultural prowess. Its Ganesh Festival and Sawai Gandharva Mahotsava are famous across the country. It is also famous for music, dance and drama. In order to promote such talents we started the 'Firodia Trophy', a competition for college students that has completed 26 years!

Pune and its surroundings have many sight seeing places but my favourites amongst them are historic forts like Sinhgad, Purandhar, Torna, Rajgarh etc. They are excellent trekking spots, for those who enjoy outdoor adventure.

Already known as Oxford of the East, and a cultural and entertainment capital, if the Enlightenment fields are well promoted Pune will attract the best talent in the country and very soon become a centre of Engineering, Electronics and Education.

Atul Kirloskar

A Mechanical Engineer by qualification, Atul Kirloskar began his career with Kirloskar Cummins Limited in the year 1978. He is presently the Chairman and Managing Director of Kirloskar Oil Engines Limited. Mr. Kirloskar has also served as the Chairman of MCCIA and CII National Committee on Defence.

It's an educational capital, an industrial hub, a pensioners' paradise, a sports city, an intellectual arena, hosts a cultured, educated and aware citizenry, is adorned with hills and encircled by lakes, is nature's decked up bride in the monsoons, is bursting with youth and hope, and is marching unabashed into the future yet mindful of its past; there are not many cities that can match this versatility of Pune, though there are many who aspire to ape it.

> Adorned with hills and encircled by lakes it is nature's decked up bride in the monsoons and

Pune has a culture of learned debate and has been a torchbearer of reform, whether it was female literacy, widow re-marriage or contraception. Reformists like Mahatma Phule, Savitribai Phule and Maharshi Karve led this city out of the shackles of ritual and regression into a reformist mindset, which pervades thought even today.

Pune proudly hosts and nurtures industries ranging from manufacturing to IT services, pharmaceuticals to biotechnology and institutes like NCL, Agarkar Agricultural Institute, NIV and Gokhale Institute to name just a few. These are testimony to the abundant intellectual resources available here.

I could go on showering honest praise and exhibiting reverence to this singular city but it would be unfair if I were to gloss over areas the city needs to pay particular attention to, if it is to continue to set the bar and live up to it.

The city's administration is unable to cope with attendant issues of traffic, pollution, water, sewage, transport and all other civic amenities. Proper roads and drainage, adequate water and power supply, etc. must precede growth and construction, not follow it.

All of us in Pune rest too easily on our laurels when our pride must goad us to better living. Our attitude today might prove the idiom 'Pride comes before a fall'.

The Pune I envision is one which has an efficient public transport system, roads which can endure traffic and rains, habitable, low cost housing which will ensure dignified living for all, protection and forestation of the hills which gird us, an administration which will take the lead in doorstep governance, a rigid adherence to rules, wide open spaces and playgrounds, safe roads for children to cycle on, and the preservation of and respect for our resplendent heritage structures.

I am fortunate to be born in this marvelous city and take immense pride in being a part of its citizenry, but I want to see Pune set the benchmark, which will ensure that quality of civic amenities and living are as critical to our country's evolution as the GDP.

B.G. Deshmukh

B. G. Deshmukh joined the IAS in 1951 and held a number of prestigious positions including that of Municipal Commissioner of Mumbai. In 1986, Rajiv Gandhi appointed him Cabinet Secretary, he then went on to become principal secretary to the Prime Minister in 1989, a post he held also under V P Singh and Chandrashekhar. At present, he is President of the Mumbai Natural History Society and President of Community Aid and Sponsership Programme (CASP).

I still remember Pune as Poona, my hometown, the place I was brought up and educated in and the place I left in 1951 to join the IAS in Delhi. Pune in those days was pleasant, friendly, interesting and surrounded by wooded hills. It had a very pleasant climate throughout the year and was even then the educational and cultural capital of the area. The Fergusson College where I was educated, College of Engineering, and Agriculture College, were pioneering institutions of India. The great freedom fighter Lokmanya Tilak worked from here, and it was home to many classical singers and famous institutions of music. The Ganpati Festival lasting ten days was a feast of classical singers and musicians coming together to perform here. In the 40 years of my absence, Pune has changed beyond recognition. It is no longer a city but almost a metropolis. It has blossomed into a place of excellence in Education, Engineering, Information Technology and basic sciences like Chemistry, Astrophysics and Defence Technology and has the largest number of foreign students in India. The number of defense establishments has also increased considerably.The city is just expanding, making the old city look like a small seed in a full-grown fruit. Clusters of multi-storied building are sprouting up everywhere, so also self-contained townships, malls and multiplexes. But I still find that Pune has not lost its essential character and culture. People no doubt love and indulge in being argumentative but they are really friendly and cosmopolitan. On any day, you can always find a classical cultural event, and also modern disco style entertainment. There is a variety of cuisine on offer not only from different parts of India, but from different countries too and you can enjoy lunch or dinner with good wines which are now produced in nearby areas. In Pune you can pick up the choicest heavy silk saris, especially the ones with rich golden embroidery called "Paithani" or the simple Puneri Sari. The city is also famous for the variety of 'Nau Wari' or nine-yards saris available. If you are lucky you might see women wearing this traditional sari. A fashion designer from abroad once told me that he found this saree to be one of the best garments to bring out feminine beauty. The old typical cap called a "Pagdi" is also an item worth collecting.

To me there is no place like Pune but you have to come and visit it to discover this truth.

The city is just expanding, making the old city look like a small seed in a full-grown fruit.

B. K. S. Iyengar

Yogacharya BKS Iyengar heads the world renowned Ramamani Iyengar Memorial Yoga Institute. Remarkably fit even in his late eighties, the Yogarcharya's disciples include J. Krishnamurthy, Jayprakash Narayan, Achyut Patwardhan, violin maestro Yehudi Menuhin, and the Queen Mother of Belgium.

I was born in Bellur, a village in Kolar about 60 km. from Bangalore. How I became a Maharashtrian and a Puneite is a question that has many pieces like a jigsaw puzzle. In 1937, Dr. Gokhale, who had seen my yoga skills at a demonstration in Belgaum, invited me to Pune, to teach and share my knowledge in educational institutions and the Deccan Gymkhana Club. This is when I came here, and created a yoga centre, which has since become a landmark in Pune city.

This city is considered a place of pilgrimage for artists, musicians, dancers, dramatists, philosophers, politicians, educationists and yogis who believe that appreciation by Pune's people means respect all over India and abroad. Pune's history is resplendent with events and personalities who have helped to transform India and bring about the progress of the nation.

Pune is surrounded by beauty and magnificent splendour, some natural, some man made. There is Sinhgad Fort, Parvati, Khadakwasla Lake, Mulshi Lake and the list never ends. Then there are places that serve *chai* (tea) that is so good it can change the course of your day.

The Oxford of India, Pune has many educational institutes where one can learn everything from agriculture to information technology. It has renowned universities and prestigious institutions like the Bhandarkar Oriental Institute. Pune has now developed as an emerging industrial capital of the region.

> This city is considered a place of pilgrimage for artists...

The most important feature of Pune is that it is the only city in India where there are no strikes in industry or educational Institutions or in any other profession.

For me, Pune is a mini world. The culture and citizens of Pune are very cosmopolitan and you will find a person from nearly everywhere in the world in this city. The people are kind, helpful and courteous, irrespective of religion, caste, gender or nationality.

The only worrying factor with the growth of the city is the rising pollution level. But I am sure that the natural beauty of Pune will be preserved by the efforts of its citizens who are proud to be living here, in our Pune city.

Christopher Charles Benninger

American born, Harvard and MIT educated architect, Christopher Benninger has been living in Pune since 1976. His design for Mahindra United World College, India has won many international architectural awards. He is presently designing the Samundra Institute of Maritime Studies, the new Taj Blue Diamond Hotel, an air-conditioned indoor stadium in Ahmedabad, a new campus for IIM- Calcutta, Suzlon Corporate campus, International school at Sahara Amby valley, the Supreme Court in Thimphu, and the Capitol complex in Bhutan.

From my early days in India, Pune held the allure of an intellectual centre, blessed with a mountainous terrain and good people. When I first visited the city in the 1960s "Poona" was known as a pensioner's paradise, a cantonment town and a provincial place where girls rode bicycles! Three hundred *wadas* from the Peshawa times still accented the quiet lanes of low-rise structures made of brick, basalt and tile roofs. Indeed when I moved here in 1976, Poona was a green city with the likes of V.M. Dandekar, Manibhai Desai, Vilasrao Salunke, and J.P. Naik on the scene, all stalwarts of India's self-generated development and inventors of a uniquely human intellectualism. The founders of global Pune were people "next door," whose enthusiasm was contagious! Adi Bathena was founding Wanson Industries (now Thermax), S.L. Kirloskar was in control of his thriving empire, and B.V. Rao was creating history in the agro-industries sector.

New institutions like the Indian Institute of Education, the Centre for Development Studies and Activities, and Systems Research Institute were blossoming, attracting youngsters like Narayan Murthy to discover themselves. Most important, Poona then as Pune now, was a forward-looking city that lived in the future!

The attraction then as the attraction now: being near Mumbai, yet away from it. Being in the centre of huge markets, the nation and all of its resources, yet free from ancient problems and mind-sets; enjoying law and order; having access to a pool of young talent emerging year by year; and living with a secular, tolerant people interested in the inherent truth of things!

Pune is a cauldron of a delightful coming together of diverse ingredients.

In a global economy, which implodes at the centre and leaves some "space" on the periphery to think and create, I find Pune offering our design house all of the big city advantages, with the relative isolation needed for new ideas to incubate. Our architectural studio needs this "in-between space" to be vibrant and creative!

As Poona morphed into Pune, its economic base shifted from manufacturing towards services, where the creation of intellectual property plays a stronger role day by day.

As Pune transforms into a global metropolis its manufacturing activities ground its intellectual products within reality. As an architectural firm we need to be close to the craftspeople who build our computer generated images. We need access to university-based academics, students and the captains of industry to be catalysed creatively. Pune is a cauldron of a delightful coming together of these diverse ingredients in a salubrious climate!

Dr. Charudutt Apte

Trained at the Christian Medical College Hospital, Vellore, Dr. Apte has been a Consultant Neurosurgeon for over 20 years and heads the Neurosurgery Department at the Pune Institute of Neurology. He is presently a Consultant Neurosurgeon at Sahyadri Speciality Hospital which he started.

I have to say that coming to Pune was a great turning point in my life. Not only has my professional life benefited but more importantly the kind of exposure I have got in Pune related to the various aspects of life such as meeting thinkers and doers in every field, interacting with academia and intellectuals, learning social responsibility from prominent activists and many more exciting things, are experiences I would never have had if I stayed on in the institute I was planning to settle in.

I would not say that Pune is the best place to work in my subject 'neurosurgery'. In fact when I came here in 1985, Pune was positively backward as far as facilities and awareness in this subject were concerned. Even now the concept of institutionalization of medicine is not all that well accepted by most professionals and people at large. The result is that in spite of developing a good professional set up, some doctors and people still tend to go by the names they have heard or know, rather than an institution which has a good and proper functioning system.

Thinking laterally is part of the culture and tradition of this city. There are many persons here who live their passions and are not at all bothered about social success, acceptance and material rewards. When it comes to their beliefs, they will never compromise. In my opinion this is something very few cities can boast about and this is the thing, that I like and appreciate most about Pune.

My favorite places in this city are its surrounding hills and the campus of the Pune University.

> There are many persons in Pune who live their passions and are not bothered about social success, acceptance and material rewards.

Pune, I believe will continue to grow robustly in most knowledge based industries and will soon become a hub for new developments in technology. A place where people from various branches of study will come together and develop new concepts and products. I find this a very thrilling opportunity for the city.

For me Pune can be compared to Paris in Europe, Massachusetts in the United States and Bangalore in India as far as confluence of cultures, intellectual camaraderie, heritage and its cosmopolitan nature are concerned.

Unique to Pune is the passion of its people and their admiration and appreciation for totally out-of-the-box thinking, this adds a distinct flavour to Pune.

Dr. S. B. Mujumdar

Dr. S B Mujumdar is the Founder President and Director of the Symbiosis Group of Institutes. The Symbiosis family consists of B-schools, a renowned mass communication institute, an undergraduate college of Arts and Commerce, a law faculty and several other institutes and courses.

Forty-three years ago I was called to join Fergusson College as a professor, thanks to the dynamic and benevolent Principal S.V.Kogekar. It was on the campus of this college that Symbiosis was born with a vision of '*Vasudhaiv Kutumbakam*' (the world is one family) and a mission to promote international understanding through quality education. Little did I realize then that one day Symbiosis would achieve the status of a University.

But such things happen in Pune.This city makes the impossible possible. Because Pune is a city of educational opportunities. Education is in its air, soil and soul.

I salute Pune where past and present are forged to create a global vision for the future.

I dream that one day Pune will become the knowledge capital of India. With over six Universities, two hundred colleges, countless schools and over one hundred institutions of national and international repute devoted to training and research, the dream may come true in the near future.

To me, the best place in Pune is the campus of Fergusson College where stalwarts like Lokmanya Tilak, Gopal Ganesh Agarkar, G.K.Gokhale and Dhondo Keshav Karve walked the talk. Where the father of the Nation Mahatma Gandhi discovered his political Guru in Gopal Krishna Gokhale.

It can rightly boast of its alumni such as Swantantraveer Sawarkar, Acharya Kripalani, and also P.V.Narsimha Rao and V.P.Singh who went on to become prime ministers of India. There is something mystical, magical and creative in the soil of that campus.

Nowhere in India is one likely to find a city like Pune where liberal arts and performing arts, science and technology, I.T. and B.T., economics and politics, humanities and social sciences are discussed and debated, criticized and appreciated. This is the city of teachers, authors, researchers and consultants.

This city is a beautiful bouquet of universities, colleges, multiplexes, research laboratories, cultural, social and political organizations, Shaniwarwada, Gaikwadwada and many newspapers and magazines. Its citizen, the Punekar, is original, insightful and practical. Its once conservative society is fast becoming a knowledge society.

If you want to know what India will think tomorrow, you should know what Pune thinks today. This is the strength of this unique city.

If you want to know what India will think tomorrow, you should know what Pune thinks today.

Dr. Vasant Gowariker

A renowned scientist, Dr. Vasant Gowariker has held a number of high-profile posts, including Scientific Advisor to the Prime Minister and Vice-Chancellor of Pune University. For his contributions in the field of science Dr. Gowariker has won many awards. Currently he is the Chairman of the Rajiv Gandhi Science and Technology Commission (Govt of Maharashtra), with a cabinet rank.

Why did I come to Pune? I didn't – I happened to be born here! Then destiny took over. I was away from Pune for over 40 years. Then I returned to my roots – only to rediscover that Pune is great.

Why is Pune great? For many reasons. It is the intellectual and educational capital of India. Pune is now the most happening place, not only for IT majors but also for corporate giants setting up multi-billion R&D units and production complexes in Pune. Already home to a strong automobile and engineering industry, Pune is a fertile ground for leadership in IT. I find that anything which I once called the best stands bettered in Pune. That's Pune's special magic and Pune's uniqueness.

My favourite places in Pune are perhaps the same as of others. But mine are laced with some fantasies! I like, for instance, the entire campus of Pune University, especially the main building with its fascinating 19th century architecture. Every time I see it my mind goes back to the days of the great Dr.M.R. Jaykar – the founding Vice Chancellor. The man who fervently pleaded way back in the 1920s for a 100 percent literate India and education for everybody, in preference to even a sizeable number of world-class individuals and the rest deprived of education. Fergusson College is my favourite again not just because of the historical Amphitheatre, but also because the college takes my mind back to the year 1885. And then I mentally see the first Principal of the College, Gopal Ganesh Agarkar, one of India's early social reformists and a truly godly man who never believed in God. I like Kesari Wada – a place which once resonated with the thundering voice of the father of unrest against the British. There are numerous such places in Pune one should not miss.

What I would like to see in future – maybe within the next four or five decades – is the reversal: Oxford to be called the Pune of the West.

I see two things in Pune of the future. One is Pune surpassing Bangalore in IT activity, to become India's IT leader in the true sense. Secondly, Pune is said to already have the highest density of educational institutions in the country and is called the 'Oxford of the East'. What I would like to see in future – maybe within the next four or five decades – is the reversal: Oxford to be called the Pune of the West (No exclamation mark).

Dr. Vijay Bhatkar

Best known for his pioneering contributions to India's Supercomputing initiative. Dr. Vijay Bhatkar is the architect of India's PARAM series of Supercomputers. He is the founder Executive Director of C-DAC, Chairman of ETH Research Lab, Chief Mentor of I²IT and Chancellor of Multiversity. A Fellow of IEEE, CSI and INAE, Dr. Bhatkar has founded many innovation based start-ups and institutions. He is a recipient of Padmashri and Maharashtra Bhushan awards and author of eight books and 80 research papers. Dr. Bhatkar did his Ph.D. from IIT, Delhi in 1972.

Since I have been associated with some very prestigious Pune-based projects, many people think that I belong here. However I stayed in many different cities such as Baroda, Delhi, Nagpur, Mumbai, and Trivandrum before 1988, but never in Pune. The first time that I came to Pune was in 1987, when India's first supercomputing initiative was taken and it was decided that the Centre for Development of Advanced Computing (C-DAC) was to be established. Since C-DAC was a very prestigious project, I remember that there was a lot of discussion on where this project should be based.

Pune is the finest city of India and in fact one of the finest in the world.

I had my reasons for choosing Pune over multiple other options being considered. Firstly, I definitely wanted this project out of the Delhi circles, where the institutes tend to become very high profile and are constantly visited by famous personalities. From my perspective, what was needed most to make this project successful was to attract the best possible talent from all over India. I needed to look for a place that was rich in academia and had a resource-rich research environment in place.

Secondly, when one tries to attract young people, one faces the question of whether good schooling would be available for their children. From both these points of view, I thought that I could get no better place than Pune. It also had a number of high quality engineering colleges; and its proximity to IIT Powai was an added advantage. The campus of the Pune University was perfect for establishing C-DAC. The temperate environment, climate and city culture also made this choice very appealing.

I have been watching this city grow and I must say that Pune is the finest city of India and in fact one of the finest in the world as well. Whenever I have been to Bremen, San Jose or Austin, I have found startling similarities to Pune, be it the hills, the strong education-base, IT industries or the temperate climate. I find that my best thinking occurs in the mornings against the serene backdrop of the Vetal Hills.

The growth of the city lies in advancing the 5 Es: Education, Engineering, Electronics, Entertainment and culture and finally, Enlightenment. With a high level of attainment in pursuits such as academia, science, music and drama, I find a perfect blend of education, culture, intellect and philosophy in this charming city.

Dr. Wilfried G. Aulbur

CEO & Managing Director of DaimlerChrysler India, Dr. Aulbur has a Ph.D in Physics from Ohio State University, USA. He has worked as a post-doctoral researcher and has over 50 publications to his credit ranging from Knowledge Management to Computational and Solid State Physics. Dr. Aulbur has headed the Business Development and Strategy function at the DCRC India, and has worked in several positions across DaimlerChrysler both in Germany and the US.

It was a beautiful morning in October 2005. I had slept little the previous night and I was filled with excitement and anticipation. The previous evening I had received confirmation that I would be taking charge of operations of DaimlerChrysler in India. My better half, Rekha was also awake early, sharing my enthusiasm and perhaps for her it was even more exciting to be in India, she being an Indian herself!

After three fulfilling years in corporate headquarters we thus returned to India and stepped out of the plane into a warm, humid Mumbai evening on November 1st, 2005. The next morning, we drove down to Pune, the home of DaimlerChrysler in India.

We soon settled down to our new life in Pune though I admit, we were a little jolted by the potholes and the traffic that seemed to be worse than in Chennai or Bangalore, cities we had lived in previously.

Pune is a city that is unique in its own way. To begin with, I was a stranger in a strange city. And now as I am beginning to have more and more friends, I realize more than ever, the camaraderie, warmth and cheerfulness that are the hallmarks of the "Punekars" as the people of Pune are referred to.

Camaraderie, warmth and cheerfulness are the hallmarks of "Punekars".

Also, Pune with its museums, forts and lovely hills lures me to the outdoors - while the variety of local cuisine contributes to my culinary experience. The Kelkar Museum and the Shaniwarwada capture the rich legacy of this city of the Peshwas, while the Aga Khan Palace stands as a reminder of the sacrifices of India and its people during the freedom movement. I also like the young and vibrant face of Pune: the night-life, the city's pubs and the new walking-plaza at MG road. Truly, weekends in Pune are never boring!

Professionally my assignment at Pune is a worthy challenge. India's booming economy and our participation in the development of the Manufacturing as well as the IT & Engineering Services industries provide me with sufficient adrenalin to last for a long time.

Thus for me Pune is an inspiring combination of friendly Punekars, an emerging IT and Outsourcing industry, the Detroit of the East, and the city of the Peshwas.

Ganesh Natarajan

An alumnus of IIT Mumbai and the Harvard Business School, Ganesh Natarajan is Global CEO of Zensar Technologies Ltd. He and his wife Uma made Pune their home in 2001.

Pune for me was a place I loved to visit throughout my career and every chance I got – whether as a consultant to Thermax and Praj in the 1980s, or as an invited speaker in IT seminars in the 1990s – I would grab the chance to get a breath of fresh air, literally and figuratively, that this town always would provide. And as the Deccan Queen steamed into Pune station, the warmth of the city would never fail to make an indelible impression on one's mind and heart!

Pune today has everything going for it – I love the fact that the traditional Kothrud Maharastrians, the genteel Boat Club Parsis, the magnificient Bajajs, Kalyanis and Kirloskars, and even the many foreign nationals who have made this city their home take every new entrant to their hearts and make us feel so welcome. The fact that, five years after moving to this city in search of new career horizons, my wife Uma and I have developed such strong relationships here that Pune has become our true home, bears testimony to the hospitality of this city.

Pune is full of favourite places for us – the once sleepy suburb of Kalyani Nagar which now throbs with the rhythm of youth, the emergence of Kharadi from a dust heap to one of the favourite IT locations in the country, the wonderful restaurants that dot Koregaon Park and Boat Club, and the homes of some great friends; the Agas, the Malhotras, the Palekars, and many more where one can find true rest and relaxation. Is there any place quite like Pune? Well maybe San Jose, California is the closest match where the contrasting colours and languages of a fluid social milieu mix with such ease! People say Pune is changing – the roads get more crowded and the industry-academia growth brings more people to settle here every week – but then that is the true strength of the city – its ability to assimilate the transitions in focus and culture and where conversation becomes the great leveler between politicians, academicians, industrialists, executives, students and the Punekar next door. Its great tolerance for minor inconveniences as the city spreads its wings and grows is matched with a spirit of positive activism and makes citizens cut across community and class barriers to come together for common causes. It is a city that reflects the best of cultural flexibility, discovery and innovation that add sparkle to all our lives. Many of us truly believe that this is where India's multicultural heart truly beats – in the city we love!

As the Deccan Queen steamed into Pune station, the warmth of the city would never fail to make an indelible impression on one's mind and heart!

Jaswinder Narang

Jaswinder Narang has been working in the hotel industry for more than 30 years. He worked in Austria and Canada for the Hilton, Four Seasons, and Westin Hotel Groups. His next position was that of general manager in a hotel in Hurghada, on the Red Sea coastline, followed by the Metropolitan Hotel, Dubai. Currently Jaswinder Narang is the GM of Le Meridien, Pune.

In 2000, I was asked to take over the reins of Le Meridien, Pune. Having spent most of my career overseas, I had only heard of Pune. It was a challenge! Le Meridien Pune was a new hotel and the hospitality industry was going through its worst phase against the backdrop of Kargil, 9/11 and then SARS. I was told that Pune is the Queen of the Deccan! My first visit to Pune was to get a feel of the city. As I traveled through the city, I was taken in by the quaint old world charm of the cantonment and the gentle dignity of the old city with its numerous temples and *wadas*. I saw the canvas of the city stretched to the gentle green hills and then, there was no turning back. I was truly captivated.

Pune is metamorphosing into a vibrant world class city.

Pune lacked the frenzied pace of Mumbai and yet I felt a strong undercurrent of vibrancy. The IT boom was just beginning. As an outsider, I believe Pune has the makings of a great world-class city. It has a sound manufacturing base and is a centre of learning and research. Excellent educated manpower is offset by a strong aspiring middle class with a gentle disposition! Over the years I have savoured what the city has to offer- Koregaon Park's old royal homes that bespeak a different era, the movies in the swanky modern multiplexes, the variety of food and restaurants available for the foodie, and the pastoral and idyllic suburbia. However, what I find most unique is the temperament of the people-warm, gentle, law abiding and unobtrusive. The awareness and commitment to social issues and advocacy when law and ethics have been covertly digressed everywhere else. Pune has great potential as a tourist destination, particularly for adventure tourism. It has numerous forts atop surrounding hills, which are a paradise for trekkers, para-gliders, and campers. The fort Sinhagad, the Aga Khan palace, Shaniwarwada and the quaint Tulsibaug are a must -see for those visiting Pune. I was truly surprised to know that so many of India's greatest institutes and research centres are based here – FTII, NIBM, NCL, NDA, CDAC, IUCAA, NARI, Agharkar Research Institute, National Institute of Virology (NIV), Automotive Research Association of India and the Institute for Tropical Meteorology. This only goes to prove the immense talent and potential of the city. Pune has now emerged as the No, 1 destination for education in India and has become the preferred city of IT and ITES. The international airport will give a boost to the status of the city. I am glad to be here, when Pune is metamorphosing into a vibrant world class city.

Jaymala Diddee

Specializing in Urban Studies Jaymala Diddee has published several research papers and edited a number of books on the subject. Her doctoral thesis on 'Central Places in Western India' has won her high acclaim. She has been a reader at the University of Pune, a visiting professor at the University of Hawaii and Bremen, and has been involved in urban research centered around Pune including a collaborative research project on the ecology of Pune's social areas.

I was born in Baroda and came to Pune first as a schoolgirl and later to go to the Wadia College - to avoid having to study Home Sciences in Baroda! While at college I met and married Naval Diddee – and Pune became my home.
I then applied to and was accepted in the Geography Dept of Pune University. Thereafter began a lifelong adventure with the city and the subject. The scholarly traditions of the city are a real inspiration, almost as if the very air one breathes fills one with the passion to achieve the impossible!
The ambience here is charged with talent and people have a generosity of spirit to share ideas and give unstintingly of their time. You feel a revving up of the spirit, almost infectious and it is impossible to remain untouched by this.
As someone for whom trekking is a passion, Pune offers many treats in its girdle of hills, but for me Sinhagad remains my favourite. The Deccan College is another favourite with its peace, tranquility and magnificent library; it is a haven where I often find myself.
I enjoy the core city, Peshwai Pune, the precincts around Shaniwarwada, Tulshibag, etc. There is also Colonial Poonah-the world of the Cantonment, its bungalows, clubs, racecourse, churches, etc. – and for the young the world of multiplexes, shopping malls. A different Pune is now growing along the urban fringe – the world of IT Parks, Call Centres and BPOs creating a new urban landscape of the city.
From the city which once had the largest bicycle population, Punekars are now traveling at high speed on the digital highway. Pune's educational institutions, its cultural eminence and its fabled environment are its great strengths – the assurance of its bright future.
One-lacuna remains the abysmal state of its infrastructure, which has simply not kept pace with the accelerating growth and which might just derail Pune's future promise.
Pune has always welcomed people and they have become a part of Pune's social, cultural and economic fabric. The fast food joints may be the icons of modern Pune yet the original flavour of old Pune remains alive in its labyrinth. where even today *vada pav* and *misal* remain gastronomic details for the original Punekars and the neo-Punekars!
There is an old saying that anyone who has drunk the water of Pune always returns to the city.

The scholarly traditions of the city are a real inspiration, almost as if the very air one breathes fills one with the passion to achieve the impossible!

Lila Poonawalla

A Mechanical Engineer from COEP, Lila Poonawalla went on to become the country's first woman CMD of an engineering company when she took over the reigns of Alfa Laval and then Tetra Pak. She has to her credit the Padmashree (1989), Mahila Jeevan Gaurav (1998), the Lifetime Achievement Award (2001) from the Indian Women Scientists Asscociation, and the Polar Star from the King of Sweden (2002), appointing her an Officer of the Royal Order. Currently she is the Chairperson of DeLaval.

Pune is a wonderful city. It has charm and value for all who live here, be it retired people, young professionals, students,art and culture lovers, housewives, single women, children, or even foreigners. Anyone who comes to this city just falls in love with it.

When we fled from Pakistan as refugees, it was my grand parents who decided that we come and live in Pune. Not for a moment have I regretted their decision. I share a very special bond with Pune and it is here that I have risen from an apprentice to become the CMD of the same company.

Pune vibrates with all possible industries.

Pune offers the best in education. It is for this reason that it is called 'Oxford of the east'. It is a home to top ranking universities and colleges, be it technical, arts, science, commerce, biotechnology, microbiology and others. Pune also boasts of a number of world class government research institutes.

The development of education has moved forward by leaps and bounds. Many new universities, colleges and institutes have been established. And with the influx of all the student population, the city has a very young look and feel.

Always a hub for the engineering industry, many multinationals have set up shop here. Now IT companies, biotechnology and pharma companies are also setting up huge establishments here. It has the largest number of SMEs to cater to the demands of the auto and engineering industry. Pune vibrates with all possible industries.

This city has tremendous scope to grow and become a city of international standard and repute. In the past few year development of IT clusters, such as Hinjewadi and Magarpatta, multiplexes, shopping arcades and malls, has made Pune a very hip city.

Pune has many places to keep the traveler occupied. Tulsibaug, Parvati, University of Pune, Shaniwarwada, Agakhan palace, Kelkar Museum, Scindia Chhatri and Sinhgad are a few of the popular favourites.

The best part of Pune is the people. A very loving and easygoing people, they are also very giving and philanthropic, always helping those in need. Ever encouraging, especially for women, the people of Pune are very endearing.

A unique thing about Pune is that every citizen is clear that 'We want to become the most sought after city in IT, BT or Auto industry, still keeping the maxim of Oxford of the East.'

N. B. Chitale

N.B. Chitale is a partner of Chitale Bandhu Mithaiwale, a renowned chain of stores selling milk products, sweets and **farsan** *in Pune. It was he who pioneered the idea of mechanizing the process of making the products* **(mithais and namkeens)** *sold at Chitale Bandhu.*

It was in 1950, when my elder brother Raghunath came here and started our first shop selling sweetmeats, that I first came to Pune. I came here to pursue my studies in commerce. In my spare time I also helped at the shop and thus was trained in handling the business.

In 1954, on graduating, my brother offered me the chance to open a branch of Chitale at Deccan Gymkhana. I accepted the offer and settled in Pune. Thus began the story of an extremely successful and flourishing business.

Punekars, I have found, have a zest for good food and good living. They accept only the best, be it art, culture, food, or clothing. They have high standards of taste and expect products to be consistent in quality.

I have lived in Mumbai and Kolhapur also, but there is something different about Pune. It is hard to define, but there is pleasure in doing business here. People are friendly and loyal and the atmosphere is that of one big family.

Pune has something for everyone; there are a variety of experiences on offer. Hill stations like Lonavala, Khandala and Matheran for people who want to relax and take it easy. The Karla Caves, Shaniwarwada, Sinhgad Fort, Raja Kelkar Museum, many temples and historic sites for those interested in history and culture.

For the academically oriented, there is in Pune such a concentration of institutes in varying fields of education and research as can be found in no other place in India. For the businessmen there are vast industrial estates producing almost everything from a pin to a car. Pune is an IT hub too. For me one of the most mesmerizing places is Tulsibaug. It is one of the must-see places in Pune. A world within a world, it is a place where modernity and antiquity come together to create a sight so special you will wonder at it for days to come.

Punekars, I have found, have a zest for good food and good living.

There are problems with transport infrastructure such as bad roads and inadequate public transport but if addressed now, these will be only minor setbacks. With the addition of an International Airport, Pune will be the obvious choice for entrepreneurs and investors alike.

Pune is a city of music, art, festivals, and innumerable opportunities to be exposed to the best, no matter in what field. All this and more makes Pune an exclusive city, yet it has retained its simplicity, honesty and charm.

Ninad Bedekar

An engineer by education, Ninad Bedekar is a renowned historian. He has published many papers, has a collection of 3,500 slides of forts in and around Maharashtra, and is an authority on the Maratha Empire and Shivaji Maharaj. He is an accomplished speaker and has to his credit more than 4,000 lectures at the local, national and international level and has received the Outstanding Young Person, Pride of Pune and the Shivabhushan awards for his excellent and pioneering work.

I am proud of having been born and brought up in this wonderful city that is the Queen of the Deccan, Pune. The city has many other sobriquets: Oxford of the East, Pensioner's Paradise, Detroit of India and now IT Capital of Maharashtra. It has now certainly become the most vibrant metropolitan centre in Western India.

The city offers enormous facilities for research and study. Many institutions over a 100 years old, with libraries that have rare books, manuscripts, documents, coins, copper plaques, etc. give a rare opportunity to interested persons to examine and study these and offer excellent references to the history of not only Pune but India as well.

I can only compare Pune with Oxford for its educational facilities, with Detroit for its auto industry, and San Jose for being an IT Hub.

The engineering industry has flourished and prospered in and around the city. Various industrial estates accommodate light and heavy industry. Trained and skilled local manpower helps industrialists make excellent, quality products.

The ambience in the city is great. Youth power is growing due to the tremendous growth in the educational facilities available here. With industries in close proximity campus interviews can be carried out and fresh graduates get jobs easily.

My favourite place in Pune is the Pataleshwar or Panchaleshwar caves. These caves, having 8th - 9th century Rashtrakuta carvings, transport you to the city's mystical past. The atmosphere here is quite tranquil, like time has stood still. Another place to visit is Vetal hill, the topmost point of Pune. It offers a panoramic view of the bustling city below.

What one should not miss in Pune is the "Light and Sound show" at Shaniwarwada. This show is the only one of its kind in Maharashtra and gives an idea about the history of the land. A visit to Raja Kelkar Museum is also a must and should not be missed. Pune is now emerging as the cyber hub of Maharashtra state. The growing IT industry and foreign investments coming into Pune are helping the city to flourish further. I see the city emerging as a powerful industrial hub of western India in the future.

I can only compare Pune with Oxford for its educational facilities, with Detroit for its auto industry, and San Jose for being an IT Hub.

Weather-wise or even otherwise Pune is unique. The weather is friendly, the heritage and culture is age-old and with no threats of volcanoes, cyclones, earthquakes, tsunamis and very heavy showers, Pune is truly unique.

Pralhad Chhabria

Chairman of the Finolex Group of companies, Pralhad Chhabria was the President of MCCIA in 1994-96. In 1994 he was presented the "Successful Businessman of the Year Award" by the Priyadarshini Academy. He is the Founder Member of the Hope Foundation and is involved in many other social causes.

I came to Pune in 1945 in search of a job. In those days the climate of Pune was serene and even in summer a fan was not required. The people in Pune were simple and the total population was about a lakh. Pune was not very crowded in those days and business, and friends were all in close proximity

Pune is a city known for its historical and cultural heritage. One can pursue any hobby such as music, drama, painting, etc. with ease. There are so many renowned and talented people in Pune from every sphere of the arts. But one can see the old culture slowly dying out. The interest for drama and music is fading away and with it Pune's rich cultural legacy too is dying.

> It is a balanced city with an equal blend of modernization and tradition.

It is a cultural, educational, science, research and development hub; a balanced city with an equal blend of modernization and tradition.

The city is well connected by air, rail and road. Pune is a business centre, a developed city with the latest technology. However the increased development and growth in the city is taking away its natural beauty and in 10 years time or even less Pune will become a suburb of Mumbai. People will prefer to stay in Pune and work in Mumbai.

Nowadays even an AC is not enough to relieve one from the heat because all the greenery, gardens and bungalows are being destroyed to make way for huge high-rise buildings. The city bureaucrats need to start checking and planning the city to ensure that it retains its greenery and beauty. We must have more open spaces with beautiful gardens in Pune.

My favourite places in Pune used to be Bund Garden, Saras Baug or even Parvati in the good old days. But today due to the city having developed rapidly they too have lost their serenity and old world charm. Hence I find it very difficult to have a favourite place.

After visiting so many places in the world, I still cannot compare Pune to any other city. It has its own culture and class. The uniqueness of Pune lies in the Puneites who still maintain their traditional practices, value their personal relationships and meet people cordially and with utmost respect.

Pratap Pawar

The Managing Director and Managing Editor of Sakal Papers Ltd., and the Chairman of Ajay Metachem Group of Industries, Pratap Pawar is also the Director of various other Indian companies. A Former President of MCCIA Pune and the first President of the Federation of Chambers and Associations all over Maharashtra, he is also a former President of The Indian Newspaper Society, New Delhi.

Part of my education was from the renowned Fergusson College in Pune after which I continued my education at BITS Pilani. For all its qualities, Pune was the obvious choice for me to start my own business and my career.

Pune has a rich heritage and tradition of reformers and academicians. Punyanagri as it was originally known, has the makings of a beautiful and great city, fair weather conditions and abundant water supply, not to forget its rich historical background; it has also been the capital of the Maratha Empire.

All these characteristics of Pune make me proud to be a Puneite.

A centre for the manufacturing and engineering industries, with a well-educated population, availability of infrastructure, proximity to the commercial capital Mumbai, Pune's growth and enhancement is inevitable, and as any other industrial city, Pune is growing very very fast. But the complete lack of planning and erratic growth is causing many worries. Soon there will not be enough open spaces for cultural gatherings, playgrounds and gardens due to this haphazard planning. The city will become like a concrete jungle and I would not like to see it like this.

Even the general public of Pune take their civic responsibilities very seriously.

There is hope however. While living in this city I have come across many persons involved in and very committed to various social and humane causes. There are a number of selfless dedicated people working towards one social mission, 'The betterment of this city and its people'. Even the general public of Pune take their civic responsibilities very seriously.

The abundance of universities, colleges and various national research institutes here has already given Pune the title of 'Oxford of the East'. We should further develop Pune as a city of knowledge and industry but this should be done without sacrificing any characteristics of Pune's rich heritage and culture.

Pratima Joshi

Pratima Joshi is the Founder-Director of Shelter Associates, an NGO working with the urban poor to facilitate and provide technical support to community-managed infrastructure projects. An architect, she also has a post-graduate degree in Building Designs for Developing Countries from Bartlett University, UK. In 2005 she was selected to feature on the BBC News website for her work as a Slum Architect, and recently was awarded the Ashoka Fellowship in recognition of her work as a Social Entrepreneur.

I moved to Pune in 1988 after marriage as my husband's family lived here. I remember feeling a mixture of apprehension and excitement not only because I was moving to a smaller city, having lived all my life in the metropolitan city of Chennai, but also because it was a homecoming of sorts - back to the city where I spent many summer vacations of my childhood visiting my grandparents.
My early memories of Pune were most certainly of Sarasbaug, which I visited every evening with my grandfather. Offering prayers at the Ganpati temple with delicious *pedhas* as *prasad,* followed by sugarcane juice, was a routine which I never tired of. We would also visit the Parvati temple in the mornings, counting the numerous steps as we climbed.
I settled in Pune effortlessly. As luck would have it my office is a stone's throw away from Sarasbaug. This city vibrates with life and there is a heightened awareness among its citizens regarding social and developmental issues that affect the city. It probably has one of the largest number of NGOs among any other Indian city, which have created a body of like-minded people with a real love for the city and a zeal to improve it. Life is easier than in other cities, even in terms of commuting from place to place which makes my work-time use most efficient!

This city vibrates with life and there is a heightened awareness among its citizens.

I love walking around the University campus and the grounds of Gokhale Institute for a breath of fresh air and I am still seized by a childlike excitement when I enter Tulshibaug. The main Mandai market and the Synagogue are also my favourite buildings and I confess that walking into some of the malls of the city is one of my most enjoyable 'chill out activities', though my favourites still remain Westside and Dorabjee's. A visit to Laxmi Road, the older parts of the city, Shaniwarwada and of course Marathi theatre is a must!
Of late however the city has become highly congested with huge traffic and pollution problems. It is now no more a city for the pensioner, but for the young with its universities and burgeoning IT industries. As an architect, I still see that we have a long way to go, when dealing with housing and services for the poor in the city
It is also a city with so many faces, young, traditional, Osho, spiritual, IT, institutions studying ancient texts and traditions...just everything, all living happily together.

Prof. S. V. Kogekar

Prof. S. V. Kogekar was a life member of the Deccan Education Society, one of the most well known educational institutions in India. He was the principal of Fergusson College and the Vice Chancellor of Tilak Vidyapeeth, the first deemed university in Pune. He is well respected in the field of education and his peers and students adore him for his insight and knowledge.

I was born, brought up and educated in Pune. I have lived here for 92 years except for a couple of years spent in England as a student at the London School of Economics, some seventy years ago.

I have watched the gradual transformation of this beautiful, old, sleepy, provincial town of pensioners and students over the last nine decades. I have vivid memories of life in Pune during my childhood. People used to live in *wadas* in various *peths* of the city, where along with the landlord several tenants had their residential premises. In every *wada* there used to be a spacious courtyard, where children could play. All the residents lived like a small community and mutual help and support was the order of the day. There were occasional quarrels among them. But by and large life in the Wada was pleasant and peaceful. Electricity had not made its debut and kerosene lamps were used for lighting. The municipal staff had to go with a ladder, a can and matches to kindle the street lights. The macadam roads were rough and became muddy and slippery during the rains. There was no public transport. Mostly people used to walk. Bicycles were very common for office goers and students. Cars and motorcycles were very few and horse driven *tongas* were used for covering long distances.

Pune has always been a great centre of education.

The primary schools were mainly conducted by the Municipality and their quality was high. Most of us went to these schools. The secondary schools were established by young, idealistic, public spirited and patriotic Indians. The first such school was the New English School established in 1880. Out of this initiative grew the Deccan Education Society. Their founders believed that education was the only effective way of bringing a tradition bound people up to the level of the most advanced countries of the world "by slow and peaceful revolutions". The same pioneering spirit was displayed in other fields of development like social reform, journalism, self-relying economic activities and political organisation and leadership. In their present avatar one sees all these nation-building efforts in the work of the NGOs which are trying to meet the felt needs of the people.

During the last fifty years or so Pune has undergone a great transformation. It has become more vibrant, dynamic, cosmopolitan and an expanding place full of hectic activity and a large influx of people with varying cultural backgrounds. The city also faces new challenges in the wake of these changes. I have no doubt that they will be adequately met in days to come.

Rahul Bajaj

Rahul Bajaj was the CEO of Bajaj Auto Ltd. (BAL) since 1968 and is currently its Chairman. He has an Honours Degree in Economics, an LL.B and MBA (Harvard) degrees. He has served twice as President of the Confederation of Indian Industry and was awarded the nation's third-highest civilian honour, the Padma Bhushan, in 2002. He is a member of the Rajya Sabha and the International Advisory Committee at the New York Stock Exchange and Brookings Institution.

Though I am from Mumbai, I have lived in Pune for over 40 years and hence this is my home. I like being, and I am happy to be called, a Punekar.

The best thing about Pune is that it lets you be yourself. Not in the anonymity of Mumbai way, but in an "I am at peace with myself" way that is most unique. I have not experienced this in any other city in the country, except, a little maybe in Chennai. I think it comes from a tradition of quality education and Pune's very Maharashtrian identity.

The best thing about Pune is that it lets you be yourself.

The temperament and the mentality of Punekars attracts me. Pune is a lovely place to live in and raise a family.

There is the usual middle class emphasis on education, and hard work but also a good work-life balance, a deep-seated sense of democracy and a serious interest in music and theatre. Not that there are no downsides to that. Low propensity to take risks, low civic involvement and too much tolerance are part of the parcel.Hence, the horrible state of our infrastructure.

However the Puneri outlook to life has important business consequences also.

The quality of employees, their ability and willingness to adapt and change are very good. This is why Pune has become and will remain an important hub for the engineering industry, and is increasingly becoming one for the IT industry. Ever since Shivaji made it his capital, Pune has flourished and will continue to flourish.

I hope that Pune retains its character and flavour of life as it grows.

I hope its powerful culture continues to strongly influence the immigrant to adopt its way of life, as it has done successfully for so long.

Rati Forbes

A director of the Forbes Marshall Group of companies, Rati Forbes has specialised in psychology and organisational behaviour. Under her guidance, the company has won the Social Impact Award 2006 instituted by SP Jain Management Institute, Mumbai; First Runner-up to Tata Steel in the inaugural year (1998) of the Businessworld Compaq Award for outstanding Corporate Social Responsibility; and the Runner-Up position at the Mother Teresa Awards in 2000.

Growing up in Mumbai, Pune was nothing more than a weekend get-away destination for me as a child; a fun place to relax, cycle around long driveways, and play hide and seek in large old homes!

I moved here when I got married twenty years ago. Living here has given me an entirely different perspective on the "small town, striving to be a big city". Over the last ten years, it has developed almost unrecognisably, becoming more and more urban while still retaining the small-town charm in areas. I have gradually fallen in love with it!

I hope to see Pune become a benchmark for other cities to replicate.

Even today, Pune continues to startle me with so many contrasts – some more obvious, some subtle and underlying.

The developed modern industrial regions, abutting the rural areas.

Heritage bungalows in the cantonment and Koregaon Park area right-angled with modern, up market buildings.

New shopping malls on Main Street, bursting with the latest goodies, alongside long established family-run stores.

Fancy new restaurants with stylised interiors alongside old Irani cafes selling the best tea and homemade biscuits.

The contrasting architecture across the Camp and Deccan areas – one so colonial and the other so Maratha – both so beautiful and striking in their own way.

The river, which divides the "City" and the "Camp" areas and the incredibly contrasting life styles of people living in those areas.

But in these contrasts, there are so many positives – a mix of cultures, diverse religions, people rich, middle income and poor all living harmoniously together.

I have come across so many businessmen of Pune – sharp, intellectual, full of acumen, and running huge industries - with equally large hearts and values when it comes to philanthropy and giving to a good cause.

What I like most about Pune, are the wonderful people I have met here and made friends with - warm, fun to be with, generous and "chilled". The environment, which is very conducive for business and the availability of talented people in almost all spheres. The support I have received from diverse quarters of society to reach out, and assist with various social initiatives I am committed to.

I could add so much more to the list.

In the future, I hope to see Pune become a benchmark for other cities to replicate.

I cannot wish anything but the best and nicest, for the wonderful town I now call home.

Ravi Pandit

Chairman and CEO of KPIT Cummins Infosystems Ltd., and the Kirtane and Pandit Group, Ravi Pandit is a fellow member of the Institute of Chartered Accounts. He is also the President of the Mahratta Chamber of Commerce, Industries and Agriculture. His interests include Community Initiatives and Corporate Governance.

The uniqueness of Pune is in the mind-set of its people.

Punekars have deep love and respect for education. In the old days, it was said that every house in Pune had two things - a graduate and a bicycle! The bicycle has now been replaced by two-wheelers (more than 55% of the families have at least one, but generally two, two-wheelers) and the graduates have increased! You can see the love for education in every stratum of the society. Speak to your milk-man, your driver, a *rickshawala,* a cobbler and they will tell you with pride how they are ensuring that their children get a good education.

Pune has a strong sense of individualism. Most Punekars have a view on everything and a pretty strong view at that! People here have a sharp intellect and an even sharper tongue. You will see this expression of individual opinion in every aspect of life. The Punekar is the quintessential "Argumentative Indian".

Punekers are connoisseurs of arts – be it music, dance, painting or sculpture. You will find ardent art-lovers and honest critics, many of who are more generous in criticism than in compliments! Therefore the Puneri compliment is very highly valued!

Pune's people are public-spirited and will actively support and participate in social activities.

Punekers are public-spirited. They actively support and participate in social activities. If there was an index of the number of public trusts per 1,000 residents for a city, I am sure Pune would score the highest in the country! Countless institutions built solely by selfless contribution of many volunteers have worked in this city for decades – Vasant Vyakhyanmala, the summer speech series, has been around for 130 years. The Ganesh festival celebration has been around for 112 years. The Savai Gandharva music festival has been around for 53 years - all these are organized and run solely by volunteers!

Punekers have strong "middle-class" values. There is a disdain for display of wealth. You can't gain respect in this city just by having a lot of money!

Pune also has a great ability to adopt newcomers into the city and the newcomers love Pune. They also love to make fun of Pune, but they would never want to leave it!

Snuggled amongst the Sahyadris, Pune has many nature lovers. People of all ages from kids to elderly people can be seen walking on the city's many hills.

Pune certainly has its own set of problems – the roads, the traffic, the pollution, but still there is no other place where I would like to be!

Sanjeev Abhyankar

A classical singer of the **Mewati gharana,** *Abhyankar is a disciple of the renowned vocalist Pt Jasraj. His first stage performance was at the age of 11, and he has since performed the world over. Abhyankar has also done playback singing for popular films like* **Maachis, Nidaan, Maqbool, Bhet, Dil Pe Mat Le Yaar** *and* **Godmother** *for which he won the Best Male Playback Singer, National Award.*

There are various reasons for my attachment to Pune, the first being that I was born and brought up here. I have traveled the world, and have visited about two hundred different cities to perform at concerts. It is after having this exposure that I have come to the conclusion that Pune is the best city for me to live in.

Culturally it is one of India's richest cities. Considering the size of the city, the number of activities happening here is phenomenal. The activities are diversified and include wide diasporas like classical music, Marathi theatre, literature, poetry, art, and the list goes on.

As a performing artist the audience one gets in Pune is very satisfying.

As a performing artist the audience one gets in Pune is very satisfying. The audience in attendance at these events is large, serious, involved in the performance and appreciative. A large number of well-equipped auditoriums and theatres in which performances can be held, make Pune an ideal city for any artist.

Pune has grown manifold and now has a population of nearly three million, but it still has the compactness of a town. It is easy to meet your friends and acquaintances often. Distance and time are not a hindrance in maintaining interpersonal relations, which are very important to me.

There is a flip side to this development. Lack of proper infrastructure to support the growing needs of the city is a problem. Quick measures need to be taken to develop proper infrastructure to match the level of development.

Pune is one of the safest places in India, and this can be credited to the cultured citizens of the city. It is an educational hub, a cultural hub and now an IT hub, and has a tremendous number of intellectuals and pioneers in varying fields, be it medicine or music.

You can find a variety of restaurants, which serve food that suits every palate. From Continental to Thai, from Kashmiri to Keralite, any kind of food is available. My favourites are Wadeshwar, Shreyas and Garden Court.

Pune has very picturesque surroundings, which encourage long drives and picnics as often as one can spare the time. Personally, I enjoy the beautiful drive to Mulshi Dam during the rains. Hill stations like Mahabaleshwar and Matheran are easily accessible from here, as also the commercial capital of India, Mumbai.

If problems such as power shortage and lack of infrastructure are addressed, then Pune will be like heaven on earth.

Sudhir Sharma

Sudhir Sharma is one of the Founder Directors of Elephant Strategy+Design, one of the largest design houses in the country. A member of the CII Design Task Force, he is also a frequent guest lecturer at national and international design seminars and institutes. His office has created distinctive looks for ICICI, Bajaj, Standard Chartered, Persistent, Sahyadri Hospital, and many more.

I heard about Pune when I was studying at NID (National Institute of Design) and to me it sounded like a fantasy place with its good weather, lush green hills, lots of young people and an extremely active populace. Nearing our graduation some of us got together to form "Elephant Design" in 1989 and we decided to start first at Pune and then expand to Delhi. Two days after the convocation, we all landed in Pune and since then none of us has left.

Initially Pune was not the best place for our work. Design at that time was considered a big city phenomenon and we wouldn't get many clients in Pune who would put big money to innovation and growth. However, in time we realized that Pune has a unique stability of growth and slowly both Pune and Elephant have progressed to a brighter future.

> Pune has a huge pool of extremely brilliant but down to earth people....

Pune has a huge pool of extremely brilliant but down to earth people, some of whom have traveled the world over and then decided to settle here. Interacting with them instilled in us self-confidence, an ethical, philosophical outlook and an awareness of the world underlined with a stark sense of realism.

This confidence, mixed with realism and Pune's fearless passion for new ideas started reflecting in our work, and our clients liked the down to earth, simple solutions that we provided to complex issues.

My office is my favorite place in Pune; located on a hillside, it is a three tiered building that reflects the layered terrain one sees in Pune. Another place I love is the NDA road where I go for my morning walk and from where you get a fabulous view of Pune.

If you get the time, don't miss an early morning walk on any *tekdi* (hill) close to you. Not many cities in the world can give you the pleasure of a clean, green, peaceful morning on a hill with a fabulous view of the city, just before you start your hectic day.

A lot of young intellectuals are setting up base in Pune, as it offers an opportunity of being in a growing city and still being able to connect with nature.

I see Pune fighting to become one of the best cities of India and I have no doubt it will attain its goal within a few years. I have come to realize that only originality and innovation can lead this city and Pune as I see it will not follow but lead in development at any level.

You can compare Pune in parts with other places but holistically Pune is incomparable.

Sujit Patwardhan

Founder member of 'Parisar' a non-governmental organization working for environmental conservation and education, Sujit Patwardhan is a renowned environmental activist. He is extremely active in issues related to sustainable urban transport, river pollution and encroachment in no-development zones.

My father being a Government officer we lived in many different towns during my school days but the years spent in Pune were the most enjoyable. The happiest times were learning to ride the bicycle on Prabhat Road and Karve Road which had a grand canopy of huge banyan trees, and riding the cycle from Dandekar Bridge to Vithalwadi.

Those were the carefree days of playing cricket on the many empty plots in and around our locality, plucking raw mangoes and tamarind, learning to swim in the Tilak Tank, going for cricket coaching classes at Deccan Gymkhana and playing tennis.

For many years changes were slow and the city retained its easy pace, pleasant climate, and green areas.

I left Pune and went to Varanasi, Nagpur and Mumbai with my parents but holidays were always spent in Pune where we would meet up with old friends, visit Sinhagad, Panhala Fort and Mahabaleshwar. For many years changes were slow and the city retained its easy pace, pleasant climate, and green areas.

When I returned to Pune in 1968 and made it my home, things had started changing. Industry and commercial establishments were opening up and the city was expanding in all directions. Although this was good for business, we were noticing the effect on social patterns. Old *wadas* and famous landmarks were being erased by the changes in economy. The city was becoming prosperous economically but slowly losing its old world charm – trees and canals and cycling paths were giving way to fast moving vehicles. Auto rickshaws wiped out the old *ghoda-gadis* (horse carts) and cycling was growing more and more dangerous.

Today the city is on the verge of collapse with civic amenities at breaking point. Traffic congestion, pollution, accidents, destruction of natural environment, green areas, public spaces, water bodies, and all parts of the city experiencing growth without planning accompanied by massive failure of governance.

The environmental pollution is also spreading to the hearts and minds of citizens – more and more people are concentrating on personal profits at the cost of the city and the community.

We have still not reached the point of no return and there are scattered examples of community oriented efforts from all sections of society which can still blossom into a force of renewal but time is short and we need to start the process of healing today if the city is to regain the great heights of yesteryears as a hotbed of social, political and educational reforms and a torch bearer to a whole generation of Indians.

Suresh Kalmadi

A Member of Parliament, (Lok Sabha & Rajya Sabha), for 24 years, Suresh Kalmadi has held many prestigious positions such as Minister of State for Railways in 1995-96 and Chairman of MTDC in 1988-89. Currently, as Chairman, he is the driving force behind the Pune Festival, Pune International Marathon, Pune Vyaspeeth and Pune International Film Festival. He has been the President of the Indian Olympic Association for the last eight years and is the Chairman of the Organising Committee, Commonwealth Games Delhi 2010.

I completed my education from St. Vincent's High School and Fergusson College. Thereafter I joined NDA where I trained to be a pilot for the Indian Air Force. My postings took me to many different places but Pune was always on my mind and thus after 10 years of service I opted for premature retirement and returned to Pune. More than anything else I wanted to do social service as I had watched my father Dr. Kalmadi Shamrao do. I decided to serve the people through a political party, thus I enrolled as a Youth Congress member, and thus began my political career. What I like most about Pune are its citizens, the Punekars! They are fiercely proud of their traditional roots, yet are not averse to modernization. It is due to the foresight of the Punekars, that Pune has so many identities: Oxford of the East, Queen of the Deccan, Sports City, Garden City, Industrial city, Cultural Capital of Maharashtra, and is now on the threshold of becoming the Information and Bio Technology Capital of the country! It is also one of the most secular cities of the country where people from all walks of life co-exist peacefully. Some places that I love to visit in Pune are the magnificent Shaniwarwada, Aga Khan Palace, Pune University, Khadakvasla Dam, Sinhagad Fort, Saras Baug and many more. Besides these tourist spots, various cultural and sports events such as the Pune Festival, Pune International Marathon, Pune International Film Festival and many more are major attractions with local and international visitors! Pune is growing at a frantic pace and as the elected Member of Parliament from this city, I am constantly trying to do things to put Pune on the international map. The city will now undergo a major transformation to get ready for the grand international event in 2008, the Commonwealth Youth Games, after which it will become a model city! Having traveled extensively to many cities of the world, I have yet to find one like Pune that has everything – history, rich culture and tradition, secular citizens, salubrious climate, natural beauty and the capability and willingness to embrace modernity, at the same time retaining her traditions and values. Anybody who has experienced even a little of what this city has to offer is bound to come back for more! Pune will now undergo a major transformation to get ready for the grand international event in 2008, the Commonwealth Youth Games.

> Anybody who has experienced even a little of what the city of Pune has to offer is bound to come back for more.

Uday Narayanrao Borawake

Farmer, entrepreneur, and Chairman of the Agriculture & Agri-Business Committee MCCIA, Pune, Uday Borawake is also an Executive Council Member of the National Institute of Agricultural Extension & Management (MANAGE), Hyderabad.

I came to Pune in 1955. I was only eight at the time, sent here to study at the SSPMS School, after which I graduated from Fergusson College in Economics.

I am proud to have been educated in the Oxford of the East, as per the wishes of my father, Raobahadur Borawake, a farmer of great talent and enterprise. An educationist and philanthropist, he actively participated in Pune's industrial development as a Director with Kirloskar Brothers and Kirloskar Oil Engines and as promoter of Krupps, India's first Indo-German venture in Pune. In 1932 he also guided 400 farmers in setting up the first co-operative sugar factory, which served as a model for future farmers and sugar cooperatives in India. Pune has always been famous for horticulture and agro-based industries. It is at the centre of the agriculture producing districts of Ahmednagar, Satara and Solapur. The diversity of agricultural output in this area is astounding. It comprises multiple agri-cash crops, horticultural produce, floriculture, poultry and dairy products, which in turn support and supply agri-produce to 1,100 food processing units. Pune's airport has facilities for exporting agri-produce bound for international destinations, a necesscity for the region.

Pune is home to a large number of institutes that generate human resources for the agriculture industry, amoung them the century old Mahatma Phule Agriculture College, Agarkar Institute, the VSI Centre and Ganeshkhind Agri/Horticultural Institute. These are the bedrock for agri business development. In Pune we also have the best, floriculture training greenhouse facility housed at the Agriculture College.

> In Pune we have the best, floriculture training greenhouse facility housed at the Agriculture College.

I established a mixed economy activity farm in Pune, and then I set up a Broiler Chicken Farm, a pioneering effort. The next step was the setting up of the Farm to Fork concept of Ready-to-Eat Borawake's Ku-Kooch-Ku Chicken. These farm based business endeavors were possible only due to Pune's consumers who are open to new ideas and value quality above all else. I like living in Pune because of its forward-looking citizens who are open to participating in the economy and creative atmosphere of the city, and forging ahead with multi-activity, multi-identity institutions that are constantly adding to its eclectic character. Pune's citizens are constantly providing creative solutions to many problems facing the city, and thus contributing to the academic and cultural ethos of Pune city.

I second *Forbes* magazine when it names Pune as one of the three best cities in the world. Its character, wisdom and climate make living in this enriched habitat we call Pune city worthwhile.

Selective Directory

Emergency Numbers

Police Control Room
26122880
Police
100
Fire
101
Ambulance
102

Ambulance Services

Ruby Hall Clinic
26123391
Columbus
25531146, 25532630
Sai Ambulance
26959308, 26959208
Shivsena Rugnavahika
26124848
YCM
27423456

Blood Banks

Jehangir Hospital
26050550
KEM Hospital
26125600
Ruby Hall Clinic
26123391
Sassoon Hospital
26128000

Generic Numbers

Electricity MSEB
1600214565
PMC Complaints Services
1913
BSNL Enquiry
198
Pune Cantonment Board
26453696
Kirkee Cantonment Board
25812893
Dehu Cantonment Board
27671222

Crematoriums

Vaikunth
24336975
Kailash
26124123
Yerawada
2661422

Places to Stay

(Hotels, Lodges, Hostels and Services Apartments)

Aundh & Surroundings

The Pichola Hotel
55/2, Ganeshkhind Road,
Aundh,
Pune 411007.
25885695
hotelpichola@ip.eth.net

Bund Garden & Koregaon Park

Bel Air Suites and Service Apartments
333, Koregaon Park,
Off North Main Road,
Near Cosmos Bank,
Pune 411001
30523333 / 30524431

Don Bosco Youth Centre
4 Koregaon Road,
P.O Box No 216,
Pune GPO,
Pune 411001.
26122813
Lodging facility available

Hotel Homeland
18, Wilson Garden,
Near Pune Railway Station,
Pune 411001.
26127659

Hotel Meru
Ladkat Wadi Road,
Off Dhole Patil Road,
Pune 411001.
26123939
tghotels@hotmail.com

Hotel Regency
192, Dhole Patil Road.
Pune 4110001.
56033611

Hotel Shalimar
12/A Connaught Road,
Sadhu Vaswani Road,
Pune 411001.
26129191

Hotel Srimaan
361/5A, Bund Garden Road,
Pune 411001.
26133535 / 26122369
srimaan@vsnl.com

Hotel Woodland
Sadhu Vaswani Circle,
Near Pune Railway Station,
Pune 411001.
26126161 / 26136161
info@tghotels.com

Le Meridien
Delux
Raja Bahadur Mill Road,
Pune 411001.
26050505 / 26122000
www.pune.lemeridien.com
sales@lemeridien.com

Seasons Service Apartments
Trinity Court,
Off South Main Road,
Koregaon Park, Pune 411001.
26140130 / 31 / 32

Sunderban
19, Koregaon Park,
Next to Osho Commune,
Pune 411001.
26124949
tghotels@hotmail.com
Heritage Hotel

Sun n Sand
Delux
262 Bund Garden Road,
Pune 411001.
26137777
sales@sunnsandpune.com

Taj Blue Diamond
11, Koregaon Park,
Pune 411001.
26125555
bluediamond.pune@tajhotels.com

The Central Park Hotel
Opp Council Hall,
Bund Garden Road,
Pune 411001.
26054000
centralpark@vsnl.net

Central Pune

Poona Guest House
P
100, Budhwar Peth, Laxmi Road,
Pune 411002.
24455679 Lodge

YMCA
P
382, New Rasta Peth,
Quarter Gate, Pune 411011.
26134842 / 26131338
Boys Hostel with amenities like swimming pool and gym.
Branch at Race Course.
26360504

Deccan & Shivajinagar

Baramati Boys Hostel
270/C Gokhale Nagar,
Pune 411004.
25658686 / 25659191

Best Western Pride Hotel
5 University Road,
Shivajinagar, Pune 411005
25534567
pune@pridegroup.net

Centurion Hotel Quality Inn
10/1A, Ganeshkhind Road,
Opp Akashvani Bhawan,
Shivajinagar,
Pune 411005
25510600

Gordon House
132A/2A, University Road,
Ganeshkhind,
Pune 411016.
66044100
e-square@e-squareindia.com

Hotel Ashish Plaza
1198, Shivajinagar,
F.C. Road, Pune 411004.
25536541 / 42 / 43 / 44

Hotel Ashiyana
1198 Shivajinagar,
F.C. Road, Pune 411004.
25538011

Hotel Coronet
1205/4, Apte Road,
Deccan Gymkhana,
Pune 411004.
25530300

Hotel Nandanvan
1212/A Shivajinagar,
Apte Road, Pune 411001.
25531111

Hotel Shreyas
1242/B, Apte Road, Deccan
Gymkhana, Pune 411004.
25532023

Kohinoor Executive
Apte Road, Deccan Gymkhana,
Pune 411004.
25532000 / 25531811

Oakwood
Good Luck Square,Bhandarkar
Road, Deccan Gymkhana,
Pune 411004.
25670011
tghotels@hotmail.com

Kondhwa Wanworie & Bibvewadi

Beverly Hills
VISA P
Service Apartments
Plot 178, 179, 180, Lulla Nagar,
Near Mount Carmel School,
Pune 411040
26837000

Kothrud & Erandawane

Hotel Senator
VISA P
54, Lokmanya Colony,
Opp Vanaz Factory, Pune 411038
25399999

R K Khadilkar Girls Hostel
79-B/2, Corner of 15th Lane,
Prabhat Road, Pune 411004
25658252

Saheli Home Ladies Hostel
P
Near Cummins College of
Engineering, Karve Nagar,
Pune 411038.
25422514

Sharda Niketan Girls Hostel
30/2B, Karve Nagar,
Pune 411052.
25444319

The President Hotel
34/11, Erandawane, Prabhat Road, Lane No 8, Behind Kohinoor Mangal Karalaya,
Pune 411004.
25431797 / 66031797
www.hotelpresidentpune.com

Pimpri - Chinchwad

Hotel Emerald Park
P 63, D 1 Block, MIDC,
Chinchwad, Pune 411019.
27477468 / 27477469

Hotel Kalasagar
Near Old Pune- Mumbai Highway, Near Vallabhnagar,
Pimpri, Pune 411034.
27125901

Panchsheel Hotel
C32, Near MIDC Office,
Chinchwad, Pune 411019.
27472012 / 27472013

Pune Cantonment

Aurora Towers
9, Dr. Ambedkar Road,
Pune 411001.
26131818
hotelaurora@usa.net

Sagar Plaza
1, Bund Garden Road,
Pune 411001.
26122622 / 12 / 23
Fax: 26122633
tsp@sarovarparkplaza.com

YWCA - Girls Hostels
5 Gurudwara Road,
Camp, Pune 411001.
26360300

Eateries

(Restaurants, Bakeries, Coffee Shops and Snack Joints)

Aundh & Surroundings

Ambrosia
Survey No. 38/2, Bavdhan Khurd, Taluka Mulshi,
Pune 411021.
22951023 / 22951571
ambrosia_resorts@vsnl.com
Multi-cuisine restaurant and bar

Banjara Hills Holiday Resorts
TIME: 9 am–11 pm.
Survey No. 20/4/B, Bavdhan Khurd, NDA Road,
Chandni Chowk,
Pune 411021.
22951019 / 22951560
safari@vsnl.net
Multi-cuisine restaurant, pub and disco

Club Oasis
Survey. No. 104/5/1,
NDA Road, Pune 411029
25286276 / 5135 / 6422
Multi-cuisine restaurant.

Faaso's
Shop No 1, Aditya Classic,
Baner Road,
Pune 411045.
27293940
Branch also at NIBM Road.

Garden Court
NDA Road, Chandni Chowk,
Bavdhan,
Pune 411029.
25283502 / 25280001
gardenresorts@indiatimes.com
Multi-cuisine restaurant and bar

Green Park
14/B, Kale Park, Baner Road,
Baner, Pune 411045.
25886265
Multi-cuisine restaurant

Kobe
ITI Road, Aundh,
Pune 411007.
25887576 / 77.
Veg and non-veg sizzlers.

Malvani Gazali
Baner Road, Pune 411045.
27291667
Konkani cuisine.

Polka Dots
D. P. Road, Aundh,
Pune 411007.
56212241
Continental and Indian cuisine.

Rajwada
15/A, Kale Park, Baner Road,
Baner, Pune 411045.
25885885 / 1881
Multi-cuisine restaurant

Sarjaa
ITI Road, Aundh,
Pune 411007.
25886177 / 25880666
Multi-cuisine restaurant.

Up and Above
9 am-11 pm.
Rambaugh, Survey No. 75,
Chandni Chowk, Kothrud,
Pune 411029.
22953272 / 9371060746
Multi-cuisine restaurant and bar

Wazwaan
Baner Road, Baner,
Pune 411045.
27292422
Kashmiri cuisine

Bund Garden & Koregaon Park

ABC Farms
North Main Road,
Koregaon Park,
Pune 411001.
25123220 / 26876555 / 999
Many restaurants offering a range of different cuisines in the same compound

Arthur's Theme
Vrindavan Apartments,
Off North Main Road,
Koregaon Park, Pune 411001.
26132710 / 24032710
French cuisine

Bombay Brassiere
11 am-11 pm.
101, City Point Boat Club Road,
Near Akshay Complex,
Pune 411001.
560111012 / 9822398749
bpune@hotemail.com
Multi-cuisine restaurant and bar

Chandini Paan Shop
Next to Sagar Plaza,
Bund garden Road,
Pune 411001.
Exclusive *paan*

Comesum
Railway Station Premises,
Pune 411001.
26141737 / 26145761
Multi-cuisine restaurant

Flags
12 noon–3 pm, 7 pm–11 pm.
G/2 Metropole, Next to Inox,
Bund Garden Road,
Pune 411001.
26141617 /18
World cuisine, restaurant and bar

Flapjack
Central Park Hotel,
Bund Garden Road,
Pune 411001.
26054000
Specializes in crepes

German Bakery
7 am-11 pm.
291, Vaswani Nagar,
North Main Road,
Pune 411001.
26136532
german_bakery@yahoo.co.in
Rolls, sandwiches burgers, confectionery and other snacks

Golconda
ABC Farms, Mundhwa Road,
Koregaon Park, Pune 411001.
26817415
Popular for its open-air ambience and biryani

Gourmet
North Main Road,
Koregaon Park, Pune 411001.
Pancakes and crepes

Hot Breads
1A/1B Gera Sterling,
North Main Road,
Koregaon Park, Pune 411001.
26133757 / 26054307
Bakery and confectionery products

Indyaki
South Main Road,
Koregaon Park, Pune 411001.
26055116 / 26055118.
Multi-cuisine restaurant

Just Baked
7 pm-11 pm.
198/3, Chandrakant Chambers,
Dhole Patil Road,
Pune 411001.
26123296 / 26127278
Bakery and confectionery products

Kapila Kebabs
B.O.Maharashtra Compound,
Next to Kapila Hotel,
Dhole Patil Road,
Pune 411001.
Kathi rolls, veg and nonveg

Koyla
Hermes Vishal Building,
Mira Nagar Corner,
North Main Road, Pune 411001.
26120102
Hydrabadi cuisine.
Branch at F. C. Road

Krishna Restaurant & Bar
11.30 pm-3 pm,
7 pm-11.30 pm.
Ashoka Mall, Bund Garden Road,
Opp. Sun 'N' Sand,
Pune 411001.
26132331 / 26113680
Specialises in seafood

La Dolce Vita
City Point, Boat Club Road,
Pune 411001.
26145555
Italian cuisine

La Pizzeria
12 noon-3.30 pm,
6.30 pm-12 midnight.
Srimaan Hotel, 361/5B Bund
Garden Road, Pune 411001.
26122369
www.littletaly-india.com
Italian restaurant & bar

Mad House Grill
Lane No 6, Pingle Corner,
Koregaon Park,
Pune 411001.
26124779
Continental cuisine, sizzlers and steak

Madhuban Restaurant
8 am-11 pm.
Dhole Patil. Road,
Near Larsen and Tubro,
Pune 411001.
Udipi and Punjabi cuisine

Mainland China
12.30pm-3pm.
7.30pm-11.30pm.
Ground Floor, City point,
Boat Club Road,
Near Akahay Complex,
Pune 411001
66013030
mlcpune@eth.net
Chinese cuisine

Malaka Spice
Vrindavan Apartments,
Off North Main Road,
Koregaon Park,
Pune 411001.
26136293
South-east Asian cuisine

Manmeet
Ganpati Chowk,
Dhole Patil Road,
Pune 411001.
30940451
All kinds of Chaat.
Branches: F.C. Road and M.G. Road

Only Parathas
11am-11.30pm.
Metropole Building,
G4 Ground Floor, Near Inox,
Bund Garden Road,
Pune 411001.
26051834 / 26051835
Chaat, parathas, Punjabi snacks, home delivery within 3 Kms.

Pizza Corner
11am-11pm
1st Floor, The Hub,
North Main Road, Koregaon Park
Pune 411001.
26055511 Pizzas

Pizza Express
11 am-11 pm.
Sohrabh Hall, 21 Sassoon Road,
Behind Railway Station,
Pune 411001.
26059002 / 30520666
sanmarzano@vsnl.net
Pizza restaurant and bar

Riverview
81/82 North Main Road,
Koregaon Park Extension,
(towards Mundhwa)
Pune 411001.
26811335 / 6
Multi-cuisine restaurant

Shisha Café
ABC Farms, North Main Road,
Koregaon Park,
Pune 411001.
56202674
Lebanese, Iranian and Mogulai cuisine

Silk Route
357/1 Lane No 6, Pingle Corner,
Koregaon Park Pune 411001.
26135793
South-east Asian cuisine restaurant with lounge

Sisa
(Some Indian Some Asian)
11 pm-12 midnight.
G1, Metropole Building,
Next to Inox, Bund Garden Road,
Pune 411001.
56091227 / 56229945
Longue bar with multi-cuisine restaurant.

Soul
ABC Farms, Mundhwa Road,
Koregaon Park, Pune 411001.
56206997/ 9823193324
Italian food and a live band

Spice Garden
12 noon-12 midnight.
Akshay Complex, Dhole Patil Road, Behind Zamus,
Pune 411001.
Restaurant and bar

Suonmoi
12 noon-11.30 pm.
11, Century Arcade,
Narangi Baug Road,
Off Boat Club Road,
Pune 411001.
30581110 / 500
Chinese cuisine

Sweet Chariot Cafe
Mit Corner, North Main Road,
Koregaon Park, Pune 411001.
26113363
Bakery & confectionery products

Swiss Cheese Garden
ABC Farms, North Main Road,
Koregaon Park,
Pune 411001.
26817413
Swiss and French cuisine

Thai House
10 am-12 noon, 7 pm-11 pm,
Sunday.
Shop No. 4 & 5,
Shankar Parvati Chambers,
Dhole Patil Road, Pune 411001.
9822517975
kritsadakh@hotmail.com
Authentic Thai cuisine

The Great Punjab
5, Jewel Tower, Lane 5,
Off North Main Road,
Koregaon Park, Pune 411001.
26145060 / 30932023.
Punjabi cuisine

Whispering Bamboo
Taj Blue Diamond,
11 Koregaon Park,
Pune 411001.
24025555
Thai and Chinese cuisine

Yoko Sizzlers

12 noon-11.30 pm.
G/3 5th Avenue,
Dhole Patil Road, Pune 411001.
30908165
Sizzlers

Zamu's

189 Nirmal Building, Dhole Patil Road, Pune 411001.
26123610
Sizzlers

Central Pune

Bedekar Missal

Near Sathe Gadikarkhanna,
Below Purandare Classes,
Narayan Peth, Pune 411030.
Missal

Coconut Grove

Near Ambedkar Bhavan,
Mangalwar Peth,
Maldhaka, Pune 411002.
26053981 / 26053982

Durvankur Dining Hall

11 am-11 pm.
Hatti Ganpati Chowk, Tilak Road,
Sadashiv Peth, Pune 411030.
24474438 / 24467067
Only veg Maharastrian *thali*

Jana Seva Dugdhalya

Near Gokhale Hall, Laxmi Road,
Pune 411030.
24453118
Maharashtrian snacks

Kawre Ice-cream

89. Budhwar Peth, Laxmi Road,
Pune 411030
24455764
Ice-cream, Mastani, falooda, snacks, etc.

Rasoi Dining Hall

324, Shaniwar Peth,Laxmi
Madhav Apartment,
Pune 411030.
24453066
Maharashtrian cuisine

Sujata Mastani

1260, Sadashiv Peth, Nimbalkar
Talim Chowk,
Pune 411030.
24474641
Mastani, falooda, snacks, etc.

Deccan & Shivajinagar

All Stir Fry

Gordon House Hotels, E-Square,
Ganeshkhind Road,
Pune 411016.
66044100
Chinese and Thai cuisine

Appa Canteen Or Deccan Gymkhana Tea Stall

Next to the Billiards Department,
Deccan Gymkhana,
Pune 411004.

Café Good Luck

Goodluck Chowk,
Deccan Gymkhana
Pune 411004.
25676893
Traditional Irani food

Chaitanya Dining Hall

12.30 pm-11.30 pm.
1199/B
Chanakyapuri Apartments,
Next to Hotel Ashish Plaza,
F.C Raod,
Pune 411004.
25520945
Famous for various types of *parathas*.
Branches at Dhole Patil road and Karve Road

Hotel Shreyas

1242 b Apte Road,
Deccan Gymkhana
Pune 411004.
25531963 / 25536903
Specializes in Maharashtrian cuisine

Kobe

Shop no 1-2-3, Business Guild,
Law college Road,
Pune 411004.
25455001 / 2
Sizzlers

Poona Coffee House

Opp PMT Bus Stand,
Deccan Gymkhana,
J.M. Road, Pune 411005.
25531256/25531970
Fast food

Poonam Pan Shop

Deccan Gymkhana,
Pune 411004.
All types of *paan*

Puran da Dhaba

The Pride Hotel, 5,
University Road,
Shivajinagar, Pune 411016.
25534567
Punjabi cuisine

Radhika

9am-10pm
927 Sanas Memories,
F.C. Road, Pune 411004.
25664393
Veg fast food

Radhika

Senapati Bapat Road,
Pune 411016
Bengali cuisine

Roopali

Fergusson College Road,
Shivajinagar
Pune 411004.
23352951
Veg restaurant serving south Indian and Punjabi cuisine

Rutugandh

638 J.M. Road, Near Z Bridge,
Decaan Gymkhanna,
Pune 411004.
25536560 / 66029201
Rajasthani and Gujarati *thali*

Shabree
Next to Tukaram Mandir, F.C Road, Shivajinagar, Pune 411004.
25531511
Maharashtrian *thali* and snacks

Shiv Sagar Fast Food
9am-11.30pm
J. M. Road, Opp Sambhaji Park, Shivajinagar Pune 411005.
25532179
Mexican, *pav bhaji*, juices, milk shakes etc.

Vaishali
1218/1 Fergusson College Road, Shivajinagar Pune 411004.
25531244
Veg restaurant serving south Indian

Hadapsar & Solapur Bazaar

Courtyard Greenview
Pune-Solapur Road, Hadapsar, Pune 411028.
Multi-cuisine restaurant

Deccan Harvest
143 Magarpatta City, Off Pune-Solapur Highway, Hadapsar, Pune 411028.
26824142
Multi-cuisine restaurant

Khadki

Royal Symphony Hotel Pvt. Ltd.
210/A, Opp. Kumar Vastu, Range Hill Road, Pune 411016.
25539061
Multi-cuisine restaurant

Kondhwa, Wanowrie & Bibvewadi

Baan Thai
Kubera Colony, Bakers Point, NIBM Road, Pune 411048.
32911907 / 3294007
Thai cuisine

Badamikar Caterers
Shop No-1, Hill View Apartments, Near Mount Carmal School Chowk, Lulla Nagar, Pune 411040.
25425191
Maharashtrian vegetarian

Foodies
Shop No 2, Bakers Point, NIBM Road, Kubera Colony, Pune 411048.
26832729 / 26850777
Fast food joint, famous for Kathi *kebabs*

Hot Gossip
9 am-9 pm.
176, Udyam Parvati, Near Parvati Hall Pune 411009.
24365830
Coffee, milk shakes, ice cream etc.

Just4U The Café
10 am-11.30 pm.
Survey No. 7/2/7, Pune-Satara Road, Near Katraj Snakes Park, Pune 411046.
24374621 / 24377621
Multi-cuisine restaurant with party and conference hall facilities

Kimling
Shop No 1, Gera Junction, Kondhwa Road, Lulla Nagar, Pune 411040.
32931635 / 56236345
Chinese cuisine

Pappu Paan
8 am- 12 midnight.
Poonam Apartment, Bibvewadi-Kondhwa Road, Pune 411048.
24260401
All types of *paan*.
Branches: Portico on Deccan, Ashish Plaza on FC Road and Sarja in Aundh

Southern Spice
Brahma Majestic, Shop No. 11, NIBM Road, Pune 411048.
26805080
South Indian cuisine

The Terrace
12 noon-11.30 pm.
3rd Floor, Brahma Majestic, Shop No. 11, NIBM Road, Pune 411048.
26805080
Multi-cuisine restaurant

ZK's
301/302 Winner Court, Kondhwa Road, Lulla Nagar, Pune 411040.
26834455
Multi-cuisine restaurant

Kothrud & Erandawane

Chinese Room Oriental
17A 4/5 Erandwane, Continental Chambers, Karve Road, Pune 411004.
25441179
Chinese cuisine

Durga
Malti Complex, Off Paud Road, Near MIT College, Pune 411038.
25450565
Coffee and snacks

Faaso's
Near Chaitanya Health Club, Ideal Colony, Paud Road, Kothrud, Pune 411038.
Fast food

Kamat
9 am-11 pm.
Kamat Building, Kothrud,
Pune 411038.
66012233
Maharashtrian, Punjabi, South Indian snacks

Kimaya
127, Karve Road, Kothrud,
Pune 411029.
56007852
Multi cuisine restaurant

Mirch Masala
Amruta Heights, Swamabaug Colony, Near Dahanukar Colony, Karve Road, Pune 411029.
25463949
Multi-cuisine restaurant

Shaukeen Paan Shop
Karve Road, Nal Stop,
Pune 411004
All types of *paan*

Pimpri - Chinchwad

Golden Palms
Patel Golden Farm,
Barber Complex,
Pune-Mumbai Road,
Near Octoroi Naka,
Nigdi, Pune 411044.
27640868
Veg, non-veg cuisine

Hotel Bhola
Block D-2, Plot No 64,
Telco Road, MIDC,
Chinchwad,
Pune 411018
27462847 / 66114023
Thali and other veg cuisine

Hotel Mayur
Opposite Jayshree Talkies,
Chinchwad, Pune 411019
27476999 / 27472071
Gujarati *thali*

Vrindavan
Kohinoor Marvel,
Near Bhakti-Shakti Garden,
Nigdi, Pune 411044
27471110
Multi-cuisine restaurant

Pune Cantonment

Bhavnagari Dry Fruit Co
7 am-9 pm.
Opp. Nehru Memorial Hall,
Dr. Ambedkar Road,
Pune 411001.
26132161
Sweetmeats and dry fruits

Blue Nile
4 Bund Garden Road, Opposite Poona Club, Pune 411001.
26125238
Moghlai cuisine

Budhani Wafers
682, Taboot Street,
Pune 411001.
26134118 / 26131264
All types of wafers, chips, and other snacks

Café Mahanaaz
M.G. Road, Near FotoFast, Opp. Hotel Aurora Towers, Sterling Centre, Camp, Pune 411001.
Tea, snacks and fast food

Cake n Counter
Shop no 15, Thakker House,
2418 East Street, Pune 411001.
26348495
Confectionery

Chinese Room
11.30 am-11.30 pm.
2434, East Street, Pune 411001.
26131336 / 26145613
Chinese cuisine

Chung Fa
12 noon-11 pm.
2435, East Street, Pune 411001.
26136678
Chinese cuisine

Coffee House
2 A Dr. Ambedkar Road, Camp
Pune 411001.
26130716 / 1282
Veg-multi cusine restaurant

Dorabjee Cafetaria
Outside Dorabjee Departmental Store, Dr. Ambedkar Road,
Pune 411001
26052882 / 83 / 84
Sandwiches, burgers, coffee, pastries, etc.

Dorabjee and Sons Restaurant
845, Dastur Meher Road,
Camp, Pune 411001.
26145955
Authentic Parsi cuisine

Hitebar
Office No. 2, Kumar Corner,
Convent Street,
Camp, Pune 411001.
26334080
Shawarma, burgers and rolls

Karachi Sweet Mart
9.30 am-9.30 pm.
Hotel Aurora Towers,
M. G. Road, Camp,
Pune 411001.
56240270 / 56248631
Sweetmeats and dry fruit shop

Kayani Bakery
7 am–8 pm, Sunday
East Street, Pune 411001
26360517
All kinds of biscuits, cakes and other bakery products

Mahesh Lunch Home
12 noon–3 pm, 7 pm–11 pm.
Ashoka Pavillion, 18 Dr. Ambedkar Road,
Next to SBI Main Branch, Camp,
Pune 411001.
26133091 / 56032230
Seafood restaurant- bar

Marz-O-Rin
Bakthiar Plaza,
M.G. Road, Pune 411001.
26130774 / 26136690
Rolls, sandwiches, burgers,

coffee and milkshakes

Mayur

East Street, Pune 411001.
26130909
Gujarati *thali*

Nawab

1st Floor, San Mahu Complex,
Bund Garden Road,
Pune 411001.
56202475/26054274
Moghlai cuisine

Pasteur Bakery

6, M.G. Road,
Opp. Bombay Store,
Pune 411001.
26137848
Cakes, bakery products and *chaat*

Royal Bakery

200, M. G. Road, Camp,
Pune 411001.
26345251
All kinds of biscuits, cakes and other bakery products

Sagar

11 pm–11 pm.
2436, East Street, Camp,
Pune 411001.
26052706
Restaurant and juice centre, serving Indian and Chinese cuisine

Sahare Dining Hall

5, Sadhu Vaswani Road,
Opp GPO, Pune 411001.
26126138
Veg restaurant specializing in *thali*

The Place Touché

Clover Centre, Dr. Ambedkar Road, Next to West End theatre,
Pune 411001.
26134632
Sizzlers, and continental cuisine

Yerawada & Nagar Road

Chokhi Dhani

Ganga Retreat Countryside,
Opp Pune Nagar Highway, Near Ramwadi Octroi post
Wagholi Pune 411007.
27051032
Rajasthani cuisine and entertainment

Kremes n Krusts

Shop No.6, Landmark Garden,
Kalyani Nagar,
Pune 411006.
26615730
Bakery and confectionery products

North West Frontier

Uttam Towers, Opp Aga Khan Palace, Nagar Road,
Pune 411006.
56619300 / 56619301
Kashmiri cuisine

Polka Dots

Metro Traders, Behind Ramvadi Octroi Post, Next to Bishops School, Kalyani Nagar,
Pune 411014.
56611739
Multi-cuisine restaurant

Saat Handi

12, Landmark Garden,
Kalyani Nagar, Pune 411001.
26612934 / 26612935.
Moghulai and Punjabi cuisine

The Bounty

Landmark Garden, Kalyani Nagar,
Pune 411006.
26613360 / 26611758
Sizzlers, continental and Chinese food

The Ship

First Floor, Forteleza, Above Megamart, Kalyani Nagar,
Pune 411006
26608777
Multi-cuisine restaurant

Chains

Coffee Shops

Café Coffee Day
26050728
Barista
25532835

Pizza Joints

Somkin Joes
26124790
Pizza Hut
25530707 / 0828
Pizza Corner
26055511
Domino's Pizza
25673877

Bakers and Confectioners

Bakers Basket
65212235
Copper Chocs
26682896
Monginis Cake Shop
25510451

(These chains have many outlets across the city; call them to find the branch closest to you.)

Shopping

(Books, Apparel, Stationery, Music, Footwear, Jewellery and Gifts)

Aundh & Surroundings

Banjaras
Sarjaa Restaurant Lane,
Off ITI Road, Aundh
Pune 411007.
25881844
Apparel for men and women, tailoring facility available

Bonsaii
Next to Ozone Dept Store,
ITI Road, Aundh, Pune 411007.
25896647 / 66033941
Apparel for kids

Crossword
ITI Road, Next to Ozone,
Aundh, Pune 411007.
66028013 / 25883501
Bookstore

Dass
Dass Electric Trading Co Pvt Ltd,
Sanghvi Nagar, D. P. Road,
Near Bremen Chowk,
Aundh, Pune 411007.
56092480 / 81 / 82.
dasselec@vsnl.com
Electronic appliances available

F-Cube
Closed on Monday.
Shirine Garden, ITI Road,
Aundh, Pune 411007.
5898018 / 4024488.
Gift articles

M Square
Closed on Monday.
Samsung Digital Home
Plot no 8, Sanghvi Nagar,
D. P. Road, Parihar Chowk,
Aundh, Pune 411007.
56096890 / 56091376 / 7
Samsung products

Natekar Sports
C3 / C4 Chaitraban Residency,
Sarjaa Restaurant Lane,
Aundh, Pune 411007.
25885556
Sports wear and equipment

Ozone
92, Anand Park, ITI Road,
Aundh, Pune 411007.
56022555 / 56 / 57, 56032559
Departmental store

Petsworld
ITI Road, Aundh, Pune 411007.
25897321
For pets and related goods

Plugin
D. P. Road, Sanghvi Nagar,
Aundh, Pune 411007.
30939299
Consumer durables chain

Sony World
Closed on Monday.
Equity Tower, D. P. Road, Sanghvi Nagar, Aundh Pune 411007.
56005336 / 25883881
www.sonyindia.co.in/sonyworld
Sony products

Spencer's Daily
Survey No 161/2/2 D. P. Road,
Aundh, Pune 411007.
25880938
Departmental store
Branches: Kothrud, Bhandarkar Road, Paud Road, Wanowrie.

Twist 'n' Tales
10:30am- 8:30pm
Closed on Monday.
Gaikwad Nagar, Aundh,
Pune 411007.
25881465
twistntales@hotmail.com
Bookstore

Bund Garden & Koregaon Park

Burgundy
1st Floor, Prem's Restaurant, Opp SBI Bank, North Main Road,
Pune 411001.
56096571/2
Ethnic wear

Cotemporary Arts
Sohrab Hall, Ground Floor,
Sassoon Road, Pune 411001.
26051177
Ethnic handicraft

Crossword
Sohrab Hall, 1st Floor,
Sassoon Road, Pune 411001
260596001 / 2 / 3
Bookstore

Curio Shops
North Main Road, Koregaon Park, Pune 411001
Metal curios, lucky gems, therapeutic stones, meditation bells, etc.

Either Or
Ground Floor, Sohrab Hall,
Sassoon Road, Pune 411001.
26050225
Ethnic wear and handicraft

Fabindia
Sakar-10, Opp Jehangir Nursing Home, Sassoon Road,
Pune 411001.
26124820 / 26124832
Ethnic wear, handicraft and household linen
Branch at Aundh

Just Antiques
Ganga Commerce,
5 North Main Road,
Koregaon Park,
Pune 411001.
9890032531 / 9370146186
Antique furniture

Magna Book Gallery and Nutrition Centre
Graphicon Arcade,
Opp Jehangir Nursing Home,
Sassoon Road, Pune 411001
56271681 / 56271682
Health food store and book store

Max 10/10 Departmental Store
Survey No. 179/1 Mundhwa Ghorpadi Road, Koregaon Park Annexe, Pune 411001
66260343
Departmental store

More Mischief
34/35 Sohrab Hall,
Opp Jehangir Nursing Home,
Sassoon Road, Pune 411001
26059393
Ethnic and western wear for men

Nature's Bounty
G 11/6 Liberty 11,
North Main Road,
Koregaon Park, Pune 411001.
26114627
Natural health care products

Para Amor
5 Sohrab Hall,
Opp Jehangir Nursing Homes,
Sassoon Road. Pune 411001.
26059696
Jewellery store

Pune Central Mall
256, Koncord Towers, Boat Club Road, Bund Garden.
Pune 411001.
56099000
Clothes, accessories, groceries, etc.

Sanskriti Arts
Sapphire Apts, EP No 347, Near Pizza Hut, Koregaon Park,
Pune 411001.
26139933
Unique show pieces and furniture

This 'n' That
Shop No. 2 Phase 2,
Liberty Society, North Main Road,
Koregaon Park,
Pune 411001.
26055146
Assorted ethnic & western wear & gift articles

Central Pune

Appa Balwant Chowk (ABC)
Budhwar Peth, Pune 411002.
A hub for textbooks, test papers, and stationery

B.N. Ashtekar Jewellers
603 Kunte Chowk, Laxmi Road,
Pune 411030.
24454176
Traditional jewellery

Butterfly
689, Narayan Peth, Bajirao Road,
Pune 411030.
24458343
Apparel for new borns and kids

Chitale Bandhu
777 Sadashiv Peth,
Opp Bank of Maharshtra,
Near Vishrambaug Wada,
off Bajirao Road,
Pune 411030.
24473208
Sweetmeats, savouries and milk products

H.V. Mehendale
Budhwar Peth,
Pune 411002.
24456665
Musical instruments

Jai Hind Collections
Kunte Chowk,
Laxmi Road,
Pune 411030.
24450105
Ethnic and western menswear

Juna Bazaar
9 am-3 pm,
Only on Wed and Sun.
Mangalwar Peth,
Near Sangam Bridge.
Flea market selling all kinds of goods

PN Gadgil
PNG House, Laxmi Road,
Pune 411030.
24435001 / 24455742
Jewellery
Branches:
Camp: 26052424
Chinchwad: 27443444.

Laxminarayan Chiwda
374 Bhawani Peth,
Opp Bhawani Mata Temple,
Pune 411042.
26454561
Speciality *chivda* - a savoury mixture prepared with puffed rice

Laxmi Road
Road extends from Tilak Chowk (Alka) to Phule Chowk (Quarter Gate).
A shopping hub for clothes and jewellery both traditional and contemproray.

Tulsibaug
Next to Bank of Maharahtra,
Janamangal Branch,
Bajirao Road, Pune 411030.
Open all days of the week.
Clothes, accessories, and utensils.

Deccan & Shivajinagar

Bottoms Up
Sagar Arcade, F.C. Road,
Pune 411004.
Apparel and accessories

Champion Sports
10am-8.30pm
759/52 Deccan Gymkhana,
F. C. Road, Pune 411004.
25674534
Sports wear and equipment

Chitale Bandhu
759/51 F. C. Road, Pune 411004.
25674214
Sweetmeats, savouries and milk products

Cotton World Corp.
Laxmi Sadan, J. M. Road, Pune 411004.
24030313
Cotton garments
Branch at Camp

Deo Sports
Deccan Gymkhana, F.C. Road, Pune 411004.
25650598
Sports wear and equipment

Handmade Paper Institute
K.B. Joshi Road, Agriculture College Compound, Shivajinagar, Pune 411005.
25337383 / 25538838
Textured paper and stationery

Hong Kong Lane
Opp. Deccan Bus Stand, J.M. Road, Pune 411005.
A collection of shops selling books, cosmetics and accessories

Kalakriti
50/ A, Shop No. 3 Bhandarkar Road, Pune 411004.
25450760 / 9890011311
Wooden and copper artifacts

P.Y. Vaidya
917/19 F. C. Road, Pune 411004.
25654819
Maharashtrian *masalas*, chutneys and other assorted food items

Popular Book Store
Next to Garware Bridge, F. C. Road, Pune 411004.
25671737 / 25678327
Books and magazines

Shoe World
Next to PMT Stand, J.M. Road, Deccan, Pune 411005.
26348891
Footwear

Shopper's Stop
B Wing, Godrej Etarnia Building, Mumbai-Pune Road, Wakdewadi, Shivajinagar, Pune 411005.
66014959
Apparel, accessories, etc.

TruMart
Abhijeet Court, Bhandarkar Road, Pune 411004.
25659627
Departmental store

United Colours of Benetton
1206/B –19 Opp UTI Bank, J. M. Road Pune 411004.
25532542
Apparel and accessories

Venus Traders
1226/1 Off F. C. Road, Near Roopali, Pune 411004.
25535757
Complete range of stationery
Branch: Nucleus Mall, Camp.

Waman Hari Pethe
Shrisht Chambers 1196 /B, Ghole Road, Pune 411005.
25537498 / 99
Jewellery

Wills Lifestyle
1204/22 Shop No. 8, Ground Floor, Kamla Arcade, J.M. Road, Pune 411004.
66019403
Apparel and accessories

Hadapsar & Solapur Bazaar

Krome Planet Furniture
Amar Manor, 32/3, Pune Solapur Road, St. Patricks Town Corner, Opp ASPT, Pune 411013
26815052/ 53
Furniture and furnishings

Big Bazaar
Fun and Shop Building, Solapur Road, Fatima Nagar, Pune 411040.
66420500 / 5608 / 3025
Apparel, accessories, groceries etc.

Vishal Mega Mart
B Wing KP City Mall, Wanowrie Road, Fatima Nagar, Pune 411040.
26822337/ 38

Khadki

Khadki Bazaar
A popular shopping area offering a variety of clothes, jewellery, furnishings, etc.
Elphistone Road, Khadki, Pune 411003.

Kondhwa, Wanowrie & Bibvewadi

KK Bazaar
Wing B, K.K. Bolsar Market, Pune-Satra Road, Dhankawadi, Pune 411043.
66500444 / 9371003457
Discount mall
Branch at Sachapir Street.

Mantra Magic
Clover Linkfield Plaza, Near Clover Village, Salunke Vihar Road, Pune 411040.
66020304 / 9373999333
Departmental store

TruMart
Konark Indrayu, Off NIBM Road, Kondhwa Khurd, Pune 411048.
26800112
Departmental store

Kothrud & Erandawane

Alurkar Music House
P
4 Swapna Nagri, Karve Road,
Pune 411004.
☎ 25440662
Wide range of Indian classical music

Gitai Shopping Mall
Ideal Colony, Near Anand Nagar,
Paud Road, Kothrud,
Pune 411029.
☎ 25455767 / 25455768

Karve Road
A popular shopping area offering a variety of apparel, jewellery, furnishings and hardware

Kheliya
P
42 Krishnaprasad Society,
Rambaug Colony,
Near Bedekar Mandir,
Paud Road, Pune 411038.
☎ 25459003
Toys and books for children.
Branch at Narayan Peth
☎ 24450547

Paud Road
Several inner city shops have opened up branches here, such as P.N. Gadgil Jewellers. Brands such as Raymonds and Megamart also have outlets here

Ranka Jewellers
❄ VISA P
Karve Road, Kothrud
Pune 411038.
☎ 24263024
Jewellery

Pimpri – Chinchwad

Kohinoor Arcade
❄ P
Nigdi Chowk, Nigdi,
Pune 411031.
(Near the new flyover)
Shopping complex

Mega Mart
❄ VISA P
Opposite PCMC Building,
Mumbai-Pune Highway, Pimpri,
Pune 411018.
☎ 27292880
Range of reasonably priced branded

Pimpri Market
This busy market has a number of stores selling good quality clothing at very reasonable rates.
Behind Pimpri Station,
Shagun Chowk, Pimprigaon,
Pimpri 411018

Pune Cantonment

Babe Boutique
❄ VISA P
6, M .G. Road,
Camp, Pune 411001.
☎ 26135239
Designer outfits and fabrics

Bombay Store
❄ VISA P
M. G. Road,
Pune 411001.
☎ 26131891 / 26131067
Ethnic wear and artefacts

Budhani Wafers
P
682, Taboot Street,
Pune 411001
☎ 26134118 / 26131264
Savoury snack items

Chandan Departmental Store
❄ VISA P
217/218, M.G. Road,
Camp,
Pune 411001
☎ 26342063
Groceries and other house hold items

Dorabjee's
❄ VISA P ♿
1-B Dr. Ambedkar Road,
Pune 411001.
☎ 26052882 / 83
Imported sauces, meats, cheese, chocolates, biscuits, etc.

Fashion Street
Between M.G. Road and East Street, Near Grand Darbar,
Camp, Pune 411001.
A collection of stalls selling reasonably priced apparel and accessories

Haji A. Gani Hiroli
P
Centre Street,
Pune 411001.
☎ 26340994
Puneri sari store

Just Casuals
❄ VISA P
Shop No 13 Tulidas Apts,
Dastur Meher Road, Camp,
Pune 411001
☎ 26125018 / 26125645
Apparel for men and women

Kayani Bakery
P
East Street, Pune 411001.
☎ 26360517
Bakery products, specialty - Shrewsbury biscuits

Main Street
P
Mahatma Gandhi Road,
Camp, Pune 411001.
Hub for apparel, jewellery, footwear, etc.

Manneys
❄ VISA P
Clover Centre, Dr. Ambedkar Road, Camp, Pune 411001.
☎ 26131683
A wide range of books and magazines

Music World
❄ VISA P
Nucleus Mall, Opp GPO, Camp
Pune 411001.
☎ 26140467
Audio cassettes, CDs. DVDs, etc.

New Kashmir Stores (Kashmir Emporium)
VISA P
323, M. G. Road, Pune 411001.
☎ 26138436
Ethnic Kashmiri artefacts

Nucleus Mall
10 am-10pm
1, Church Road,
Opp. Police Commissioner's Office, Camp, Pune 411001.
26120790 / 56096262
Range of apparel and accesories stores

Om to Home and More
11 am-8 pm.
Virwani Plaza, 11 East Street, Camp, Pune 411001.
26332038
Furnishings and artefacts

Pantaloons
3 Castellino Road, Off East Street, Camp, Pune 411001.
26330467 / 26363430
Apparel and accesories

Pin-a-Kin
261, M.G. Road, Camp
Pune 411001.
26342243
Apparel for children

Planet M
Above Dorabjee's Departmental Store, Dr. Ambedkar Road, Camp, Pune 411001.
26141707 / 0809
Audio cassettes, CDs. DVDs, etc.
Branch at Pune Central

Pyramid
1978, Convent Street, Camp, Pune 411001.
1600-1199-11
Apparel, accessories, groceries, etc.
Branch at Senapati Bapat Road

Royal Bakery
200, M. G. Road, Camp, Pune 411001.
26345251
Cakes, biscuits and other bakery products, speciality - Shrewsbury and ginger biscuits

Shivaji Market
Gaffer Street, Sharbatwalla Chowk, Camp, Pune 411001.
Meat, vegetable and fruit vendors

Stout Footwear
10 am-1 pm, 4 pm-8 pm
349, Centre Street, Camp. Pune 411001.
26340189
Kolhapuri slippers and jutis

Sudhan Jewellers
Wonderland Building, M. G. Road 7, Pune 411001.
26133378
Range of exquisite gems, silver and gold jewellery

Toy World
60, M. G. Road, Camp, Pune 411001.
26342022
Toys, prams, books for children

Westside
Next to Dorabjee Departmental Store, Dr. Ambedkar Road, Camp, Pune 411001.
26119920
Apparel and accessories for the family.

World of Toys
2417/A, Exhibition Road, East Street. Pune 411001.
26341534 / 26343109
Range of toys and games for children

Yerawada & Nagar Road

Ishanya Design Mall
Opp. Golf Course, Shastri Nagar, Yerawada, Pune 411006.
66458000 / 26680679
A mall with everything for home interiors

Mariplex
Survey No 15, Wadgaon Sheri,Kalyani Nagar 411014.
56092698 / 99
Multiplex, eateries and other stores

Nilgiriwalas Mega Shoppe
Blue Hills Society, Nagar Road, Pune 411014.
26690364
Departmental store

Sports & More
C-1, Chinar Building, Floriana Estate, Kalyani Nagar. Pune 411006.
27036577
Sports wear and equipment

Entertainment
(Theatres, Auditoriums, Resorts, Amusement Parks, Clubs, Parks and Gardens, Pubs and Discos, Art Galleries, Museums, Stadiums and Libraries)

Aundh & Surroundings

Anandban Club
Anand Park, ITI Rd, Aundh, Pune 411007.
25884455
A family club with a swimming pool, tennis courts and gymnasium

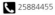

Indiaart Gallery
11 am-7 pm.
Sarjaa Restaurant Lane,
Off ITI Road, Aundh,
Pune 411007.
25896503
Venue for painting exhibitions.

Jagtap Library
P
Gaikwad Nagar, Aundh,
Pune 411007.
Wide range of books.

Jungle Book
❄ P
10 am-1 pm, 3 pm-7 pm
Avni Arcade, Gaikwad nagar,
Aundh Pune 411007.
25882223.
Thrusday closed
Library and activity centre for children

Konark Park
11 am-6 pm.
Pirangut Road,
Near Chandni Chowk,
Bavdhan, Pune 411044.
22951203
Aviary and restaurant

P40
10.30 am-1 pm,
4.30 pm-8.30 pm.
Clarion Park, Aundh.
30948175.
Houses a diverse selection of English books and magazines

PanCard Clubs
VISA P
Baner Hills, Baner Village.
Pune 411007.
27290182 / 83
Amenities include sports centre, amphitheatre, discotheque and go-karting etc.

Shiv Chhatrapati Sports Complex
P
Balewadi,
Dehu Road-Katraj Bypass,
Pune 411045.
Sports Complex

Vaishwik Art Environment
Survey No 246, House No 1982,
Saket Society, D. P. Road, Aundh,
Pune 411007.
27298182
Art gallery for artists, potters, sculptors, calligraphers, etc.

Bund Garden & Koregaon Park

Alankar
❄ P
Near Pune Railway Station,
Pune 411001.
26123333
Movie theatre (Hindi)

Bund Garden
P
Bund Garden Road,
Pune 411001
Garden

Club Polaris
❄ VISA P 🍸
Hotel Taj Blue Diamond,
Koregaon Park, Pune 411001.
26125555
Night club for members only

Inox
❄ VISA P
Bund Garden Road,
Opp. Council Hall, Pune 411001
26111010
Multiplex with 4 screens, eateries and shops

Lush
❄ VISA P 🍸
Shop 14-19, City Tower Building,
Dhole Patil Road, Pune 411001.
Lounge and disco

Nirvana
❄ VISA P 🍸
Ground Floor,
Metropole Building,
Bund Garden Road, Next to
INOX, Pune 411001.
66024733 / 66025733
Lounge and disco

Osho Teerth Nullah Park
Koregaon Park, Pune 411001.
66019999
Garden

Royal Connaught Boat Club
❄ P 🍸
7/8 Boat Club Road,
Pune 411001.
26113512 /13 / 14
Club with sports and entertainment amenities

The Residency Club
❄ VISA P 🍸
3 Queens Garden Road, Next to
Wadia College, Pune 411001.
26362226
Club with sports and entertainment amenities

Saks Art Gallery
P
4/5 Kalpataru Gardens,
9/A Boat Club Road,
Pune 411001.
26123255
Art gallery and exhibition centre

Satwa Art gallery
P
Adit Enclave Building,
South Main Road,
Koregaon Park, Pune 411001.
26056078
Art gallery and exhibition centre

Scream
❄ VISA P 🍸
Le Meridien Hotel,
Raja Bhadur Mills Road,
Pune 411001.
26050505
Disco

Sphinx
❄ VISA P 🍸
Plot No 396/398 Sphinx House,
South Main Road, Greefeild Park
Koregaon Park, Pune 411001.
30583338
Lounge and disco

Ten Downing Street (TDS)
❄ VISA P 🍸
2nd Floor Gera Plaza, Boat Club
Road, Pune 411001.
26128343
Lounge and disco

Zanzibar
❄ VISA P 🍸
Central Park Hotel, Bund Garden
Road, Pune 411001.
26054000
Lounge and disco

Zinc
A/1 Gera Centre, Bund Garden Road, Opp Wadia College, Pune 411001.
26136447
Lounge and disco

Central Pune

Abhiruchi Village
P
Bhide Baug, Sinhagad Road, Wadgaon-Budruk, Pune 411046.
24392483
Entertainment resort

Alka Theatre
P
81 Tilak Road, Navi Peth, Pune 411030.
24333038
Movie theatre (English)

Apollo Theatre
P
549, Rasta Peth, Pune 411011.
26120550
Movie theatre (Hindi)

Art 2 Day
Tilak Road, Hirabaug, Shukrawar Peth, Pune 411002.
24452706
For exhibition and sales of paintings and artwork

Baburao Sanas Athletic Ground
Near Saras Baug, Sadashiv Peth, Pune 411030.
Sports ground

Bharat Itihas Samshodhak Mandal
1321, Sadashiv Peth, Next to Bharat Natya Mandir, Pune 411030.
24472581
Library

Bharat Natya Mandir
P
1320, Sadashiv Peth, Pune 411030.
24471614
bharatnatyamandir.org
Auditorium

Mahratta Chamber of Commerce, Industries and Agriculture
P
Tilak Road, Pune 411002.
4440371 / 4440472 / 4444639 / 4445604
Has library facility

Nagar Vachan Mandir
181, Laxmi Road, Budhwar Peth, Pune 411002.
24450526
Libaray

Neelayam
P
Parvati, Near Peshwe Park, Sadashiv Peth, Pune 411030.
24335301
Movie theatre (Hindi)

Nehru Stadium.
P
Tilak Road, Sadashiv Peth, Pune 411030.
24440641 / 24444739
Cricket stadium and gymnasium

P. L. Deshpande Park
P
Next to Parvati Water Works, Sinhagad Road, Pune 411030.
Garden

Peshwe Energy Park
10 am-8 pm, Closed on Wed
Peshwe Park, Tilak Road, Sadashiv Peth, Pune 411030.
24332388
Display of alternative energy sources

Prabhat Talkies
681, Budhwar Peth, Near Appa Balwant Chowk, Bajirao Road, Pune 411002.
24458856 / 24454841
Movie theatre (Marathi)

Raja Dinkar Kelkar Museum
P
10 am-5 pm, Closed on all Govt. holidays
1378, Shukrawar Peth, Natu Baug, Raja Kelkar Museum Street, Pune 411002.
24482101

Sahitya Parishad Library
P
C/o Sahitya Parishad, Tilak Road, Sadashiv Peth, Pune 411030.
24475963
Library

Saket Library
P
19, Tulsibaug Colony, Sahakarnagar, Pune 411009.
24221285
Library

Saras Baug
P
2170, Sadashiv Peth, Near Peshwe Park, Pune 411030.
24332388
Garden with Ganesh temple in the compound

Sudarshan Art Gallery
P
421/422 Shaniwar Peth, Pune 411030.
24490188
For exhibition and sales of paintings and artwork

Sudarshan Rangmanch
P
421/422 Shaniwar Peth, Pune 411030.
24490188
Auditorium

Tilak Smarak Mandir
P
Tilak Road, Pune 411030.
24339920 / 24334004
Auditorium and exhibition centre

Vijay Chitramandir
P
310, Laxmi Road, Pune 411030.
24454830
Movie theatre (English)

Deccan & Shivajinagar

Balgandharva Art Gallery
P
Next to Sambhaji Park, J. M. Road, Pune 411005
25532959

Balgandharva Rangmandir
Next to Sambhaji Park,
J. M. Road,
Pune 411005
25532959

British Council Library (BCL)
917/1, F. C. Road, Pune 411004.
25654351/ 25654352
bl.pune@in.britishcouncil.org
Library

Chitaranjan Vatika
P
Model Colony, Shivajinagar,
Pune 411015.
Garden

Deccan Gymkhana
P
759/2, Shivajinagar,
Pune 411004.
25670217 / 25663861
Sports centre and club

E-Square
132 University Road,
Pune 411016.
56044141/2/3
www.e-squareindia.com
Multiplex with 5 screens, eateries and shops

Indiaart Gallery
P
Kala Chhaya Campus, Opp Vikhe Patil School, Patrakar Nagar ,
Senapati Bapat Road,
Pune 411016.
25662854
Art Gallery

Jagtap Library
P
Model Colony,
Pune 411015.
Library

Kamala Nehru Park
P
Bhandarkar Road,
Pune 411004.
Garden with many small eateries

Mahatma Phule Vastu
P
Sangrahalaya (Museum)
1203, Ghole Road, Shivajinagar,
Pune 411004.
25532750
Museum

Mangala
111, Shivajinagar, Pune 411005
25533468
www.clicktickets.com
Movie theatre (Hindi)

Model Colony Lake Natural Reserve
Model Colony, Shivajinagar,
Pune 411015.
Natural reservoir

PYC Hindu Gymkhana
766 Bhandarkar Institute Road,
Deccan Gymkhana, Pune 411004
25121894 / 25663007
Club and sports centre

Sambhaji Park
J. M. Road, Pune 411005.
25532514 / 25338553
Garden with many small eateries

Sambhaji Park Aquarium
P
9 am-11 pm 4 pm-11 pm.
Next to Shambhaji Garden,
J. M. Road, Pune 411005.
25532514 / 25338553
Aquarium located in the garden

Sawai Gandharva Auditorium
Opp. Police Grounds, Unversity Road, Shivajinagar, Pune 411005.
25535570
Concert hall and auditorium

X'tasy
Best Western Pride Hotel, 5 University Road, Shivajinagar,
Pune 411005.
25534567
Fax: 25533228
Lounge and disco

Hadapsar & Solapur Bazaar

Boating Park
Campus of the SRP Group 2,
Near Army School of Physical Training (ASPT)
Ramtekdi, Hadapsar,
Pune 411028.
Lake with boating facitility

Sanskruti
Opp. Indian Oil Corporation,
Sholapur Highway, Loni-Kalbhor,
Pune 412201
26915156 / 7 / 8
Entertainment resort and restaurant

Vaibhav Theatre
P
Pune Solapur Road, Hadapsar,
Pune 411028.
26870211
Movie theatre (Hindi)

Khadki

Kiva
Symphony C Building, Range Hills Road, Bhosale Nagar,
Pune 411020
25538339
Lounge

Jaihind
Pune–Mumbai Highway, Near Khadki Railway Station, Khadki,
Pune 411003.
25817741
Movie theatre (Hindi)

Kondhwa, Wanowrie & Bibvewadi

3D Gaming Centre
Sujay Garden, Mukund Nagar,
Pune 411037.
66027777
Bowling alley and video games

Angraaz Water Park
11 am-6 pm
Kondhwa Budruk, Survey No 37, Kahdi Machine Chowk, Pune 411041
26932921
Water Park and restaurant. Rs. 200 for adults, Rs 150 for children

Corinthian Club
Off NIBM Road, Nyati County South, Pune 411028
26970900
Club with sports and entertainment amenities

Cyclone
Above Fulora Restaurant, Market Yard, Pune 411037.
24265847
Disco and bar

Friends Library
P
Salunke Vihar, Crystal Castle Building, Shop No 2, Pune 411040.
26855124
Library

City Pride
Pune Satara Road, Pune 411009.
24212355 / 24213291
Multiplex with 3 screens and eateries

Gool Poonawalla Jogging Park
Salisbury Park, Gultekdi, Pune 411037.
Garden and jogging track

Havi Arts
261, W-2, Clover Citadel, Salunke Vihar Road, Wanowrie, Pune 411040.
9860092454.
www.haviarts.com
Art gallery

Jagtap Nursery
3, Phayre Road, Near Golibar Maidan, Behind S.M. Joshi Hindi High School, Pune 411040.
26363432
Nursery with wide range of plants for sale

Laxmi Narayan
P
Near Swargate, Pune 411040.
24448181
Movie theatre (Hindi)

Nilayan Library
P
12, Sevanand Colony, Santnagar, Aranyeshwar, Pune 411009.
Library

P40 Library
P
Opp. Salunke Vihar, Salunke Vihar Road, Pune 411040.
56217560
Library

Rajiv Gandhi Zoological Park
P
Opp. Katraj Dairy, Pune Bangalore Highway, Pune 411043.
24370747
Snake park and zoo

Kothrud & Erandawane

City Pride
Karve Road, Erandwane, Pune 411038.
25458875 / 76
Multiplex with 4 screens, eateries and shops

Gandhi Bhavan
10 am-5 pm.
Near Kirloskar Cummins, Kothrud, Pune 411038.
25385091
Museum

Joshi's Museum of Miniature Railways
P
17/1 B/2, G A, Kulkarni Road, Near Sangam Press, Karve Road Pune 411038.
25435378
Museum of toy trains

Kshipra Sahniwas Hall
Kshipra Sahniwas Society, Karve Nagar, Pune 411052.
25440120
Auditourium

Major Tathawade (Tatya) Udyan
6 am-11 pm, 4 pm-8 pm.
Opp Tol Hospital, Karve Nagar, Pune 411052
Garden

Manas Holiday Resorts
Bhugaon, Taluka Mulshi, Paud Road, Pune 410042.
9822657659 / 32933863
Boating, Go-Karting, restaurant

Purna Library
P
11 Shri Niketan Society , Opp. Marathe Nursing Home, Kothrud, Pune 411029
25435054
Library

Smriti Van
Behind Kirloskar Cummins Factory, Karve Nagar, Pune 411052.
Plantation area

Tathawade Garden
6 am-11 pm, 4 am-8 pm.
6 am-11 pm, 4 am-8 pm.
Opp Tol Hospital, Karve Nagar, Pune 411052.
Garden

Yashwantrao Chavan Natyagruha
P
Karve Road, Karve Putla, Throat Udyan, Pune 411038.
25395232
Auditorium

Pimpri – Chinchwad

Abhinav Vachanalaya and Library
P
1147/1, Vijaynagar, Kalewadi, Pune 411033.
27612374
Library

Appu Ghar Amusement Park (Indira Gandhi Udyan)
P
Indira Gandhi Udyan, Pimpri Chinchwad Muncipal

Corporation Sector 23, Nigdi,
Pune 411044
27854040

Ashoka Chitra Mandir
Pimprigaon, Pimpri 411018
27460908
Movie theatre (Hindi)

Bahinabai Choudhary Zoological Park
Vrindavan Society, PCMC,
Chinchwad, Pune 411019.
27496036
Garden and zoological park

Bhakti-Shakti Statue Park
Near Jakat Naka,
Mumbai-Pune Road, Near PCMC
Building, Nigdi, Pune 411044.
Garden

Bhosari Lake
Bhosari, PCMC, Pune 411039.
27121791

Delux Cinema
469, Pimpri, Pune 411017.
27454304
Movie theatre (Hindi)

Dolphin Water Park
Pradhikarn, Pimpri
Chinchwad Municipal
Corporation, Nigdi,
Pune 411044.
66303433 /
9890037435
Amusement park

Durgadevi Hill Park
Pune-Mumbai Highway, Nigdi,
Pune 411044.
Garden

Environment Heritage Park
T Block, MIDC, Bhosari,
Pune 411026.
Garden

Fame Jai Ganesh Multiplex
Off Mumbai Pune Highway,
Chinchwad.
27442744.
Multiplex with 3 screens

Jayashree Talkies
Pune Mumbai Highway,
Chinchwad, Pune 411019
27473494
Movie theatre (Hindi)

Poly House Project
Talawade Gairan, Dehu-Alandi
Road, PCMC, Pune 411025.
Garden

Public Library
P.C.M.C Bhavan, Pimpri,
Pune 411018.
27477777

Rajershi Shahu Udyan
Shahu Nagar, Chinchwad,
Pune 411019.
Garden

Sai Udyan - Butterfly Park
Vrindavan Society, PCMC,
Chinchwad, Pune 411019
Garden

Sanjay Library
58/1, Masulkar Colony, Pimpri,
Pune 411018.
27475662

Vishal Chitra Mandir
206/1 By Road Pimpri 411018.
27470440
Movie theatre (Hindi)

Yashwantrao Chavan Rose Garden
T Block, MIDC, Bhosari,
Pune 411026
Garden

Pune Cantonment

Aqua Lounge
Aurora Towers, 9,
Dr. Ambedkar Road,
Pune 411001.
26131818
Lounge and disco

Chitari Academy Of Fine Arts
Atur Foundation House 4 Dr
Ambedkar Road, Pune 411001.
26121297
Art gallery and school of fine arts

Edward Albert Library
East Street, Next to Victory
Theatre, Camp,
Pune 411001.
Reading hall and library

Empress Garden
Prince of Wales Drive, Near Race
Course, Camp,
Pune 411001.
26361840 / 26331193
Botanical garden

Gulati Hall
St Vincent's School Campus, St
Vincent's School Road, Opp St
Anthony's Chapel
Pune 411001.
26352135
Concert Hall

J. J. Garden
Dastur Meher Road, Behind
Aurora Towers, Camp,
Pune 411001.
Garden

Khushbu Art Gallery
Sterling Centre, M.G. Road, Opp
Hotel Aurora Towers, Camp
Pune 411001.
26130924

Ladies Club
3, Lt. Col. Tarapore Road,
Camp,
Pune 411001
26362674
Club with entertainment
facilities

Land Records Museum
4 pm–6 pm.
213, New Admin Building, Opp.
Council Hall,
Pune 411001
26050006/1886

Leather Lounge
9-20 321A Amba Commercial
Complex,
M. G. Road,
Pune 411001.
66012013 / 11 / 12
Lounge

Mazda Hall
Dastur School Campus, 2
Lt. Col Tharpore Road,
Opp Ladies Club, Pune 411001.
26362634
Concert Hall

Nehru Memorial Hall
Ambedkar Road, Pune 411001.
26128560 / 8558
Auditorium

Parsi Gymkhana
33, Off Kahun Road,
Near Kendriya Vidyalaya,
Pune 411001.
26361206
Club with entertainment and sporting facilities

Poona Club Ltd
6, Bund Garden Road,
Pune 411001.
26360083
Club with entertainment and sporting facilities

Rajendra Singhji Institute (RSI)
Ashoka Marg,
Near Circuit House,
Pune 411001.
26361105
Club with entertainment and sporting facilities

Rani Laxmibai Udyan
Off M.G. Road, Bata Chowk,
Camp, Pune 411001.
Garden

The Royal Western India Turf Club
1, Solapur Road, Race Course,
Pune 411001.
26362666
Club with entertainment facilities

Thousand Oaks
2417 East Street,
Pune 411001.
26343194 / 26345598
Lounge with restaurant.

Tribal Cultural Museum
10 am-5.30 pm.
28, Queen's Garden Road,
Camp,
Pune 411001.
26362071
Entry Fee: Rs. 5

United Services Library
6, Bund Garden Road,
(Poona Club Compound)
Pune H.O.,
Pune 411001.
26331419
Wide range of fiction books

Victory
2429, Gen Thimayya Road,
Camp,
Pune 411001.
26132975
Movie theatre (Hindi)

Waves Art Gallery
B 204, Parmar Trade Centre,
Sudhu Vaswani Chowk,
Pune 411001.
50064059

West End Theatre
9, Dr. Ambedkar Road, Camp,
Pune 411001.
56031447
Movie theatre (English / Hindi)

Yerawada & Nagar Road

Aga Khan Palace
Gandhi National Memorial,
Nagar Road.
Pune 411006.
26680250 / 1834
Museum

Diamond Water Park (formerly Splash Mountain)
Water Park Road, Lohegaon,
Pune 411047.
56300509
Water park with restaurant

Fire and Ice
Metro Traders Compound,
Behind Ramvadi Octroi Post,
Next to Bishops School,
Kalyani Nagar,
Pune 411014.
26695861 / 26615056
Lounge and disco

Gunjan
Airport Road, Yerawada,
Pune 411006.
26694484
Movie theatre (Hindi)

Jogger's Park
Opp. Baron's Health Club,
Kalyani Nagar,
Pune 411014
Park with jogging track

Mariplex Gold Adlabs Mariplex Mall,
Marigold Complex, Kalyani Nagar, Pune 411006.
56096464 / 56096565
Multiplex with 3 screens, eateries and shops

P-40
Kalyani Nagar, Pune 411014.
Library

Pune Golf Course
Airport Road, Yerawada,
Pune 411006.
26689351
Eatery & golf goods shop

Sohos
Behind Ramvadi Octroi Post, Next to Bishops School, Kalyani Nagar,
Pune 411014
26681987
Restaurant and lounge

Places to Visit

(Temples and Heritage Buildings)

Aundh & Surroundings

Balaji Temple
P
Near Mont Vert, Sus Road,
Pune 411021.

Loyola Chapel
Loyola High School,
Dr. Homi Bhabha Road, Pashan,
Pune 411008.

Pashan Lake
P
NDA-Pashan Road,
Near Bharat Electronics.
Best time to visit:
November and February

Shiva Temple
P
Someshwarwadi, Pashan Road,
Pune 411021.

Bund Garden & Koregaon Park

Maulana Abdul Kalam Memorial
P
9 am-8.30 pm.
Plot No 296, Koregaon Park,
Near Bund Garden,
Burning Ghat, Pune 411001.
Free Admission

Osho International Meditation Resort
VISA P
Koregaon Park, Lane 1,
Pune 411001.
66019999
Guided tours of the resort and its facilities available.

Tribal Cultural Museum
P
28, Queen's Garden Road,
Pune 411001.
26362071
Display on culture and art of the tribes of western India

Central Pune

Belbaug Mandir
Shivaji Road, Budhwar Peth,
Pune 411002.
Temple dedicated to Lord Vishnu

Dhakta Shaikh Salla Dargah
Near Kumbhar Ves Chowk,
Mangalwar Peth,
Pune 411001.

Goadiji Parasnath Temple
203 Bhawani Peth, Nehru Road,
Pune 411042.
26451756
Jain temple

Kesari Wada
568 N. C. Kelkar Road,
Narayan Peth, Pune 411030.
24459051
Houses offices of *Kesari* and mementos of Lokmanya Tilak

Khunya Murlidhar Temple
Sadashiv Peth,
Pune 411030.
Temple dedicated to Lord Radha and Lord Krishna

Lal Mahal
Near Jijamata Udhyan Pune,
Kasba Peth, Pune 411011.
Home of Chhatrapati Shivaji

Mazumdar Wada
Mazumdar Path, Near
Shaniwarwada, Shaniwar Peth,
Pune 411030.
24489364
Houses manuscripts of music. (Not open to the public without prior permission.)

Nana Wada
Behind Shaniwarwada,
Next to Sakal Office,
Budhwar Peth,
Pune 411002.
Houses a school and government offices

Omkareshwar Mandir
Omkareshwar Chowk,
Near Vishnukrupa Hall,
Shaniwar Peth, Pune 411030.
Temple dedicated to Lord Shiva

Parvati Temple
Parvati Hill, Pune 411030.
24443520
Temple and museum complex on Parvati Hill

Raste Wada
Rasta Peth, Near Apollo Theatre,
Pune 4110011.
26055603
One of the last few surviving *wadas* in the city

Shaniwarwada
P
Shanivar Peth, Pune 411036.
24335597
Fort ramparts and Sound and Light show

Shrimant Dagdusheth Halwai Ganpati Mandir
250 Budhwar Peth, Shivaji Road,
Pune 411002.
24479222 / 24452049
Temple dedicated to Lord Ganesha

Succath Shelomo Synagogue
93 Rasta Peth, Pune 411001.
Not open to public

Tambadi Jogeshwari Temple
Near Appa Balwant Chowk,
Budhwar Peth, Pune 411002.
Temple dedicated to Goddess Jogeshwari

Thorla Shaikh Salla Dargah
Near Shaniwarwada, Kasba Peth,
Pune 411011.
Place of worship for Muslims

Trishund Ganapati Temple
139, Somwar Peth, Near Kamala
Nehru Hospital, Pune 411011.
Temple dedicated to Lord Ganesha

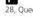

Tulshibaug Temple & Complex
Shree Ram Sansthan Trust, 1225, Tulsibaug, Budhwar Peth, Pune 411002.
Temple dedicated to Lord Rama, Lord Ganesha and Mahadev

Vishrambaug Wada
Opp. Bank Of Maharastra, Bajirao Road, Sadashiv Peth, Pune 411030
☎ 24457750
Museum documenting Pune's history

Deccan & Shivajinagar

Chaturshringi Temple
P
Senapati Bapat Road, Pune 411016.
☎ 25639032
Temple dedicated to Goddess Amba (Durga)

Jungli Maharaj Temple
P
Jungli Maharaj Road, Pune 411005.
Temple dedicated to the Hindu ascetic Jungli Maharaj

Pataleshwar Caves
P
Jungli Maharaj Road, Pune 411005.
8th century rock-cut cave temple

Khadki

All Saints Church
P
All Saints High School, Elphinstone Road, Opposite Khadki Business Centre, Khadki 411003.
☎ 25813969

Gurudwara Shri Gurusingh Sabha
P
Elphinstone Road, Khadki Bazaar, Khadki, Pune 411003.
☎ 25822732

Kali Bari Durga Temple
P
254B Park Road, Near Khadki Station, Pune 411020.
☎ 25693533

St. Ignatius Church
P
General Timaya Road, Bombay-Pune Road, Khadki, Pune 411003.
☎ 25817179

Kondhwa, Wanowrie & Bibvewadi

Mahadji Shinde Chhatri
P
Survey No, 75, Wanowrie, Pune 411040.
☎ 26852141
Built in memory of the great Maratha general Mahadji Shinde

Padma Vilas Palace
P
Opp. Shinde Chhatri, Wanowrie, Pune 411040.

Kothrud & Erandawane

Dashabhuja Ganapati Temple
Paud Phata, Karve Road, Pune 411029.
☎ 25434353
Temple dedicated to Lord Ganesha

Mrityunjayeshwar Mandir
Kothrud, Karve Road, Pune 411029.
☎ 25430992
Dedicated to Lord Shiva

St. Crispin's Church
P
Near Sharda Centre, Karve Road, Pune 411004.
☎ 25456979

Vitthal Mandir
Raja Ram Bridge, Kothrud, Pune 411052.

Pimpri – Chinchwad

Chapekar Wada and Chapekar Smarak
Pagechil Talim Road, Chinchwad, Pune 411033.
☎ 27441218
Houses a museum

Morya Gosavi Temple
Mangal Murti Wada, Ahead of Chapekar Chowk, Chinchwadgaon, Pune 411033.
☎ 27453138 / 3123
Named after Moraya Gosavi, the temple houses a Ganesh idol found by him

Pune Cantonment

Babajan-Ki-Dargah
P
Babajan Chowk, Off M.G.Road, Camp, Pune 411001.

Hanuman Temple
Shree Astha Siddhi Hanuman Mandir, 343 Sachapir Street, Camp, Pune 411001.
☎ 26340047 / 26340027

General Post Office (GPO)
P
Sadhu Vaswani Road, Pune 411001
☎ 26125516

Hare Krishna Temple (ISKCON)
P
Lt. Col. Tarapore Road, Next to Dastur Primary School, Camp, Pune 411001.
☎ 26331044

Holywood Gurudwara
P
Gurudwara Road, Near Race Course, Camp, Pune 411001
☎ 26360919

Lal Deval (Ohel David Synagogue)
Dr. Ambedkar Road, Camp, Pune 411001.
Not open to public

Pune Archives (Peshwe Daftar)
P
Bund Garden Road, Opp. Council Hall, Pune 411001
26127307
Land records from the Peshwa era

Sir J.J. Agiary (Fire Temple)
826, Dastur Meher Road, Opp. J.J. Garden, Camp, Pune 411001
26135514
Not open to public.

St. Patrick's Cathedral
P
1-B Prince of Wales Drive, Near Race Course, Pune 411001.
26332329

St. Paul's Church
P
2 Church Road, Behind Police Commissioner's Office, Near G.P.O,
Pune 411001.
26120757

St. Xavier's Church
P
2007, St. Vincent's Street, Opp. Shivaji Market,
Pune 411001.
26356776

Vasupujya Swami Jain Temple
P
657 Jain Mandir Path, Sachapir Street, Camp,
Pune 411001.

Yerawada & Nagar Road

Aga Khan Palace
P
Gandhi National Memorial, Nagar Road. Pune 411006
26680250 / 1834
Museum and memorial

Central Jail
Central Building 1, Yerawadaa Prision, Jail Road,
Yerawadaa, Pune 411006.
26696115
Not open to public.

Parnakuti Temple
Yerawada, Pune 411006.
Temple complex situated atop a hill

Education

(Schools, Colleges, Institutions, Research Centres, and Hobby Classes)

Aundh & Surroundings

DAV Public School
Opp. Spencer's Daily, D.P. Road, Aundh, Pune 411007.
5893377 / 25890081.
CBSE Board

Indira Group of Institutes
85/5 - A Tathawade,
New Mumbai-Pune Highway,
Near Wakad Police Chowkey,
Pune 411033.
22933279 / 80 / 81 /
Fax: 229342633
www.indiraedu.com
Graduation and post graduation courses in mass communication, management and various other fields

Kalaniketan Institute of Fine Arts
Atushataj' Plot 113, Anand Park, Aundh, Pune 411027.
25883248
Bharatnatyam dance classes

Loyola High School
Dr. Homi Bhabha Road, Pashan,
Pune 411008.
25656699
SSC Board

Mercedes-Benz International School
Pune Infotech Park,
MIDC, Phase 1,
Hinjewadi 411057.
22934420 / 30
International Baccalaureate

National Chemical Laboratory (NCL)
264 Main Building,
Dr Homi Bhabha Road, Pashan,
Pune 411008.
25893300 / 25893053
Research Institute

Orchid School
Baner Road, Baner,
Pune 411045.
27292701 / 02 /
30926464
www.theorchidschool.org
CBSE Board

Spicer Memorial School and College
Aundh-Khadki Road,
Aundh,
Pune 411007.
College: 25691383.
School: 25692384
25882140
HSC Board, affiliated to Pune University

St Joseph's High School
Dr Homi Bhabha Road,
Pashan,
Pune 411008.
25655505
SSC Board

Vidya Valley School
Sus Road, Pashan,
Pune 411021.
56339986 / 56339985
ICSE Board

Yashwantrao Chavan Academy of Development Administration (YASHADA)
Raj Bhawan Complex,
Baner Road,
Pune 411007.
25608000 / 25608612
Training institute

Bund Garden & Koregaon Park

Anjuman Islam, Peer Mohamed High School,
Bund Garden Road,
Pune 411001.
26122549
SSC Board

Army Sports Institute (ASI)
Mundhwa Road, Koregaon Park Annexe, Pune 411001.
26102926
Training institute

Cinderella Dance School
Parmar Trade Centre,
Pune 411001.
Ballroom dancing classes

J N Petit Technical High School
Bund Garden Road,
Opp Sun 'N' Sand, Pune 411001.
26124104
SSC Board

Kalanidhi
10, Galaxy Society,
Boatclub Road, Pune 411001.
26122710
Kathak dance class

Max Mueller Bhavan
14/3 B, Boat Club Road,
Pune 411001.
26131340
German language coaching

National Institute of Naturopathy
'Bapu Bhavan', Tadiwala Road,
Pune 411001.
26059682 / 3 / 4
Yoga classes and health centre

St. Felix School
4 Boat Club Road,
Pune 411001.
26128693 / 26123616
SSC Board

St. Mira's School
10, Sadhu Vaswani Road,
Pune 411001.
26127841
SSC Board

St. Mira's College for Girls
6, Koregaon Park, Pune 411001.
26138604 / 26124846
HSC board, affiliated to Pune University

Tata Management Training Centre (TMTC)
1, Mangaldas Road,
Pune 411001.
26139246
Training centre

Wadia College
E-19, V. K. Jog Path, Bund Garden Road, Pune 411001
Commerce College
26127024
Arts and Science College
26122944
HSC Board, affiliated to Pune University

Central Pune

Abhinav Kala Mahavidyalya
2043, Sadashiv Peth, Tilak Road,
Pune 411030.
24335428 / 24320599
Training in Fine Arts

Ahilyadevi High School for Girls
Shaniwar Peth,
Pune 411030.
4450690
Marathi medium school established in the year 1939

Bharat Natya Sanshodhan Mandir
1320, Near Perugate Police Chowki, Sadashiv Peth,
Pune 411030.
24471614
Training in theatre

Gandharva Mahavidyalaya
495 Mehunpura, Shaniwar Peth,
S.P. College,
Pune 411030.
24450795
Training in Hindustani classical music

HHCP High School
Laxmi Road, Pune 411030.
A premier Marathi medium girls' school

Jnana Prabhodhni School
Jnana Prabodhini Trust, 510,
Sadashiv Peth, Velhe Taluka,
Pune 411030.
24477691 / 24478095
CBSE Board

Kalavardhini
1582 Sadashiv Peth, Tilak Road,
Pune 411030.
24333107
Bharatnatyam dance class

Nad Roop
1534, Leela Chambers,
Sadashiv Peth, Tilak Road,
Pune 411004.
24477465
School of Kathak dance and music

National Institute of Virology (NIV)
20-A, Dr. Ambedkar Road,
Post Box No.11, Pune 411001.
26127301 / 26124386
Research Institute

St. Helena's School
8, Sorabji Road. Near GPO,
Pune 411001.
26126796
ICSE Board

S.P. College
Tilak Road, Sadashiv Peth,
Pune 411030.
24321462 / 24332479
HSC board, affiliated to Pune University

Deccan - Shivajinagar

Alliance Française de Poona
Indo-French Cultural Centre,
270-D, Patrakar Nagar Road,
Pune 411016.
25657848 / 25676509
French language classes

Bhandarkar Oriental Research Institute (BORI)
812, Shivajinagar, Pune 411004.
2656932
www.bori.ac.in
Historical & sociological research institute

Bharatiya Vidya Bhavan School
407/408 Senapati Bapat Road,
Pune 411016.
25653413

Brihan Maharashtra College of Commerce (BMCC)
Off Fergusson College Road,
Pune 411004.
25654943
HSC Board, affiliated to Pune University

Centre for Development of Advanced Computing (C-DAC)
Ganeshkhind Road, Pune University Campus,
Pune 411007.
☎ 25704100
Fax: 25694004
Affiliated to Pune University

College of Agriculture
Ganeshkhind Road,
Shivajinagar, Pune 411005.
☎ 25537889 / 25537038
Affiliated to Mahatma Phule Krishi Vidyapeeth

College of Engineering, Pune (COEP)
Wellesley Road, Shivajinagar,
Pune 411005.
☎ 25507214
Deemed College

Fergusson College
Fergusson College Road,
Pune 411001.
☎ 25654212
HSC Board, affiliated to Pune University

Film & Television Institute of India (FTII)
Law College Road, Pune 411004.
☎ 25431817, 25433016.
Training in direction, scripting, cinematography, sound engineering and acting

Gokhale Institute of Politics and Economics
846, BMCC Road, Shivajinagar,
Pune 411004
☎ 25654288 / 25654289

Indian Law Society (ILS) Law College
ILS Law College, Law College Road, Pune 411004.
☎ 25678678 / 25656775
25658665
ilslaw@vsnl.com
Affiliated to Pune University

Indian Meteorological Department
'Simla Office', Ganeshkhind Road, Shivajinagar, Pune 411005.
☎ 25535211 / 25535245
www.education.vsnl.com
www.imdpune.org
Research centre

Institute of Modern Music
1010, Deep Bungalow, Model Colony, Pune 411016.
☎ 25652336
Hindustani classical music institute

Inter-University Centre for Astronomy and Astrophysics (IUCCA)
Post Bag 4, Ganeshkhind,
Pune University Campus,
Pune 411007.
☎ 25604100 / 25704100
Fax: 25604699
webm@iucaa.ernet.in
Affiliated to Pune University

Kamayani School for Mentally Challenged Children
270, B1, Gokhale Nagar,
Pune 411016.
☎ 25651588

Lalit Kala Kendra
University of Pune Campus,
Pune 411007.
☎ 25692182
B.A. and M.A. in dance, drama or music

Maneesha Nirtyalaya
870/2, Rasik, Bhandarkar Road,
Pune 411004.
Classical dance class

Modern College
Shivajinagar, Pune 411005.
Arts, Science and Commerce College

National Centre for Radio Astrophysics (NCRA)
Tata Institute of Fundamental Research, Pune University Campus, Post Bag 3, Ganeshkhind,
Pune 411007
☎ 25697107 / 25691384
www.ncra.tifr.res.in
Affiliated to Pune University

National Film Archives of India (NFAI)
P.O. Box No. 810,
Law College Road,
Pune 411004.
☎ 25652259
www.nfaipune.nic.in
Archives, library and research centre

Nritya Bharati Kathak Dance Academy
1256 Shivajinagar, Deccan Gymkhana, Pune 411004.
☎ 25536335

Ramamani Iyengar Memorial Yoga Institute
1107 B/1 Hare Krishna Mandir Road, Model Colony, Shivajinagar, Pune 411015.
☎ 25656134
www.bksiyengar.com
Yoga classes and fitness centre

Siddha Samadhi Yoga
Ghole Road, Pune 411005.
Yoga classes

Symbiosis Group of Institutions
Senapati Bapat Road,
Pune 411004.
☎ 25676875 / 25676876
Deemed University

Symbiosis School
Lane No. 15, Prabhat Road,
Pune 411004.
☎ 25665935
SSC Board

University of Pune (UoP)
Ganeshkhind Road, Pune 411007
PRO
☎ 25601191
Vice Chancellor
☎ 25693868
www.unipune.ernet.in

Vidya Bhawan High School
Model Colony, Shivajinagar,
Pune 411016.
☎ 25654917
Co-ed, SSC Board

Vikhe Patil Memorial School
Senapati Bapat Road,
Patrakar Nagar, Pune 411016
☎ 25660550
SSC Board

Hadapsar & Solapur Bazaar

Annasaheb Magar Mahavidyalaya
Hadapsar, Pune 411028.
☎ 26990376
HSC board, affiliated to Pune University

Army School of Physical Training (ASPT)
Ramtekdi, Hadapsar,
Pune 411028.
☎ 26873522

Sadhana Vidyalaya
Hadapsar,
Pune 411028.
☎ 26999871
SSC Board

Khadki

All Saints High School
Church Road,
Khadki 411003.
☎ 25813969
SSC Board

College of Military Engineering (CME)
Bombay-Pune Road,
Pune 411031.
☎ 27145194
Civil, electrical and mechanical engineering.

Queen Mary's Technical School for Disabled
Park Road, Khadki,
Pune 411020.
☎ 25816779
Vocational training to disabled soldiers and army officers and their dependents

Shanta Sangeet Academy
33 Bhau Patil Road,
(Shanta Apte Bungalow),
Khadki, Pune 411020.
☎ 25816730
Music institute

St Joseph's Boys High School
Khadki, Pune 411003.
☎ 25813325
SSC Board

St Joseph's Convent Girls High School
36 Burr Road, Khadki,
Pune 411003.
☎ 25822141
SSC Board

St Thomas Public School
Swastik Road , Near Railway Station, Khadki, Pune 411003.
☎ 25815304
SSC Board

Symbiosis Institute of Management Studies (SIMS)
Plot No. 6,
Opposite EME Workshop,
Range Hills Road, Khadki
Pune 411020.
☎ 30213200
www.sims.edu

Tikaram Jagannath (TJ) College of Arts, Commerce and Science
491, Elphinstone Road,
Khadki, Pune 411003.
☎ 25811491 / 8246
Affiliated to Pune University

Kondhwa Wanowrie & Bibvewadi

Bharatiya Vidyapeeth
Katraj- Campus, Pune
Satara Road, Pune 411043
☎ 24362516 / 24373226
www.bharatividyapeeth.edu
Deemed university

Billabong High School
Dorabjee Paradise,
Corinthian Club Road, Extention
NIBM, Pune 411048.
☎ 39525552
ICSE and IGCSE Board

Delhi Public School (DPS)
Nyati County,
Village Mohammadwadi,
Kondhwa, Pune 411028.
☎ 26970418 / 26970428
26970988
www.dpsfamily.org
CBSE Board

National Institute of Banking Management (NIBM)
Kondhwe Khurd, NIBM P.O.,
Pune 411048
☎ 26833080 / 87
Fax: 26834478
www.nibmindia.org

Tilak Maharashtra Vidyapeeth
Vidyapeeth Bhavan, Gultekadi,
Pune 411037.
☎ 24461856 / 24464 699
24467888 Fax: 24466068
Deemed university

Vishwakarma Institute of Technology (VIT)
666, Upper Indiranagar,
Bibvewadi, Pune, 411037.
☎ 24281594 / 24282294
www.vit.edu

Kothrud & Erandawane

Abasaheb Garware College
Karve Road, Pune 411004.
☎ 25450796
HSC board, affiliated to Pune University

Abhinav Vidyalaya English Medium High School
Karve Road, Nal Stop,
Pune 411004
☎ 25442812
SSC Board

Cummins College of Engineering for Women
Karve Nagar, Pune 411052.
☎ 25467210
Fax: 25465869
cumminscollege@yahoo.co.in
Affiliated to Pune University

Indian Institute for Aeronautical Engineering & Information Technology
140/6, Near Warje Chowk,
NDA Road, Warje Malwadi,
Pune 411052
☎ 25292151 /4197 /4347
enquiry@iiaeit.org

Kala Chhaya
759 / 94b 1st Lane Prabhat Road
Pune 411004.
25433153
Dance Institute

MES Bal Shikshan Mandir
Mayur Colony, Kothrud,
Pune 411029.
25435260
SSC Board

Millennium National School
18, Hill Side, Karve Nagar,
Pune 411052.
25436239

MIT College
S.No.124, Paud Road, Kothrud,
Pune 411038
25431795/ 25432767
Fax: 25442770
info@mitpune.com
Engineering college

MIT School
127/1, Paud Road, Kothrud,
Pune 411029
25442166
SSC Board

National Defence Academy (NDA)
Khadakwasla, Pune 411023.
25290333
Fax: 25292200
Defense training for all three wings of the Armed Forces: army, navy and air force

New India English School
Kothrud,
Pune 411038.
25280291
SSC Board

Dr. Kalmadi Shamrao Karnatak High School
Dr Ketkar Marg, 36 Erandwane,
Pune 411004.
25434300 / 3136
SSC Board

P. Jog High School,
Beside UTI Bank, Mayur colony,
Kothrud,
Pune 411029
25431065
Marathi and English medium school

Rosary International School
Madhav Baug Shiv Tirth Nagar,
Paud Road, Kothrud,
Pune 411029
25410446 /107/108
Katraj Dehu Road Bypass,
Warje, Pune 411052
ICSE / SSC Board

School of Fashion Technology (SOFT)
Near Cummins Engineering
College, Karve Nagar,
Pune 411052
25444328 /25442782
Fax: 25444328
softpune@vsnl.net

SNDT College
Maharishi Karve, Vidya Vihar,
Karve Road, Pune 411038
25420528
HSC board, affiliated to Pune University

Vedacharya Ghaisas Guruji Ved Pathshala (Ved Bhavan)
Chandni Chowk, Pune 411021.
25282568
Conducts studies of Vedas

Pimpri – Chinchwad

Dr. D. Y. Patil Group of Institutes
Sant Tukaram Nagar, Opp. H.A.
Company, Pimpri, Pune 411018.
27421095
www.dypatil.com
Medical, Engineering, and colleges of other educational streams

Dyana Prabodhini Secondary School
Pradhikaran, Nigdi, Pimpri-
Chinchwad, Pune 411044.
27654380 / 27657508
CBSE Board

Jai Hind High School
Pimpri, Pune 411017.
27415273
SSC Board

Judson High School
Near Pimpri Station, Pimpri,
Pune 411018.
27475736
SSC Board

Manghalmal Udharam College of Commerce
Pimpri, Pune 411017.
27413943
Affiliated to Pune University

Maharashtra Academy of Engineering
Dehu Phata, Kelgaon,
Alandi Dehu Road, Pune 412105.
27185857 / 5514 /
www.mitpune.org/mae
Training for all streams of engineering

National AIDS Research Institute
73, G Block, MIDC, Bhosari,
Pune 411026
27121342 / 43 /
27121280 / 27121071 / 72
www.nari-icmr.res.in
Research institute

Pimpri-Chinchwad College of Engineering
Anandibag, Opp Beck Company,
Nehru Nagar Road, Pimpri,
Pune 411018.
27653168 / 27653166
www.pccoepune.com
Training for all streams of engineering

St Ursula's High School
Post office, Akurdi,
Pune 411035
27652669 / 27641122
SSC Board

Pune Cantonment

Armed Forces Medical College (AFMC)
Pune-Solapur Road, Camp,
Pune 411040.
26811205 / 26306010

Hutchings High School
7, Phayre Road,
Pune 411040.
26352764
ICSE Board

Sardar Dastur Group of Schools Trust Office
2, Lt. Col. Tarapore Road, Camp,
Pune 411001.
26362630
SSC Board

St. Anne's School
Convent Street, Camp,
Pune 411001
27690519
SSC Board

St. Mary's School
5-B,General Bhagat Marg, Camp,
Pune 411001
26156282
ICSE Board

St. Vincent's School
St. Vincents Street,
Near Shivaji Market, Camp,
Pune 411001
26352135
www.stvincentspune.com
SSC Board

The Bishop's School
5-A, General Bhagat Marg,
Camp,
Pune 411001.
26360437/ 26330261
ICSE Board

Yerawada & Nagar Road

Amritanjali School Of Bharatanatyam
10/10 Kumar City, Kalyani Nagar,
Pune 411014.
27032700
Dance Institute

Deccan College
Yerawada,
Pune 411006.
26682982 / 26680104 / 26689794 / 26680113
College and Research Institute

Erin Nagarvala High School
12, Kalyani Nagar,
Pune 411006.
26681166
Co-ed, SSC Board

International School of Business & Media
Ashoka Plaza, S No 32/2 ,
Next to Weikfield Company,
Nagar Road
Pune 411014
26633444 / 46
Deemed college

Jail Officers Training School
Near central Jail, Jail Road,
Yerawada,
Pune 411006.
26692417

Symbiosis Centre of Design
Next to Weikfield Company,
Viman Nagar, Pune 411014.
26634547 / 48
Training for various branches of design

Symbiosis International School
Viman Nagar,
Pune 411014.
26634550
International Baccalaureate

The Bishop's Co-Ed School
Plot No. 78, Yerawada Town Planning Scheme, Kalyani Nagar,
Pune 411006.
56212204 / 56212205 / 56237656
ICSE Board

The Lexicon International School
Lexicon Estate, G No. 726,
Wagholi, Pune Nagar Road,
Pune 412207.
27051818

Classes

Aptech
25531317 / 25538061
Computer training institute

Arena Multimedia
26053428 / 29
Graphics and design inst.

Career Forum
30616677 / 88 / 99
Coaching for GRE, GMAT, CAT and CET

Dilip Oak's Academy
Malati Madhav, 819, Bhandarkar Institute Road, Pune 411004.
25656237 / 25678066
Training for GRE, GMAT, TOEFL, IELTS

MAAC (Maya Academy of Advanced Cinematics)
303, Choice Arcade, Opp Ruby Hall Clinic, Dhole Patil Road,
Pune 411001.
32544171
Range of computer graphic courses

NIIT
26131581 / 24842849
Computer training institute

(These classes have branches across the city; call them to find the one nearest to you.)

Health and Fitness

(Hospitals, Clinics, Medical Stores, Opticians, Gyms and Salons)

Aundh & Surroundings

Aundh Chest Hospital
P
9 am-1 pm (Sunday closed).
Aundh Camp, Aundh,
Pune 411027.
27280237
Fully equipped hospital

Beauty in Toto
10:30 am-6 pm.
Shanker Smriti Apartments,
Near Ozone, Anand Park,
ITI Road, Aundh, Pune 411007.
56611791
Salon

Bellezza
Solaris Health club, ITI Road,
Aundh, Pune 411007.
25893565 / 25887464
Salon

Callipygian Fitness Inc.
❄ P
D. P. Road, Aundh, Pune 411007.
📞 25896195
Gymnasium with trainers and fitness centre

Indiana Health Club
❄ P
Baner Road, Pune 411045.
📞 27291620 / 21
Gymnasium with trainers and fitness centre

Kotbagi Hospital
P 24
163, D.P. Road, Aundh, Pune 411007.
📞 25882770 / 71
www.kotbagihospital.org
24 hrs emergency services, fully equipped hospital

Kushal Medical Store
P
273/5 Sankalpa Building, Baner Road, Aundh, Pune 411007.
📞 27292265
Chemist

Lifeline
24
9 am-9 pm.
157, Near Union Bank of India, 'Legacy', D.P. Road, Aundh, Pune 411007.
📞 25882053 / 25896942
Emergency services, fully equipped hospital

Medicare Drug House
P
Shop No. 4, Shree Siddheshwar, ITI Road, Aundh, Pune 411007.
📞 25899341
Chemist and druggist

Medipoint Hospital Pvt. Ltd.
P 24
D.P. Road, Aundh, Pune 411007.
📞 27297337 / 27297688
Emergency services, fully equipped hospital

Mobius Fitness
❄ P
Opposite Kundan Garden Mangal Karyalaya, Baner Road, Aundh, Pune 411007.
📞 27292354 / 66242551
Gymnasium with trainers and fitness centre

Poona Chest Hospital
♿ P 24
9 am-1 pm, Sunday closed.
Aundh Camp, Aundh, Pune 411027.
📞 27280237
Emergency services, fully equipped hospital

Salon Headlines
❄ P
Anand Park, ITI Road, Aundh, Pune 411007.
📞 27298586
Salon

Sanjay Health Club
❄ P
6 am–1 pm, 2 pm–9 pm.
Sanjay Residency, Someshwarwadi Corner, Baner Road, Pune 411008.
📞 25889072
Gymnasium with trainers and fitness centre

Smitz
❄ P
Sukhwani Prestige, Near Ramnagar Colony, Near Hotel Saffron, Bavdhan, Pune 411021.
📞 32600006
Gymnasium with trainers and fitness centre

Solaris Fitness Club
❄ P
Supreme Centre, ITI Road, Aundh, Pune 411007.
📞 25893565 / 25887464
Gymnasium with trainers and fitness centre

Bund Garden & Koregaon Park

Cut In Time
3, Siddharth Court, Dhole Patil Road, Pune 411001.
📞 26120787
Men's hair salon

Endurance Fitness Club
❄ P
120, Sohrab Hall, 21 Sassoon Road, Pune 411001.
📞 26054477
Gymnasium with trainers and fitness centre

Gazelle
❄ P
Block A, 1st Floor, Mayfair Towers, Dhole Patil Road, Pune 411001.
📞 26120526 / 26128307
Health spa, salon & academy

Inlaks and Budhrani Hospital
❄ VISA P 24
Lane 1, North Main Road, Koregaon Park, Pune 411001.
📞 26129080
Emergency services, fully equipped hospital

Jehangir Hospital & Medical Centre
❄ VISA P 24
32, Sassoon Road, Pune 411001.
📞 26050550 / 26122551
Emergency services, fully equipped hospital

Kalyani Medicals
P
Shardaram Park, Sassoon Road, Opp Ruby Hall Clinic, Pune 411001.
📞 26138114
Chemist and druggist with home delivery

Krishna Medicals
P
A Wing, Shangrila Gardens, Bund Garden Road, Pune 411001.
📞 26052832
Chemist and druggist with home delivery

Ruby Hall Clinic
❄ VISA P 24
40, Sassoon Road, Pune 411001.
📞 26123391 / 2
Emergency services, fully equipped hospital

Central Pune

Hind Medico
P 24
80 Kasturi Chowk, Raviwar Peth, Pune 411042.
📞 24470434
Chemist

Kamla Nehru Hospital
33 Mangalwar Peth,
Pune 411011.
26121202
Emergency services, fully equipped hospital

Kelkar Gymnasium and Fitness Centre
1428/1 Sadashiv Peth,
Pune 411030.
24475877

K.E.M. Hospital
TDH Building, Sardar Moodliar Road, Rasta Peth, Pune 411011.
26125600
Emergency services, fully equipped hospital

K.E.M. Medical Store
Rasta Peth, Pune 411011.
26126500
Chemist

Kerala Ayurveda Chikitsalayam
21/302 Lokmanya Nagar, LBS Road, United Western Bank, Navi Peth, Pune 411030.
24331294
Ayurvedic treatment for all ailments

Kothari Medicals
479, Near Shaniwarwada, Shaniwar Peth, Pune 411030.
24451347
Chemist and druggist

N. M. Wadia Hospital
283 Shukrawar Peth, Near Telephone Bhawan,
Pune 411002.
24479502
Emergency services, fully equipped hospital

Poona Hospital & Research Centre
27, Sadashiv Peth, Near Alka Theatre, Pune 411030.
24331706
Emergency services, fully equipped hospital

Sassoon Hospital
Near Pune Railway Station,
Dr Ambedkar Road,
Pune 411001.
26128000
Emergency services, fully equipped hospital

Deccan & Shivajinagar

Deendayal Memorial Hospital
926, F.C. Road, Shivajinagar,
Pune 411004.
25652497 / 25651613.
Emergency services, fully equipped hospital

Endurance Fitness Club
E-Square, Level 6, 132, University Road, Ganeshkhind,
Pune 411016.
24044111
www.endurancefitness.com
Fitness club with trainers and gymnasium

Gazelle
Bhandarkar Institute Road,
Deccan Gymkhana,
Pune 411004.
25650788
Health spa, salon & academy.

Hardikar Hospital
1160/61 Ganeshkhind Road,
Shivajinagar,
Pune 411005.
25535326 / 25530027
Emergency services, fully equipped hospital

Jai Medico
1184 /4 F.C. Road,
Shivajinagar,
Pune 411005.
25535908
Chemist

Joshi Hospital
778 Shivajinagar,
Kamla Nehru Park, Pune 411004.
25672565 / 25672563
Emergency services, fully equipped hospital

Kanchan Medical Store
966/A Chitra Apartments,
Kusalkar Road, Shivajinagar,
Pune 411016.
25652775
Chemist

Papillon
Bhandarkar Institute Road,
Pune 411004.
25673994
Hair salon for women

Prakash Medicals
1187/66 J.M. Road,
Shivajinagar,
Opp Balgandharva Rang Mandir,
Pune 411005.
25535473
Chemist and druggist

Prayag Hospital
1247, Deccan Gymkhana,
Pune 411004.
25532812 / 25532490
Emergency services, fully equipped hospital

Ratna Memorial Hospital
968, Senapati Bapat Road,
Pune 411016
25651037 / 25657564
Emergency services, fully equipped hospital

Sancheti Institute for Orthopaedics and Rehabilitation
16, Shivajinagar,
Pune 411005.
25533333 / 25536666
Emergency services, fully equipped hospital

Sheela's
Shop No. 26, Sagar Arcade,
F.C. Road,
Pune 411004.
25539581 / 25510435
Unisex hair salon

Talwalkars Fitness Fellowship
B-4 925, F C Road,
Shivajinagar,
Near Deendayal Hospital,
Pune 411004
25651013
Fitness club with trainers and gymnasium

Techni Art
5 Rachna House, 1st Floor, Near Sagar Arcade, F.C. Road,
Pune 411001.
25532540
Unisex hair salon

Hadapsar & Solapur Bazaar

Nisargopachar Ashram Nisargopachar Gramsudhar Trust
Urulikachan,
District Pune 412202.
26926298
Yoga and ayurvedic treatment centre

Prem Medico
1/A Jawaharlal N Building, Opp Rupali Hotel, Hadapsar,
Pune 411028.
26811027
Chemist and druggist

Rajendra Medical
Fatima Nagar, Bhairoba Nala, Hadapsar, Pune 411013.
26873003
Chemist and druggist

Khadki

Amrit Medicals
156, Old Bazar, Near Bank Of Maharashtra, Khadki,
Pune 411003.
25815506
Chemist and druggist

Military Hospital
Near EME Workshop,
Range Hills Road, Khadki,
Pune 411020.
26363901 / 25803169
Hospital for army personnel and family

Paraplegic Rehabilitation Centre (PRC)
Park Road,Near Durgamata Mandir, Khadki, Pune 411020.
25820505
Rehabilitation centre for army personnel

Kondhwa, Wanowrie & Bibvewadi

Fernandes Medicals
Shop No 16, Parmar Nagar,
Wanworie, Pune 411013.
26813928
Chemist and druggist

Noble Hospital
Near Fakhri Hills, Kondhwa Road,
Kondhwa, Pune 411040.
24003201
Emergency services, fully equipped hospital

Pawar Hospital
49/22, Balaji Nagar,
Behind Ellora Palace,
Dhankawadi,
Pune 411043.
24372008 / 24373196
Emergency services, fully equipped hospital

Saisneh Hospital and Diagnostic Centre
Pune-Satara Road, Near PMT Depot, Katraj, Pune 411046.
26959208 / 308
www.saisneh.com
Pathology lab and hospital

Shanti Diagnostic and Polyclinic
Sukhsagar Nagar, Pune 411046.
56784077
Pathology lab, sonography, X-Ray, etc.

Kothrud & Erandawane

Abhishek Medicals
Shop No 35 Girija Shankar Vihar,
Karve Nagar, Pune 411052.
25445624
Chemist

Chaitanya Health Club
Rambaug Colony, Paud Road,
Pune 411038.
25460799 / 25455197
Fitness club with trainers and gymnasium

Chiranjeev
Mata Chambers, Near Mhatre Bridge, Erandwane,
Pune 411004.
25451497
Chemist

Choice Health Club
Survey No 127/1, A3 Karve Road,
Kothrud, Pune 411038.
25434191
Fitness club with trainers and gymnasium

Cipla Cancer and AIDS Foundation
Survey No. 118/1 Bangalore Highway, Opp Popular Nagar,
Pune 411029.
25231131
Research and treatment centre

Deenanath Mangeshkar Hospital
Erandwane, Near Mahatre Bridge, Pune 411004.
256023900
Emergency services, fully equipped hospital

Jog Hospital
46/2b/2, Paud Road, Pune 411038.
25889234 / 25431758
Emergency services, fully equipped hospital

Krishna Hospital
2 Anjanwel, Prashant Society, Paud Road, Pune 411038
25460625
Pharma shop

Sahyadri Hospital
30/ C Karve Road, Opp Garware High School, Erandwane, Pune 411004
25443000
www.sahyadrigroup.com
Emergency services, fully equipped hospital

Solaris
Mayur Colony, Kothrud, Pune 411029
25468778 / 25468779
Fitness club with trainers and gymnasium

Pimpri - Chinchwad

Dhanashri Medical Store
9/4 Pawana Niwas Pimpri, Pune 411018.
27290040
Chemist

Lokmanya Hospital Foundation & Lokmanya Medical
Near Chinchwad Station, Chinchwad, Pune 411033.
27456496
Emergency services, fully equipped hospital

Mahavir Medical Store
Chinchwad Station, Pune 411019.
27474436
Chemist and druggist

Niramaya Hospital
Near Post Office, Behind Jaihind Petrol Pump, Chinchwad Station, Pune 411033.
27441860
Hospital and chemist

Padmashri D.Y. Patil Medical College and Hospital
Mahesh Nagar, Mumbai Pune Highway, Pimpri, Pune 411018.
27420605
Emergency services, fully equipped hospital.

Talera Hospital
Chaphekar Chowk, Chinchwad, Pune 411033.
27610054
Emergency services, fully equipped hospital

Pune Cantonment

Abs
Nucleus Mall, Pune Camp, Pune 411001.
Fitness club with trainers and gymnasium

Artificial Limb Centre (ALC)
Southern Command, Wanowrie, Pune 411040.
26306191
Hospital for army personnel and family

Cardio Thoracic Centre (CTC)
Golibar Maidan, Pune 411040.
26306178
Hospital for army personnel and family

Command Hospital
Southern Command, Wanowrie, Pune 411040.
26306138 / 196
Hospital for army personnel and family

Poona Drug Store
M.G. Road, Camp, Pune 411001.
26130913
Chemist and druggist

Yerawada & Nagar Road

Baron's Health Club
Opposite Jogger's Park, Kalyani Nagar, Pune 411014.
Fitness club with trainers and gymnasium

Kataria Hospital
Nagar Road, Yerawada, Pune 411006.
26697183
Emergency services

Laxmi Medicals
29, Pune-Nagar Road, Ramwadi, Pune 411014.
27034250
Chemist and druggist

Mangesh Medical Store
Ganesh Nagar, 47/3 Vadgaonsheri, Pune 411014.
27032818
Chemist and druggist

Yerawada Mental Hospital
Nagar Road, Opp. Yerawada Jail, Pune 411006.
26692543
Facility for mental illness

Travel Info

(Travel and Tour Agents, Foreign Exchange, Bus Services and Car Rentals)

Aundh & Surroundings

Genesis Tours and Travels

Survey No. 37, Building 2, Patil Complex, Office 2/B Aundh Road, Pune 411020
25695457
Flight and bus bookings, foreign exchange, visa applications, car hire, etc

LKP Forex

Hinjewadi, Pune 411027.
22934871
Foreign exchange bureau

Travel Ventures

Indumati Apartments, Sanewadi, Aundh, Pune 411007.
25885357
International and domestic tour and package bookings

Vishal Tours and Travels

N.D.A. Road, Raste Nagar, Bavdhan, Pune 411021.
22952901 / 22952992
Daily bus service to Goa, Nagpur, Hyderbad, and other cities in India

Bund Garden & Koregaon Park

Ajanta Travels Pvt. Ltd.

9.30 am-1 pm, 2 pm-6 pm.
A/122 Sohrab Hall, 21, Sassoon Road, Pune 411001.
26059091 / 56011032
www.ajantagroupindia.com
Air ticket booking and foreign exchange service

Centrum Forex Ltd.

Office No. 108, Sohrab Hall, Sassoon Road, Pune 411001
26059402/3
Foreign exchange bureau

Cool Cab Taxi

24
Sassoon Road, Near Railway Station, Pune 411001.
26121090 / 26145365
A/c taxi for outstation destinations

International Travel House India Ltd.

24
B8/9, Ground Floor, 5th Avenue, Near Regency Hotel, 177/3, Dhole Patil Road, Pune 411001.
32516182/ 99
www.travelhouseindia.com
National and international travel bookings, tour arrangements and cars for hire

Maitreya Travel Lines Pvt. Ltd.

24
9 am-7.30 pm, Sunday.
197, Dhole Patil Road, Pune 411001
32939555 / 26052222
National and international travel bookings, tour arrangements and cars for hire

Prasanna Tours & Travels

9 am-11 pm.
Sadhu Vaswani Road, Near Pune Station, Pune 411001.
66015180
Phone booking for tours all over India and passport assistance

Pune Railway Station

P 24
Station Road, Pune 411001.
26126575 / 133

Pune Railway Station Bus Stand

P 24
Station Road, Pune 411001.
26126218
Buses to Mahabaleshwar, Goa, Kolhapur and other cities. Asiad buses to Mumbai depart every 30 minutes

Raj National Express

9 am-11 pm.
G-7 Metro House, Mangaldas House, Opp. Tata Management Training Centre, Pune 411001
325811414 / 15 / 16
Buses to Mumbai, Indore, Ahemdabad and other cities

Satnam Travels

9 am-11 pm.
Shardaram Park Shop No 10, Sassoon Road, Opp. Ruby Hall Clinic, Pune 411001
26122420 / 26145140
Luxury bus service

Travel Corporation India Pvt. Ltd.

10 am-6 pm.
TCI House, 170 Dhole Patil Road, Pune 411001.
32519000
www.tciindia.com
Assistance with all travel needs

Central Pune

Neeta Volvo

8 am-10 pm.
Mangalwar Peth, Maldhakka Chowk, Pune 411011
25458393
Daily bus service to various cities

Nehal Travels & Exchange Pvt. Ltd.

10 am-7 pm.
14, Rajendra Nagar, Near Mahatre Bridge, Suvarnagad Apartments, Navi Peth, Pune 411030
24536511 / 2422
nehaltravels@hotmail.com
International and domestic tour and package bookings

Prasanna Travels Pvt. Ltd.

24
396, Shaniwar Peth, Behind Ahilyadevi Girls High School, Pune 411030.
24454919
Ticket booking, tour arrangements, cars and taxis on hire

Royal Tourist Services
10 am-10 pm.
12, Shanti Vihar, 10/3, Rasta Peth, Near Hotel Shantai, Pune 411011
26132333 / 26114321
Daily bus service to Indore, Amarawati and other cities; cars on hire also available

Shri Sai Tours & Travels
9 am-11 pm.
Shukrawar Peth, Near Tilak Road, Pandit Automobile, Pune 411002.
39516426
Tour and travel bookings

Swargate Bus Stand
At Tilak Road-Shankarsheth Road Junction, Pune 411037
24441591
Buses to Mumbai, Bangalore, Mahabaleshwar, Solapur, Mangalore, and other cities

Deccan & Shivajinagar

Girikand Travels Pvt Ltd
9.30 am-8 pm
759/90/B, Deccan Gymkhana, Pune 411004.
25659970 / 71 / 72 / 73
www.girikand.com
All travel related services, including bookings, visas, hiring cars, etc

PMT Bus Stand
J.M. Road, Near Deccan Gymkhana, Pune 411005.
24440417

PMT Bus Stand
Near Pune Municipal Corporation Building, Shivajinagar, Pune 411005.
24440417

Prasanna Tours & Travels
9 am-8 pm.
1199/A/1 F.C. Road, Hotel Parichay, Pune 411005.
56029999
www.prasannaholidays.com
International and domestic tour and package bookings, car hiring facility, etc.

Shivajinagar Bus Stand
Shivajinagar, Pune 411005.
25536970
Buses to Aurangabad, Nasik, Ahmedabad, Vadodara, Lonavala, and Nagpur

Shivajinagar Railway Station
Shivajinagar, Pune 411005.
25536092
Local and intercity trains

Shweta Travels International
Dhanlaxmi No. 3, Hanumannagar, Senapati Bapat Road, Pune 411016.
25655858
ureshkalra46@hotmail.com
International tour and package bookings

Silver Jubilee Travels
Shop No. 5/6, Alankar Bhavan, Near Lalit Mahal, Shivajinagar, Pune 411004
25663706
traveler@pn2.vsnl.net.in
Air ticketing, foreign transfer, package tours etc

Star Holidays
9 am-7 pm
Kamala Arcade, 4th Floor, J.M. Road, Pune 411005
25510108 / 25531170
Air ticketing, foreign exchange, visa applications, car rentals etc

Hadapsar & Solapur Bazaar

Divya Tours and Travels
C /23 Hrishikesh Apartments, Malwadi Road, Hadapsar, Pune 411023.
26815655
Daily bus service to various cities

Khadki

Khadki Railway Station
Elphinstone Road, Khadki, Pune 411003.
25816658

Laxmi Tours and Travels
10 am–7 pm.
45, Aundh Road, Khadki, Pune 411003.
25690097
Daily bus service to various cities of India

Nageshwar Travels
8 am-8 pm.
10/1A Tilak Road, L.K. Road, (Tilak Bhavan) Khadki, Pune 411003.
25813739
Cars and buses for hire

Kondhwa, Wanowrie & Bibvewadi

Navrang Roadlines
9 am–9 pm. Sunday.
Survey No. 83/2A/3/1, Mumbai-Banglore Highway, Kanchan Nagari, Katraj, Pune 411046.
24377891 / 24377892
Daily transport service all over India

Prasanna Travels Pvt. Ltd.
10 am-10 pm.
440 A/1 & 2, Opp. Walvekar Lawns, Pune Satara Road, Pune 411037.
24231600
Bus, train, Volvo, flight bookings and packaged tours

Sana Travels
10 am-10 pm.
Survey No. 588, Ganesh Market, Market Yard, Pune 411037.
24269567
Ticket Bookings, A/C, Non A/C, buses and cars available on hire

Shakun Tours & Travels
9 am-9 pm.
47/2, Pune-Satara Road,
Pune 411009.
24219740
Car hire, air and bus ticketing

Tejas Tours and Travels
9 am-11.30 pm.
Shop No 41, Bharati Vihar, Opp. PCIT College, Bharati Vidyapeeth Campus, Katraj, Pune 411046.
30961751 / 30932270
Flight, train, bus, taxi bookings, and tour arrangements

Western Union Money Transfer
Gajraj Building, Kondhwa Road, Lulla Nagar, Pune 411048.
26832550
Money Transfer and Exchange

Kothrud & Erandwane

Anunkar Tours & Travels
8 am-11 pm.
Nandan Pride,
Opp. Karve Statue,
Karve Road, Kothrud,
Pune 411038.
32936228
Domestic & international travel arrangements

Neeta Volvo
9 am-11 pm.
Shop No. 2, Ideal Colony,
Opp. BPL Mobile Gallery,
Paud Road, Kothrud,
Pune 411029.
25458993
Daily bus service to various cities of India

S.R. Travels
Shop No. 4, Shivamrut Apartments, Bhusari Colony, Paud Road, Kothrud,
Pune 411038.
25286673
Daily bus service to Gujarat, Goa, Karnataka, and others

Travel Masters Pvt Ltd
9.30 am-6 pm
94/16 Butte Patil Classic,
Prabhat Road,
Pune 411004.
25673550 / 1 / 2
www.travelmastersonline.com
Domestic & international travel arrangements

Vaishnav Tours & Travels
Shop 8, Sunita Housing Co-Op. Housing Soc., Shewale Complex, Bhusari Colony, Paud Road,
Pune 411038
9326828531
Volvo service to Mumbai

Pimpri - Chinchwad

Bright Travels
PJ Market Near PCMC Auditorium, Chinchwad,
Pune 411033.
27488102
Daily bus services, car rental, package tours, hotel bookings, etc.

Pandit Tours & Travels
Shitole Chambers, Pune-Nashik Road, Near PMT Chowk, Bhosari,
Pune 411039.
27127696
Daily bus service, package tours and other bookings

Pintu Tours & Travels
H.O. Main Road, Shrinagar, Rahatane Corner, Kalewadi,
Pimpri, Pune 411017.
56344052
Daily bus service, package tours and car rentals.

Prasanna Tours & Travels
9 am-11 pm.
Shop No. 5, Vikram Chambers, Opp. Elpro Company,
Chinchwad, Pune 411033.
56114120
Car rentals, package tours, hotel bookings, etc.

Shri Balaji Tours & Travels
9 am-11 pm.
Shop No. C6 Premsagar Nagar, Near PCMC Auditorium,
Chinchwad, Pune 411033.
56322886
Package tours, bus services, hotel bookings, etc.

Thomas Cook India Ltd.
C-8, Pune-Mumbai Road,
Chinchwad, Pune 411019.
27456733 / 27456734
Foreign exchange bureau

Vijay Travels
Near Ganesh Super Market,
Nashik Phata, Kasarwadi,
Pune 411034.
27125842
Daily bus service to various cities in India

Pune Cantonment

A Three Visa Services & Consultants
Shop No. 37 Kumar Plaza, 8,
M.G. Road, Camp, Pune 411001.
26124803
Airline bookings, visa applications and tour arrangements

Central Railway Booking Office
10 am–6 pm.
Shankarsheth Road,
Near Swargate, Pune 411037.
26136666
Computerised Central Railway booking office

Lancer Travels
9.30 am-5.30 pm.
Shop No. 19, Ground Floor,
Hotel Aurora Travels,
Dr. Ambedkar Road,
Pune 411001.
26133189
www.lancertravels.com
Airline bookings, visa applications and tour arrangements

LKP Forex
4, Thakkar House, 2418 East Street, Pune 411001.
26347041
Foreign exchange bureau

New Shree Raj Travels
10 am–10 pm
102, Mukta Apartments,
Swargate, Pune 411002.
24446550
Daily bus service to various cities, and ticket booking

Shrinath Travel Agency
10 am–6 pm.
Shatrunjay Darsan,
Shop No. 3&4, Plot No. 299,
Opp. Poornima Travels,
Shankarsheth Road,
Pune 411042.
26443399
Daily bus service to various cities

Thomas Cook India Ltd.
13, Thakkar House, 2418,
General Thimayya Road, Camp,
Pune 411001.
26330978
Tour and travel agency and foreign exchange bureau

Yerawada & Nagar Road

Airport
Lohegaon, Pune
26612598 / 26689433

Apple Travels
1, Commercial House, Central Avenue, Opp. Preet Mandir,
Kalyani Nagar,
Pune 411006.
26616883 / 26616885
appletravels@vsnl.net
Ticket booking, tour arrangements, cars and taxis on hire

AS Tours and Travels
18, A/B, Indira Park, Nagar Road,
Opp. Yerawada Police Station,
Yerawada,
Pune 411006.
26612242 / 56279007
Volvo coach service, buses, Qualis, Indicas and Sumos for hire

Maitreya Travel Lines Pvt Ltd
Pune Nagar Road, Near Bus Stop,
Yerawada,
Pune 411006.
26611385
maitreyatravellines@vsnl.net
Daily bus services, cargo services, car rental, package tours, etc.

Tirupati Travels
Shop No. 24, Airport Road,
Near Vishrantwadi Bus Stop,
Yerawada,
Pune 411006.
26613493
Cars on hire, package tours and other services

Vitesse Travels
115 Victoria, Forteleza,
Kalyani Nagar,
Pune 411006.
56229402
Ticket booking, tour arrangements, cars and taxis on hire.

Wings Travels
6 am–12 midnight.
Survey. No. 111/1 Plot No. 34,
Opp. Hotel Landmark,
Alandi Road, Yerawada,
Pune 411006.
wings@vsnl.com
Bus services, car rentals, package tours, etc.

Communication
(Post offices and Courier services)

Akurdi Post Office
Akurdi, Pune 411035.
27652669 / 27641122

Aundh Post Office
Next to Rakshak Society,
Aundh-Sanghvi Road,
Pune 411027.

Chinchwad Post Office
Chinchwad,
Pune 411019.
27472460

City Post Office
Laxmi Road,
Pune 411002.
24475058

Deccan Gymkhana Post Office
Next to Chitale Bandhu, Opp. Deccan Gymkhana,
Pune 411004.
25670939

General Post Office
Sadhu Vaswani Road,
Pune 411001.
26123220

Hadapsar Post Office
Pune-Solapur Road,
Pune 411028.
26993619

Katraj Post Office
Somnath Niwas, Katraj,
Pune 411046.
26959746

Khadki Post Office
Range Hills Road,
Pune 411016.
25819010

NCL Post Office
Dr. Homi Bhabha Road,
Pashan,
Pune 411008.
25439491

Paud Road Post Office
Ex-serviceman Colony,
Paud Road, Pune 411037.
25437360

Pimpri Post Office
Pimpri,
Pune 411018.
27472460

Pune Cantonment Post Office
East Street, Camp,
Pune 411001.
26343617

Speed Post Centre
1st Floor, RMS Building,
Railway Station Compound,
Pune 411001.
26121570 / 26114019
www.indianpost.org
www.speedpost.org

Shivaji Market Post Office
Sachapir Street, Near
Shivaji Market, Camp,
Pune 411001.
26340252

Shivajinagar Post Office
J.M. Road, Next to Revenue
Colony, Shivajinagar,
Pune 411005.
25533505

S.P. College Post Office
Near S.P. College, Tilak Road,
Sadashiv Peth, Pune 411030.
24339922

Wadia College Post Office
Wadia College,
Bund Garden Road,
Pune 411001.
26055220

Yerawada Post Office
Yerawada, Pune 411006.
26684866

Courier Services

Aramex India Pvt. Ltd.
G/5 Parmar Chambers, Sadhu
Vaswani Chowk, Pune 411001.
26125678 / 26114675
26114677

Blue Dart Express Ltd.
Nityanand Complex, Shop No.
9-14, 247/A, Bund Garden Road,
Pune 411001.
26111234
Fax: 26122465

DHL
Atur House, 16A, Dr. Ambedkar
Road, Pune 411001.
1600-11-1345

Desk To Desk Cargo (DTDC)
Shop No.1, Hidayatulla
Complex, Off. Shankar
Sheth Road, Pune - 411 042
30580192 / 30580193

Overnite Express Ltd.
Shop No 8, Parwaaz Bldg, Opp.
Dhobi Ghat, Shankersheth Road,
Pune 411001.
56200975 / 31026484
www.overnite.com

The Professional Couriers
Shop No. 8 & 9, Graficon Arcade,
Sassoon Road, Opp Jehangir
Hospital,Pune 411001.
26050424

(These courier services have branches across the city; call them to find the one nearest to you.)

Others

(Government Offices, Community Associations, Old Age Homes, War Memorials and Orphanages)

Aundh & Surroundings

Gangadham Vrudhashram
P
172, Shivamjali Society,
Near Eden Garden, Wakad
Goan, Near Baner,
Pune 411045.
27273328 /
9890155661
Institution for the aged

Raj Bhavan
P
Ganeshkhind, Aundh,
Pune 411007.
2565 0188 / 1330
Residence of the Governor of Maharashtra

Rural Police Headquarters
P
Dr Homi Bhabha Road,
Chavan Nagar, Pashan,
Pune 411008.
25657878

Sakshi Siddharth Nurses Bureau
P
Sutarwadi Shriram Chawl, Tapkir
Padaal, Pashan Circle, Pashan,
Pune 411021.
9850085557

Bund Garden & Koregaon Park

Botanical Survey of India (BSI)
P
7th Western Circle,
Koregaon Road, Pune 411001.
26141491

Central Excise Office
41-A, ICE House, Sassoon Road,
Pune 411001.
26050793

Road Transport Office (RTO)
Raja Bahadur Mills Road,
Sangam Bridge, Pune 411001
26120808 / 26051840

Shreevatsa Sanstha
Room No. 87, Sassoon General
Hospital, Pune Station Road,
Opp Central Building
Pune 411001.
26120762
Orphanage

Central Pune

Pune Malayalee Federation
P
RR Chambers, 461, Nana Peth,
Pune 411002.
25539499 / 25537550
pnambiar@pn2.vsnl.net.in

Sindhi Association
C/o Noble Enterprises,
G-1, Shivganga Chambers, 686,
Budhwar Peth, Pune 411002.
24454494 / 24454233
noble1@vsnl.com

St. John's House
P
808, Panch House,
Guruwar Peth, Pune 411042.
24471736
Orphanage

Deccan & Shivajinagar

Andhra Association
P
Wrangler Paranjape Road,
Deccan Gymkhana,
Pune 411004.
25531410

Criminal Investigation Department (CID)
P
Near Sangam Bridge,
Old Mumbai-Pune Highway,
Shivajinagar, Pune 411005.
25511443
cid@mahacid.com

District and Sessions Court
P
Shivajinagar, Pune 411005.
25539985/ 25539355

International Convention Centre (ICC)
❄ P
403-A, Senapati Bapat Road,
Pune 411016
25679072 / 3
Office complex and exhibition centre

Pune Municipal Corporation (PMC)
P
Shivajinagar, Pune 411005.
25501000
Administrative offices of the local government

Hadapsar & Solapur Bazaar

Kashmiri Hindu Sabha
C/o Suvi Hatcheries Pvt. Ltd.,
Hadapsar, Pune 411028.
2671818 / 2670088

Khadki

Kalibari Bengali Association
P
Khadki. Pune 411013.
25813533

Kirkee War Cemetery
8 am–4 pm.
Mula Road, Khadki, Pune 411003.
25814462
War memorial for martyrs of World War II

Kondhwa, Wanowrie & Bibvewadi

Satyanand Hospital
Opp Konark Pooram,
Kondhwa Khurd, Pune 411048.
26930194 / 26934179 / 9822057624
Institution for the aged

Kothrud & Erandawane

Matoshri Vrudhashram
Next to Vitthal Mandir,
Opp Rajaram Pul,
Karve Nagar, Pune 411052.
25412375
Institution for the aged

Nivara Vrudhashram
Off Lala Bahadur Shastri Road,
Near Vaikunth Smashan Bhumi,
Mhatre Bridge, Pune 411030.
24328429
Institution for the aged.

St Crispin's Home
P
S No 10/12, Karve Road,
Near Bhosale Arcade, Nal Stop.
25430985
Orphanage & school

Pimpri – Chinchwad

A One Nurses Bureau
P
A One Nurses Building,
Pune Mumbai Highway,
Behind Bhaji Mandai, Kasarwadi
Pune 411034.
27124161 / 27111130

Priya Darshani Shishu Griha
P
Dr Balsha Hospital, Bhosari,
Aadinath Nagar, Dunkirk Lines,
Pune 411014.
27122630
Orphanage

Pune Cantonment

Circuit House
❄ P
18, Queen's Garden,
Solapur Road, Pune 411001.
26361802 / 26361803
Rest house for visiting government officials and dignitaries

Police Commissioner's Office
2, Sadhu Vaswani Road, Next to
GPO, Camp, Pune 411001.
26125396 Ext: 201
Also houses the Foreigners Registration Office

Poona Parsee Panchayat
M. G. Road, Camp,
Pune 411001.
yazadtravels@yahoo.com

Preet Mandir
P
Dr. Coyaji Road, Camp,
Pune 411001.
26360081 / 26330602
Orphanage

Punjab Cultural Association
P
290, M G Road, Camp,
Pune 411001.
26341994
434, Gultekdi,
Pune 411037.
26054346

War Memorial
P
Prince of Wales Drive,
RSI Golf Course,
Pune 411001.

Zoroastrian Youth Association
P
Ardeshir Baug, Pune
Camp, Pune 411001.

Yerawada & Nagar Road

Preet Mandir
P
Survey No. 212, Plot No. 59,
Central Avenue, Kalyani Nagar,
Pune 411014.
26698708 / 26685811 / 26685812 / 26685816
Orphanage

Websites

http://209.235.195.56/index.asp
(PCMC web portal)
www.bsnlpune.com
www.egovpmc.com
www.intach-pune.org
www.maharashtra.gov.in
www.mcciapune.com
www.midcindia.org
www.punecantonmentboard.com
www.punecity.com
www.punecitymag.com
www.punediary.com
www.punelifestyle.com
www.virtualpune.com
www.webindia123.com

General Index

N

O

P

Q

R

Acknowledgements

Special Contributors
Arti Kirloskar, Ravi Pandit, Nitin Kareer (PMC), Sharad Mahajan (Mashal), Madhuvanti Anantharajan, Sharvey Dhongde, Kiran Kalamdani (Kimaya), Jaymala Diddee, Shivani Maheshwari, Ashvina Vakil, Shubha Gadkari, Sakal, INTACH, MCCIA.

Special Assistance
Aishwarya Mavinkurve, Amrit Sadhana, Osho Times, Anand Upalekar (Green map), Archana Dahiwal, Arindam De (Hadapsar Flying Club), Ashok Khamkar (MTDC), Colonel Rajput (Salunke Vihar), Dileep Athavale, K. R. Dixit, Jutta Dixit, Dr. S. K. Joshi (F. C., Department of Geology), Dr. Sharma (Poona Club), Eric Menezes (Wings and Flights), Huned Contractor, Kalindi Kokal, Lt. Col. Shirish Karajgi, Malini Nair, Manjula Narayan, Manisha Gutman (Kalpavriksh Environment Action Group), Manohar Lal Bahanwal (War Cemetery), Mr. Kadam (Directorate of Economics and Statistics), Pravin Gedam, V. A. Khadwadkar, Karen Anand, Neelimkumar Khaire, Ninad Bedekar (Historian and author), Prachi Bari, Professor Nalavde, Rashmi Ranade (Design at Work), Sanjay Deshpande (Deccan College), Sanjay Godbole (Historian and archaeologist), Savita Bharati (CEE), Madhav Gokhale (The Maharashtra Herald), Shyam Dhavale (Heritage Cell, PMC), Vijay and Vinita Mahajani (Association of the Friends of Germany), Y. S. Khaire (Superintendent of Gardens), Anchal Sondhi (Environmental activist).

Institutes & Associations
College of Agriculture, Deccan College, Directorate of Education, Khadki Cantonment Board, Pimpri Chinchwad Municipal Corporation, Police Commissioner's Office, Pune Cantonment Board, Pune Municipal Corporation, Pune Municipal Transport, Regional Transport Office, Symbiosis College, Thomas Cook, University of Pune, Yuvashakti.

Bibliography
Pune Queen of the Deccan by Jaymala Diddee, Samita Gupta, Glimpses of Pune's Heritage – A Mosaic by Samita Gupta, The INTACH Pune Heritage Map- INTACH Pune, Pune City Tourist Guide- Utkarsh Prakashan by Dr. S. G. Mahajan, A Road Guide to Pune-TTK, The Times of India,The Indian Express, The Maharashtra Herald, punediary.com, virtualpune.com, punecity.com, aroundpune.com

Photographs
Sandesh Bhandare, Sakal, INTACH, Abhijeet Khedgikar (Forts), Narendre Dengle, Osho International Foundation, Sanjay Deshpande (Deccan College).

Elephant Team

Project Guidance
Partho Guha, Ashwini Deshpande, Ashish Deshpande.

Coordinator
Seema Sharma

Content
Dhun Patel, Neha Thakurdesai.

Layout, Maps and Design
Shantanu Biswas, Pravin Mutkekar, Rochana Deb, Milind Dahale, Pravin Kale, Saurav Das, Alex Martin, Rishikesh Palekar, Rashmi Pandit.

Network Systems
Ranbir Singh, Tushar Ambekar.

Administration
K. Shashi Nair, Anjali Kamat, Vaishali Khoje, Jayashree Babar, Manisha Nair, Yogesh Gaikwad, Sadashiv Kambale, Yamanappa Dodamani.

Mahratta Chamber of Commerce, Industries and Agriculture

Mahratta Chamber of Commerce, Industries and Agriculture was established in 1934 by visionary founder Shri. A. R. Bhat. It was a time when Pune was not quite on the industrial map of India. Except for some large industries like the Kirloskars, Ogales Paisa Fund, etc., the region was overwhelmingly dominated by Small and Medium Enterprises. These entrepreneurs needed a representative at the Government level a think-tank for policy direction, a financier for their growth and a trainer for helping them move towards a brighter future. The conception of MCCIA (or the Chamber as it is fondly referred to) was Shri. Bhat's answer to all these problems. Under the aegis of the Chamber, Shri. Bhat provided critical direction for promotion and protection of the smaller industries. MCCIA was crucial in helping establish the Bank of Maharashtra in 1935, a time when local industries suffering from recessionary trends were starved of credit. So forward looking was this leader that he realized that the role of the Chamber would have to move beyond just representing industries; the Chamber would have to encourage and actively help in training new entrepreneurs, pro-actively invite investment to Pune - it would, in essence, have to be a friend, guide and philosopher for the industries in Pune.

Over a period of time, MCCIA has evolved into an institution synonymous with the growth of Pune. Today, it is the first contact point for businesses wanting to set up operations in the area. The Chamber has indeed positioned Pune as a world-class investment destination. With a committed staff of 40 people, it constantly interacts with the industry on matters such as foreign trade, finance, direct and indirect taxation, infrastructure, power, etc. The Chamber believes that Pune can become an important centre for the Manufacturing Information Technology Industry and Agro-based industries. Through nearly 200 annual topical training programs and workshops, MCCIA is instrumental in providing training to the industry. It carries out surveys and studies and publishes the Industrial and Commercial Directory, which is a comprehensive database of all enterprises in Pune. Through the Pune Expo, the largest regional trade fair in the country, the Chamber provides a platform for the local industry to attract global clients and to network with strategic partners. The Chamber has also promoted several industry-relevant institutions in Pune such as the Centre for Electronics and Test Engineering (CETE), the National Agriculture and Food Analysis and Research Institute (NAFARI), the Auto-Cluster and the International Convention Centre (ICC), which will also be its new place of operations.

With a futuristic outlook, the Chamber is now interested in promoting an International Exhibition Center and an International Airport at Pune. It is also promoting Janawani (voice of the people) to improve the civic amenities within the City. True to its spirit and in tribute to its Founder, MCCIA is now establishing the Shri. A.R. Bhat SME Research Foundation, which will carry out research, policy and advisory activities for the benefit of the SMEs.

Mahratta Chamber of Commerce
Industry and Agriculture
505 & 506, A & B Wing, 5th floor,
MCCIA Trade Tower,
International Convention Center,
403 - A, Senapati Bapat Marg,
Pune 411016
Tel: 25709000
Email: info@mcciapune.com
Website: www.mcciapune.com

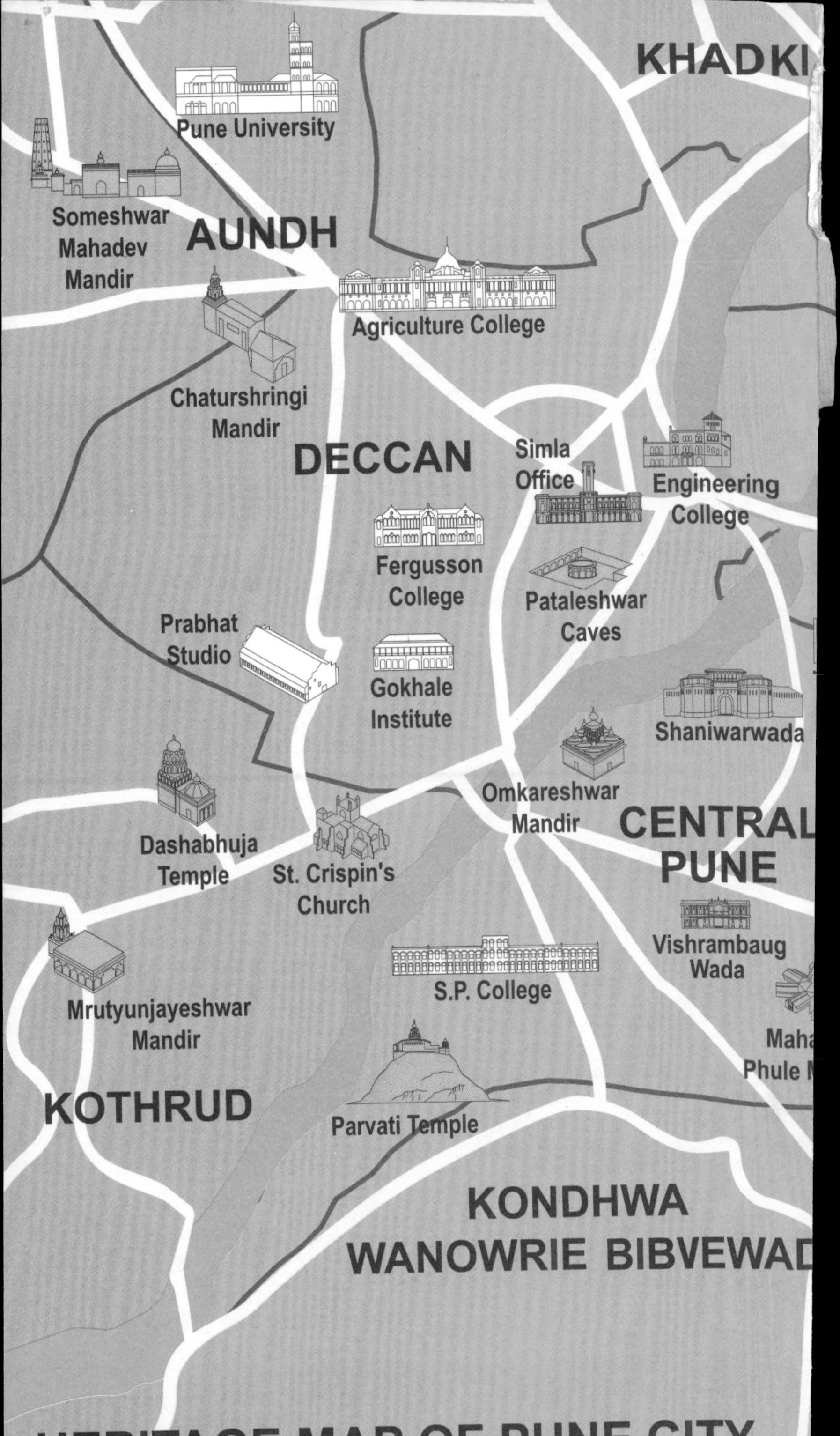

HERITAGE MAP OF PUNE CITY

Source: Intach, Pune Heritage Map